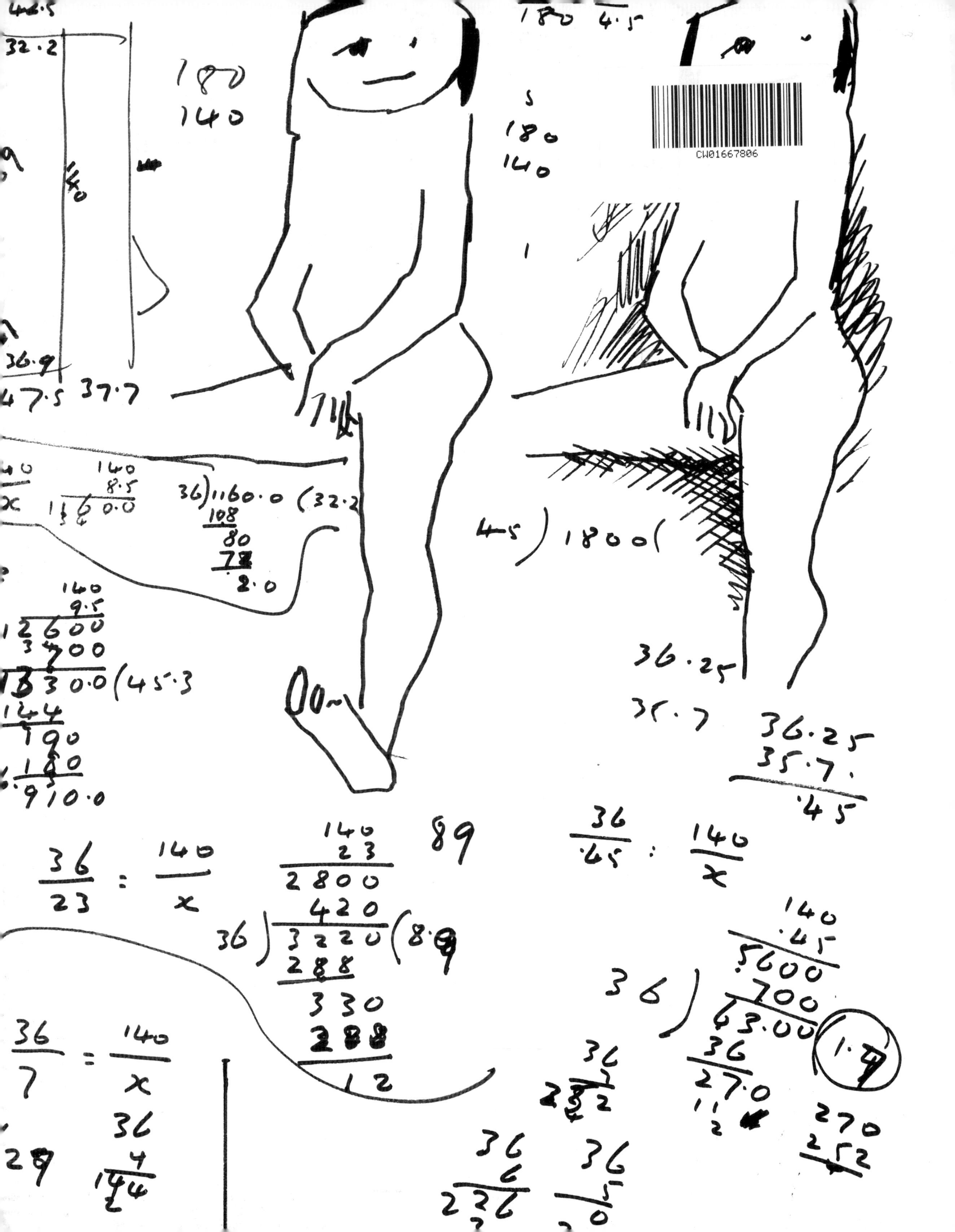

180
140
36)1160·0(32·2
45)1800(
36·25
35·7
·45
89
36)3220(8·9

Kenneth Armitage Life and Work

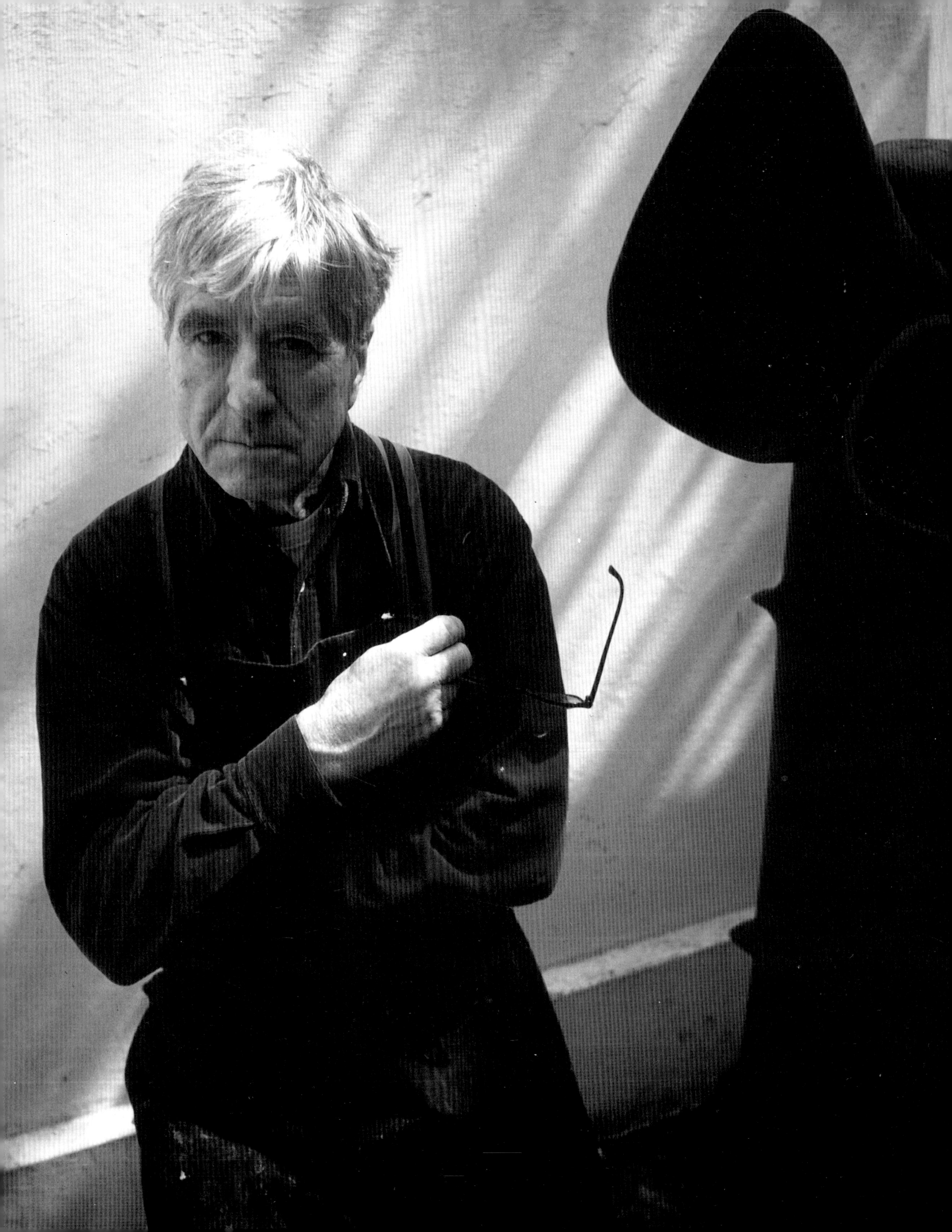

Kenneth Armitage Life and Work

with a Foreword by Alan Bowness

and a text edited by Tamsyn Woollcombe
in association with the Artist

The Henry Moore Foundation
in association with
Lund Humphries Publishers, London

First published in Great Britain in 1997 by
The Henry Moore Foundation
Dane Tree House
Perry Green
Much Hadham
Herts SG10 6EE
in association with
Lund Humphries Publishers Ltd
Park House, 1 Russell Gardens
London NW11 9NN

The text of 'Kenneth Armitage: My Life and Work'
is based on tapes of the artist recorded
by John McEwen and Tamsyn Woollcombe
for the National Life Story Collection's
'Artists' Lives' project in 1991.
The full recording may be heard at
the British Library's National Sound Archive.

British Library Cataloguing in Publication Data
A catalogue record for this book is available from the British Library

ISBN 0 85331 702 X

Designed by Alan Bartram
Typeset in Monotype Gill Sans
Made and printed in Great Britain by
BAS Printers Limited, Over Wallop, Hampshire

Frontispiece: Portrait of the artist, 1994

The endpapers are reproduced from sketchbook pages. The
front endpaper shows calculations by the artist when enlarging
from a small model to full scale, involving cut-up sheet metal.
The back endpaper is an assortment of ideas for models, including
some of those reproduced in this volume.

Distributed in the USA by
Antique Collectors' Club
Market Street Industrial Park
Wappingers Falls
NY 12590
USA

British Sculptors and Sculpture Series

Series Editor: Alan Bowness

Pre-Raphaelite Sculpture: Nature and Imagination in British Sculpture 1848-1914
Edited by Benedict Read and Joanna Barnes

The Sculpture of Phillip King
by Tim Hilton

The Sculpture of Robert Adams
by Alastair Grieve

The Sculpture of Austin Wright
by James Hamilton

The Sculpture of Frank Dobson
by Neville Jason and Lisa Thompson-Pharoah

The Sculpture of Stephen Cox
by Stephen Bann

Bernard Meadows: Sculpture and Drawings
by Alan Bowness

The Sculpture of David Nash
by Julian Andrews

Contents

Foreword
Alan Bowness

At the end of the remarkable text which Kenneth Armitage has provided for this book, the sculptor refers to a discussion of two ways of thinking – one practical, and the other playful: 'wholly gratuitous, generating no direct consequence, throwing off a feeling'.

It is of course precisely this second, playful, quality that we so admire in Armitage's own sculpture and drawing. Somewhat ruefully, perhaps, he admits to the fact that many find a humorous element in his work, and indeed one often smiles at his figures. And why not? This is no indication of a lack of seriousness: on the contrary, it is a realisation, unusual in twentieth-century art, of something profound and fundamental to human existence.

Armitage is half Irish, and he seems to have inherited some kind of magic gift which is apparent in those very early sculptures with which he immediately attracted international attention. In the early 1950s, sculptures such as *People in the Wind* and *Family going for a Walk* appeared out of nowhere. No doubt there was much thinking about sculpture during the enforced six-and-a-half years of War service, but there is no period of preliminary work in Armitage, nor are there signs of anyone influencing him. He just happened to create a series of extraordinary sculptures throughout the 1950s which marked him out as one of the most original artists of his generation. Effortlessly it seems, and much to his own surprise I think, by the time of his Venice Biennale exhibition in 1958 Kenneth Armitage was internationally famous.

Armitage did not exploit this success. Having witnessed the creation of a market for his work he turned away to do other things. Personal freedom means much to him, and now we see that his art is essentially an expression of this. His adherence to the playful, adventitious quality of life has shaped his whole career.

I have known Kenneth for forty years, and one of his most attractive (and unusual) characteristics as an artist is that he never seems to show much personal ambition, and has been prepared to accept both success and neglect as they came to him. He has done things that have taken him out of the public eye, such as self-exile, and leaving an established gallery and the support system that it provides. He has not sought commissions, and when accepted they have been in remarkably inaccessible places. He has never cultivated collectors, critics or museum directors – indeed he has always treated the art world with suspicion and made friends outside it.

Though always hard-working and totally devoted to sculpture Armitage is not prolific. There are 279 sculptures (plus editioned bronzes) in the only listing he has compiled of his work – and his records are modest, making it impossible at present to compile a complete catalogue. This small production reflects the fact that when he has nothing to say he has been silent. We should admire him for this. There have been times when he has perhaps pursued a wrong direction, or has found it difficult to make sculpture at all because of an unsympathetic artistic climate. It is typical that he should have found welded sculpture to be 'cruel' (and even cruelty in Armitage – as in the *Legend of Skadar* – has a playful edge).

Despite the relatively small œuvre, the actual achievement is considerable. This is clear when the work is gathered together, as it was at the Yorkshire Sculpture Park in the summer of 1996, or in the pages of this book. And the drawings have their own importance, particularly when grouped into series as in the wonderfully funny and touching Chaucer illustrations.

A note about Kenneth Armitage's text. It may not be generally known that under the direction of Cathy Courtney the National Sound Archive (a part of the British Library) has for several years been conducting in-depth interviews with artists. 'Artists' Lives' are done for the record, and are available for public listening, and, in transcript form, for reading. Kenneth Armitage talked for several hours to John McEwen and to Tamsyn Woollcombe, and it is from this material that Tamsyn Woollcombe has with considerable skill and devotion, and under the artist's personal supervision, edited the remarkable and self-revealing text that follows. Like many British artists (Augustus John and Ben Nicholson for example) Armitage has a gift for words. Even those who know his work well will be sure to find illumination in Kenneth's candid, honest account of his own career.

Following the pattern established in other Lund Humphries monographs on British artists, the sculptor's own contribution has been considerable. He has chosen the photographs, helped with the layout, and provided a better introduction to the work than anyone else could have made. The editors, Lucy Myers and John Taylor, are most grateful to him.

Miss Pauncefort sang at the top of her voice
    (Sing tirry-lilly down the lane)
And nobody knew what she sang about
    (Sing tirry-lirry lirry all the same)

The Songster, Stevie Smith

Kenneth Armitage: My Life and Work

Edited by Tamsyn Woollcombe in association with the artist, 1996
Based on tapes of Kenneth Armitage recorded by John McEwen and Tamsyn Woollcombe for the National Sound Archive, 1991

I know hardly anything about my father's family, but I know a great deal about my mother's.

My mother's maiden name was Quin, and she was born in County Longford, in southern Ireland, which is very quiet with no spectacular features in it; it is pastoral land, cattle and the like. Originally it was occupied by the O'Quinns and the O'Farrells, who were Catholic landowners. My great-great-grandfather changed from being a Catholic to a Protestant. At the end of the eighteenth century and the beginning of the nineteenth, Irish people were subjected to restrictions of all kinds, especially the Catholics, who were really about eighty or ninety per cent of the population. They were excluded from standing for political office and education had to be of the most elementary kind, but the main limitation was in ownership of land, and they were allowed only a very little of the least fertile. As a landowner, my great-great-grandfather, O'Quin, married a Dean's daughter, making it quite clear that he had become a Protestant, and brought his children up as Protestants. To make it even clearer he dropped one 'n' off his name, which shows the effort he made to keep the land which, alas, was going to be lost by his grandson.

My great-great-grandfather's son was called William Henry Quin, and he became a naval captain and was always known to us as Captain Quin RN. He built Lackan, two Irish miles from Edgeworthstown. While he was in the Navy, although the slave trade had been abolished by Wilberforce, there were still slavers operating in the Atlantic, and his job was to intercept them and escort them back to Africa. During one of these voyages, while in Africa, he was thrown from his horse and was badly wounded; he was taken aboard his ship, which set sail for England and he died at sea in 1840. The Quin family always maintained that as the Captain's ship, HM Sloop of War *Britomart*, had put in at St Helena, my great-grandfather was, out of convenience, laid in the now empty grave of Napoleon (who had been removed to Les Invalides) where the officers planted a laburnum tree out of respect. No Quin tomb was found but the name was entered in the church records. Thus the story is unproven one way or the other. But how did my family know about the laburnum tree? The first cinema film I ever went to was with my uncle in Dublin. It showed Napoleon's tomb on St Helena, and my uncle pointed out the laburnum tree he had been told about. A friend, browsing among the *bouquinistes* on the quays by the Seine, accidentally found a *Petit Journal* illustrated supplement of 1901 showing troops looking at the grave of Napoleon with the laburnum tree behind.

My grandfather, also called William Henry, went into the Navy as well and was sent to Nelson's flagship, HMS *Victory*, moored at Portsmouth and used as a training ship. He told me when he was ninety, lying on the sofa in Lackan, that he could not stand the harsh discipline of the Navy – 'All hands drummed on deck to witness a flogging' – so he resigned and returned to live on the land his father had left him.

He tried to earn a living from the land and, as many Irish people do, he took to gambling. He fathered nine children, one of whom was my mother. My grandfather gambled on the land, until he got down to about fifty acres, a kind of smallholding round the house. Then he made one last desperate bid, gambled on the house, and lost. My mother told the story of how all the furniture was brought out, put on a wagon, and the nine children had to climb on top, under the watchful eyes of the bailiffs, when up rode at speed a relation with money to pay off the debt, or most of it, and so they moved back into the house again.

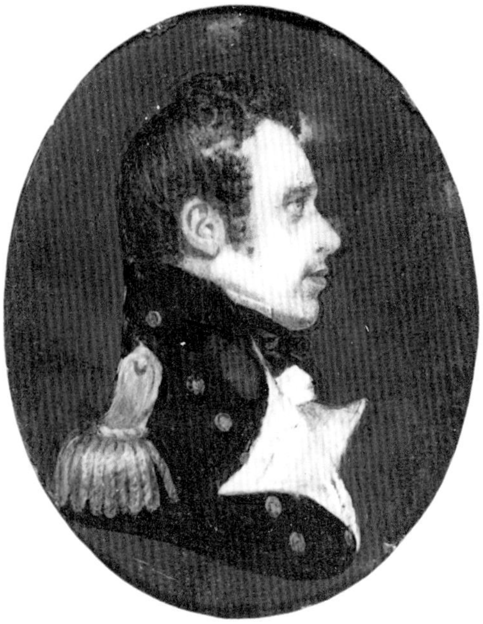

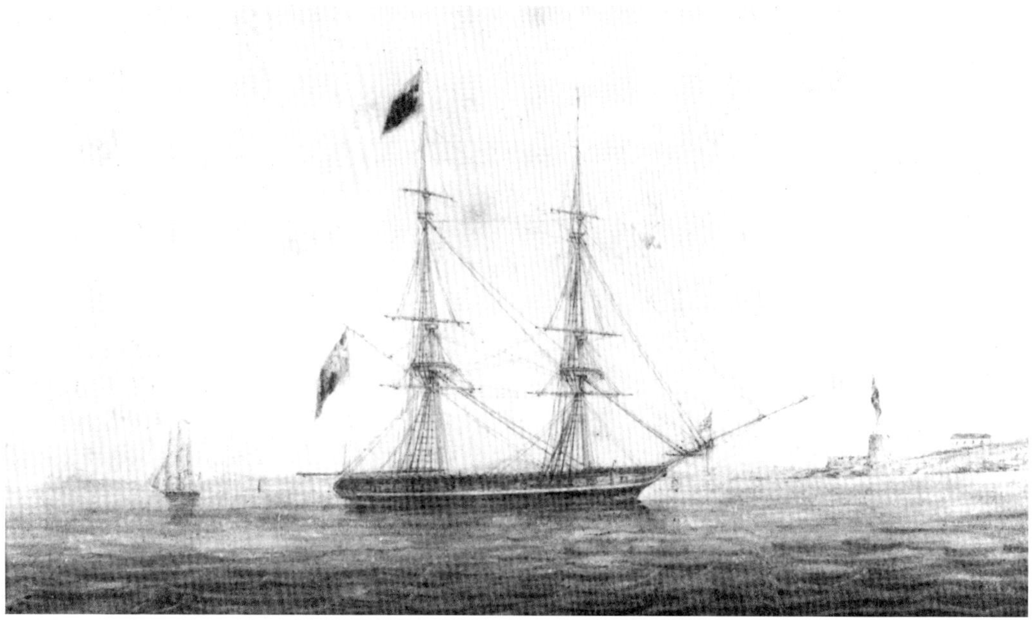

(*above*) Captain William Quin RN, builder of Lackan. Died 1840, buried St Helena

(*right*) HM Sloop of War *Britomart*, commanded by Captain Quin, 1834

My mother never criticised my grandfather for losing everything by gambling. She was the sixth of the nine children and as she had to look after the young ones, she hardly went to school at all; she was very badly educated and had difficulty with reading all her life. She went to Bradford as an under-nurse in a house with a big family; it must have been a shock to go from carefree Ireland to the blackened stone houses of Bradford, and it was there that she met my father, who had been born in Manningham.

My father was a long-suffering man, and although reserved he was very intelligent and moral, but not as dynamic as my mother. His parents had died when he was about twelve, and he had two slightly older sisters whom he had to help support by earning a living. He had wanted very much to take up music; in fact his schoolteacher encouraged him to do so, and somehow he came to the notice of the organist at York Minster, who said that he would give him free lessons if he could get to York, but he couldn't afford the fare. He moved to Leeds, where he joined an oil refinery, Filtrate Oils, and eventually became a director.

I had two older sisters: Doreen was fifteen years older than I was, and the other one, Norah, died when I was four. She had TB, and I can remember her sitting in her wicker invalid chair; she had an inhaler and often sat with a towel over her head clearing her chest. She was astonishingly talented and I still have a beautifully drawn still-life painting by her up in my bedroom. My mother was passionately fond of her and a few years later, when she died, my mother took up Christian Science, and took to it like a fanatic. Her theory was that as doctors had not been able to save Norah, she would put her faith in God instead. Christian Science believes totally in the power of prayer as a cure for sickness. So it was dinned into me from the age of nine that doctors couldn't cure me, only God could; I found this rather frightening, for I couldn't quite believe that God was going to bother with me either if I had a child's disease. It was because I had sinned, and I had to pray for forgiveness. My father accommodated her passion.

Later on I found by chance in the public library Nietzsche's *Also Sprach Zarathustra*, on the third page of which Zarathustra asks, 'Have you not heard that God is dead?'. I bought a copy of it and kept it in my pocket for comfort. Years later I found that Dalí had noticed this same detail. By then I had returned to an open mind about religion.

My sister Doreen did not turn out very well, and because my mother's affection was given to the daughter who died, she felt left out because I, as the boy, was the next in line for my mother's attention.

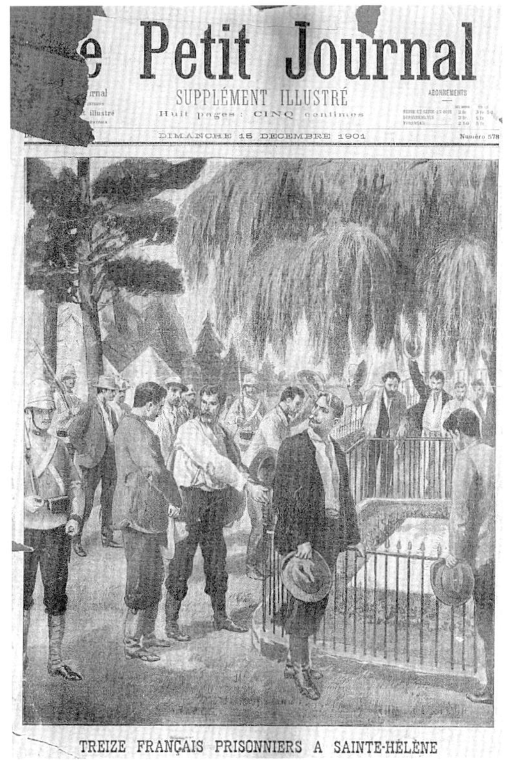

Napoleon's tomb on St Helena, from *Le Petit Journal*, December 1901

The first school I went to was in a field very near to where we lived, in Roundhay on the edge of Leeds where I was born; it was called the Tin School, because it was clad with corrugated iron, with one small room, one teacher, and a girl helping her. I went there from the age of five to ten, and I enjoyed every minute of it. The headmistress said in her report when I left, 'Shows marked artistic and inventive abilities in connection with handwork'. I made little pictures at home like mad, but 'Meccano' was the thing: like all boys I thought it was absolutely marvellous.

My family started going to Filey and Flamborough Head, and I saw for the first time the 'coble', the famous, elegant Yorkshire fishing boat thought to be descended from the beach ships of the Norsemen who had invaded the whole of that coast. This boat really fascinated me; it had a flat bottom, and it had bilge-keels at either side, or 'storkels', as they called them. To launch it, it would be poled out to deeper water, through the breakers; therefore the bows were very deep and it was broad in the beam and small in the stern, and for the rudder to be effective it had to be extended five feet below the bottom of the boat, which was thirty feet long. It took three men to sail her. The mast was then shipped – it had a simple lugsail and had brightly coloured strakes along the hull. And it used to fish five or six miles out for cod and ling. The fishing extended right up the coast and the coble was often on my mind.

After the Tin School I was sent, to toughen me up, to an elementary school further into the city, set in the remnants of an industrial era, with rows of terraced houses. It was a tough school, and they were tough children. I was then sent to a much better secondary school, nearer my home, and near Roundhay Park. The school had playing fields and, to my great delight, an art department. The art teacher, Mr Walker, took a tremendous interest in me and we used to go back after school and experiment with sculpture, which neither of us knew how to make. It was he who suggested that I took a scholarship to Leeds College of Art, so I went in for it and got it, but my mother said no, you must get a job. Unknown to me, 'Foxy' Walker went twice to my mother to try and persuade her to let me go to the art school and this is why I am eternally indebted to him. In the end she gave in, so I had the scholarship.

I left school at seventeen having decided the year before to take up art. I had a friend with whom I used to walk home from school; one day, aged sixteen, we were discussing what we were going to do and he said, 'I'm going to be an architect', and he did become an architect, and I said, 'I'm going to be an artist', and I did become an artist. And that was all decided in the quarter of an hour it took to walk home.

From my earliest years my mother took me to her home, Lackan, in Ireland. I learnt to walk there. I was born in 1916, which was the time of the Easter Rising. My very earliest visual impressions were in Ireland: following the silhouetted grown-ups on grass slopes against a setting sun, where their long shadows stretched beside and past me. First of all my Uncle Willie met us in a pony and trap at Edgeworthstown station and took us to Lackan. Following the Rising, on another Irish visit, he drove me in his Tin-Lizzy past the Dublin General Post Office, which had recently been burned down, and we saw the blackened walls still standing. Then we drove west on the road to Lackan, manœuvring around trenches dug across the road and trees felled to deter or prevent deployment of the Black-and-Tans. In one village an artillery piece was left standing in the middle of the green as a silent, threatening symbol of power.

At night, when I was sent to bed earlier than the grown-ups, my uncle would come up to my bedside and talk for a quarter of an hour every night. For example, he would say, 'Do you hear that?' and it was the Dublin train going to Sligo; 'Can you hear it straining?' and it would be puffing up the gradient, and you could just hear it on a summer night far away. We had a great rapport. In my adolescence my uncle took me to the old Abbey Theatre, in Dublin, before it was burnt down, where I saw *The Playboy of the Western World*.

As there were only fifty acres left at Lackan, Uncle Willie needed to earn more money, so he became a 'gentleman' commercial traveller for a margarine firm in Limerick. He was a great conversationalist; it was like being paid for pleasure for him, and he went out only when he felt like it. I used to love going with him, and would wait in his car while he went off on business. He tried to get me interested in farming, and when I accompanied him we used to try and judge how good the land was (whether it was the height of the grass or the colour, I cannot remember), and I would say, 'That's good land', and he would say, 'Yes, that's good land'. It made it all very interesting, he knew Ireland like the back of his hand.

I adored Lackan (it had this effect on all people) and during the Second World War, while in the army, I had moments of dreaming of how it had been the happiest time of my life and how lovely it would be to go back one day. It was rich in other ways, for the land in front of the house ran down to a point by the Longford road, but just before they met, there was a neolithic barrow up which I used to climb; wild daffodils grew up its banks in spring-time. At the end of the drive to the road there used to be high, double iron gates, which were removed when the road was widened, as were the tall trees on the Lackan side. Across the road was a farm, in front of which was a large, circular Iron Age bank showing a settlement had been there. From Lackan the road followed the banks of a high esker running east–west almost to Longford town, on top of which were three or four barrows at intervals. The linear eskers were deposits from the retreating ice, four or five of which crossed Ireland. In those early days (the 1920s) my uncle said there had been hardly any interest in Irish archaeology and all was yet to be uncovered. On the lawn was a high outcrop of grey limestone contrasting nicely with the green grass, which was something I then always liked, like Ingleborough in Yorkshire and the Cheddar Gorge in the south-west.The annual Lackan visits laid the foundations for my later life, especially my interest in the land and archaeological sites. I love the land more than people really; I love the shape of the land. I have come to think that in fact my heart more and more lies with Ireland than with Yorkshire, where I was born.

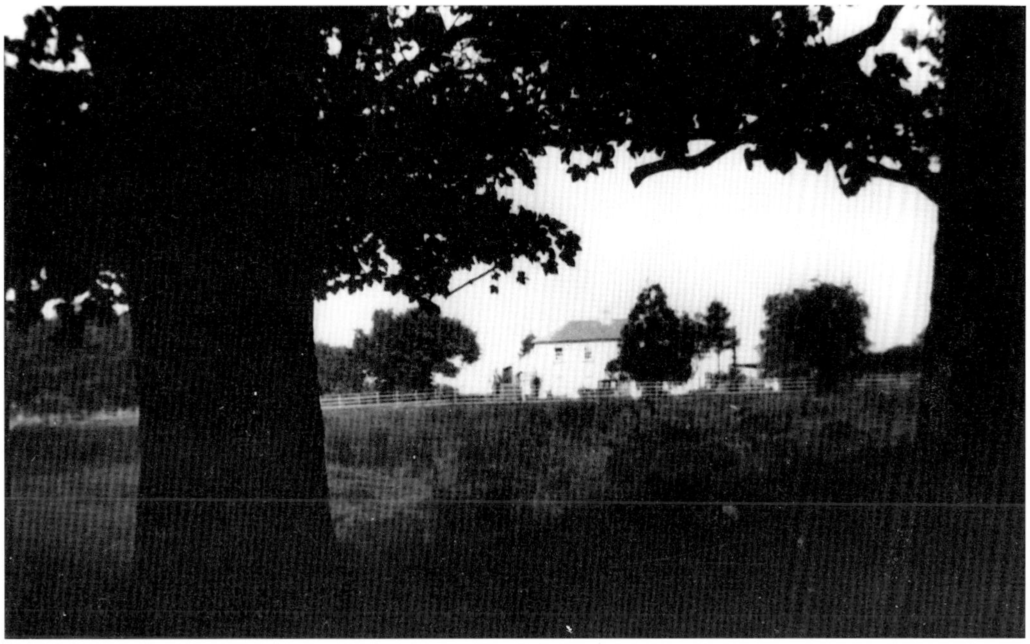
Lackan House, Edgeworthstown, Co. Longford, Ireland

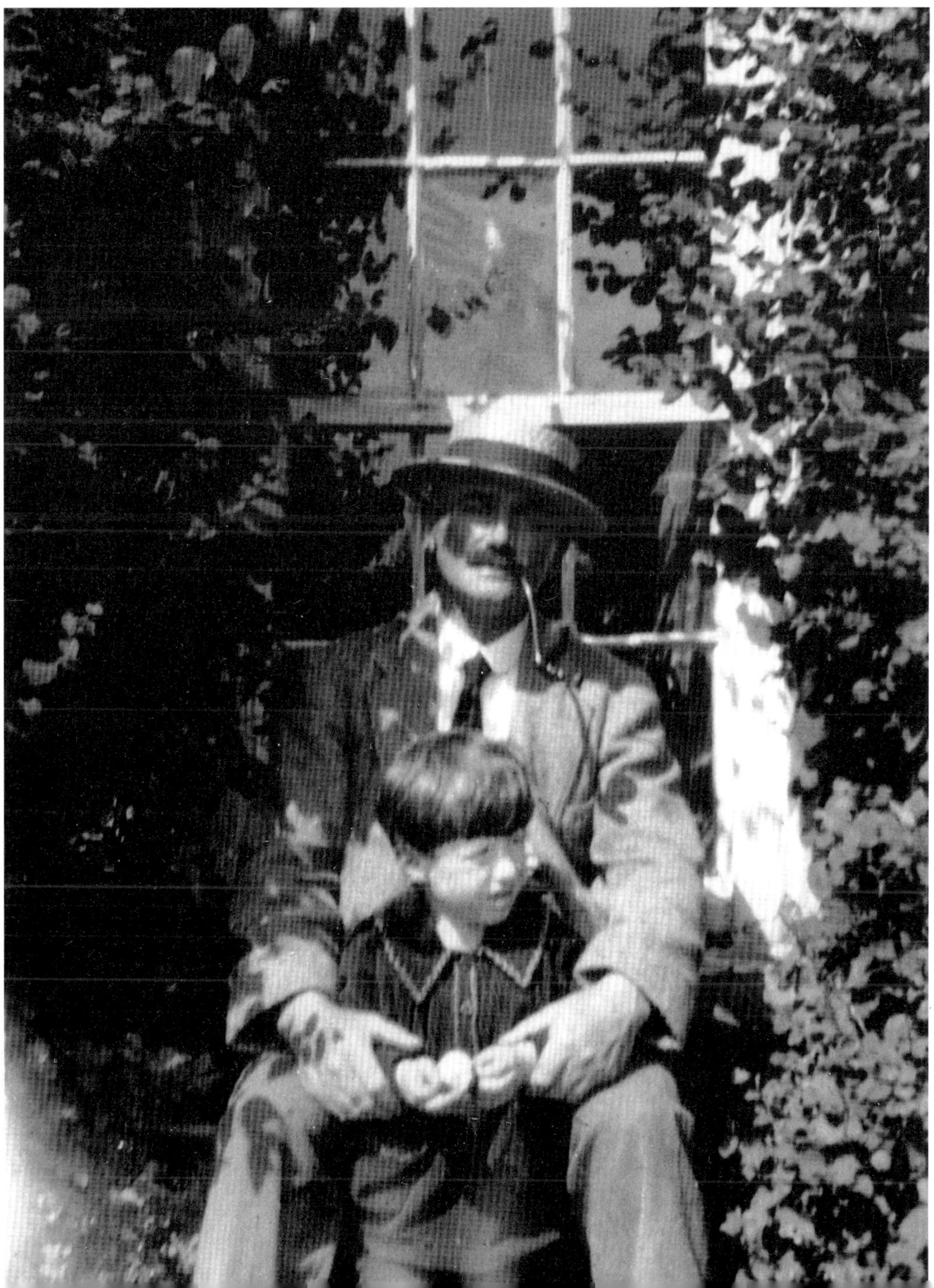
KA with Uncle Willie at Lackan House, about 1921

I returned to Lackan recently with friends, and as we drew near we found it had gone: it had been razed to the ground. It was a terrible shock because the great link with my past in Ireland had been broken.

At Leeds College of Art I spent the first year drawing and then, as I wanted to do sculpture, I moved to the sculpture class, a small class of about six people; they were very much a clique and I was shy and felt the odd man out so I joined the painting class for one year, which was a ridiculous thing to do.

Leeds College of Art was not the most dynamic art school at this time and Leeds was not a very attractive city, but it did have an extraordinary square, with a large, equestrian bronze statue in the middle, the Black Prince, with half a dozen or so great nymphs around it which I used to look at because of their physique – their feminine shapes were very attractive to a boy of seventeen.

I still lived at Roundhay while I attended the art school, and nearby was a marvellous park which had two lakes and woods which I often visited. We seemed to have cold winters, and there was often skating on the lake. The country round about was marvellous, especially Almscliff Crag, the great volcanic outcrop full of enormously deep fissures, on the way to Harrogate.

At Leeds College of Art there was an annual art exhibition and I was very thrilled to win two prizes for a carving I had made at home, of a crouched figure, in Portland stone bought from a local stonemason. The judge was Philip Hendy, then Director of the Leeds City Art Gallery, whom I was later to meet once again prior to the 1952 Venice Biennale.

It was traditional for certain students to go from Leeds to the Royal College of Art, as Henry Moore and Barbara Hepworth had done. We applied, and to my horror, I didn't get a scholarship, I was not even accepted. So I stayed on another year at Leeds and did a year of teacher-training still based at the College of Art. In 1937 I went to the Slade School of Fine Art, London, on a Leeds scholarship.

At the Slade my teacher was A. H. Gerrard, who had a fine piece of sculpture on the Headquarters of the London Underground building at St James's Park, along with Epstein's figures. Gerrard was very interested in carving, of which I had got relatively little experience at Leeds, as no one else had done any carving there. The new way of carving since the First World War was what they called 'direct carving', truth to material. In the Edwardian and Victorian days, if a sculptor did a carving he modelled the thing in clay first. It was then cast in plaster and professional stone carvers would reproduce it in stone, by means of a very simple device called a pointing machine, to within maybe a quarter of an inch of the surface, and then the sculptor would add the final, the masterly touch. That all went by the board; you couldn't do that with so-called modern art, and so, like Epstein, Gerrard continued to carve direct. It was therefore natural for me also to carve.

I worked in slate and I recall I made one piece in Hopton-wood stone. During the two years at the Slade I went with Jo [Joan Moore, see below] and two other girls from the Slade to the stone quarries at Worth Matravers, on the Dorset coast. The quarries are really part of the same bed of stone as Portland Bill, not far away, and it was like going into Palestine. They would

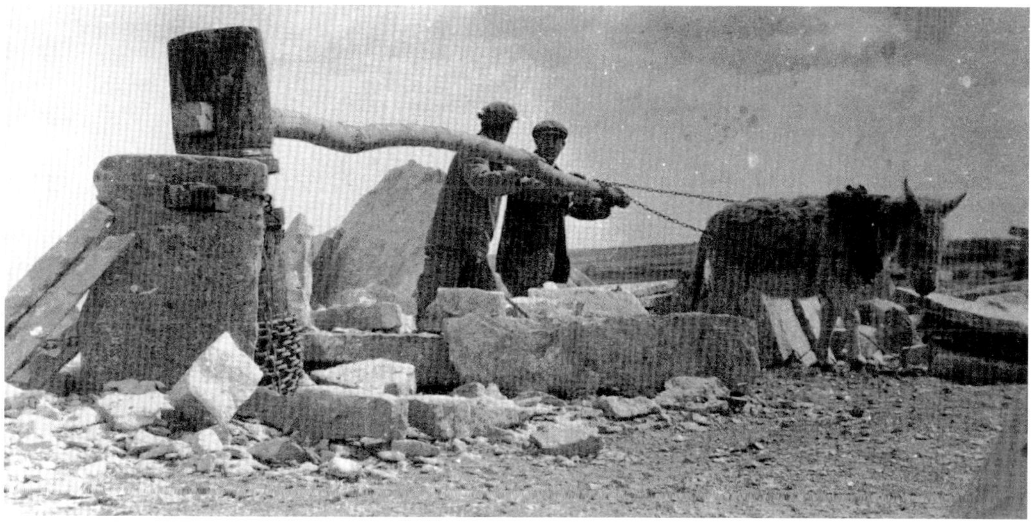

Stone quarries at Worth Matravers, Dorset, where KA and three friends worked in the summer of 1938

dig a shaft down about twenty feet into the ground and then ease the blocks out, and the cubic shape would then be hauled up by the donkey. It was very interesting there, because it was an old firm, father and son (with Queen Anne mining rights) and we were really squaring up; rather than saying 'getting it true' they said 'getting it out of winding'. We stayed at a marvellous pub called the 'Square and Compass', where Augustus John used to go a lot only shortly before. I think we did more bathing from the rocks than carving.

I also took a course in bronze casting (1938-9) at the Central School of Arts and Crafts, in the basement, which was taken by a marvellous man called Galizia, who had a bronze foundry in London. I later had many of my works cast in bronze by him after the war.

The British Museum being very near the Slade, I made a visit every week to the Egyptian Hall. The amazing amount of carving, in the hardest known stones of granite, basalt and even diorite, was very exciting to see. I thought perhaps I was seeing it too much. People say that Egypt is just wrapped up in death, because of the pyramids and the tombs, but in fact I think that the Egyptians loved life so much that they wanted to keep a hold on it, and mummify it. For example, the wonderful eye make-up of the women, with the line going out almost to their ears; the enormous wigs, the transparent dressing, painted fingernails, each finger a different colour, and marvellous jewellery. So there was a real feeling of life, in spite of the despotic nature of the civilisation, and one must remember it was 3000-5000 BC.

I had seen the great Surrealist Exhibition of 1936, but the thing that moved me most was Epstein at the Leicester Galleries. There were of course the portraits in bronze; no one has ever had any trouble with them, they are always vivid likenesses, modelled in a loose way. But his carvings offended people. And the two absolutely stunning carvings I saw were *Adam* and *Jacob and the Angel*, both in alabaster, both about seven or eight feet high, of enormous impact. They were titanic in their feeling and unique in character. Of course his *Rima* in Hyde Park, commemorating W. H. Hudson, was tarred and feathered, which is the only time I heard of such a thing. Epstein didn't mind being vulgar and this is why he's different from Henry Moore, who, while powerful, was more polite. This is the trouble with art. If you depict women in a

(*opposite*) While a student at the Slade in 1937-9, KA moved into Joan Moore's studio. Her work is in the foreground. They were married in 1940.

way that does reveal their attractive points, those which are attractive to men, people can say it's obsessive or pornographic, whereas it might just be that all men happen to admire women's corporeal reality. If they did not, we would have no children.

During my first year at the Slade a young woman turned up to see Gerrard and I started talking to her and liked her very much. Her name was Joan Moore. She was sharing a real studio with a friend, not far away from the Slade, near the Euston Road. I soon began to share her studio, which was marvellous for me, because I could work away from the Slade at night as well. Jo had been to Paris the year before and had brought back a copy of *Lady Chatterley's Lover* and James Joyce's *Ulysses*, neither of which of course I had read, because they had been very firmly banned in England. *Ulysses* made a tremendous impact on me, partly because Joyce was Irish, and partly because I knew what he was talking about in Dublin. The first chapter describes his characters, Stephen Dedalus and Buck Milligan, living briefly in the Martello tower at Dalkey, about two miles south of Dublin, next to an inlet in the rocky coast called the Forty-Foot Hole, which I remember swimming in when I was a child. A friend, Michael Scott, Ireland's leading modern architect, bought the Martello tower and exhibited Joyce's memorabilia there.

While I was at Leeds College of Art I had become fascinated by a book by R. L. Praeger called *The Way that I Went: An Irishman in Ireland.*[1] Praeger was a botanist who knew all the learned societies in Dublin. He had tramped all over Ireland making notes, measuring things, and collecting plants. I was thrilled with this book, in which he wrote about the Burren in County Clare. This was the first I had ever heard of the Burren and the book led to my great interest in the place.

During my first summer at the Slade I planned a visit to Ireland: I wrote to Praeger, care of his publisher, saying that I was going to Ireland and that I would love to meet him if he could spare the time. And he very kindly wrote back at once and said that if I could get to Roundstone in Connemara, he would be glad to meet me.

I also wanted to do something else: being involved with carving I thought of the marble quarries there in Connemara. The marble was hideous when polished, but I knew that if it was left unpolished it was an attractive grey, with a very slight hint of green and blue in it. I had the idea that it might be possible to ship the marble from Galway Bay to the south coast or the Thames and I thought I would try and find the quarries. So when I was staying at Lackan with my uncle, I borrowed a bike from the store in Edgeworthstown, and made the first of many visits to Connemara. I met Praeger, who was perhaps disappointed that I was a young student.

I had found the track to the quarries, which had not been used for a long time, when suddenly I heard a woman singing: this I thought strange, as there were no houses for a mile. I climbed further up the bank, looked over the top, and there was a young woman with black hair and a striking face, stooping slightly, using a sickle to gather fodder for her donkey which was grazing nearby. And she wore a Connemara skirt down to her ankles, a heavy woollen skirt dyed a russet colour either from berries or from seaweed on the coast; it was the only time I have ever seen such a skirt. And she was singing in Gaelic. I listened to her for a few seconds and then I slipped away, careful that she did not see me.

I kept in touch with 'Foxy' Walker until he died. While on holiday from the Slade in Leeds I made a portrait of his daughter Angela, modelled in plasticine, and many years later had three casts made, one of which I gave to Angela.

1. R. L. Praeger, *The Way that I Went: An Irishman in Ireland*, first published Hodges Figgis & Co, Dublin and Methuen & Co, London, 1937, reprinted 1947

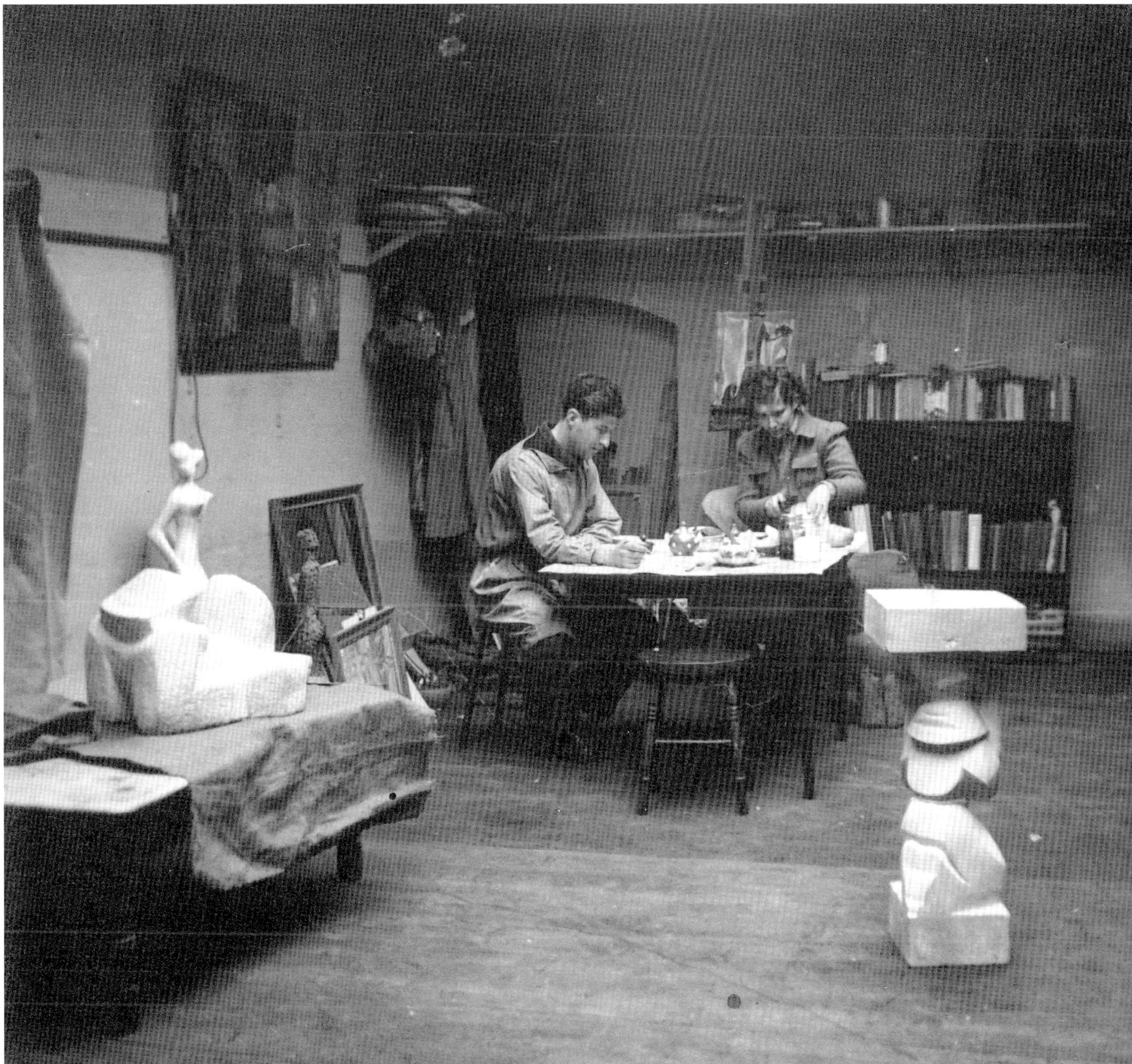

(*opposite*) *Angela Walker,* plaster 1938, cast 1985 (KA1)
H 36 cm (14 in), bronze
A portrait of KA's art teacher's daughter

At the Slade I met Stanley Spencer, whom I liked very much. I got to know his work, and was very impressed. The thing about those days was that if you were a student you were terribly impressed to meet someone famous, whereas these days one is rather ignored. The sculpture studios and the Painting School were on different floors so the students rarely mixed. Patrick Heron and Bryan Wynter were painting students while I was there but we did not meet until later.

The Slade Professor was Randolph Schwabe. I remember him talking to me about a carving I had done, which was slightly humorous (in fact a lot of people have said that some of my work can easily be humorous), and I said to him that maybe I would not get my Slade Diploma if I carried on doing this type of sculpture. But he said, 'What on earth do you want a Diploma for?'. He was not thinking of it as a teaching qualification, he was thinking of it as art. The Slade had a tradition (which came from Paris) of drawing and painting, to produce artists and painters. The Royal College of Art, from my later contact with it, is very much geared to having qualifications when you leave, so there was a slight distinction between the colleges.

Following my two years at the Slade, the idea was that I should have a travelling scholarship from the City of Leeds, but this was cancelled, as the political situation was too uncertain. So just before war was declared I went back to Leeds and stayed with my parents; I had no money and needed a job. There were three million unemployed, and the population then was much smaller than it is now. There were no teaching jobs in Leeds at all; the only job that I could get was selling Hoovers door to door, but I balked at that. Then Hitler invaded Poland, war was declared on 3 September 1939, and I had to decide what to do.

It was a worrying time, because I had been brought up with people talking to me about the slaughter of the First World War. And I really thought that my days were numbered when war came; I thought that I should be called up anyhow in a year or two, and that there would be conscription. The other thing was, if I joined up immediately I would not be a burden on my parents, so the day after war was declared I volunteered. The Army seemed pleased to see someone so prompt, because I would not have been called up for another year, at least. I was allowed to choose what part of the Army I could go into and I selected the Royal Artillery; within a few days I was sent to a field training regiment at Deepcut, a camp north of Aldershot. Field artillery was rather the élite of guns at that time, as opposed to anti-aircraft or anti-tank; it was a mathematical business because you shot at targets which were out of sight by map-reading and calculation.

In a very short time I was made a specialist, and was posted to an officer-cadet training unit at Catterick, near Richmond in Yorkshire. I was rather proud of my battery commander's report: 'Eccentric, untidy and should be curbed'. My final report was much better, and I was commissioned. The man in the next bed to me, Ainslie Ellis, was interesting: he was a poet and knew all about Surrealist art. He had worked in a gallery before the war, owned by E. L. T. Mesens. He became a very brave soldier and before D-Day he was dropped by parachute into France to direct Naval gunfire. He survived but was badly wounded and his comrades were all killed.[2]

Then Jo came up to be married in Richmond. I didn't have any money, and we used a curtain ring. It was a wartime marriage.

2. He has remained a friend ever since

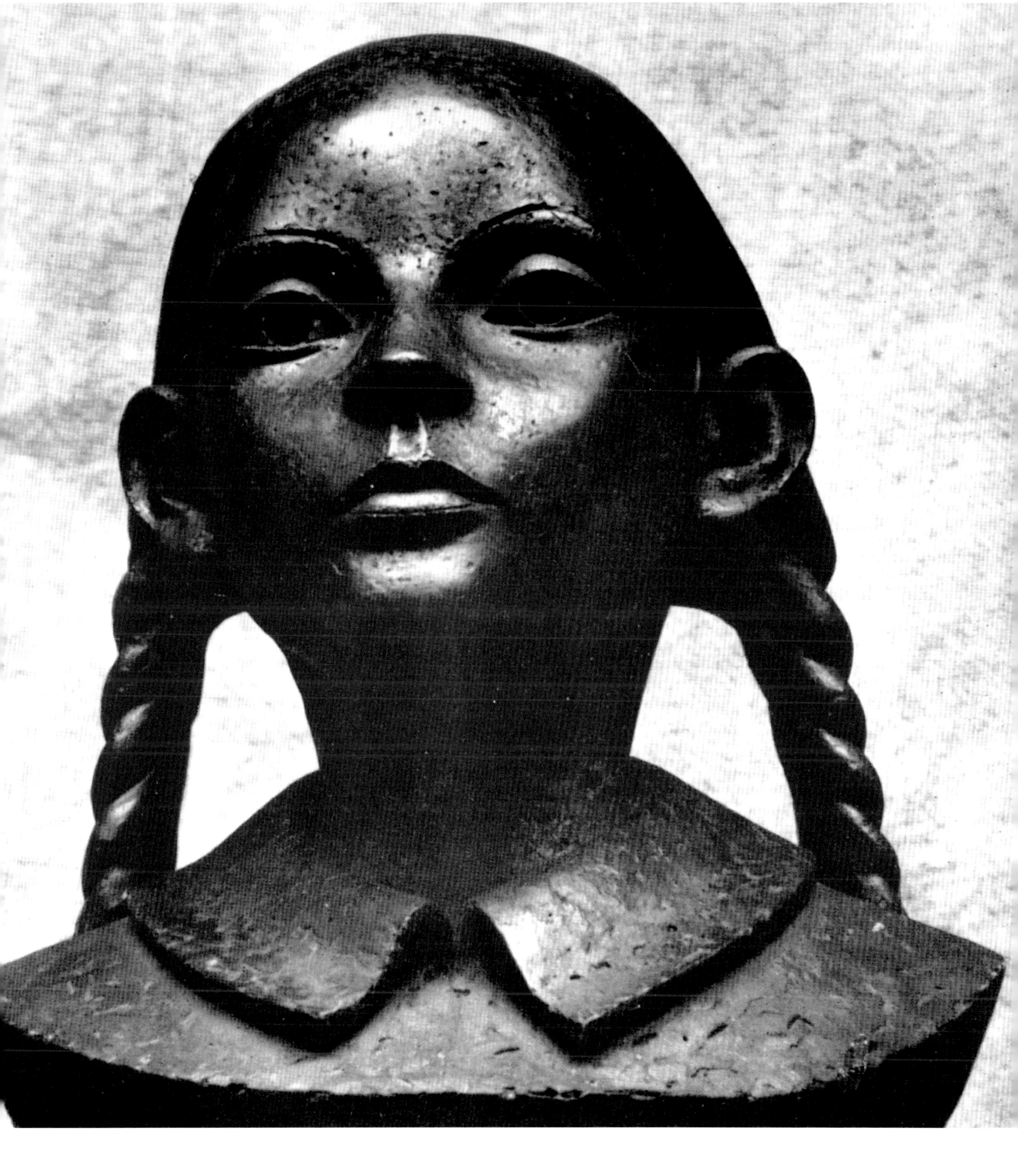

When I finished my cadet training, I was sent to have gunnery practice on Salisbury Plain, where I saw Stonehenge from the officers' mess two miles away, in the sunlight, glowing; the impact was tremendous. It was a wonderful thing to see, and then to walk around. It was not until I got to Corsham that I became more familiar with it and with Avebury too.

After the miracle of Dunkirk we lost all the equipment and I was posted to a unit in Devonport which we were defending. We had two types of guns: 25-pounders, like the one I had been trained on, and 6-inch howitzers, but we had the wrong ammunition due to Dunkirk. All day long there were dog fights in the sky, with Spitfires and Messerschmitts and Hurricanes making vapour trails – just like the Paul Nash painting *Battle of Britain* (1941) in the Imperial War Museum – with bits of shrapnel landing on the parade ground outside: this was the Battle of Britain. There would be no possibility of a land battle for a long time. We had lost everything, except the men, and I thought the thing to do was to change to anti-aircraft, which was the only valid defence. I remembered Colonel Buckland, then involved with anti-aircraft gunnery, who had previously been friendly with me at Deepcut even though I was only a recruit. I decided to write to him, and my letter must have impressed him because within ten days I was posted back to Deepcut. I was soon sent on a simple course on aircraft identification, because we had been shooting down our own planes in the evacuation of Dunkirk. I did very well there I think, because I had been involved with shape as an art student. I returned to my camp, and almost simultaneously another course started there in aircraft identification, and I was second in command. We taught by means of silhouettes and models and made visits to the Royal Aeronautical Establishment at Farnborough, where they had many British and captured enemy planes. On one occasion, at night, there was a most extraordinary roaring noise, a sound I had never heard in my life before. The following day we saw what it was: a little plane with square cut wing-tips, streaking across the sky. This was the first jet engine, designed by Frank Whittle, which was thrilling to see. I was also asked to teach tank identification, as we had been shooting up our own tanks as well, so we made regular visits to the tank range behind Pirbright, the Coldstream Guards' training camp, where we could see both captured German tanks and our own.

I was eventually made captain (later major) and put in charge of the unit, until one day I found out that Olga, the Belgian wife of Major Jackson from a nearby unit (whom I knew), had disappeared. She had been dropped by parachute into France and had joined the Resistance. She was also very friendly with the Free French here, as was 'Barmy' Buckland. He invited them to Deepcut, and he and I went to see them in London, but I never met de Gaulle. Olga's bravery worried me and I felt that my life was too soft in the circumstances, so I went to Colonel Buckland, and I told him that I wanted to volunteer to be a commando. Anyone else would have said: 'Very good, that's fine Armitage, we'll see about a posting'. Not so Barmy, the old soldier. He thought a bit, then he said, 'Better be a live donkey than a dead horse. No one will thank you for this in twenty years' time', and he told me to go away and think about it and come back the next day. I was not desperate to be killed: I wanted to get on with sculpture, if I could, after the war; at least I had made myself available. I do not know what I said when I went back – something like that I would not make a very good commando – but the result of it was that I remained a hard-working donkey until the end of the war.

Some years later I was on a bus on Kensington High Street when I heard a familiar voice shouting 'Armitage', and there was Barmy, sitting on the back seat. We had two bus stops' conversation: 'Probably,' he said, 'I saved your life'. After I had volunteered to be a commando, there was the disastrous attempt to capture the bridge at Arnhem, and I suppose there would have been more than a fifty per cent chance that I would have been killed.

I was still at Deepcut, about three months before the war ended, when one day in the officers' mess a friend tossed me *The Times* and said, 'There's a job that might interest you here'. It was an advertisement for a post teaching at Bath School of Art with 'Opportunities of unusual interest', and I wrote at once, asking what the opportunities were. Clifford Ellis, the Principal, replied very quickly. He was asking a wide range of people to apply and was well-supported by people who knew the school already. He did not say anything about what the opportunities were, but he did say that he wanted to reorganise the school. So I went for an interview in Bath; I could not say when I was going to be demobbed so I did not get the job, but as I was leaving, Clifford said, 'Look, when you know definitely when you are going to be released, let me know and I will see what I can do'.

So in 1946, when I was released from the Army, I went to teach at the Bath School of Art, in Sydney Place. I used to stay four nights a week at a little lodging house near the station, and return to our flat in Redcliffe Square in London for the rest of the week.

Immediately after the end of the war my wife and I had found a large flat in Redcliffe Square. We let part of the flat to a friend of Ainslie Ellis's, Hugh Gordon Porteus. Although he was a recluse, Hugh had many professional contacts, including Wyndham Lewis, but more interesting to me was Orwell, whom I met once. As I spent a lot of my time teaching at Corsham I missed some of these people. I did meet T. S. Eliot, Ezra Pound, Count Potocki, Arthur Waley and Gerald and Lawrence Durrell. Jo particularly liked Gerald. Count Potocki I had previously seen at the British Museum during my Slade period. Now he looked rather different: he was not dressed in medieval court robes but wore a suit. At my first somewhat premature exhibition of drawings at the Mayor Gallery in 1947, he used his printing press to produce the one-page catalogue with a list of drawings; at the bottom of the page, in tiny characters, he had 'Printed by Vladislav V, King of Poland and Hungary, Hospodar of Moravia, Defender of the Faith. 22 Devonia Road, London, N1'.

Another visitor was Tambimuttu, the Ceylonese poet and editor of *Poetry London*, a beautiful illustrated publication to which contemporary artists like Graham Sutherland and Henry Moore contributed.

It was daring of Clifford Ellis to take me on. I had spent six-and-a-half years in the Army, and before that I had been a student; he had some kind of intuition. After a few weeks I began to understand what Ellis was planning. We made a trip out to Corsham, which is an ancient little town nine miles east of Bath, with fourteenth-century weavers' cottages, and Corsham Court – the Elizabethan manor belonging to Lord Methuen, with its great estate and park designed by Capability Brown (who had also made alterations to the house).

Ellis already knew Lord Methuen, who was a painter and had once been a pupil of Sickert. Sickert himself had taught at Bath School of Art when Ellis was Principal, one day a week from

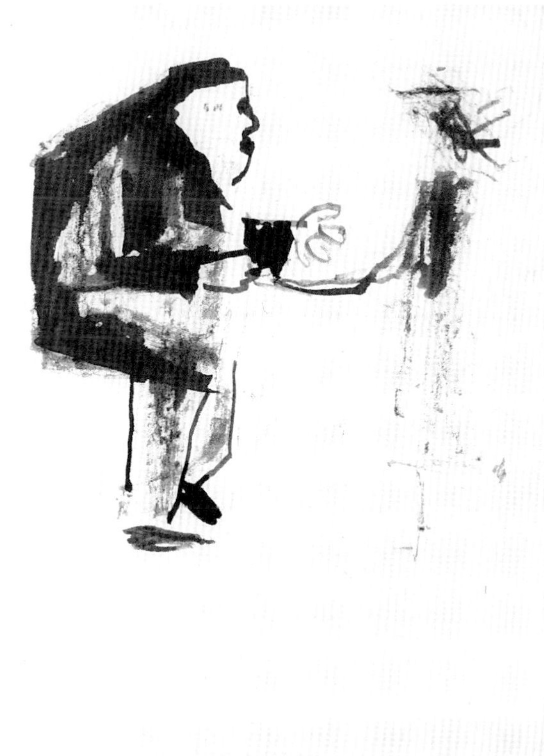

David Sylvester dancing at Redcliffe Square, c.1948, brush and wash

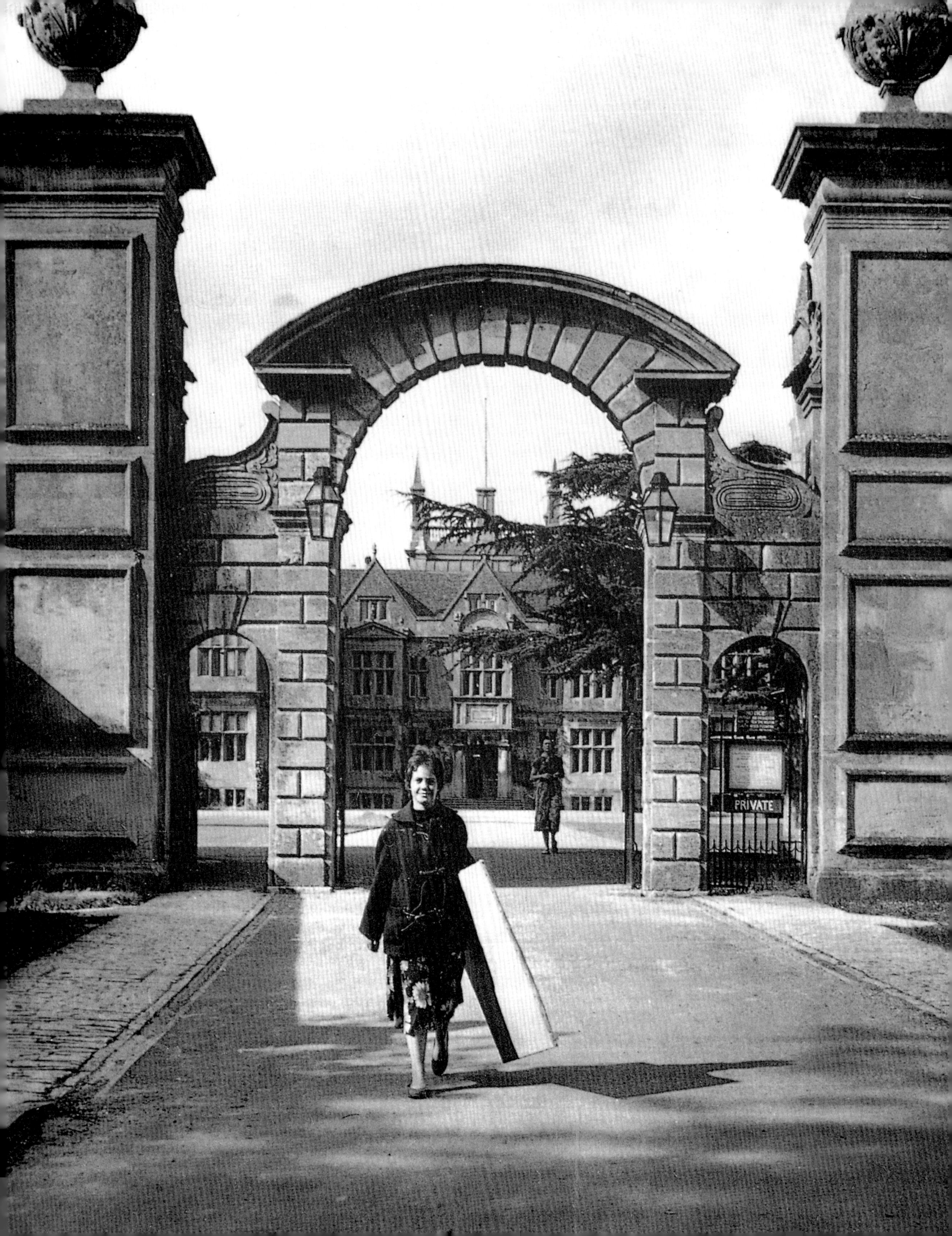
PRIVATE

(*left*) Bath Academy of Art at Corsham Court, Corsham, Wiltshire, 1950s

Moon Figure 1948 (KA3)
H 86 cm (34 in), plaster model

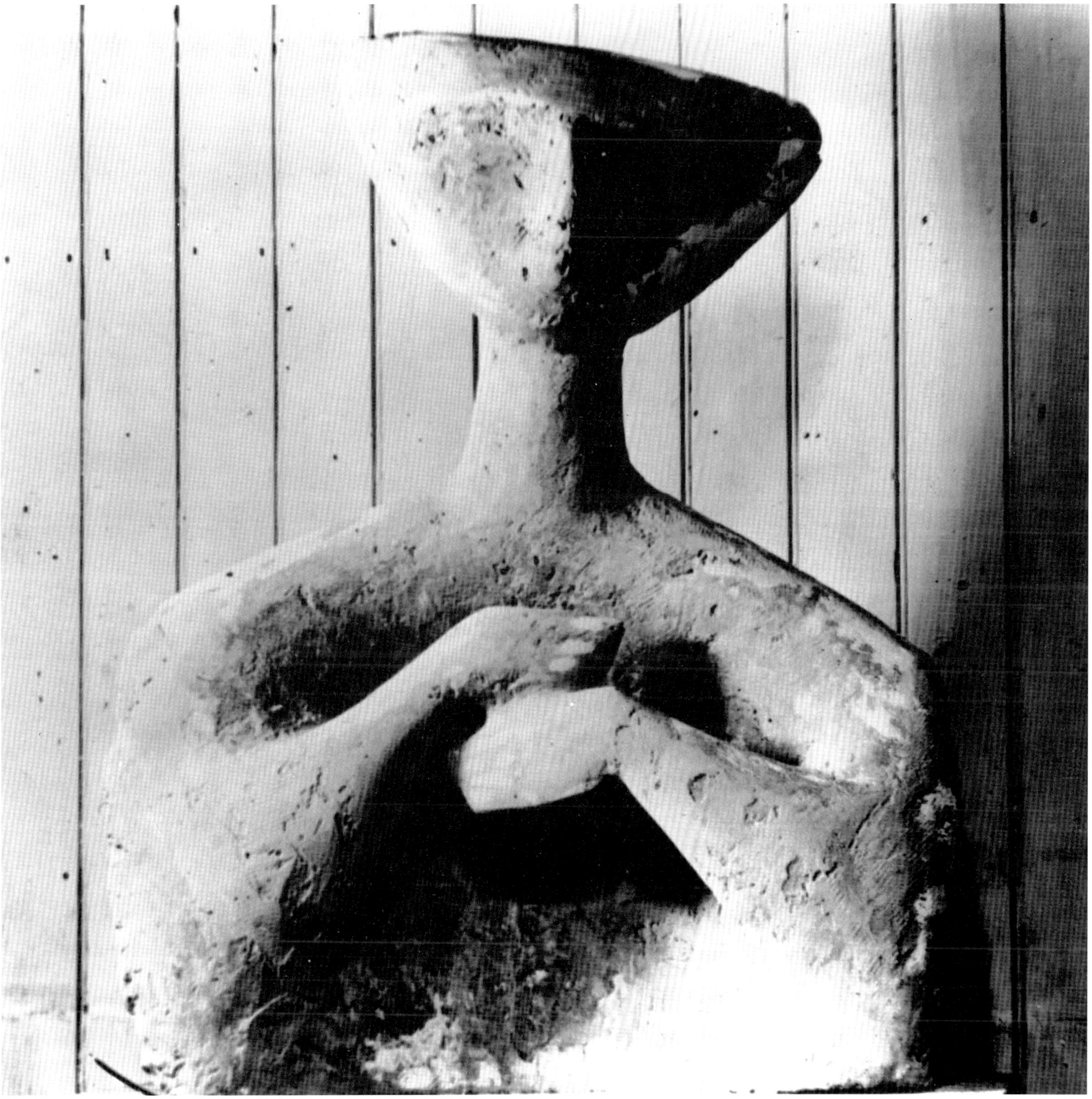

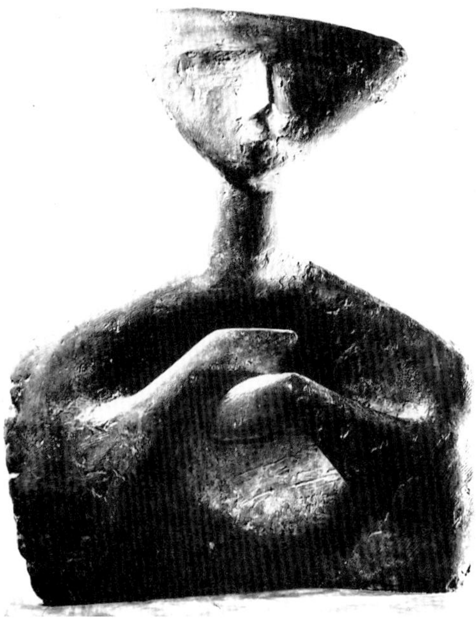

Moon Figure 1948 (KA4)
H 86 cm (34 in), bronze

(*opposite*) *Linked Figures* 1949 (KA5)
H 28 cm (11 in), bronze

1939 until shortly before he died in 1942. Ellis knew the Director of Education in Bath, who was an exceptional man, very far-seeing and bold, and these three decided what they would do. Methuen liked the idea of his home being used as an art school or training college, and Ellis had clear ideas as to how it should be realised. He felt it would be a social experiment: the young students had been deprived of much during the war, and they would now at least be able to see and work within the environment of a privileged way of life, in the magnificent house and its grounds.

After the war there was a shortage of teachers and so there were generous Government funds to help set up the school, which Ellis called the Bath Academy of Art. Hitherto, people who had gone to art schools had fallen back on teaching as a way of earning a living, without any interest in teaching at all. Ellis's idea was to set up a teacher-training course in its own right with a wide range of subjects, including painting, sculpture, pottery, music, drama, literature, print-making as well as teaching practice. In addition to this, about a quarter of the total number of students would follow the normal National Diploma in Design course. Ellis recruited onto the staff exceptional painters and sculptors, theatre designers and musicians and Corsham soon acquired a reputation for producing outstanding teachers, as well as gaining respect in the art community.

William Scott was Head of Painting and I was Head of Sculpture, using the former riding stables. It was double work: I was learning how to make sculpture myself and I had at the same time these students, open-mouthed, waiting for information.

One of the first things I made when we moved to Corsham was a piece I called *Moon Figure* (1948), which had some resemblance to a moon. The head had a crescent shape, it was flattish, and it was developed from an unfinished carving in Portland stone of a figure down to the waist, which I made in the basement of the Bath School of Art. *Moon Figure* was modelled, although it had very much a carving look about it.

While at the Slade, I had noticed something strange: when people made half life-size or even life-size terracottas, if there was an extended arm, or an arm down by the side of a body, they would place a bridge half-way down, linking the arm with the body, a kind of little neck, so that the arm would not snap off. Or, if they had two figures, there would be strange joinings here and there, rather as I imagine Siamese twins are joined together. The memory of these fascinated me, to such an extent that the models I made after a while became joined.

The year after *Moon Figure* I made two figures which I called *Linked Figures* (1949), and that was before I made *People in the Wind* (1950). In *Linked Figures* the figures were definitely merged together: instead of having two bodies they were all one, with arms and legs on the outside. And so in a sense that was a very important break with my previous work. After that, I don't know how it changed; I started making screen-like pieces. *Moon Figure* and *Linked Figures* had no connection with what I had been doing before the war, but by 1950, the aircraft identification that I had been involved with for six years in the Army had begun unconsciously to come out.

When I left the Army, was demobbed and went to Corsham, I pulled a blind down in my mind over the whole of the six-and-a-half years in the Army; I did not want to think about it. I was longing to get on with art. On the other hand, I didn't realise that those years had a

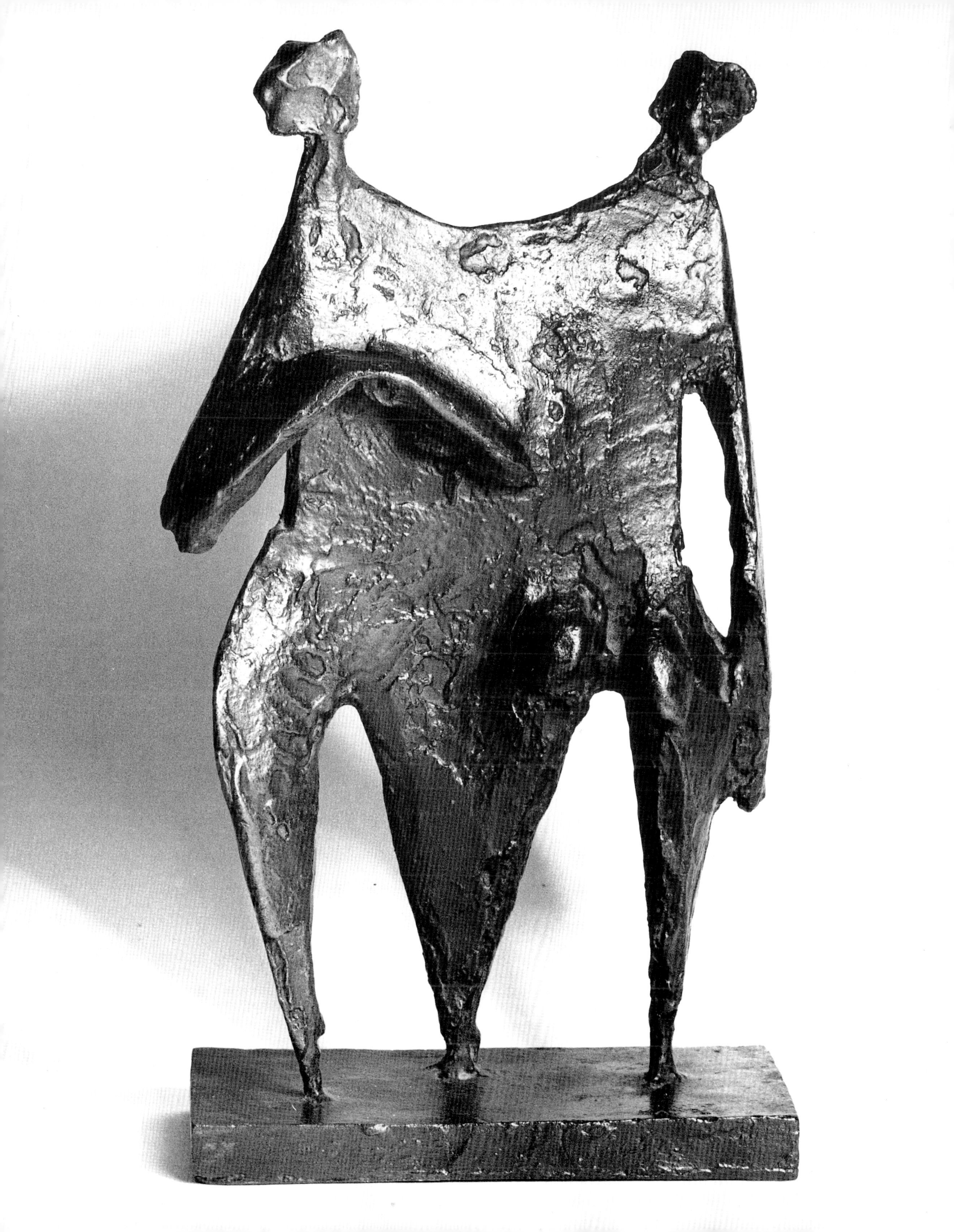

(*opposite*) *Linked Figures* 1951 (KA13)
H 99 cm (39 in), bronze

(*overleaf p.28*) *People in the Wind* 1950 (KA8)
H 65.5 cm (25½ in), bronze

(*overleaf p.29*) *People in the Wind* 1950 (KA7)
H 65.5 cm (25½ in), plaster

tremendous effect on me, because I had been looking at shapes of aircraft and tanks all that time, every day, every week, every month. There was a constant awareness of shape, particularly of aircraft, and these shapes of aircraft came into my work when I started making sculpture at Corsham. No one knew where it had come from; even I didn't realise until later.

I had gone to Bath for one reason really, apart from the job of course, and that was because of the limestone belt crossing England, south-west to north-east. Bath was at one end of that with very thick seams of Bath stone underground. Remembering the Slade I thought that I would be carving for the rest of my life, so to speak; in fact I made only two more carvings, one during the two terms I taught in Bath, and one when I got to Corsham, after which I made no more.

I used to catch the train to Bath from Paddington. The whole train line was designed by I. K. Brunel, who also designed the fabulous Clifton Suspension Bridge over the Clifton Gorge in Bristol, which seemed like one of the wonders of the world at the time. The bridge had a profound effect on me. It was suspended by chains, and its structure was very apparent. And there was I, carving away, and I became dissatisfied. The other thing was, I was looking at modern architecture and reading *The Architectural Review* with its photographs of modern architecture in Italy by Ernesto Rogers, and I became fascinated with Le Corbusier. Now this affected my work, and so instead of carving I started making little models, maquettes, of things with an armature, and I gave up clay modelling, and modelled directly with plaster over wire netting with scrim for stiffening on top. I started joining figures together compulsively and did it more and more. Two or three figures would be unified into one mass, and then I could arrange the arms and legs as I wanted, because if you look at a crowd, you do not count the arms and legs, you just see odd arms swinging and the odd leg moving. So I could use the arms as I wanted in the design of the maquette. And then, one day in London, looking out of the window on a very windy day I saw a woman walking, holding two children, all three leaning against the wind, and this gave me an idea: I started making tiny maquettes with, I think, three figures with long necks, and they had a little bunch of arms in the front, extended forward with hands. There were two or three things involved in this piece. First, seeing the actual people in London with their clothes flapping out in the wind, rather like washing on a line; second, the studio door at Corsham had a little plant outside it, which I saw every day, and it had half a dozen stalks coming up from a small stem, absolutely upright and straight, but opening out at the top, and this impressed me. In addition to the maquette of *People in the Wind*, which had an edition of six, I made two larger versions.

Then something else happened of great interest to me. Clifford Ellis knew the Principal of the Architectural Association, who asked if they could hold a summer school at Corsham where they could use unlimited space. I volunteered to be part of the staff, and a really excellent month it was. About five or six of the architecture students volunteered to come to me in the riding school and make something out of sculpture – the rest were doing things you would expect of young architects, making space frames out of bamboo, cantilevered out from walls. It was hard to know what to do with them: how could people who had never done any sculpture before make something in one month? I had some of my earlier maquettes which were more figurative, and suggested they arranged them into little groups, to see if they could

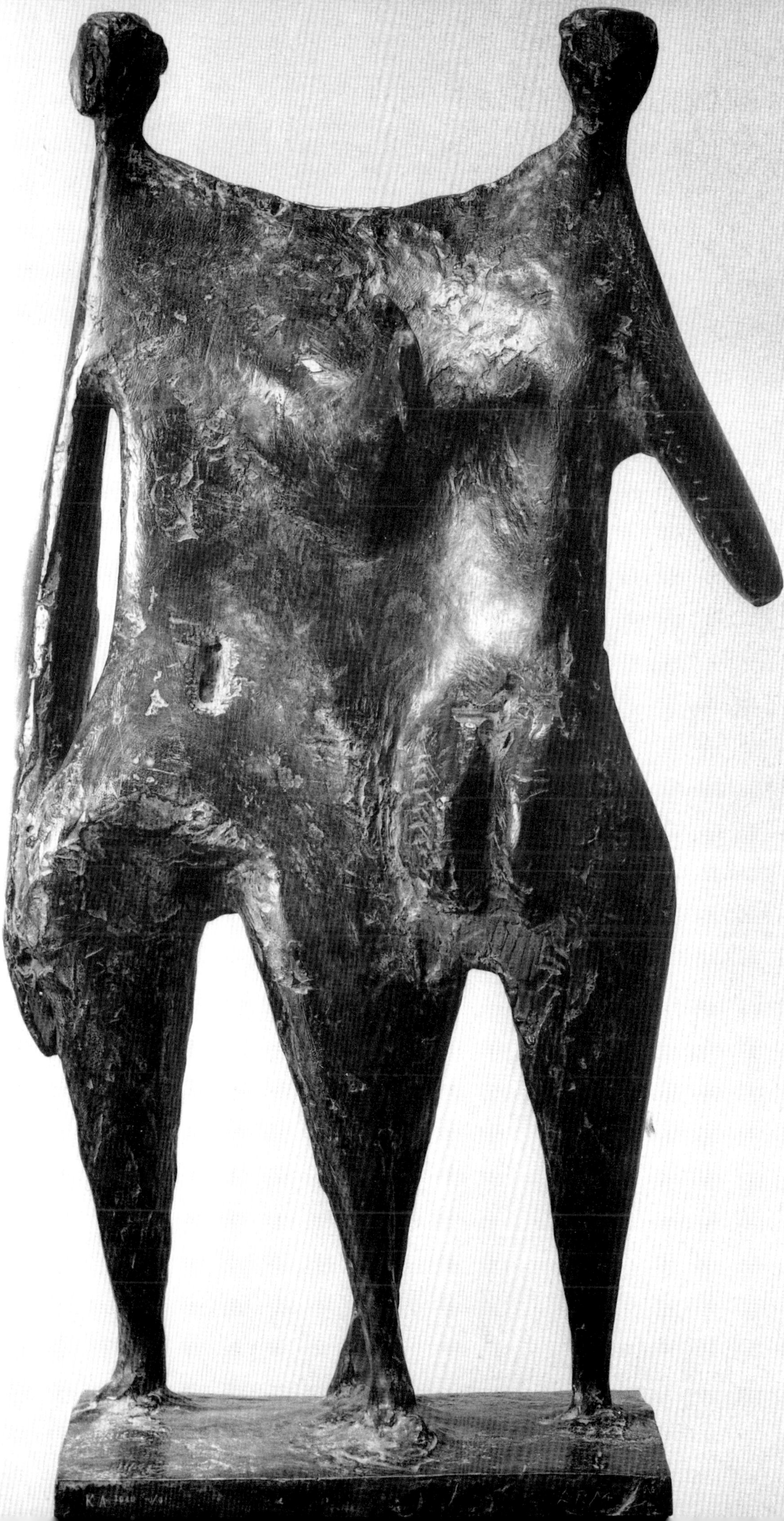

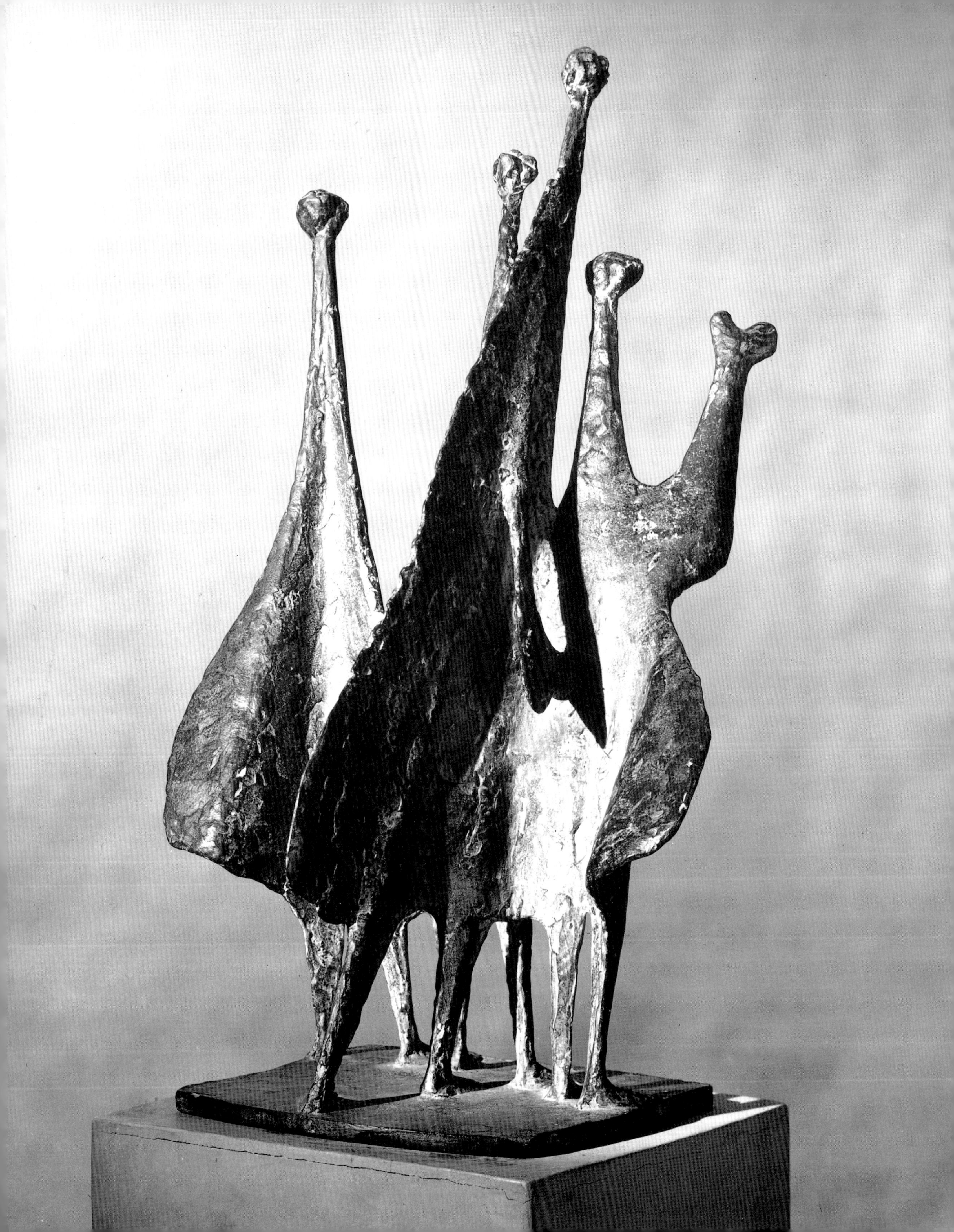

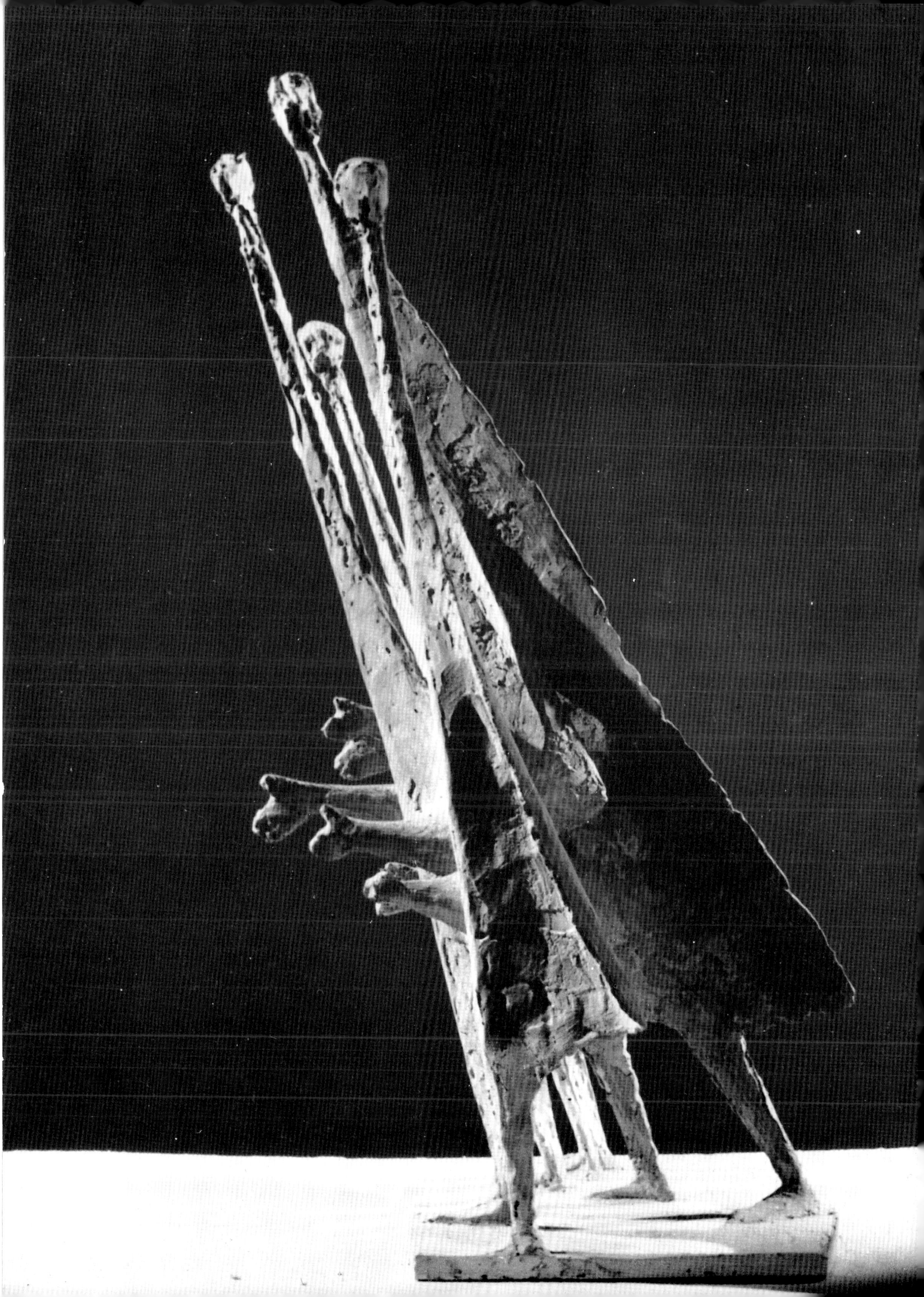

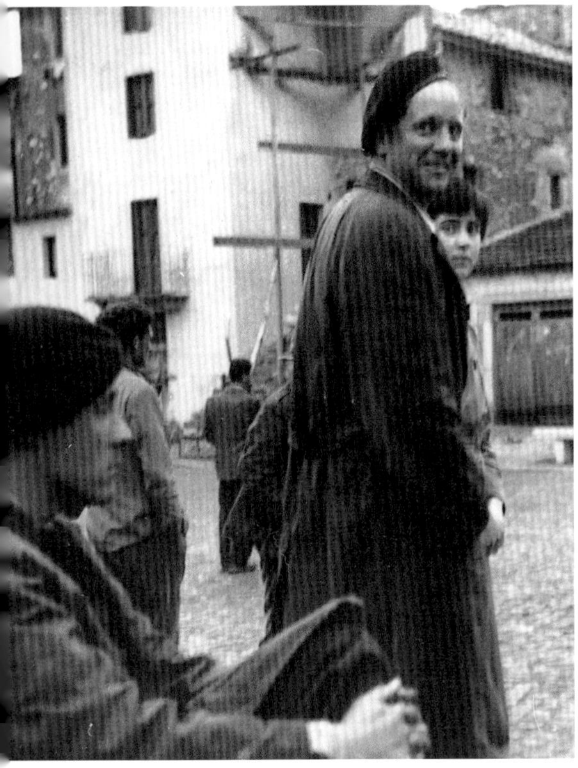

Patrick Heron (*left*), Peter Lanyon (*centre*), and Anne Severs, KA's friend from Corsham (*behind Lanyon*), at Anticola Corrado, Italy, in the early 1950s

(*opposite*) *Family going for a Walk* 1951 (KA15)
H 74 cm (29 in), bronze

make shapes they liked. In the end they decided to make a frieze of about four or five standing figures, about six feet long and four feet high. At the end of the Architectural Association summer school, they had made a hot-air balloon, which was great fun, and they launched it on an August night . . . you could see its burner flickering in the distance. And they also had a firework display, which was probably the first I had ever seen in my life. I noticed the rockets were doing just what my plant was doing outside the back door; three or four rockets would go off and open out until they reached the height of the parabola, and then they would fall to the ground.

I think it was Peter Potworowski who introduced me to the hut in Priory Street belonging to a Miss Spackman,which had previously been used as an infant school. She agreed to let me take it as a studio for £1 10s a week so I could do my own work in there, completely free from students. She left some bits of furniture at one end, and I had two or three folding screens made, with little thin legs, onto which I tacked some corrugated cardboard to conceal the pile of furniture. Various things had influenced me unconsciously; the screens did. Although they were there I never thought about them, but I actually started making real screens. As a result of having looked at aircraft with their wings, the screens appeared as if they were almost flying. The screen has fascinated me all my life, because the folded screen is a shape that is extremely stable, but as it is made of membranes it has very little mass. It is a very light structure.

There was one piece I made, *Roly-poly* (1955), which was lumpy with legs in the air, and that really came from the tanks. Also I made earlier a piece called *Family going for a Walk* (1951), which was slightly heavier; they were slabs rather than thin membranes, but again, with economy in mass.

I was asked if I would teach at the Architectural Association in London,which I was very tempted to do because I liked the students, and it would mean I would be in London, but I realised Corsham had many more opportunities for meeting all kinds of people to do with art.

Peter Potworowski had arrived to teach at Corsham a bit later than I did. He was a good painter and became a very close friend, more so even than William Scott, whom I had known briefly before the war. I also particularly liked Peter Lanyon, and I stayed twice with him in Cornwall. It was not that our work was similar in any way, but I found him stimulating and friendly, I liked being with him. Another friend was James Tower, who taught pottery; we shared our first exhibitions at Gimpel Fils.

One of my first group of students at Corsham included Hubert Dalwood. He was bright from the very first day, and knew what he wanted to do: he was not interested in making drawings from plants, or in all the other things like music, he just stuck to sculpture. He was a good person to teach. He had a kind of jokey abrasiveness and one thing that endeared me to him was that he was always loyal to me. He did extremely well, and one doesn't know what he might have done had he lived longer.

One didn't feel out of touch at Corsham because Ellis invited visiting lecturers all the time; an outstanding one was William Glock, a musicologist who was of the greatest interest. He had learnt to play the piano from Schnabel in Berlin and had run the summer school at Dartington, and just after he lectured at Corsham, he was made Controller of Music at the BBC. I think he

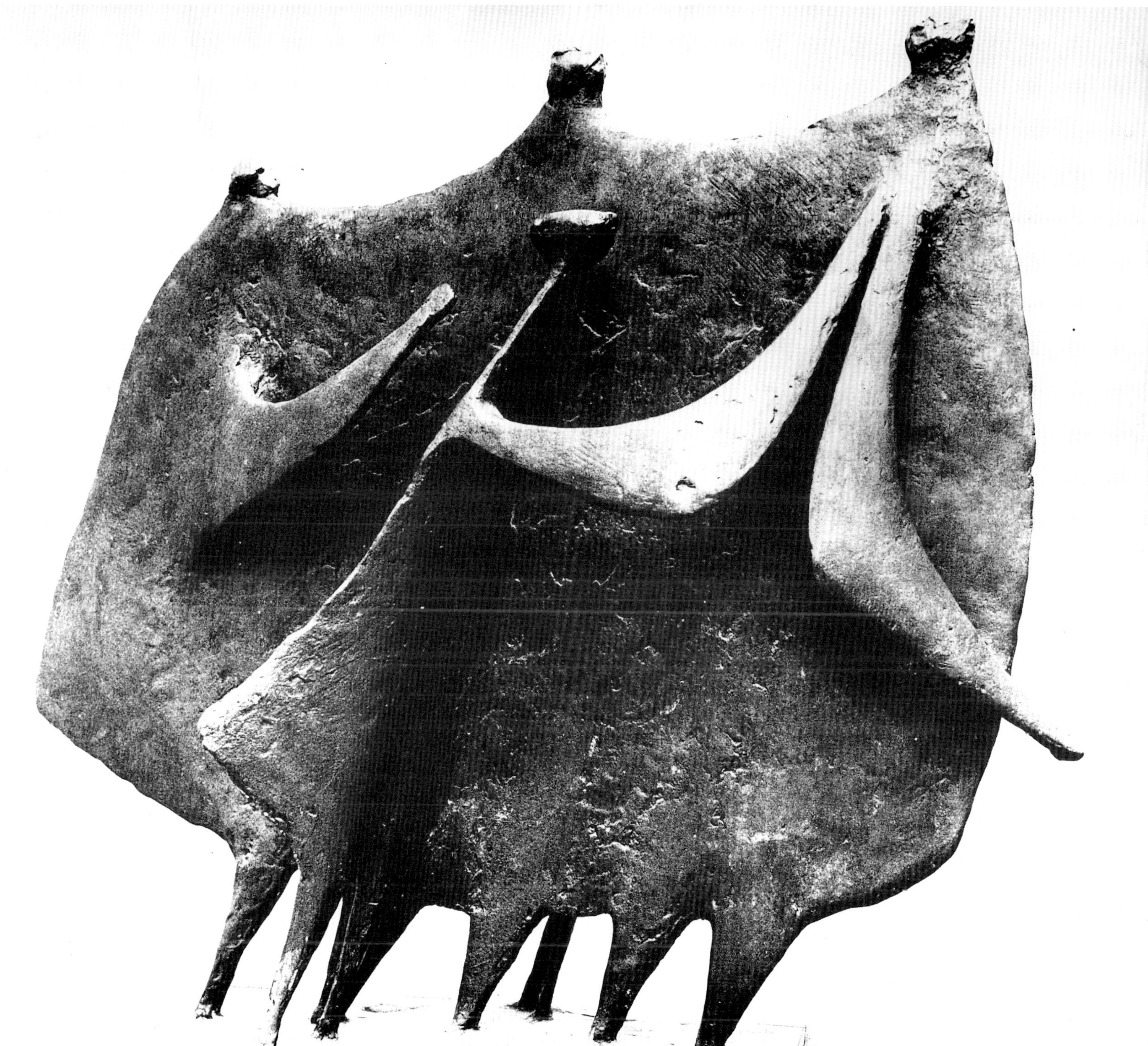

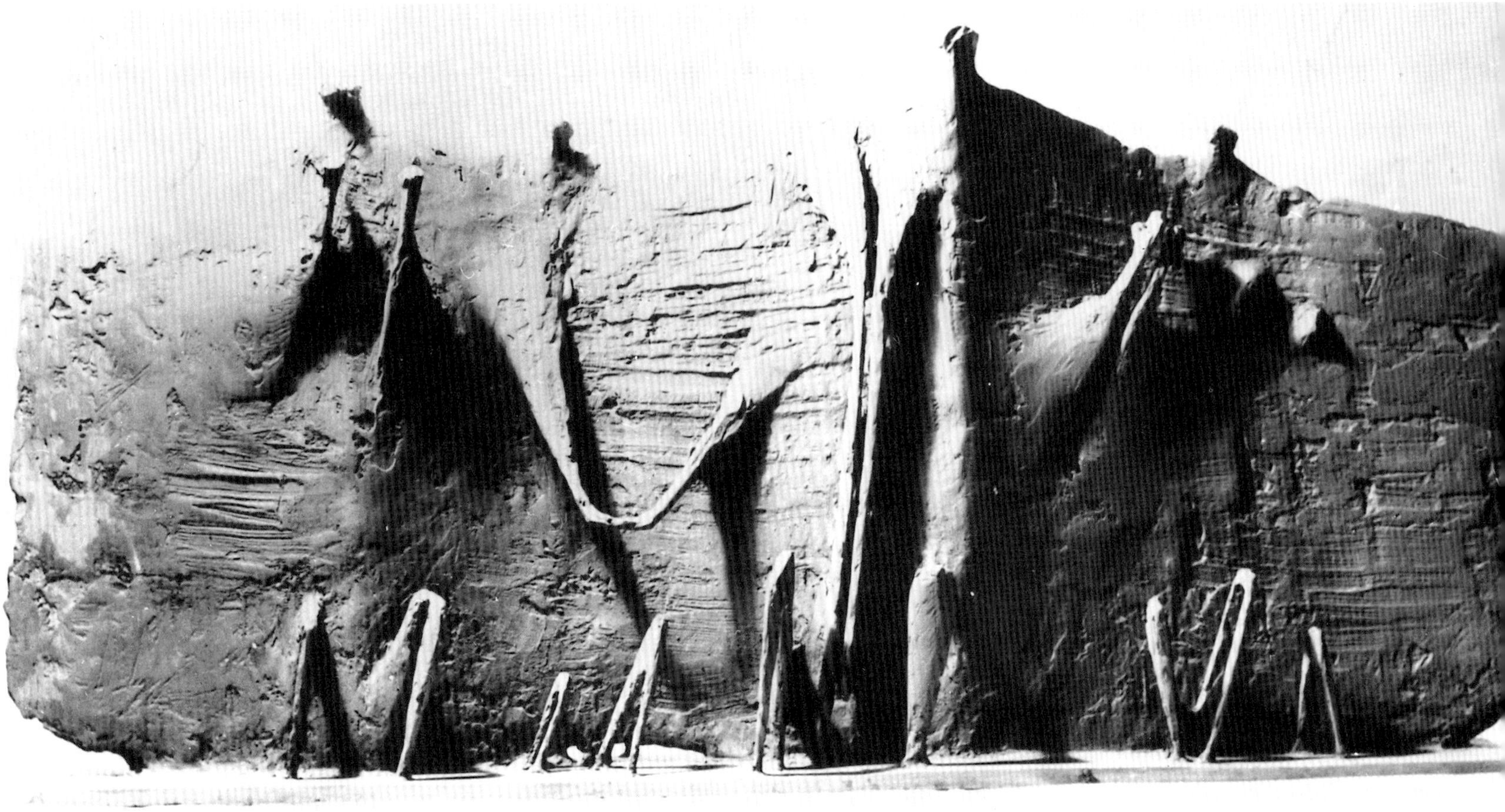

Seated Group listening to Music 1952 (KA23)
L 117 cm (46 in), bronze

(opposite) Friends walking 1952 (KA26)
H 56 cm (22 in), bronze

gave about five or six lectures in the Music Room, with its big organ, where he talked in his buoyant, wonderful way, accompanying himself on the piano. I don't know how many people benefited from it, but I thought it was wonderful, because I have been very attracted to music all my life, as my father had been. Sometimes at night I would go alone into the music room to play records, and I discovered Bach's 'Die Kunst der Fuge' ('The Art of Fugue'); from that moment to this day it has been my number one Desert Island Disc.

I began to be a bit worried that I had been seven years at Corsham, and sometime around 1953 I was offered a Gregory Fellowship in Sculpture at Leeds University. It was both a good and a bad thing for me: it would be an opportunity to make a break with Corsham; I didn't want to leave but I thought I ought to, so I went to Leeds, which of course I knew already. It was the first of many instances in which artists were attached to institutions. The Fellowship was founded by Peter Gregory, Chairman of the publishers Lund Humphries. While I was there John Heath-Stubbs was Gregory Fellow in Poetry and Martin Froy was the Fellow in Painting, followed by Terry Frost, and we each received £500 a year.

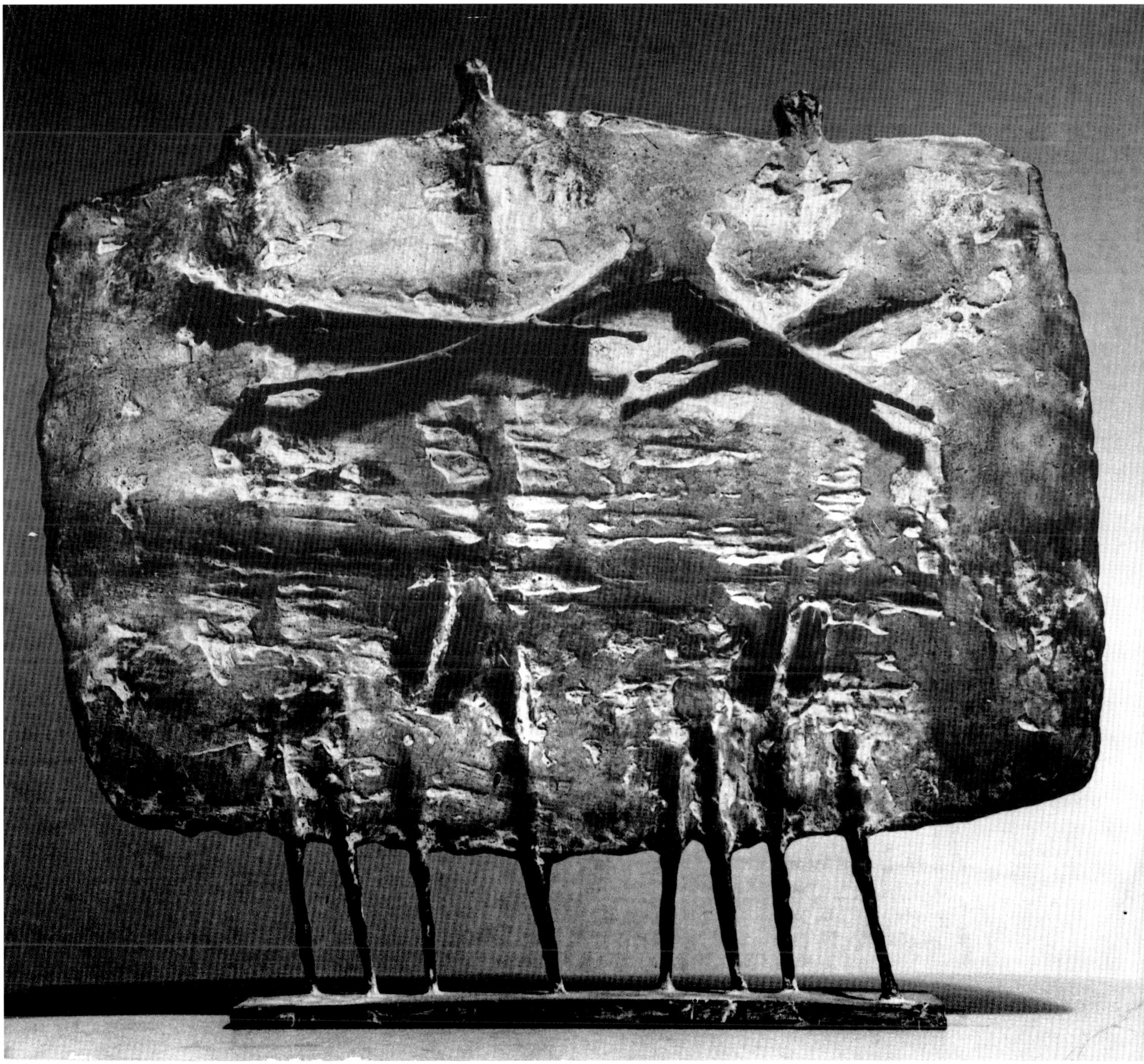

(*opposite*) *Standing Group 2* (large version) 1952 (KA28)
H 104.5 cm (41¼ in), bronze

The landscape itself in the West Riding is completely bare. There are no trees, no houses, just hills covered with heather, and the sides of the hills are lined with dry-stone walling, which gives a kind of section line to the shapes, and nothing else at all except gullies of icy cold water that feed the rivers in the valleys. The valleys by contrast are thick with industrial activity dating from the Industrial Revolution. These buildings still stand, black buildings, rows of black windows, surrounded by terrace houses for the workers, back-to-back with white washing hanging between the buildings, and over all the black chimneys, belching smoke, pulled away by the wind in big curves. This is the landscape of contrast, black and white, and shapes always clearly defined.[3]

Perhaps there is something in the character of the bleak Yorkshire landscape which has a bearing on the making of sculpture. There is this time-lag in sculpture of thinking of an idea, of assembling materials, of going through various stages, which do not necessarily have any visual bearing at all on the final product, all of which requires a kind of sustained effort, and almost slave-like activity. This I somehow link in my mind with the dogged Yorkshire character. It is supposed that the Yorkshire people were never totally suppressed by the Danes; the Brigantes they were called.

It was only later that I realised that Barbara Hepworth, Henry Moore and I were all born within about nine miles of Leeds. And Herbert Read was born a little further over in the North Riding.

I still made visits to Corsham from Leeds and with my colleague Bernard Meadows, who had joined the staff there, we built our own small bronze foundry, just before I ended the Gregory Fellowship. I was able to break my links with Corsham gradually and I resigned officially, as it were, in 1956 and about a week or two later William Scott did too.

After six-and-a-half years of Army service during the Second World War it had been a sheer delight to work at Corsham with its great house and estate, and beyond it the wide countryside of green fields and grey stone houses. But more than that it was close to the richest archaeological area in England with astonishing artefacts such as Silbury Hill, the largest man-made mound in Europe; Avebury stone circle, even larger than Stonehenge; and Stonehenge itself, the most magnificent Stone Age structure in Europe. Windmill Hill, with its important Beaker-folk pottery, and the Kennet Long Barrow were also near. So it was an area which was stimulating to be in, which was another reason why I stayed so long at Corsham. What was interesting was that eventually I got to know an architectural historian, Alastair Service, very well, who brought me much nearer to it all.

My working space in Leeds was minuscule, which restricted my work, and so this was not a very productive period, but I found it a useful intermediate phase. Towards the end of my time in Leeds I found some old stables in London behind Notting Hill Gate, where I then lived and worked for four years. This was really the most creative period of my life.

It was a slum, there were dirty old mattresses left outside. But I loved it there. My neighbours didn't talk for a bit, and after a year a young woman with a baby in a little house opposite suddenly said, 'Hi Ken!' – not Kenneth, or Mr Armitage or something, but 'Hi Ken', and it was lovely to have been accepted like that.

A new gallery, Gimpel Fils, had arrived in London from Paris, and I had been to see them

3. Kenneth Armitage in Warren Forma (ed.), *Five British Sculptors (Work and Talk)*, Grossman Publishers, New York, 1964

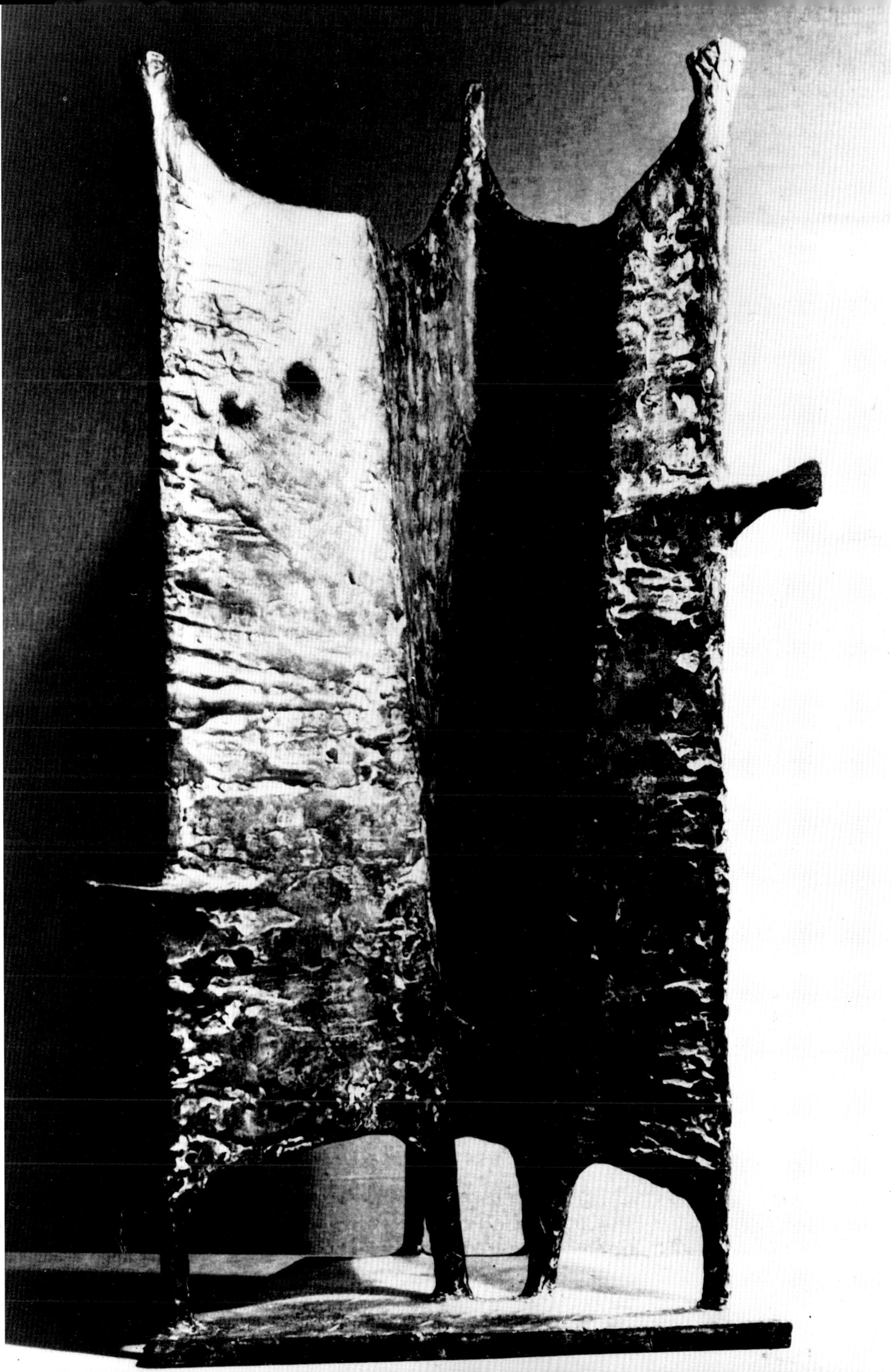

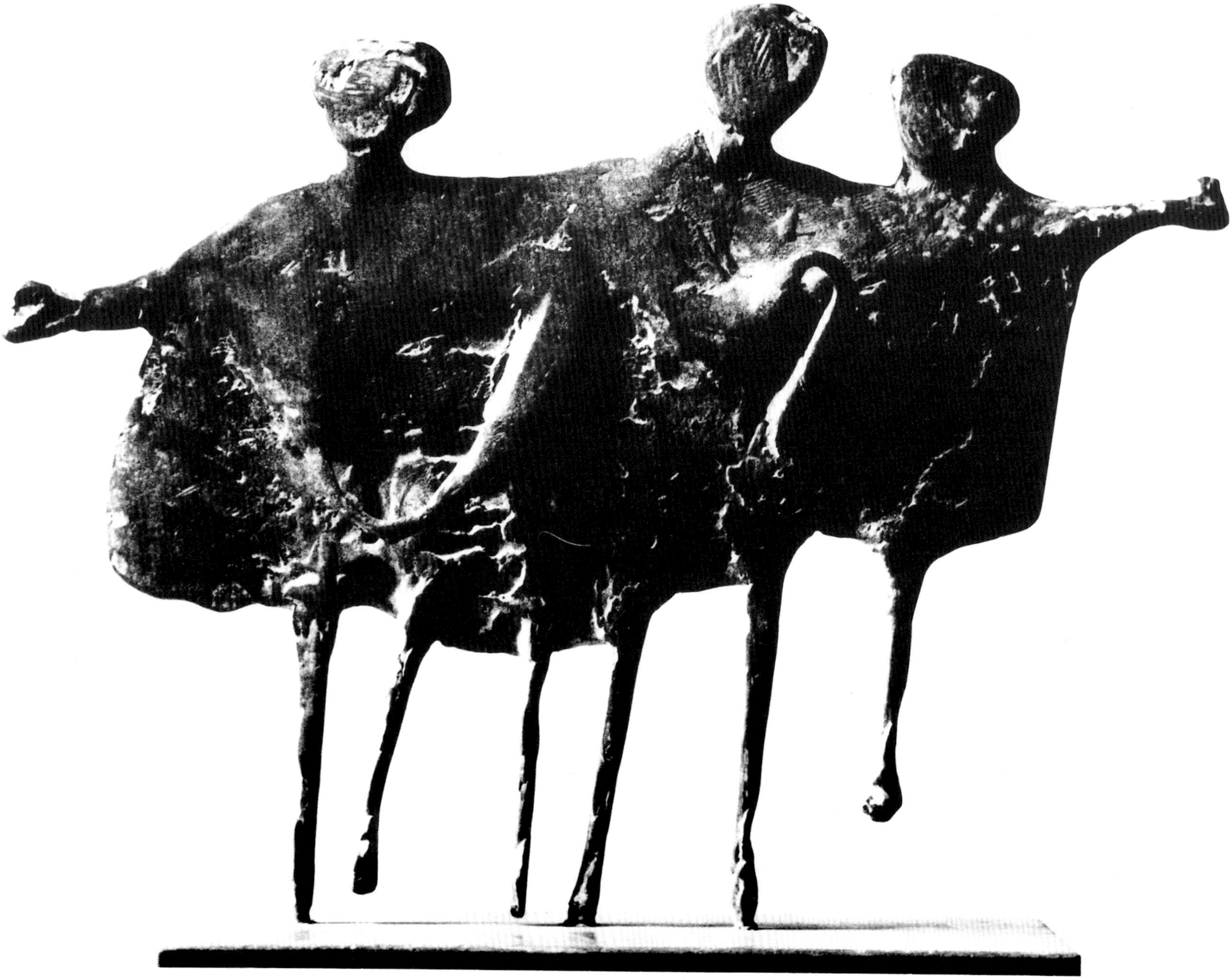

(*above*) *Children playing* 1953 (KA31)
L 42 cm (16½ in), bronze

(*opposite*) *Standing Figure* (*Life Study*) 1953 (KA33)
H 110 cm (43½ in), bronze

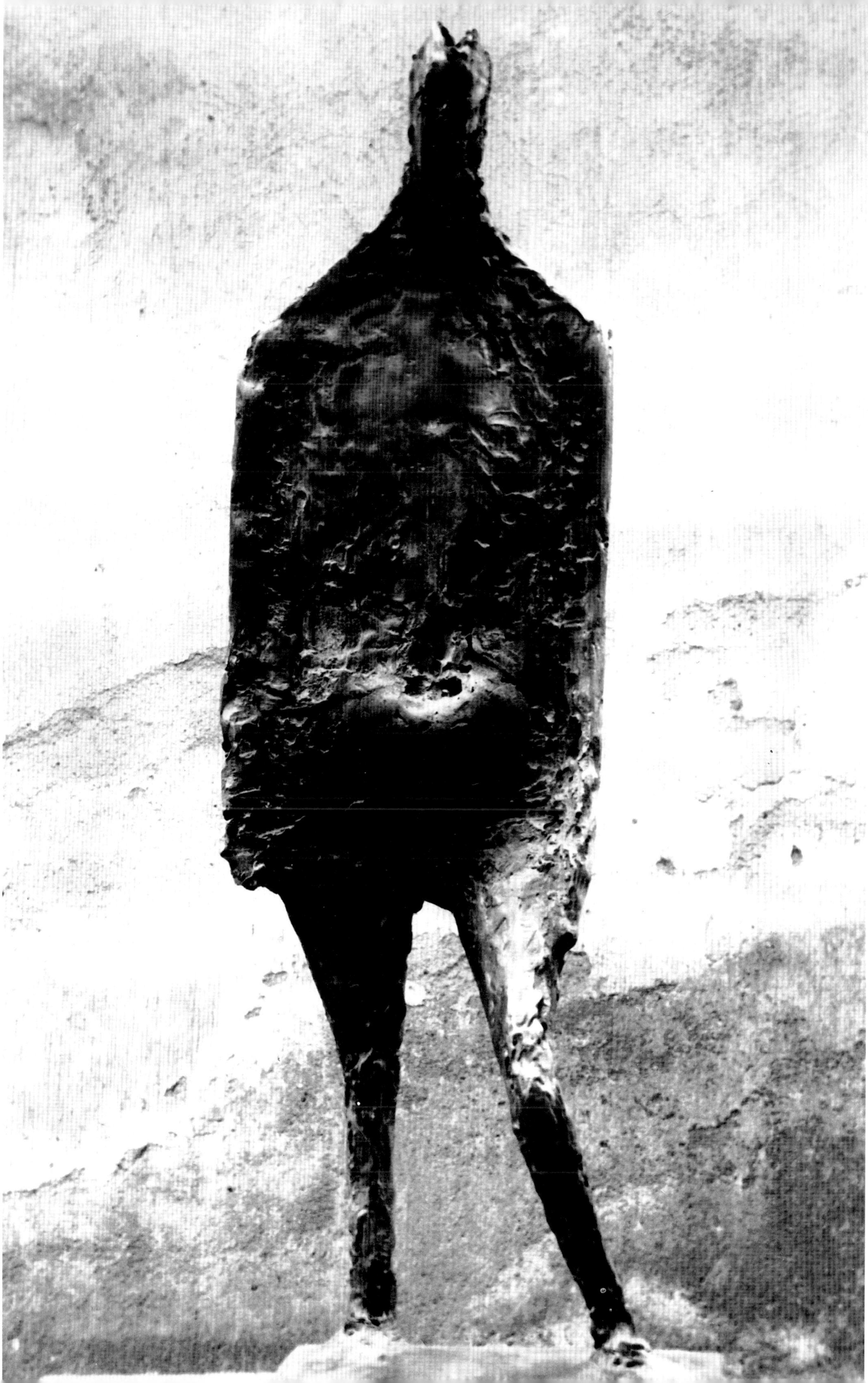

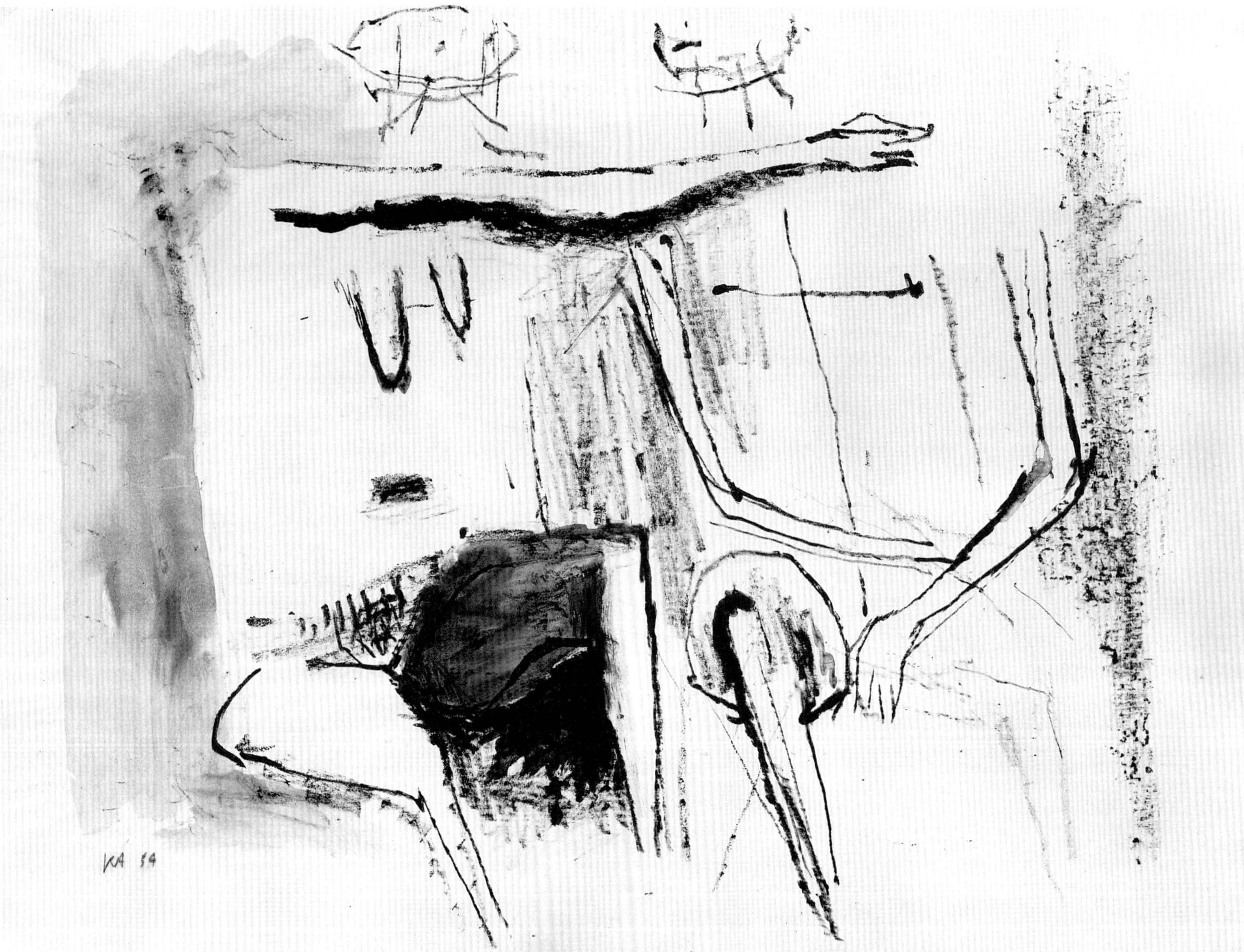

Friends sitting 1954
lithographic chalk and wash

before I went to Leeds; they looked at my work, and said, 'Well, we can't sell that', flicking it with their finger. But they must have thought otherwise, because they did take some work and not only that, they did something for which I am forever grateful, they showed my work to Lilian Somerville, Director of the Fine Arts Department of the British Council, and she liked it. She chaired the selection committee for the 1952 (26th) Venice Biennale, which comprised Philip Hendy, then Director of the National Gallery, and Sir John Rothenstein, Director of the Tate Gallery, and also Herbert Read. I was the last artist to be selected. At the selection meeting Philip Hendy brought out his cheque-book and bought my little maquette of *People in the Wind* on the spot. He called it, rather wittily, 'The Reception Committee'. The exhibition in

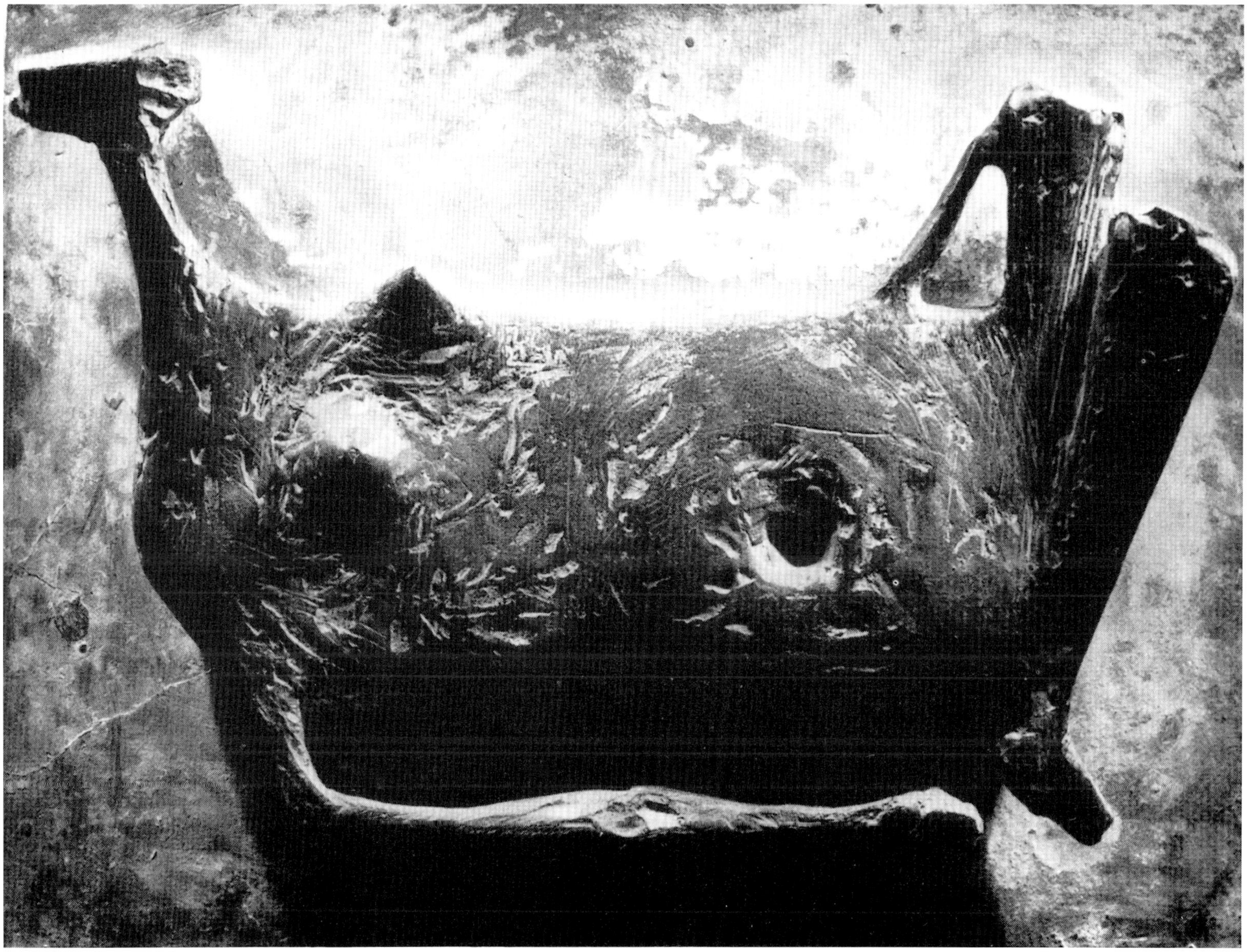

Reclining Figure 1953-4 (KA47)
H 69 cm (27 in), bronze relief
Gift to the Royal Academy of Arts, London, 1995

the British Pavilion at the 26th Venice Biennale, *Aspects of British Sculpture*, was an instant success. I sold practically everything. The first person there to buy was Peggy Guggenheim; the second, Madame Schiaparelli, and the Museum of Modern Art, New York bought *People in the Wind* and *Family going for a Walk*. The Museum of Modern Art in Rome bought something, and others did too. The exhibition was a sell-out. It was really the beginning of my professional life. Among my co-exhibitors were Robert Adams, Reg Butler, Lynn Chadwick, Geoffrey Clarke and Bernard Meadows. I was totally unknown before that, and in those few weeks I became a known name internationally.

Lynn Chadwick and I were very friendly at first until I found that our different priorities

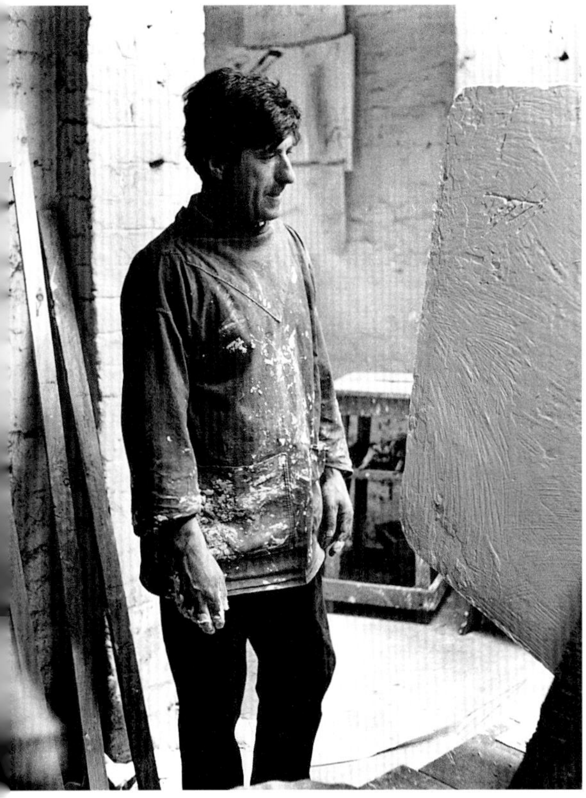

Kenneth Armitage, 1957

(opposite) Diarchy 1957 (KA79)
H 174 cm (68½ in), bronze

made it difficult to continue our friendship. I had a real feeling for Reg Butler's work, although we were never close friends. Reg was an extremely clever man. During the war he had been a conscientious objector, and he had been put to work in a blacksmith's forge; it was that which gave him the idea to weld sculpture out of iron. Erica Brausen was showing him at the Hanover Gallery at that time.

Butler, who was a kind of puritan at heart, I felt, thought that although he knew all about architecture and engineering, artists had models and so on, and so he thought he would make nudes, and he did this marvellous work *Girl* (1953-4). He became more and more figurative and it is interesting that in his *Unknown Political Prisoner* he had tiny little figures about an inch or two high, called 'Watchers', and these grew and grew and grew in size; he forgot all about the welding. He was technically brilliant: he made casts and finished them off impeccably; he then drilled millions of little holes in the scalp and threaded real hair in so that they had wigs. He used ceramic eyes, which he turned in a lathe, and they were somehow let into the bronze, the whole thing was painted, and they were in fact very erotic and luscious. But there were some strange things about them. Their positions were often grotesque, and I believe this was because he used a manikin (the kind sold in art shops,which you can arrange as you like); the knees are jointed, so he could find the position he liked. This was the reason why some of them were in almost impossible positions. Maybe he liked that, but they did make one a bit uneasy. The other thing that made me uneasy was that in spite of the enormous naturalism of the hair on the head and the paint of the body, and the eyeballs, and the lips and everything, which were dazzling, there was no pubic hair. And this had, to my mind, an almost decadent effect. There are prostitutes who shave; there are maybe men who do not like pubic hair. But I thought, well, there are two reasons for this. One, he liked it like that; the other, I have a feeling that he had not shed his basic puritanism. Whereas I have always used the pattern made by pubic hair – this very beautiful triangle on a woman, advertising her nudity – which is an eye-catcher. It is very interesting that the Japanese never include it in their prints – even in their *ukiyo-e* prints you will never see any pubic hair.

Just after the 1952 Venice Biennale, I had a letter from a well known dealer from New York called Curt Valentin, who also wrote to Gimpels, saying he would like to do business with me. Valentin was an exceptional man who worked very hard; he loved sculpture and everybody loved him. In fact he really helped make Henry Moore and Marino Marini into international figures. Gimpels did not approve and advised me not to agree to let him show my work, so I did not. Had I gone to Curt Valentin my life might have been different.

While I was in the Notting Hill studio (1955-9) I worked constantly, generally on larger work which seemed to go in series, but I made one piece you might call 'King and Queen' of two seated figures, again a slab joined together. I also made a bigger sculpture with three figures, nine feet long, and I did not know what to call them. One had two heads and one had three heads, and an approximate number of arms and legs, and it was Gerald Forty at the British Council who suggested the titles: 'Diarchy is rule by two, Triarchy is rule by three'. I was not so much interested in the ruling business; it reminded me of Henry Moore's *King and Queen*, which I never really liked very much anyhow; I had seen them at the foundry, and I liked his

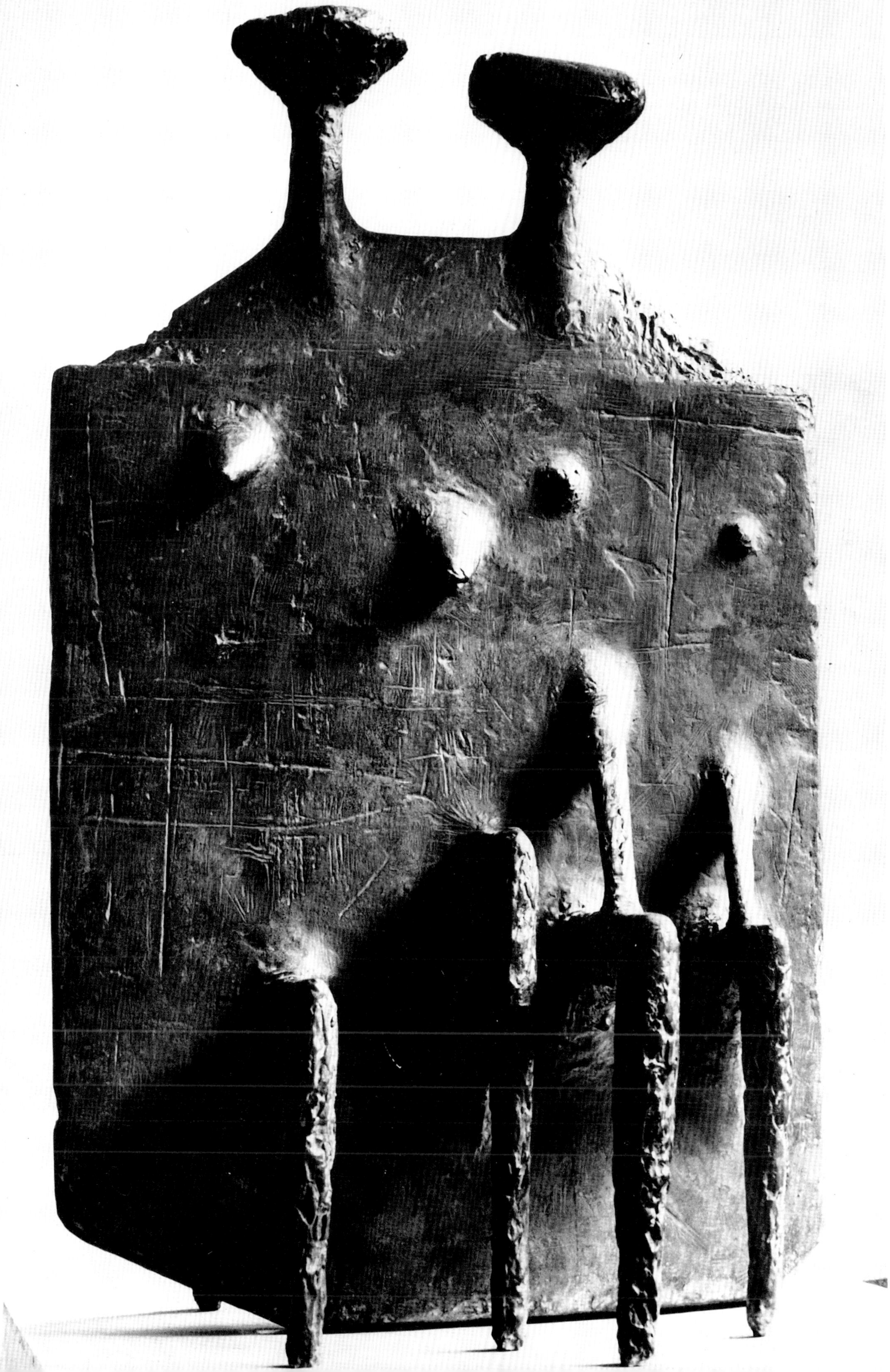

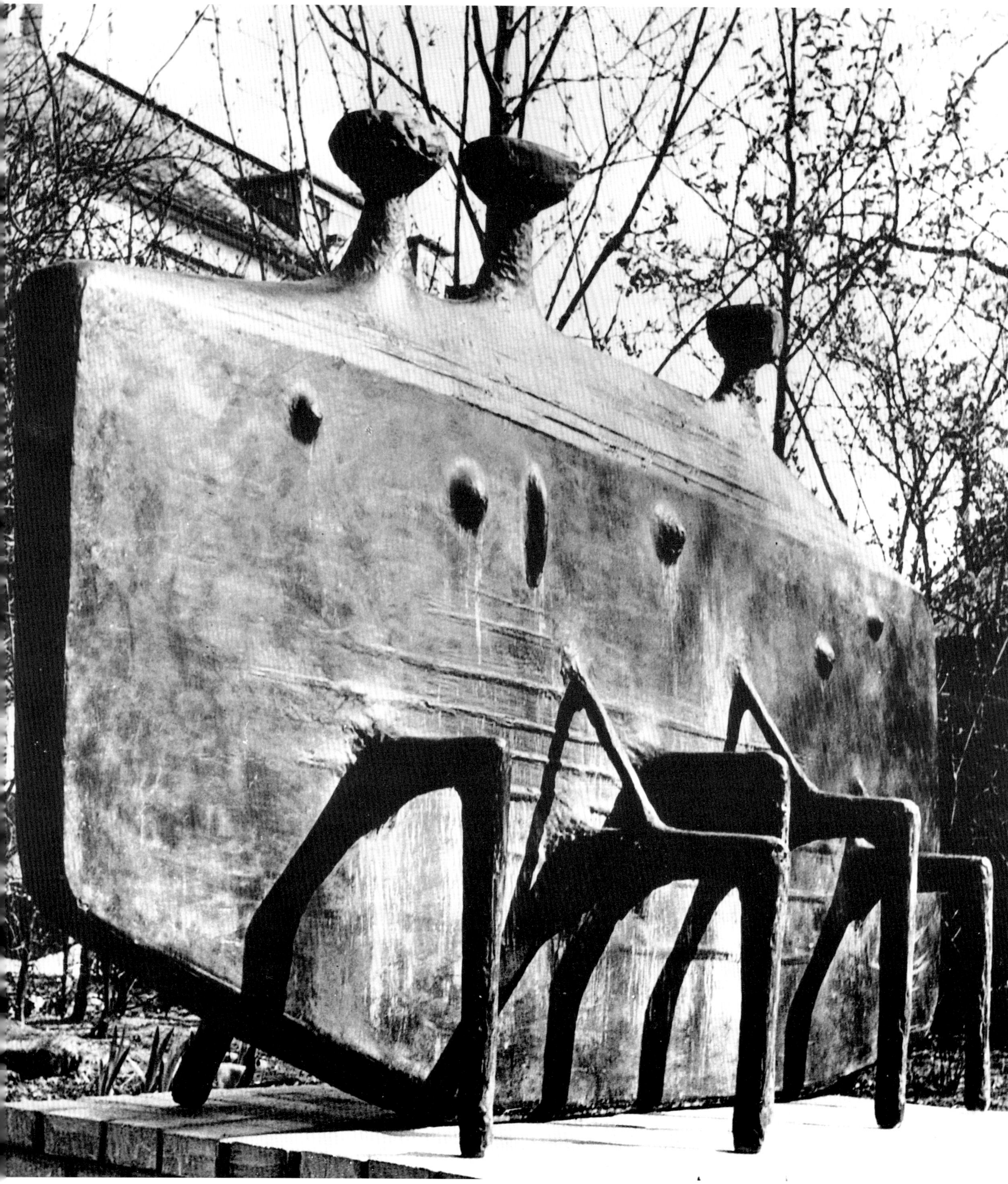

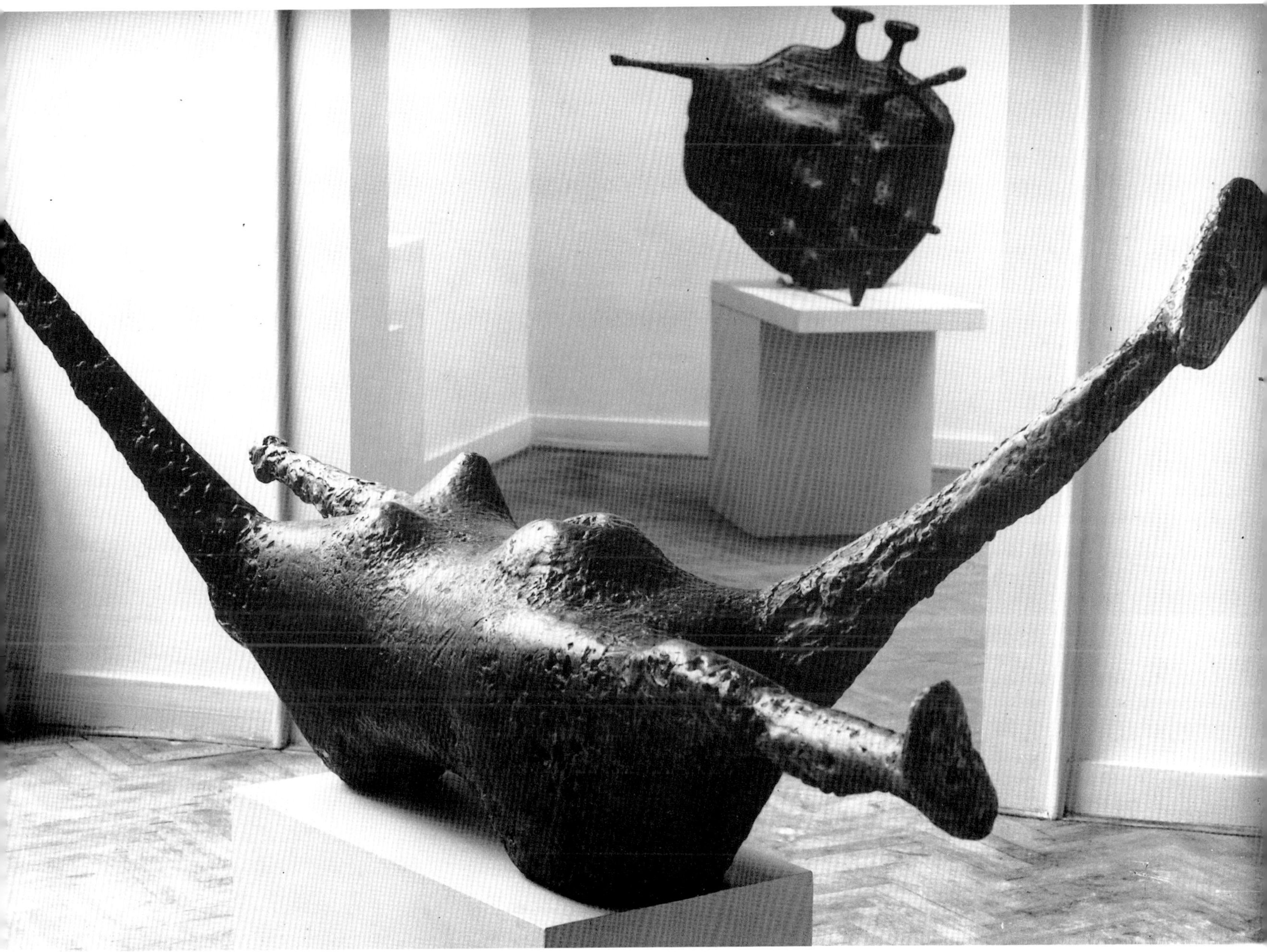

other work much better. But *Diarchy* and *Triarchy* were suitable titles for both, and they were shown in the Venice Biennale of 1958.

I also made a series of reclining figures (I think there were four), two or three of which I also showed in the 1958 Venice Biennale, and there were one or two standing figures. And I made a big piece called *Sprawling Woman*, which was almost nine feet long, and several smaller things, working constantly.

In 1956 I had made a piece called *The Seasons*, and a bit like *People in the Wind* it was an

(*above*) *Sprawling Woman* (large version) 1957 (KA81)
L 258 cm (101½ in), bronze
This illustration shows the work exhibited in the British Pavilion at the 1958 Venice Biennale. In the background is *Two Seated Figures* (large version) 1957 (KA68).

(*opposite*) *Triarchy* 1958-60 (KA86)
L 247 cm (97¼ in), bronze
This illustration shows the work in the Armitage exhibition at the Kestner-Gesellschaft, Hanover, 1960.

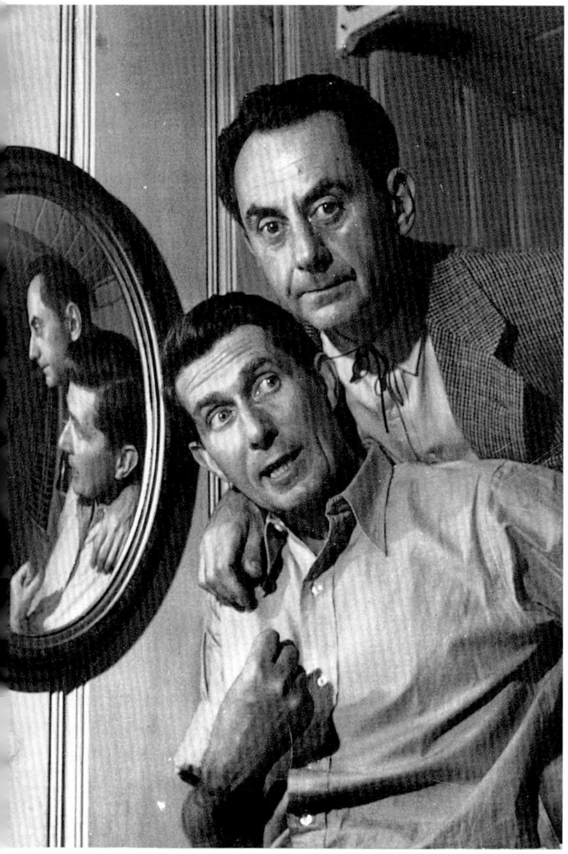

Man Ray (*top*), with Roland Penrose, Los Angeles 1946

(*opposite*) *The Seasons* 1956 (KA59)
H 86 cm (34 in), bronze (partly painted)
at the Venice Biennale, 1958

immediate best-seller. It was rather like bagpipes, with arms and legs reaching up and down. The first cast had painted areas on it in black and white, which I think was the first time I used colour on a sculpture.

At the Venice Biennale of 1958 (29th Venice Biennale) William Scott, William Hayter and myself each had one-man exhibitions in the British Pavilion. In those days the Venice Biennale was very important indeed and Chillida got the first prize. I was delighted, because I liked him, and I liked his work, and he became a great friend. At the previous Biennale Lynn Chadwick had won the first prize, beating Giacometti. A man called David Bright, who liked my work very much and bought a lot of it, created the David E. Bright Foundation Award for the best sculptor under forty-five, thinking of me.

After that the exhibition toured widely to national museums. When it reached Paris, Roland Penrose was the British Council representative there. It was wonderful to be there with him because he gave parties and he would ask, say, Giacometti and Miró, and other artists he knew; it seemed he knew everybody. I met Man Ray several times. At the end of the tour, in 1959, I had a retrospective exhibition at the Whitechapel Art Gallery.

In 1959 I moved to my present studio, where I live, near Olympia in West London, which was designed as a sculptor's studio by the Edwardian architect James Maclaren. (I met my friend Alastair Service after he had included material on the house in his book on Edwardian architecture.)

London seemed to be smaller in those days. I knew people like Hugh Gaitskell and Tony Crosland, who became a friend, and it was at a party where he lived in The Boltons that I met Robert Colquhoun and Robert MacBryde. Roger Hilton became a close friend and he moved next door to me in Notting Hill so I got to know him well. We used to drive down to the 'Queen's Elm' pub where we knew everybody.

In 1955 I made *Seated Woman with Square Head*. It was sixty-one centimetres high, a dumpy fat figure, a cast of which is owned by the Tate. A square head was used on a later work for the Mouton Rothschild commission. So far as I know, I have never been influenced by any contemporary work; one does one's work because it comes from inside and not because of anyone else. But in this case I was struck by Sidney Nolan's series of paintings based on the infamous Australian bandit Ned Kelly with his black steel helmet. Sidney Nolan's paintings were haunting. Titles are very difficult; sometimes it is very natural to call a piece by what is most striking about it, if there is some means of identification, such as a square head, a *Sprawling Woman* or a *Figure lying on its Side*, which you cannot mistake.

There were five versions of *Figure lying on its Side*, and for the first time I began to be aware of relating sculpture to the ground; isolated in rooms in galleries and in people's homes, sculptures seem to have no bearing on the ground or gravity. The natural thing for me with sculpture is to be very conscious of the vertical and the horizontal, and I very often had in mind a three-dimensional cross. So here in *Figure lying on its Side* were pronounced lines made by the limbs, reduced almost to sticks. *Sprawling Woman* (1957) was a female figure lying on her back, with a very arched back; her arms and legs were spread out, but there was a pronounced horizontal line.

In 1958-9 I made a piece called *Girl without a Face*. Instead of a face, there is an empty space

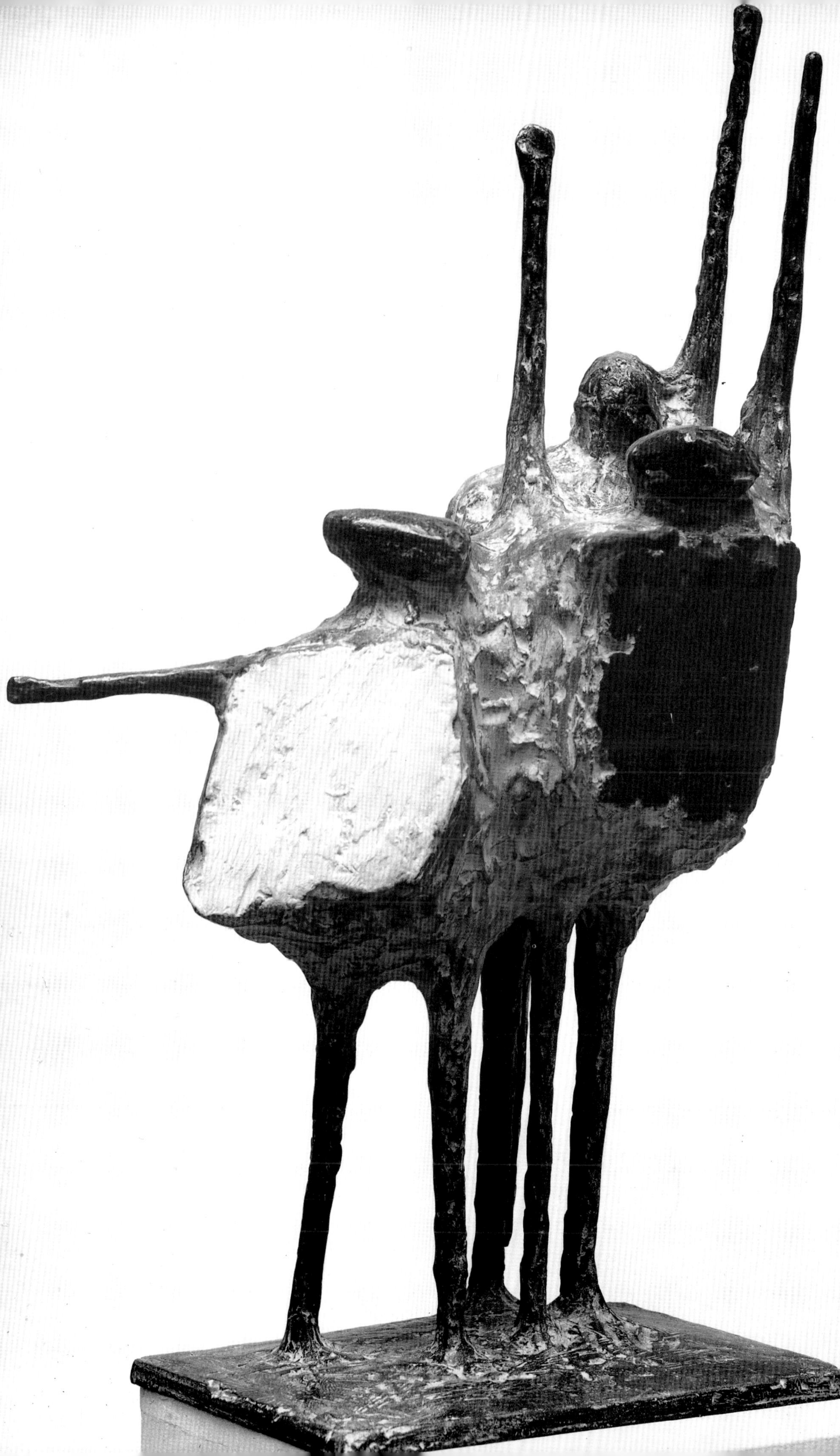

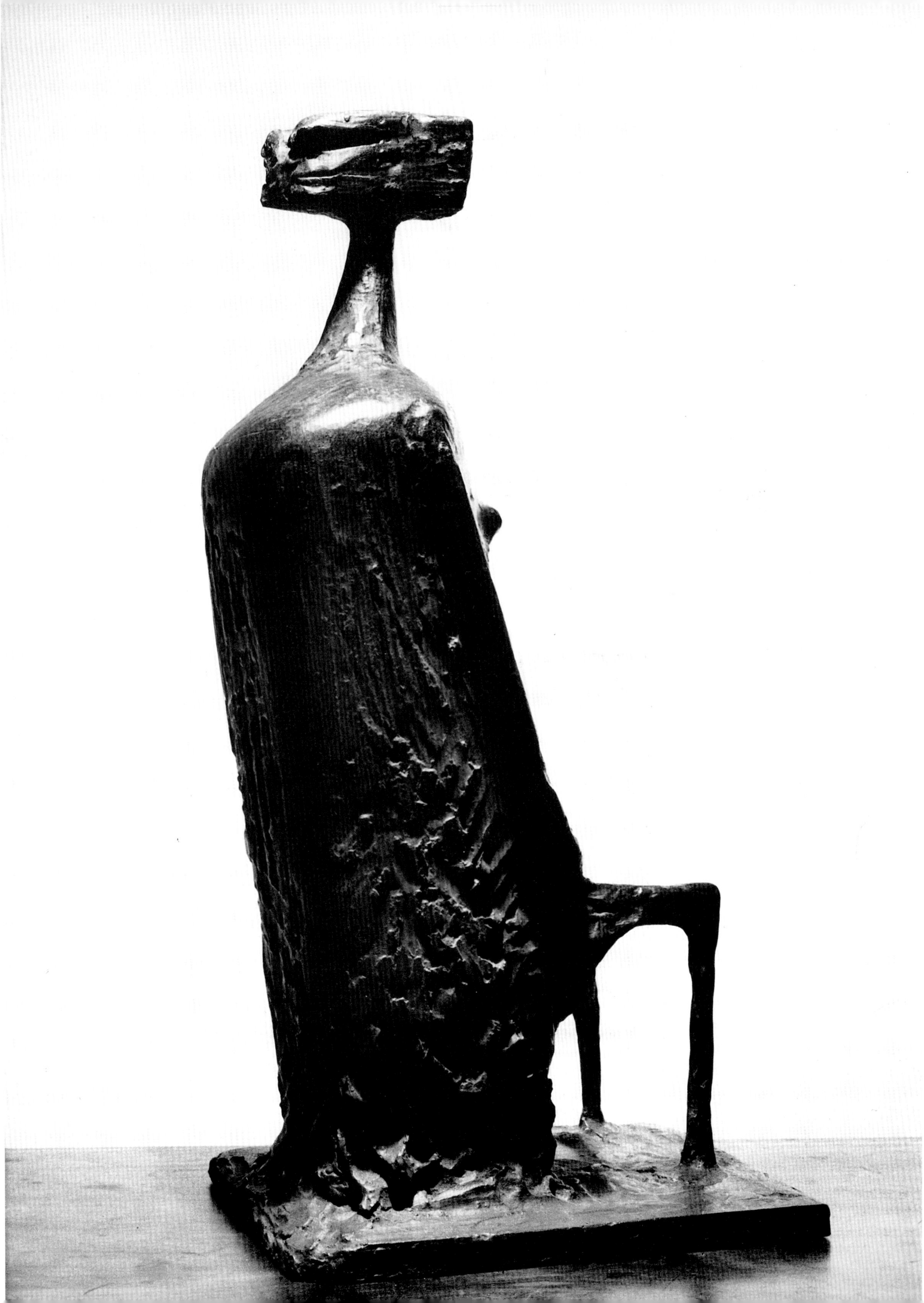

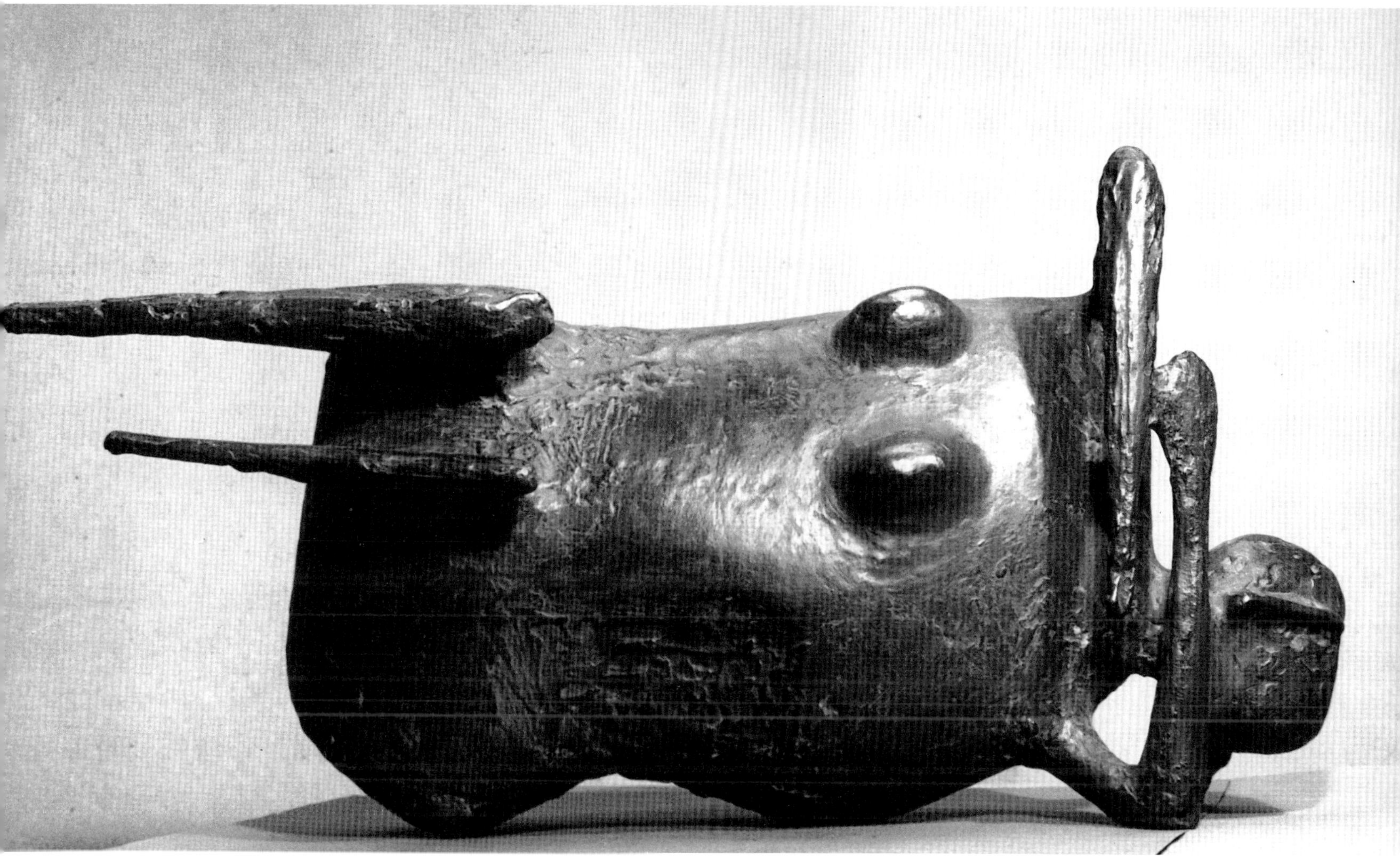

under the hat which goes right back to the bronze at the back. And I remember this started because I was looking, as one did every Saturday, at *Picture Post*, the illustrated magazine with all kinds of excellent topical photographs, published by Teddy Hulton. I remember finding a photograph of a row of models with big hats, and because their faces were partly in shadow I made drawings from the photo and automatically drew a strong shadow under the hat, where the face would have been. It was an odd idea, to have no face.

(*above*) *Figure lying on its Side* (version 5) 1957 (KA67)
L 84 cm (33 in), bronze

(*opposite*) *Seated Woman with Square Head* 1955 (KA54)
H 61 cm (24 in), bronze

The shadow idea was included in my next piece. Just before I left the studio at Notting Hill Gate, the poet Stephen Spender rang asking if he could call by, having just returned from Mouton, the vineyard in France, with a message for me from Philippe de Rothschild. Baron de Rothschild had just seen two or three of my sculptures in the Museum of Modern Art in New York, one of which was *Diarchy*, and he decided to commission me to make a piece featuring the sun for the pediment on the façade of his château at Mouton.

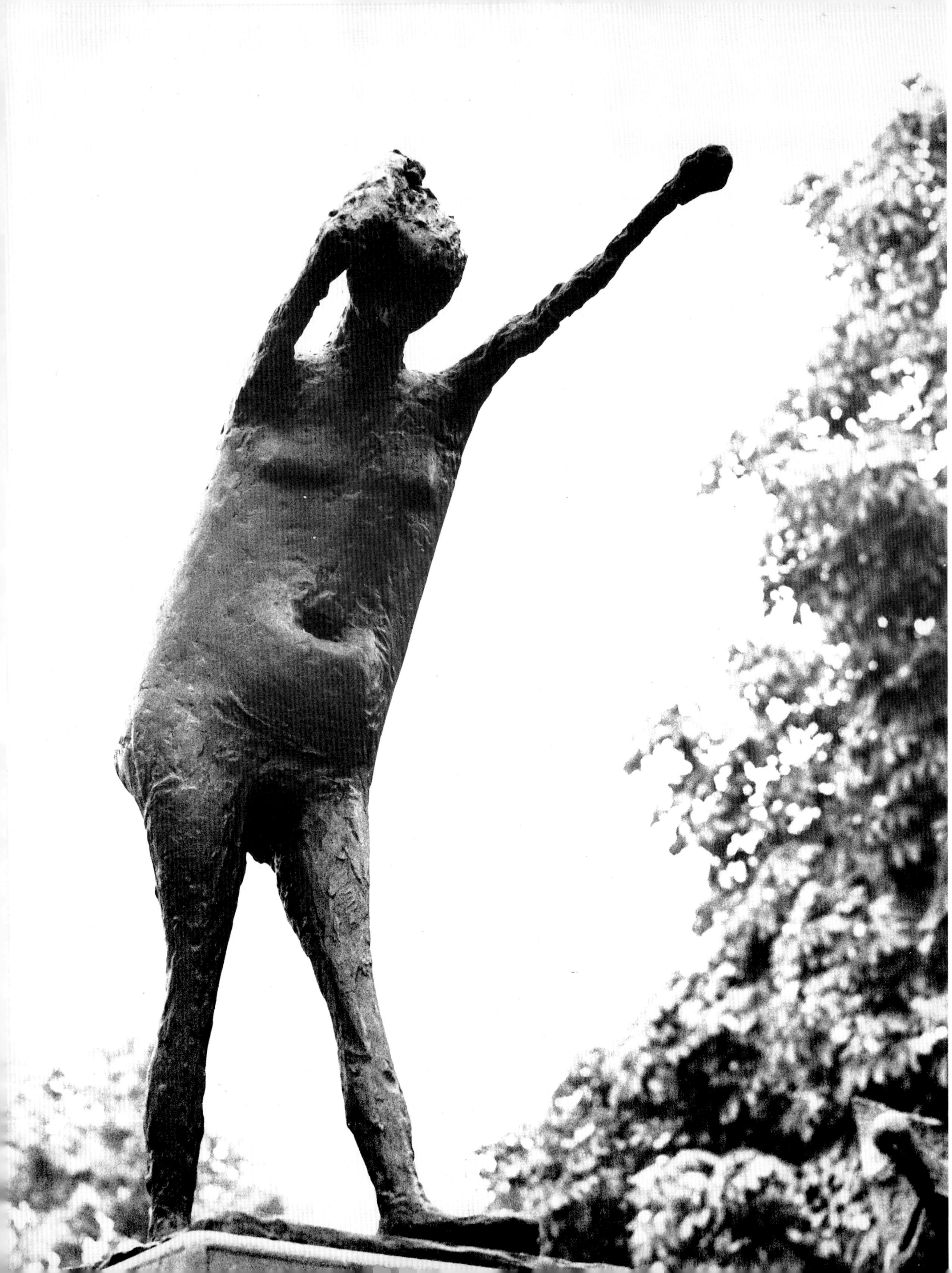

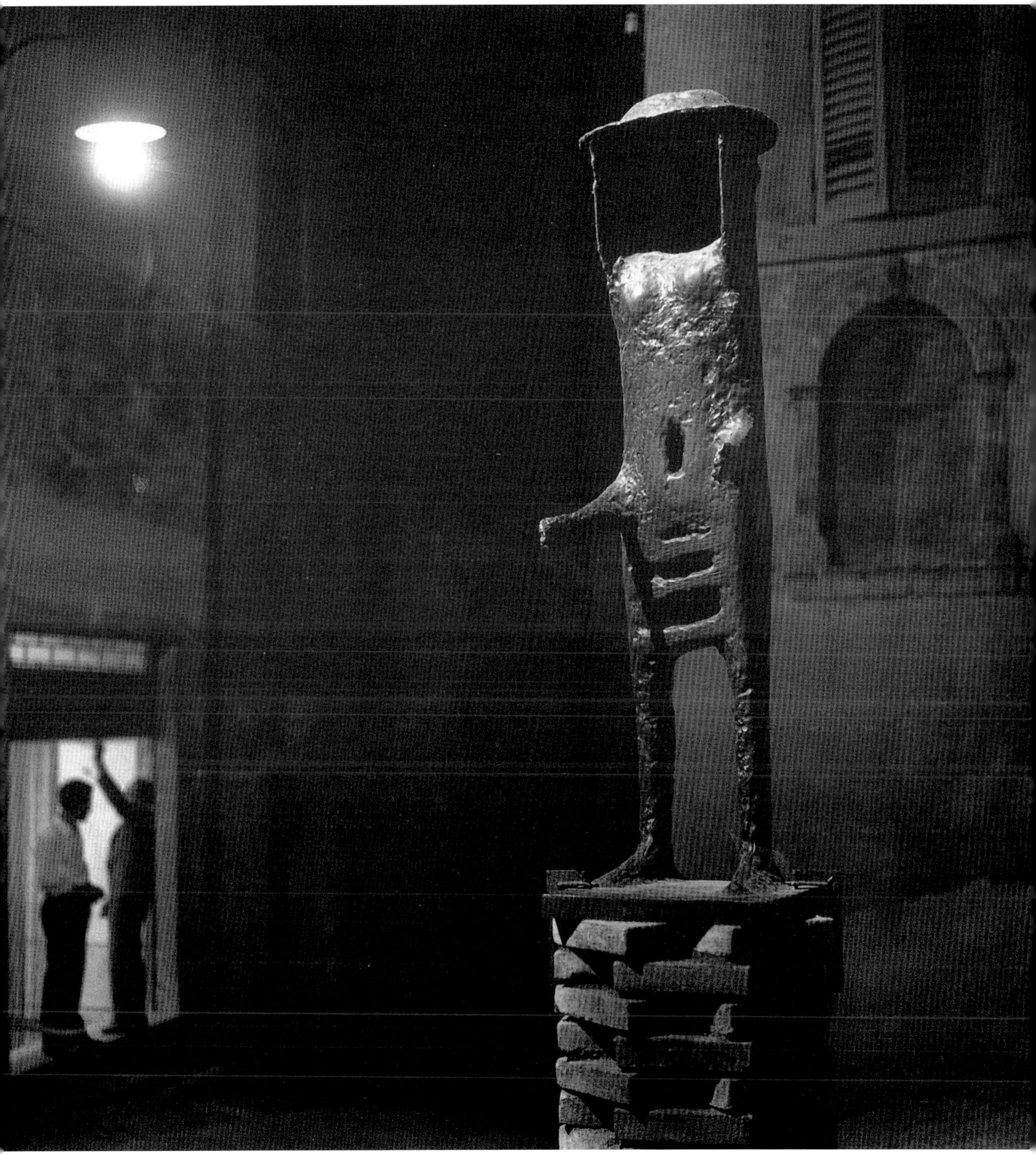

(*opposite*) *Standing Figure* 1956-7 (KA64)
H 122 cm (48 in), bronze

(*above*) *Girl without a Face* (large version) 1958-9 (KA85)
H 166 cm (65$\frac{1}{2}$ in), bronze
shown here at the Spoleto city sculpture exhibition, 1962

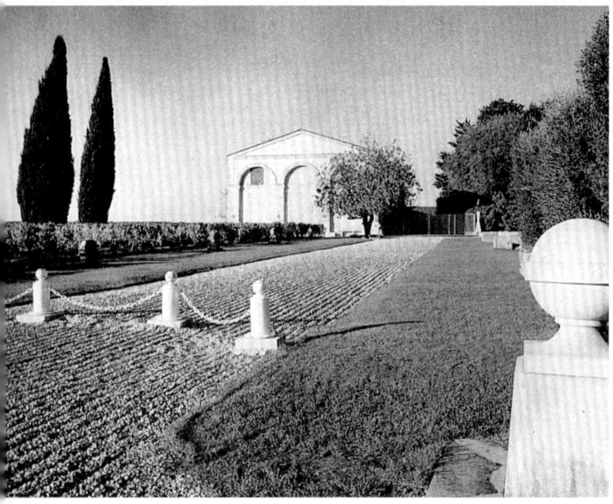

Château Mouton Rothschild, Pauillac, Bordeaux

Previously I had found the idea of commissions difficult; I was always working with ideas as they grew inside, and to compromise with a setting was not easy. But here was a commission of spectacular qualities, to do with the production of wine, and the vineyards, and France. So I agreed with delight.

I made six or seven visits to the site and as many maquettes, and decided that I would make a nine-feet-long sun, about seven feet high. I thought that I would make it in aluminium because it would be a heavy piece, and slightly cantilevered out from the wall. Philippe insisted it had to be bronze and he wanted it gilded, but since it was going to be covered in gold-leaf, it could have been made from aluminium anyway. I applied tints of grey paint in the shadows, so that it had a varied gilding, with only the projecting parts shining, and this made it much more sympathetic than it would have been.

The overall shape of *Mouton Sun* was an irregular oval, and this came from my tank identification during the war, because to identify a tank seen side-on at a distance, as well as the number of bogies, you go by the dark shadow at the side where the tracks are. The tracks run on bogies, so there is always an irregular shape, and this was stuck in my mind and became the oval of the piece. Onto the oval shape I mounted some horizontal projecting ledges based on the bracket fungus I had seen on trees in the woods at Corsham years before; it was a whitish fungus which grows out, absolutely horizontal, in a cluster up to about six or seven inches in a series of four or five. I had made sketches of this which I thought I might be able to use one day, so I used them for *Mouton Sun*. The idea was that the façade faced south, so that as the sun rose in the morning and set at night it would cast shadows during the day rather as a sundial would. And so this was an attempt to be part of the world: the ground with the horizontal lines, and the shadows from the sun.

I had thought it was going to be a straightforward commission but it proved otherwise. Philippe, and Pauline his wife, were strong characters and were not always in total agreement with each other. Once I said, 'I don't think I can go on. Why don't you get Picasso to do this thing?', and he said, 'We would if we wanted to': money was no object. So I carried on, and instead of making it in aluminium, as I had wanted, I made it in bronze, and this was fatal: the cast proved to be double the estimated weight. It was originally to have been cantilevered out on two thick rods, which had to penetrate the wall and be clamped to it inside, but this was now impossible. I had constantly asked Philippe to get the resident architect to probe the wall, and what I guessed was correct: the stonework on the outside was only about nine inches thick, the inside being rubble and not load-bearing.

Mouton Sun was then stored in the stables with the oxen used for walking along the vines to collect the grapes (which I quite liked). Philippe built another building behind which he called 'Le Club', with a strengthened wall onto which the sculpture was placed. It is there until this day, but incorrectly placed, as the flanges were not horizontal, defeating the idea behind the piece.

Towards the end of his life Philippe de Rothschild invited me to design a wine label, as Braque and Chagall had done, but sadly the project was never realised, for he died shortly after.

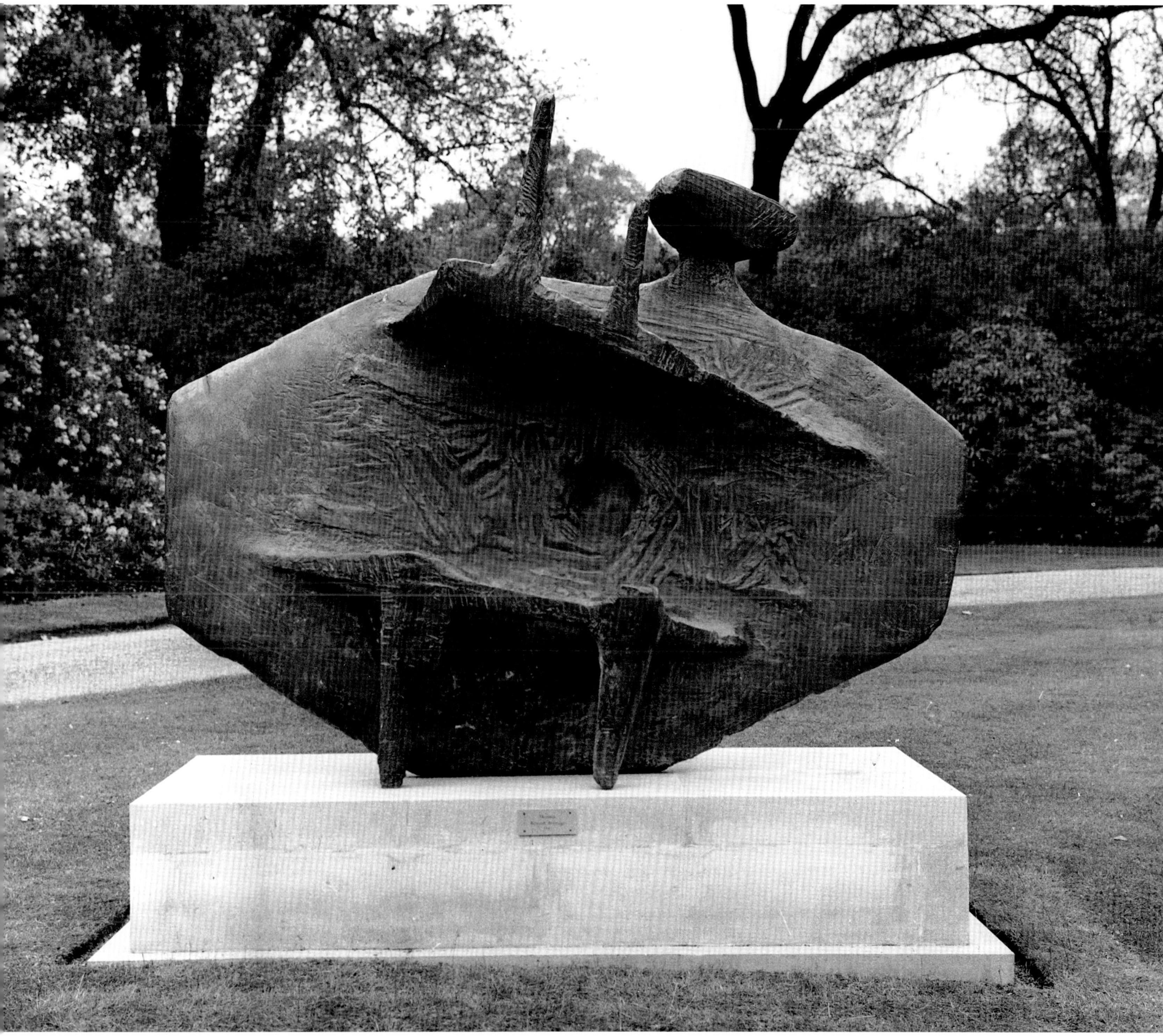

(*above*) *Monitor* 1961 (KA98) in Battersea Park
L 198 cm (78 in), bronze

(*overleaf p.52*) *Seated Figure with Arms Raised*
(large version) 1957 (KA74)
H 122 cm (48 in), bronze

(*overleaf p.53*) *The Sentinels* 1955-6 (KA56)
H 114 cm (45 in), bronze

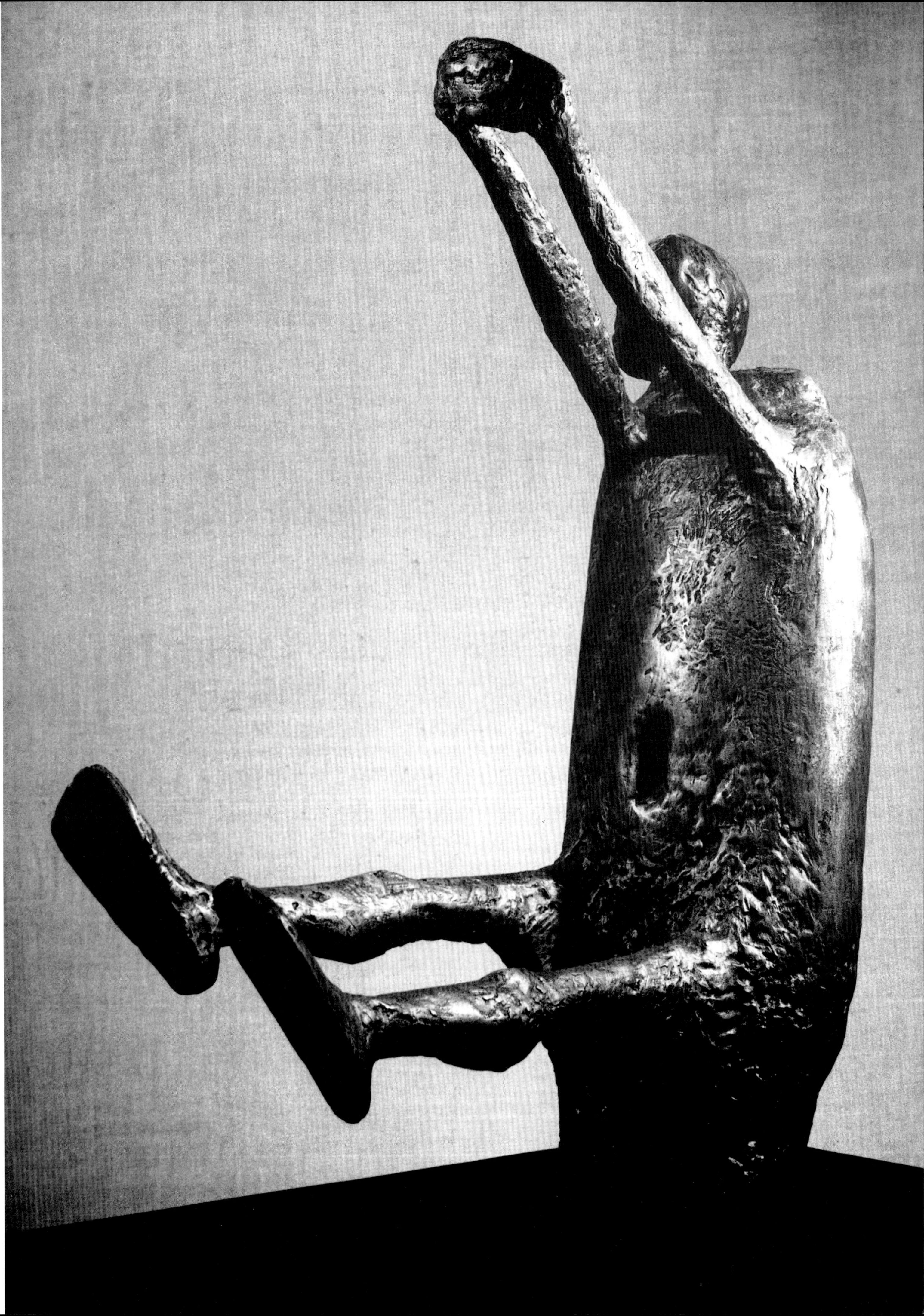

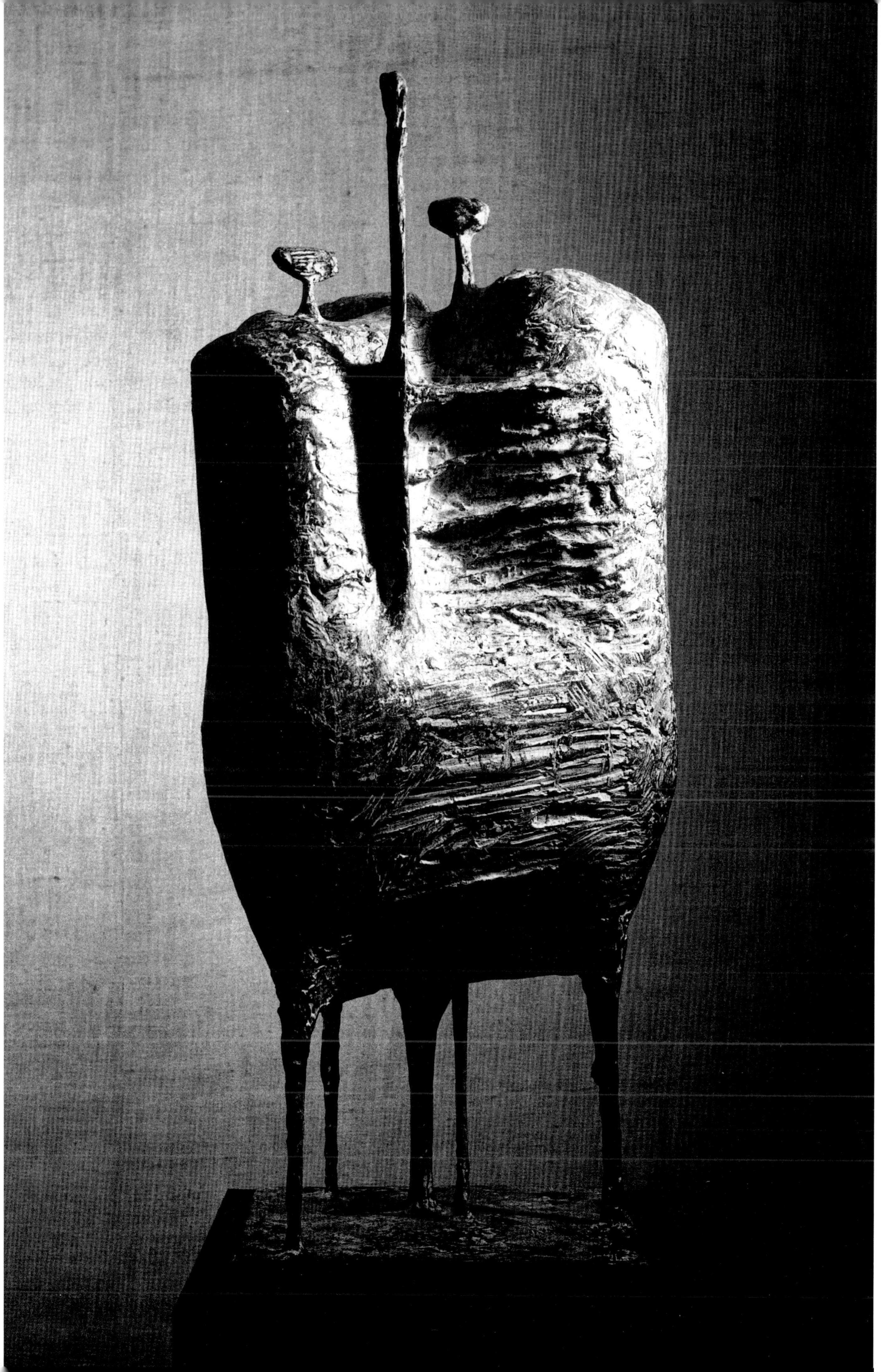

(opposite) Model for Krefeld Monument 1956 (KA62)
H 34 cm (13½ in), bronze

(overleaf pp.56 and 57) Two more views of the *Model for Krefeld Monument*

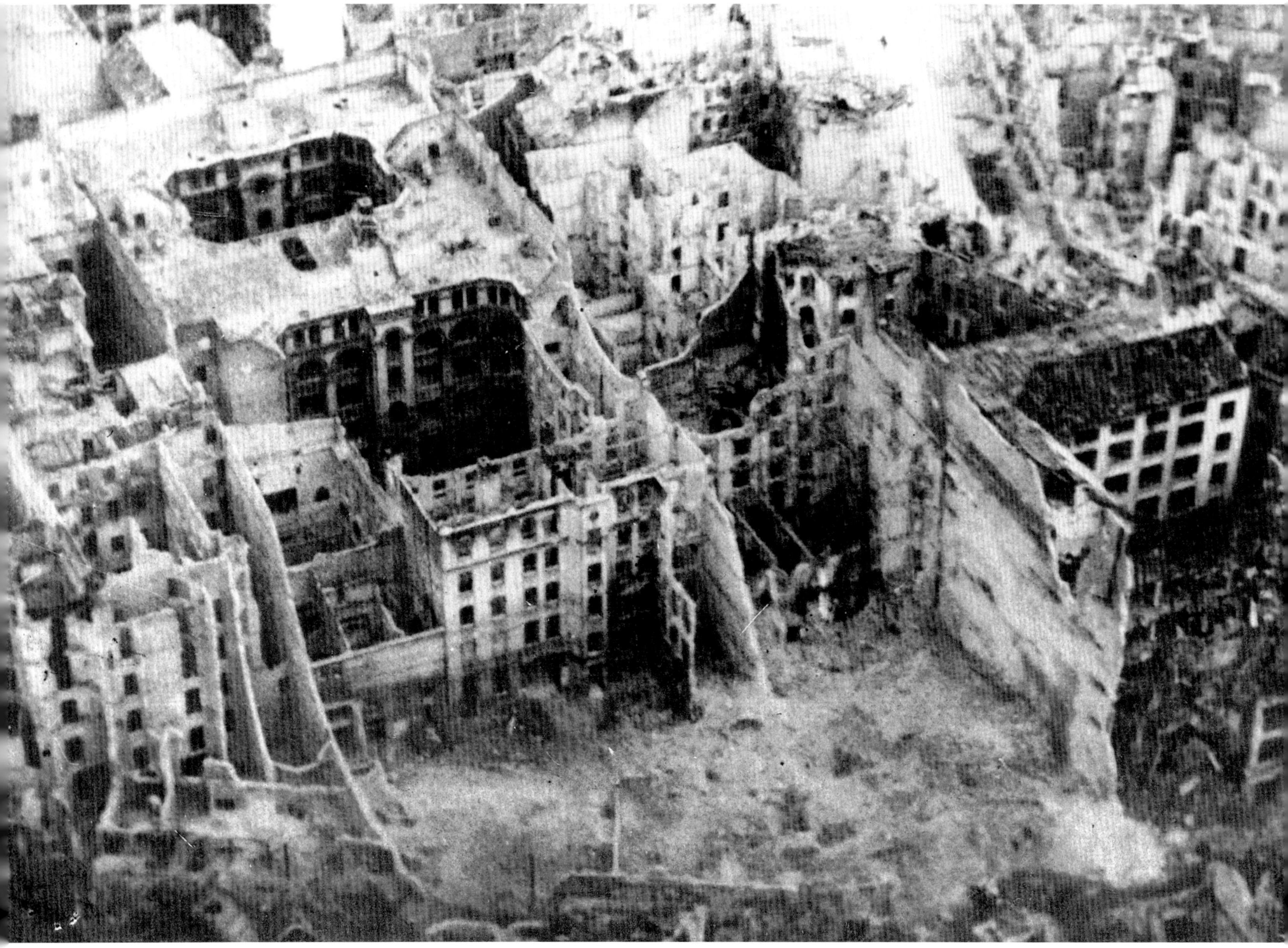

First official RAF photograph of Berlin after its fall, 1945, taken by low-flying Mosquito from RAF Film Production Unit. Later, in the early 1950s, the devastation revealed, and the buttressed cellular structure of the remaining buildings, had a profound effect on KA.

In 1956 I had been approached by the director of the Kaiser-Wilhelm Museum in Krefeld, Germany, who had the idea that they should have a war memorial there. He invited sculptors with international names: Marino Marini submitted a model, but I won first prize. I was delighted, but nothing came of it. There was an outcry in the Krefeld press that an English sculptor, a former enemy, should win the prize, and understandably the scheme fell through. A cast of the model, now called *Krefeld Monument* (1956), was purchased by Margaret Gardiner, who founded the Pier Gallery in Orkney, with its selective collection of work by Alfred Wallis, Ben Nicholson and the like.

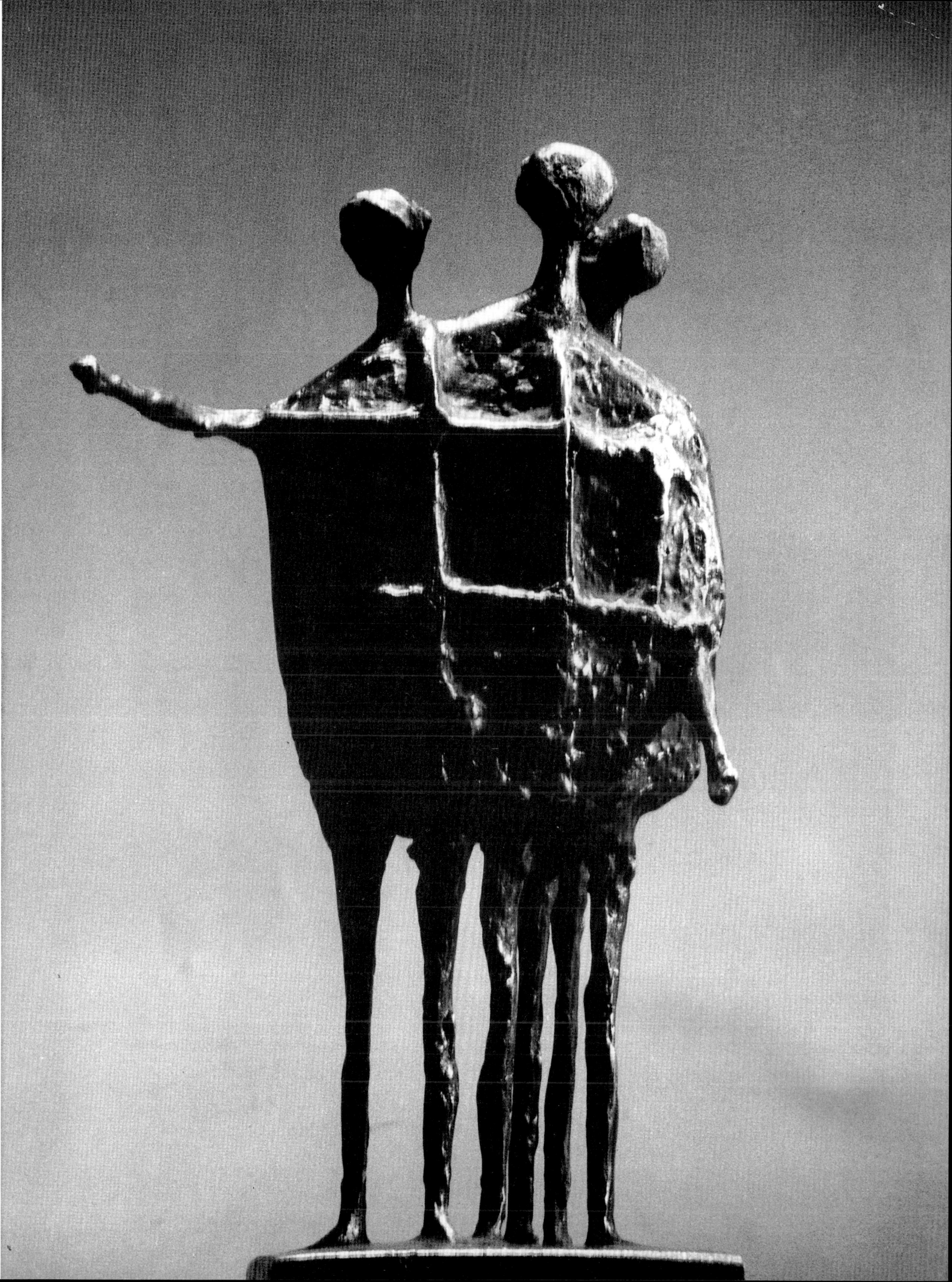

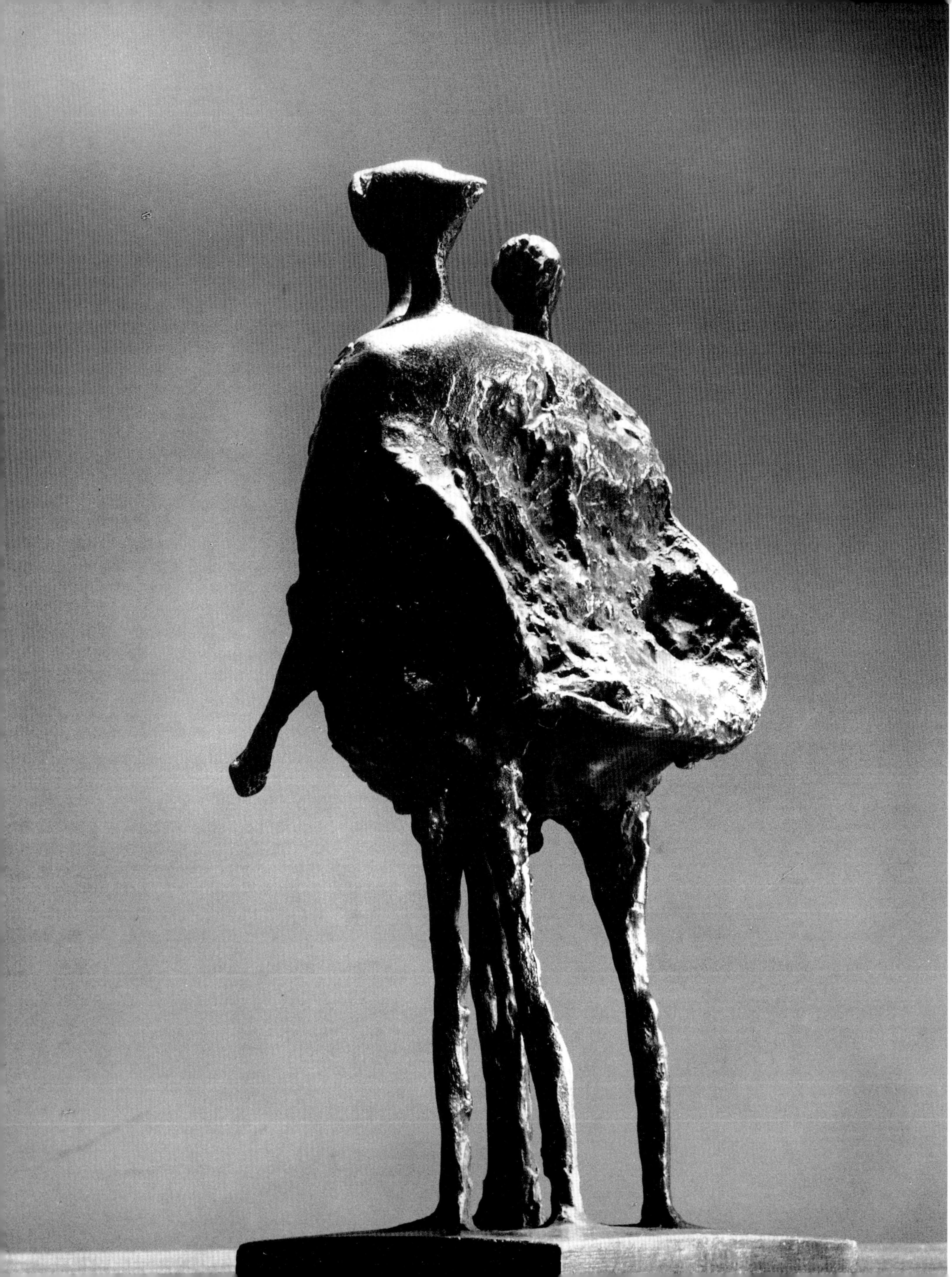

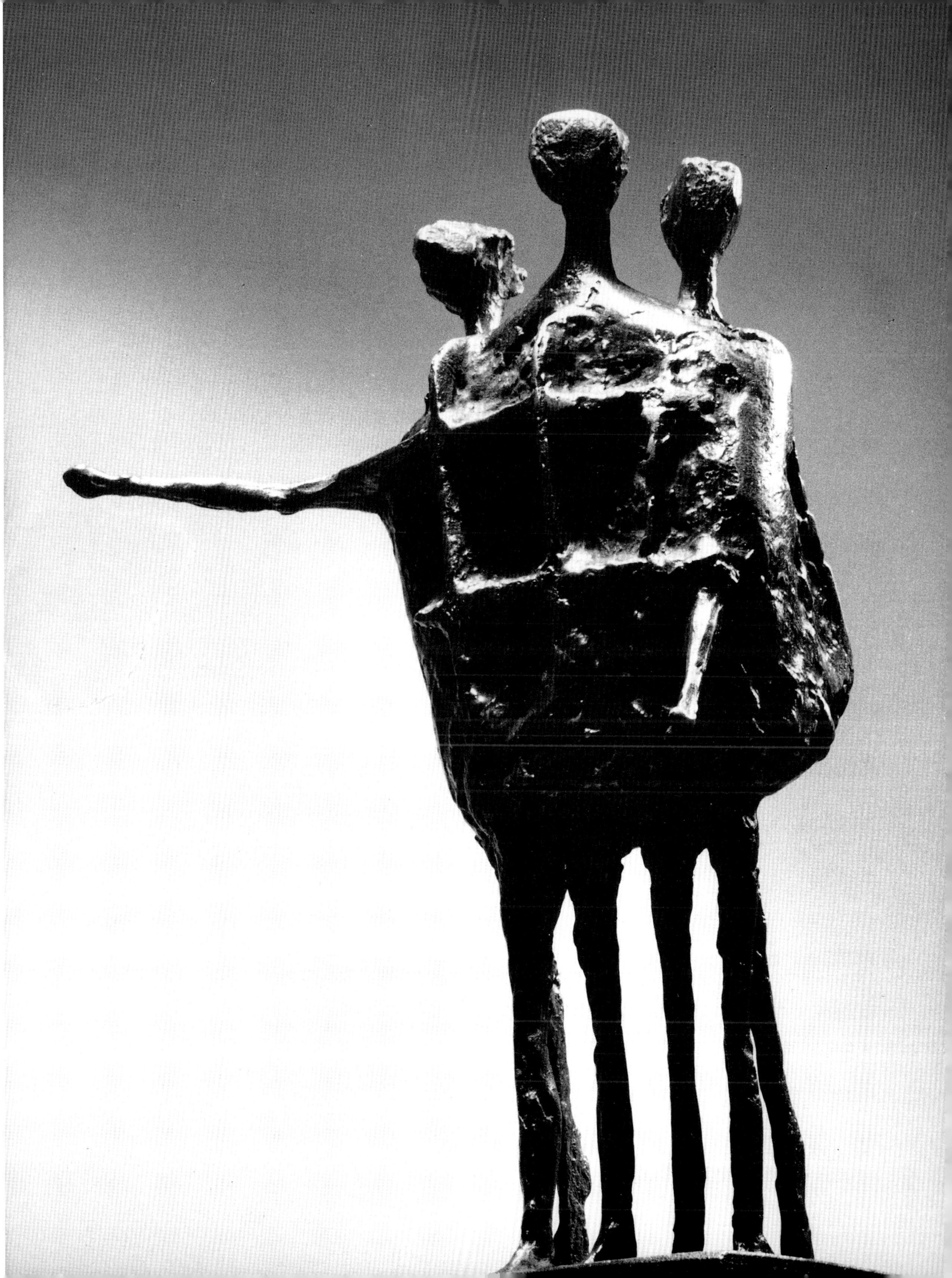

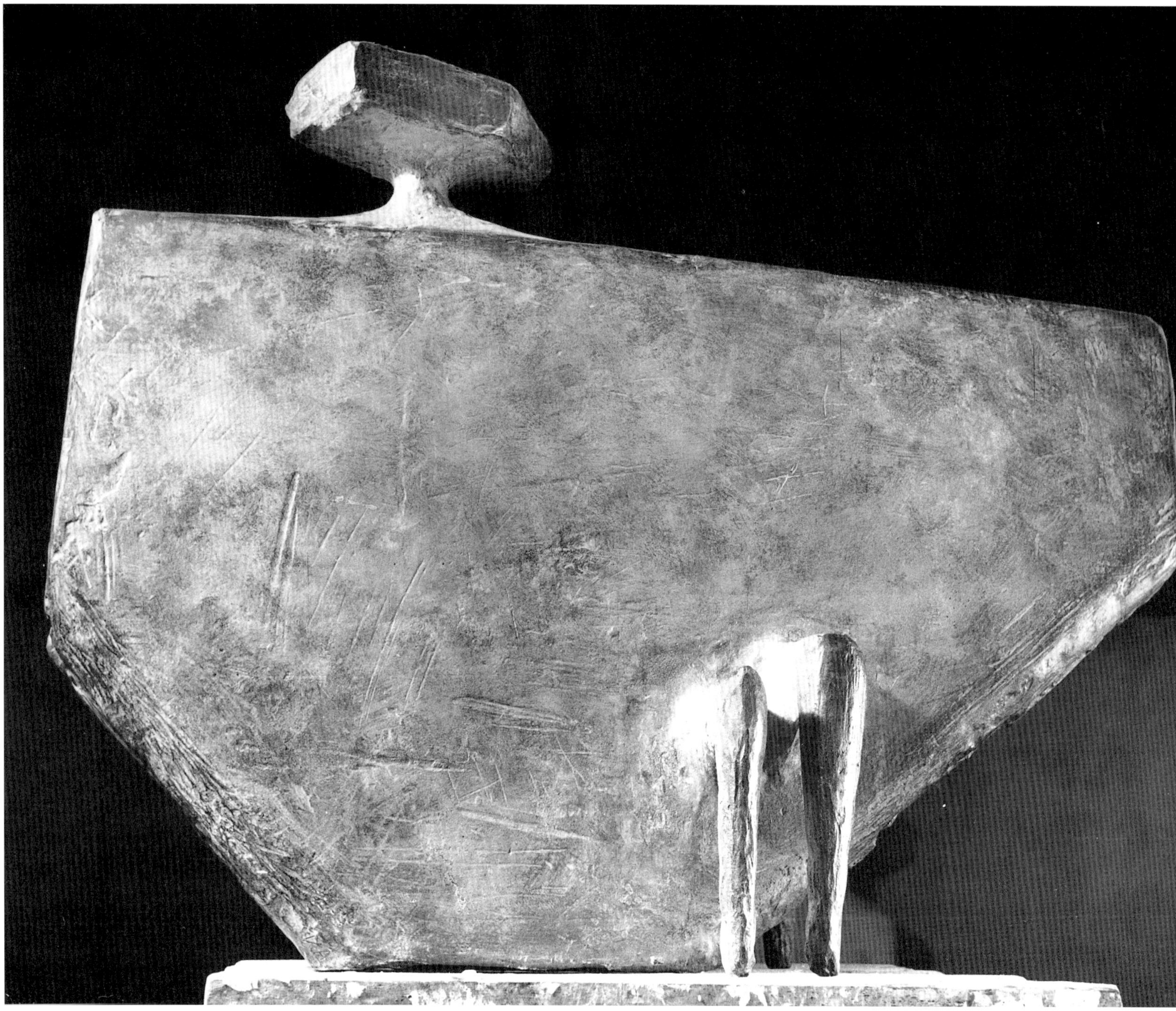

Slab Figure 1961 (KA105)
H 72 cm (28½ in), bronze

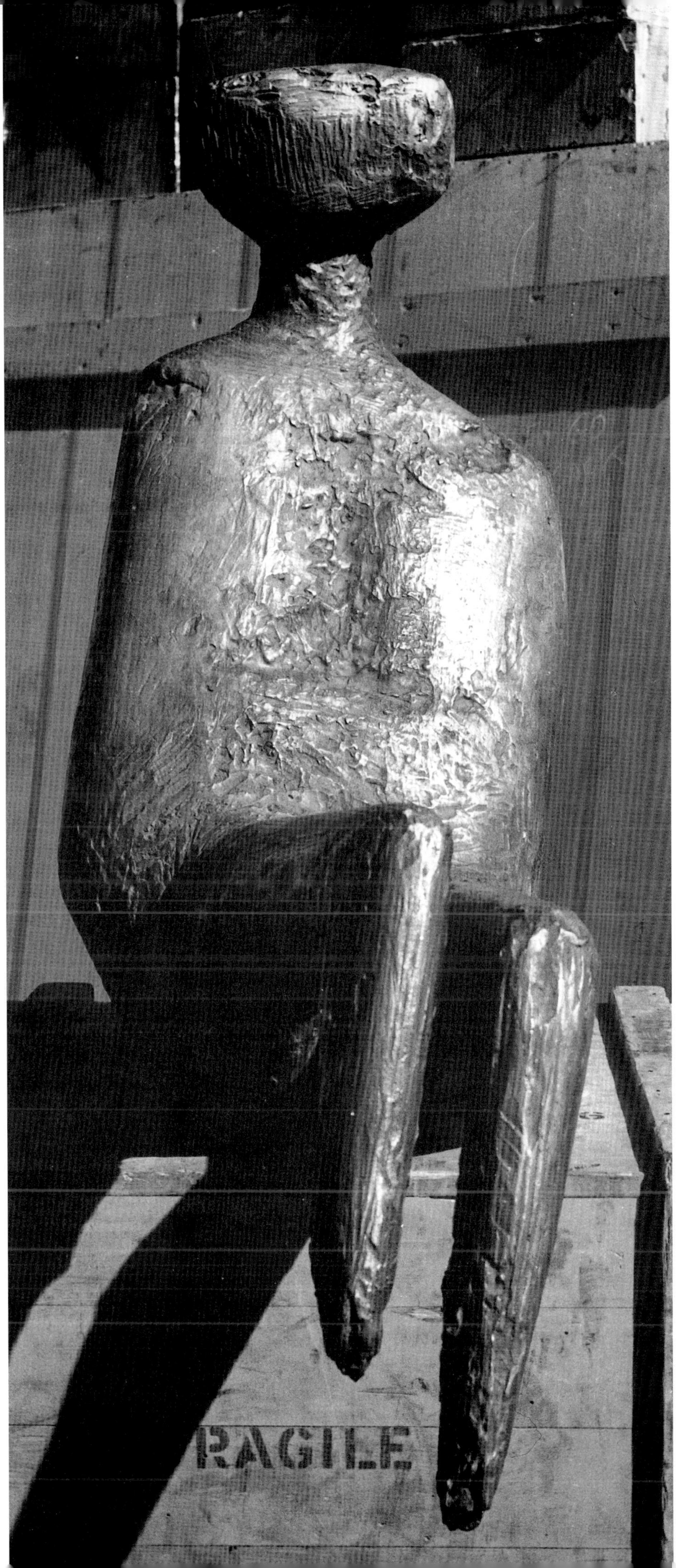

Balanced Figure 1961 (KA92)
H 130 cm (51 in), bronze

(*opposite*) *Standing Figure* 1961 (KA96)
H 173 cm (68 in), bronze

In 1959 I was invited to join the Marlborough Gallery, which meant leaving Gimpel Fils. I was the third artist to be taken on by the gallery. Lucian Freud had joined before me and Henry Moore and Graham Sutherland were approached at the same time. The Marlborough were very bold, and they were good for a while; I stayed twelve years. I was in a very good position before I joined them: I had Gimpels in London, two galleries in Canada and one in New York, and I had Claude Bernard in Paris. So joining the Marlborough resulted in leaving Gimpel Fils, which caused ill-feeling. Harry Fischer asked me if I would set out what I required in a contract. It was Fischer who introduced Moore and myself to the excellent Noack bronze foundry in Berlin, which Hermann Noack's grandfather had started.

One of the reasons for surrendering to the Marlborough (I say surrendering because it amounted to that) was that it took over all the office administration. Marlborough replaced my previous galleries, although I retained Rosenberg in New York. But when Marlborough opened up in New York they insisted I leave Rosenberg.

I had started showing in New York with Bertha Schaefer in 1954 and went to the opening of my first exhibition there. Bertha had an excellent assistant called Ilse Getz, who knew everybody, and she introduced me to many people. In fact I met all the Abstract Expressionists, whom I liked enormously. They were all wonderful men: I met Franz Kline, Rothko, de Kooning, Jackson Pollock, Philip Guston and the sculptor David Smith, several times, and liked them all. They were all generous, suggested that I went to live in New York and offered to find me a working loft. If I had been a young man in the 1950s I would have gone like a shot, but sculpture is not so easy, and the other thing is, I had interests other than sculpture. I was interested in history. And I loved England – the land.

Franz Kline was the most friendly; he loved English people. His paintings were big black and white streaks over huge canvases. And I remember one night he gave a party for me and the Gimpels (Gimpels were great fun in those days) and he made pork and bean stew in a big earthenware pot – it was delicious. Rothko was more of a philosophical person, quiet, not like the others, who were rumbustious. With reference to his tragic suicide, one of the contributing factors could have been that he possibly felt trapped, for he could neither move from the gallery, nor change his work because there would have been a terrible outcry. Philip Guston's painting was more European when I knew him. But he changed magnificently, and the collectors were all furious because they had owned previous work. Guston said, 'Well oddly enough I want to do what is a sin: I want to tell a story'. He made the break. I never met such a bunch of artists. They were not bitchy, not jealous of each other. They were big-hearted and it was great to know them.

I had four one-man shows in New York, two with Bertha Schaefer, and during one of the two exhibitions I had at Rosenberg Gallery, in 1962, Alexander Calder was exhibiting some older mobiles and some stabiles at the Perls Gallery next door. I met Calder there and said to him, 'You weld beautifully', and he replied, 'I don't weld them, stupid, I make them out of plywood or cardboard, and I hand them to a professional firm of welders, and they do the rest'. He was so friendly, and invited me to his home and to see his workshop; unfortunately I was only on a short visit so I was unable to go, but I always wish I had done so.

In 1960 and 1961, I made two standing figures, just over life-size: *Standing Man* and *Standing Figure*. A lot of the works I make are thought out in my mind, but these two figures were

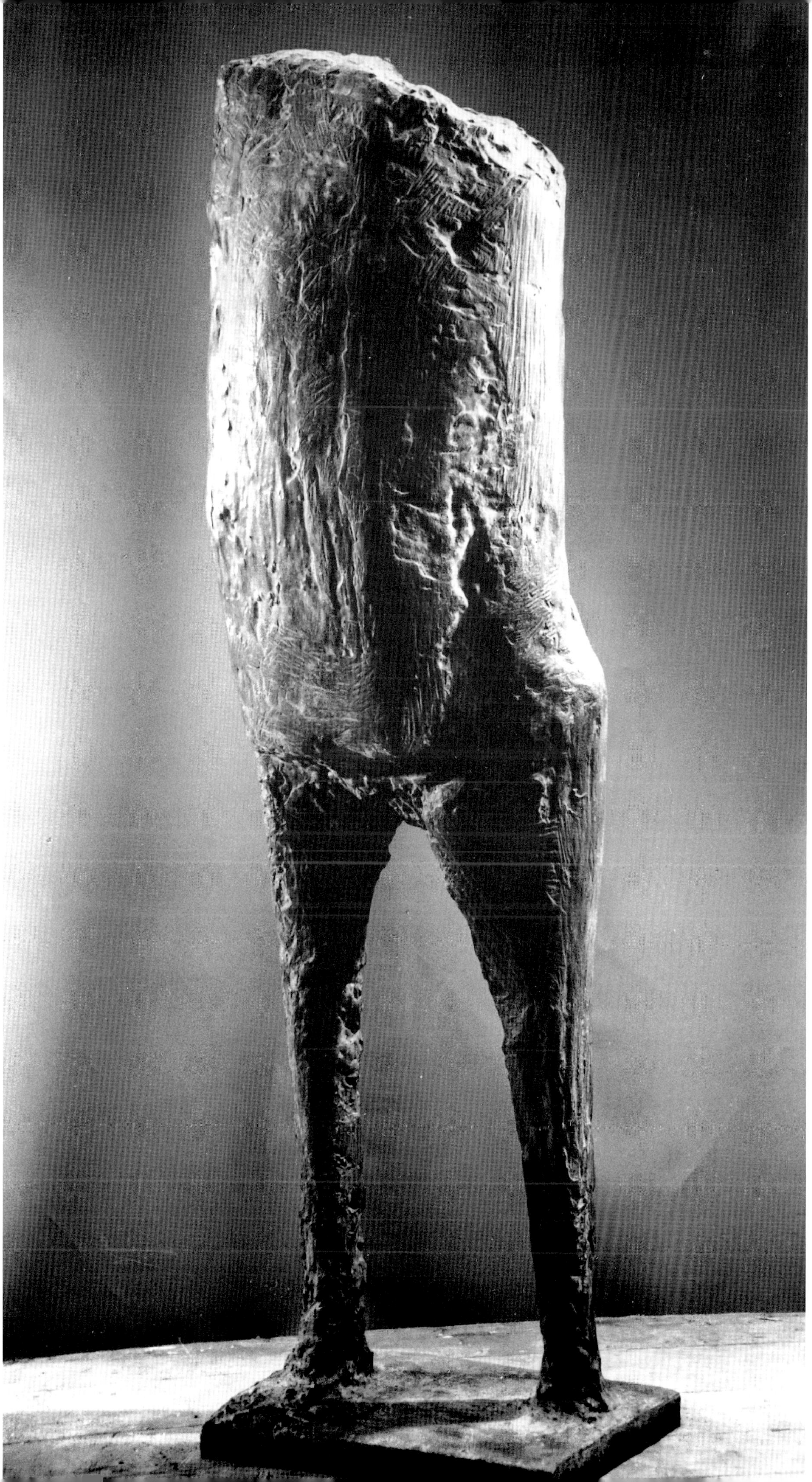

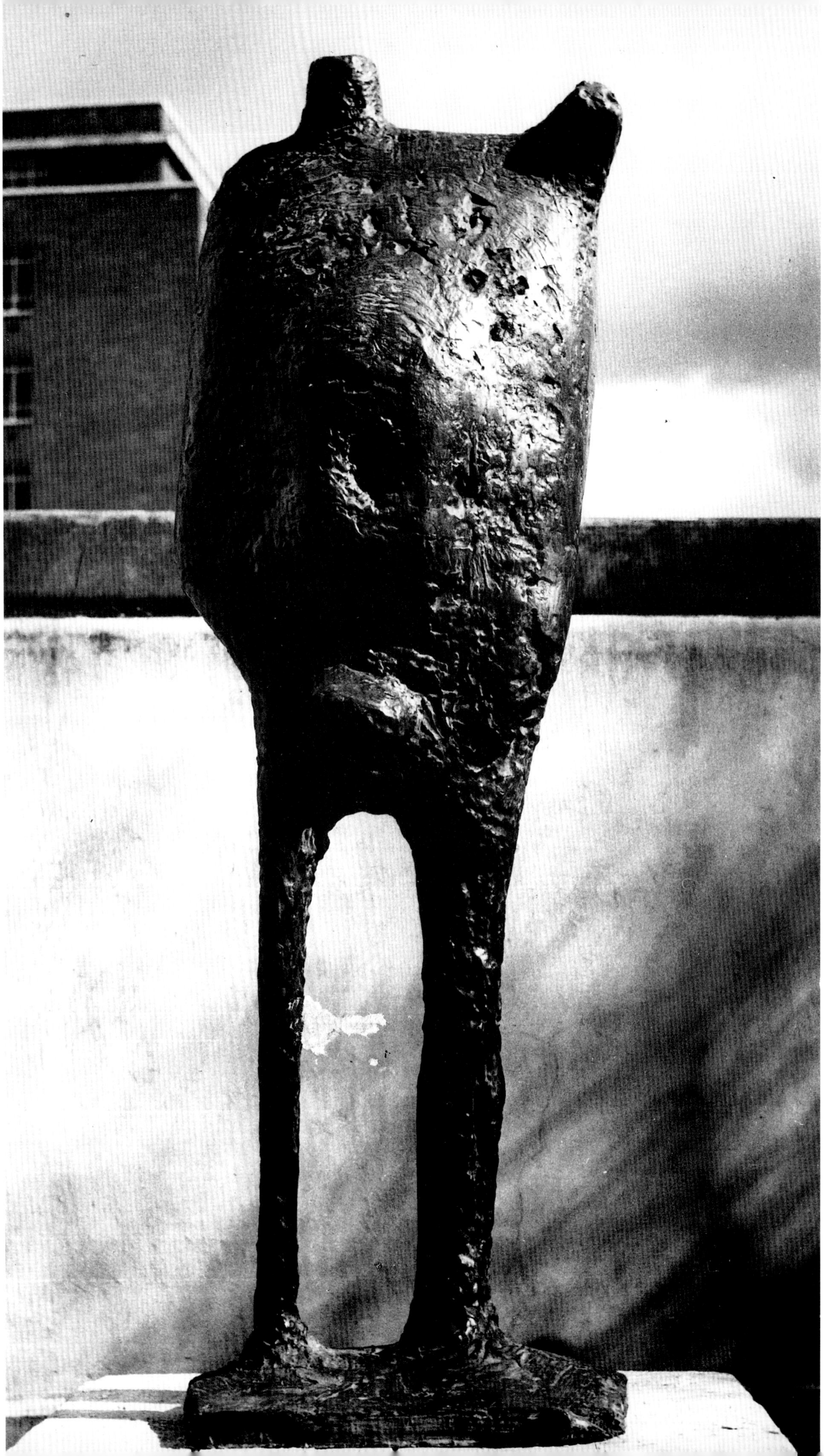

worked on more as a landscape painter works, sitting in front of a landscape and surrendering himself to what he sees. They are figurative in their own way: one figure has one enormously thick leg and one thin leg.

Then in 1961, I began a series of figures I called *Sibyls*, which have a strange link with what I feel sibyls look like. It's hard to define why, but the title seems to me appropriate. They had a feature which I used in the *Mouton Sun* for the Rothschild commission, that is, a shelf sticking out, which had come from the bracket fungus I had seen on the trees at Corsham, and they had enormous navels.

In 1962 there began a series of work which took about two years. These pieces were very different from anything else, except for one thing, the use of shadow. Like *Girl without a Face*, these works also had a confined shadow which I liked to use.

Just before I left Notting Hill in 1959, I met a very good sculptor, George Fullard, who lived nearby. We used to meet up quite often and talk about sculpture. He said that he felt that in a bronze cast everything was on the surface, like a skin, and inside it was hollow; I had to agree with that. And from 1962 I began to make these things which had a tall tower-like shape, with funnels piercing through (the *Pandarus* series). The idea of the funnel was two-fold: you could see the thickness of the metal at the edge of the funnel, and the funnel also made confined shadows. These pieces were to do with communication and were like trumpets.

Most of them were cast in brass. I was going through a phase when I was not always wanting to make things cast in bronze (whereby the sculptor makes a model in plaster and then hands it over to a foundry for the lengthy casting process and it comes back as a replica in bronze). I wanted to be involved at every stage so that it was all my own work; only the furnace element would be dealt with by the foundry. I was weary of the usual chocolate-covered patina of Victorian bronze casting; I know that bronze is a noble alloy, but in this series I felt that yellow brass was more suitable. Because I was so involved in the casting, and because time was short, these were 'one-offs' – only one cast was made of each. Manzú is the only other sculptor I know of whose preference was not to work in an edition.

There were twelve versions of the *Pandarus* series, and most of them were made by an unusual method, explained below. The advantage of this was that the cast was less expensive; it also ensured that I was fully involved except for fixing the runners, doing the kiln work and pouring in the metal. I preferred this to the traditional way of making the idea in clay, casting it in plaster and then handing it over to the foundry for the lengthy casting process, the finished piece being returned to me.

By this method, the five- to six-feet-high columns were first modelled in clay, then covered with plaster to the required thickness in sections. When the columns had been separated and cleaned, their inner surfaces were painted with wax to a quarter of an inch thick. The wax tube sections were then cast at the foundry and the resulting brass rings brazed together to form the whole. The funnels were cast in the same way.

The title *Pandarus* came from my favourite Chaucer tale, 'Troilus and Cressida', which I enjoy reading aloud in Middle English. It is very moving and poetic. There is a character in the tragedy called Pandarus, who is the go-between. He is a noisy but kind individual who tries to help the lovers. I thought that this was a good title for the brassy series.

(*opposite*) *Standing Man* 1960 (KA87)
H 178 cm (70 in), bronze

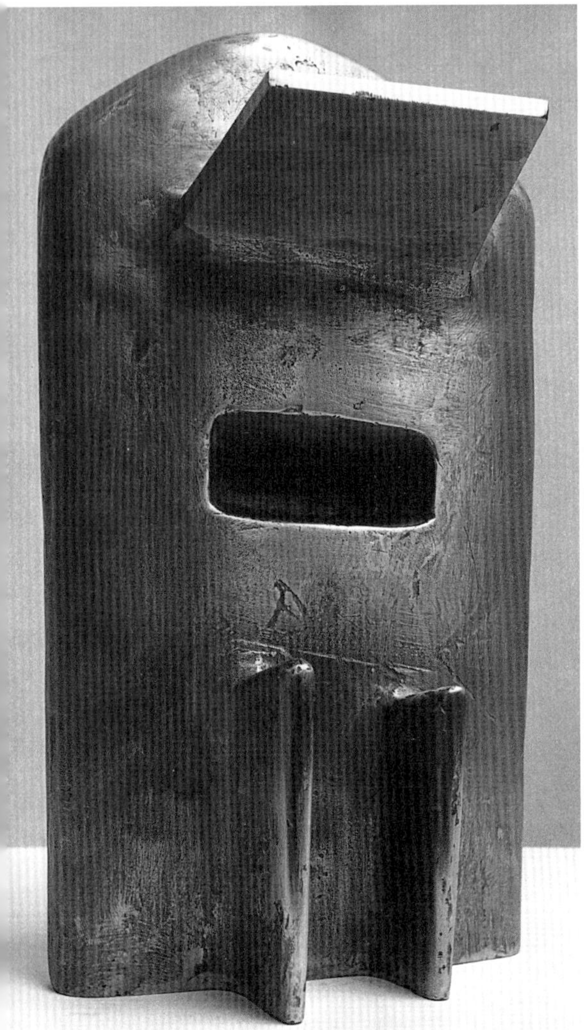

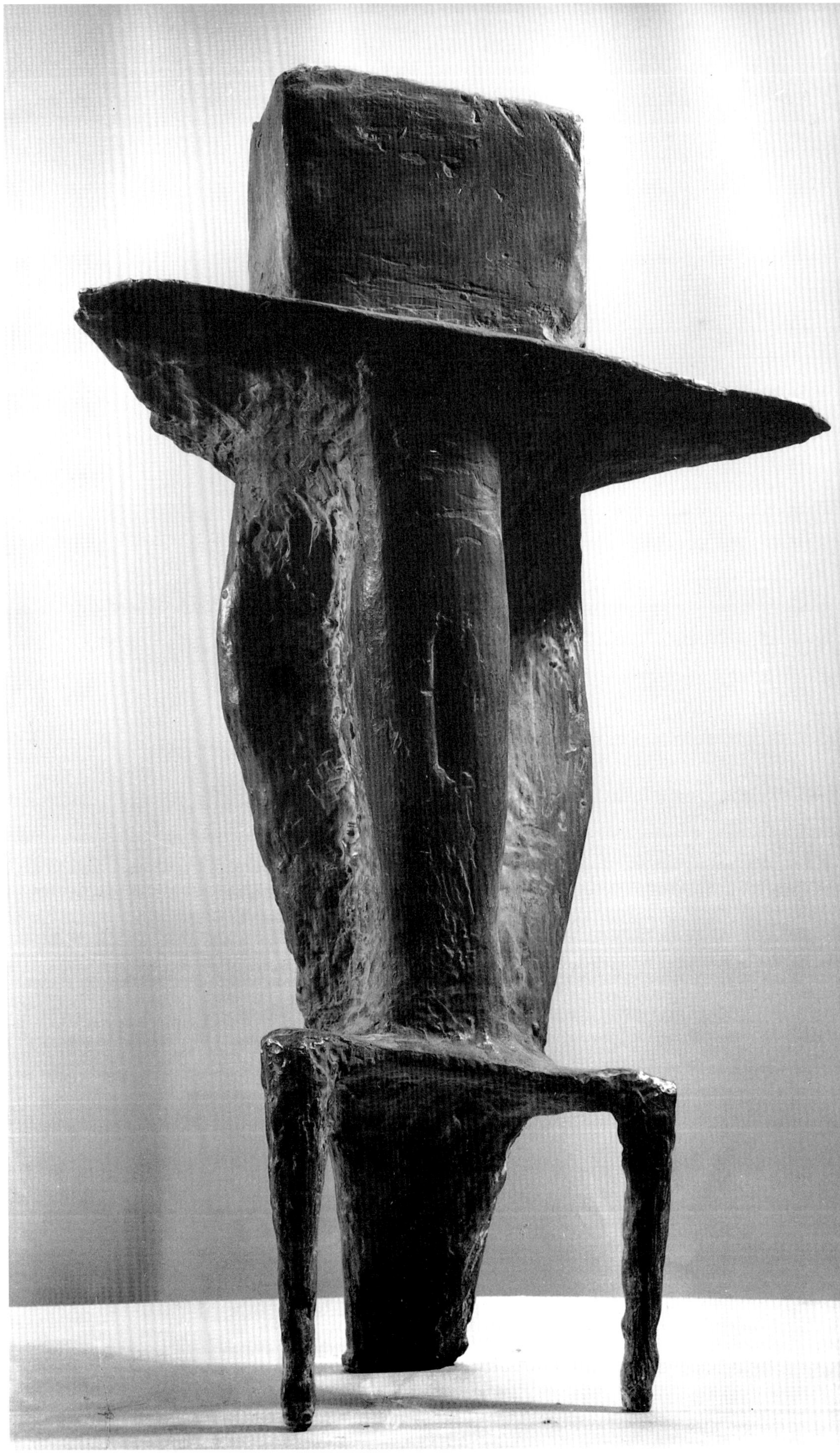

(*above*) *Prophet* (small version 2) 1962 (KA115)
H 32 cm ($12\frac{1}{2}$ in), yellow bronze

(*right*) *Sybil* (version 3) 1961 (KA108)
H 103 cm ($40\frac{1}{2}$ in), bronze

(*opposite*) Two works shown at *Documenta III*, Kassel, Germany, 1964:
on the left, *Figure on its Back* (large version)
1961 (KA111)
L 163 cm (64 in), bronze;
on the right, *Mouton Variation*
1964 (KA133a)
H 252 cm (99 in), brass

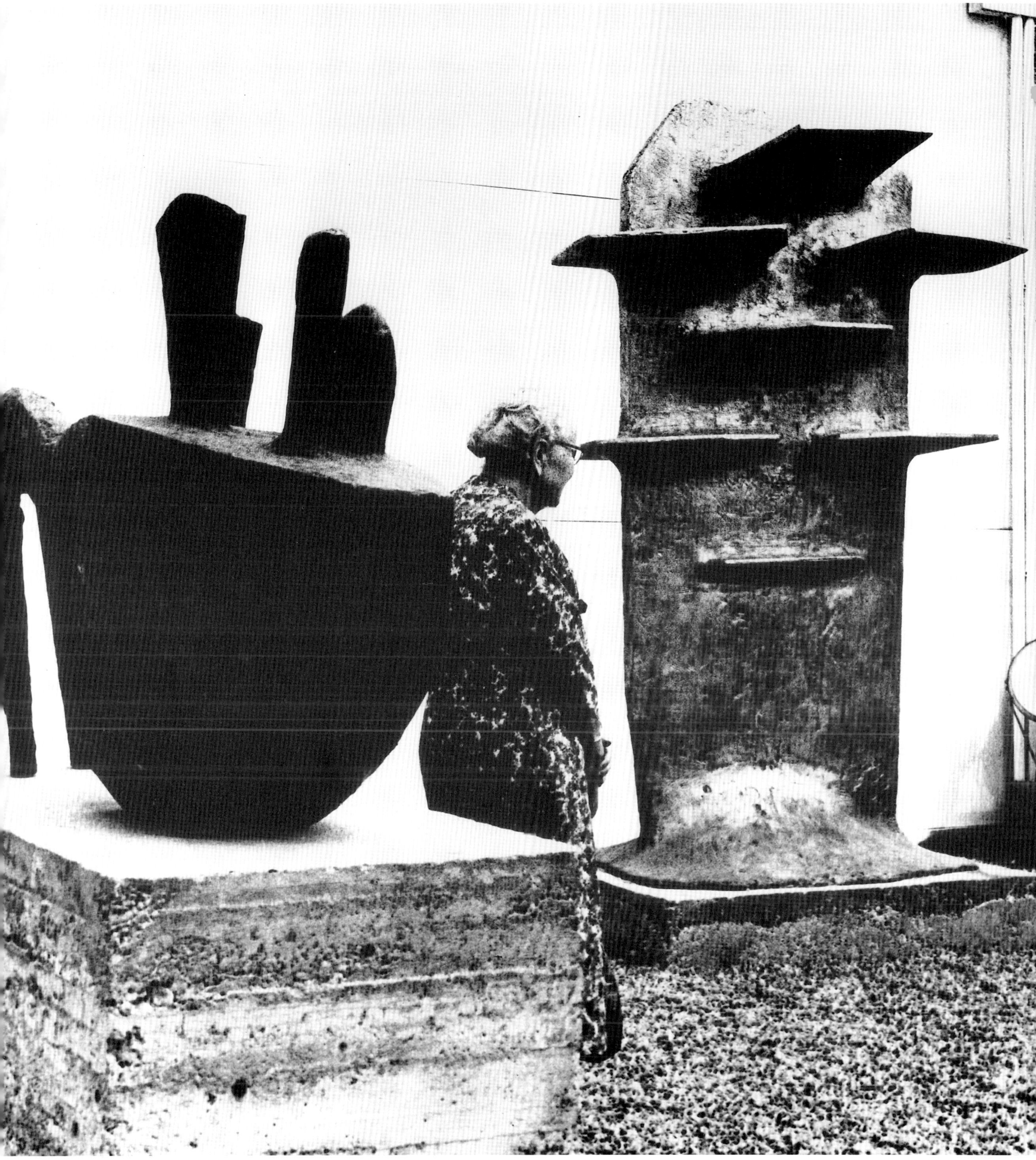

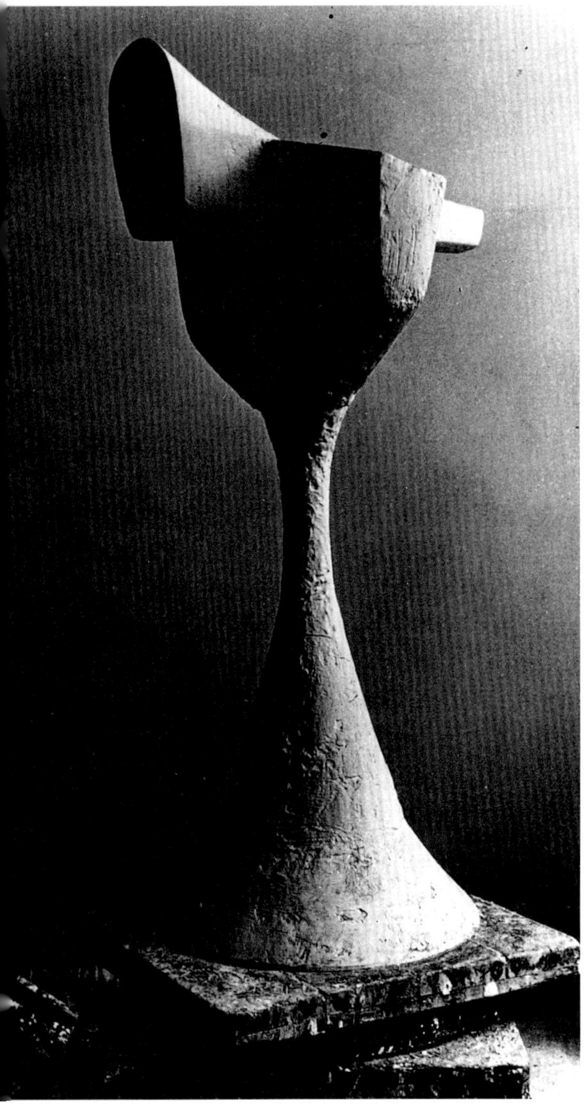

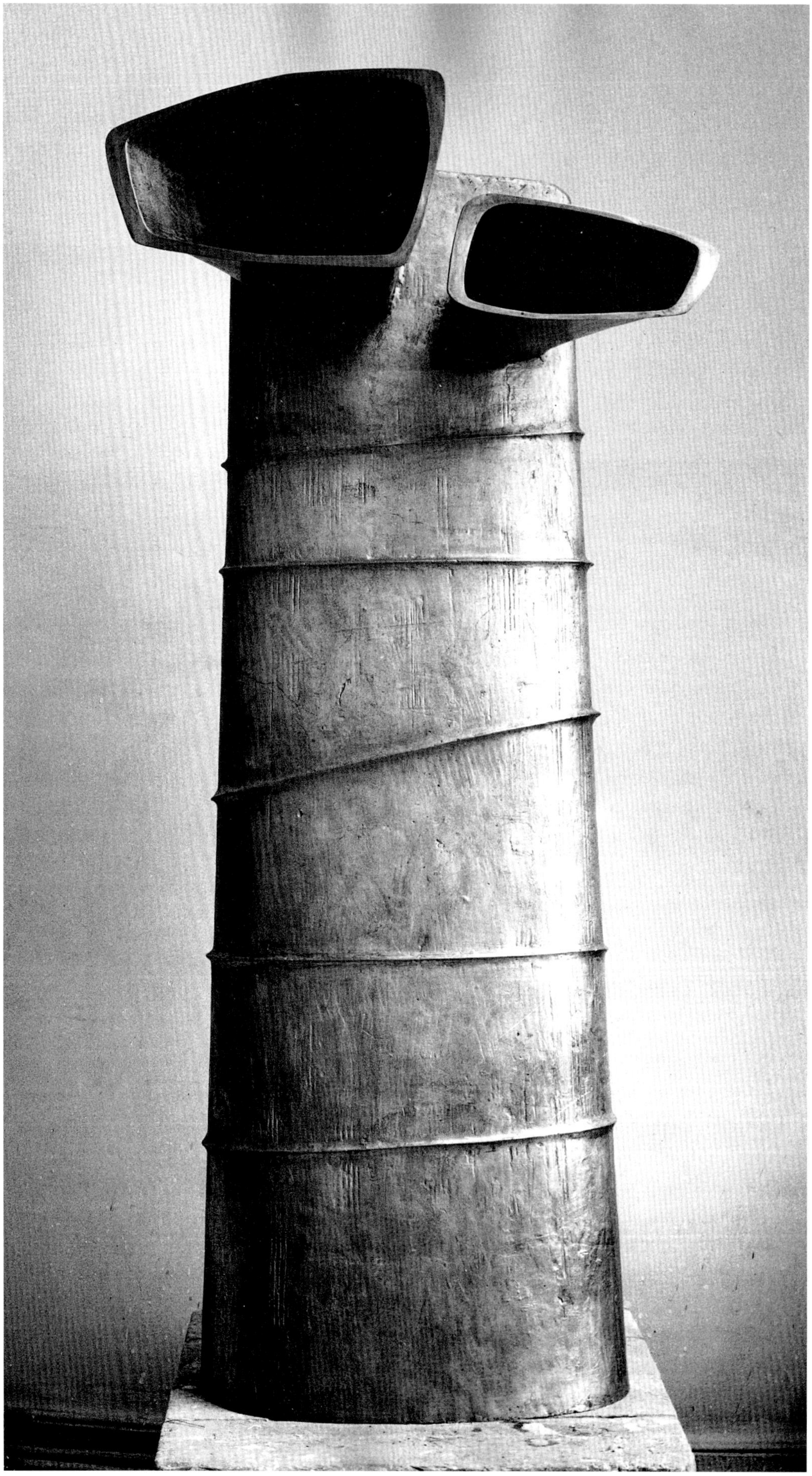

Pandarus (version 2) 1962 (KA119)
H 192 cm (75½ in), plaster model

(*right*) *Pandarus* (version 11) 1964 (KA133)
H 224 cm (88 in), brass

(*opposite*) Two works installed at Middelheim Park, Antwerp:
on the left, *Wall* 1965 (KA148)
H 190.5 cm (75 in), bronze
on the right, *Pandarus* (version 8) 1963 (KA125)
H 178 cm (70 in), brass

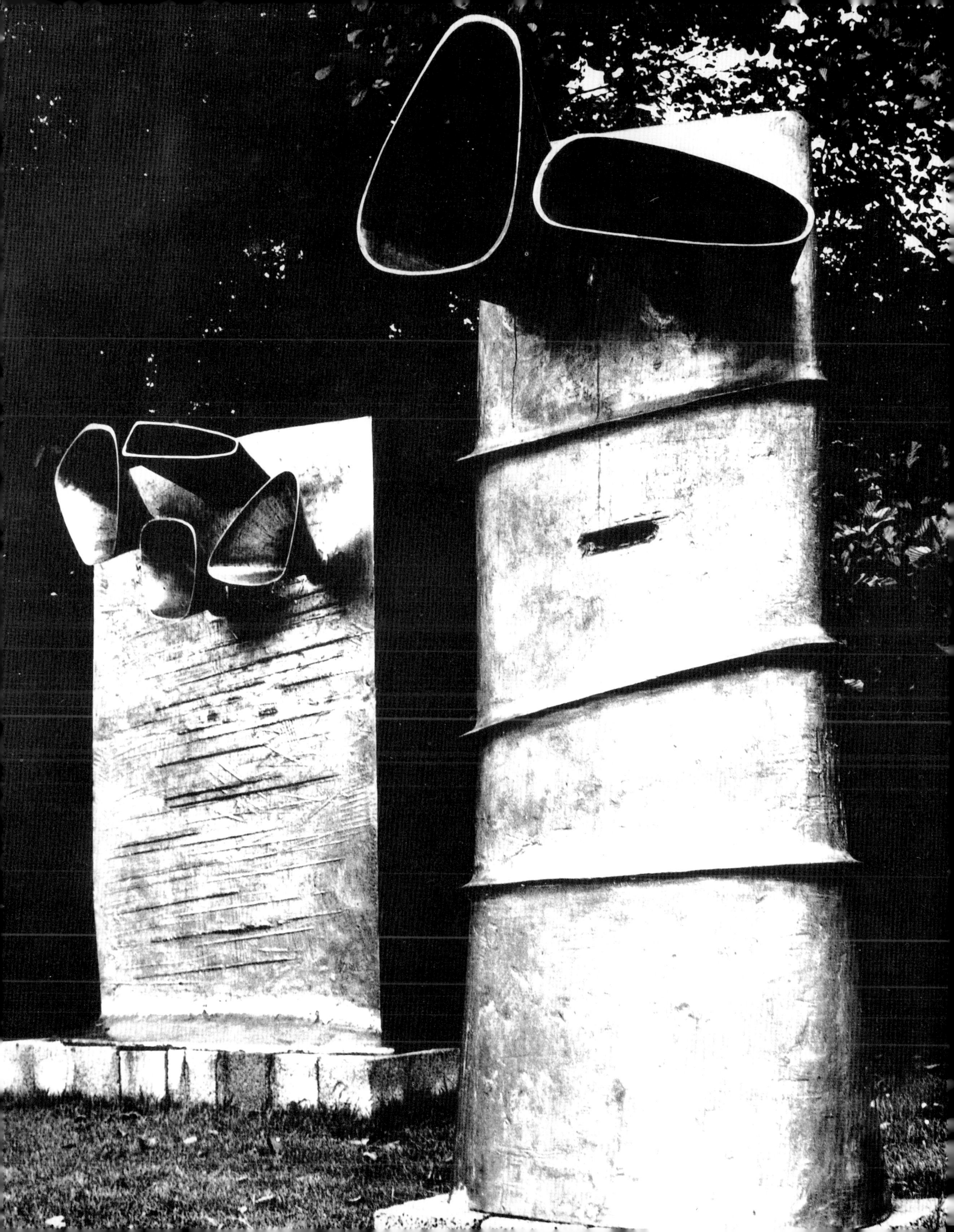

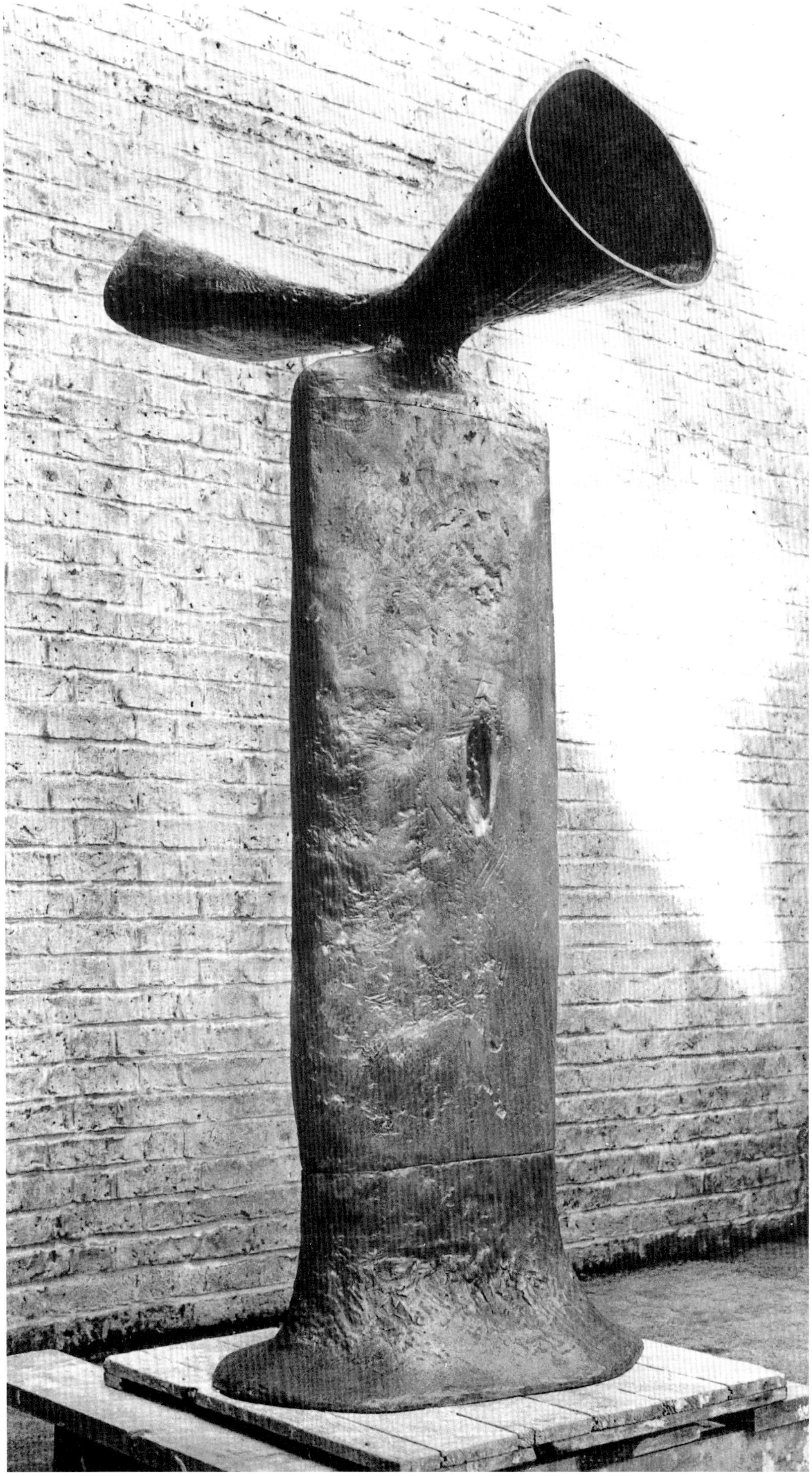

(*right*) *Pandarus* (version 9) 1964 (KA131)
H 185 cm (73 in), brass

(*opposite*)
left to right:
Pandarus (version 9) 1964 (KA131)
H 185 cm (73 in), brass
Pandarus (version 8) 1963 (KA125)
H 178 cm (70 in), brass
Wall 1965 (KA148)
H 190.5 cm (75 in), bronze

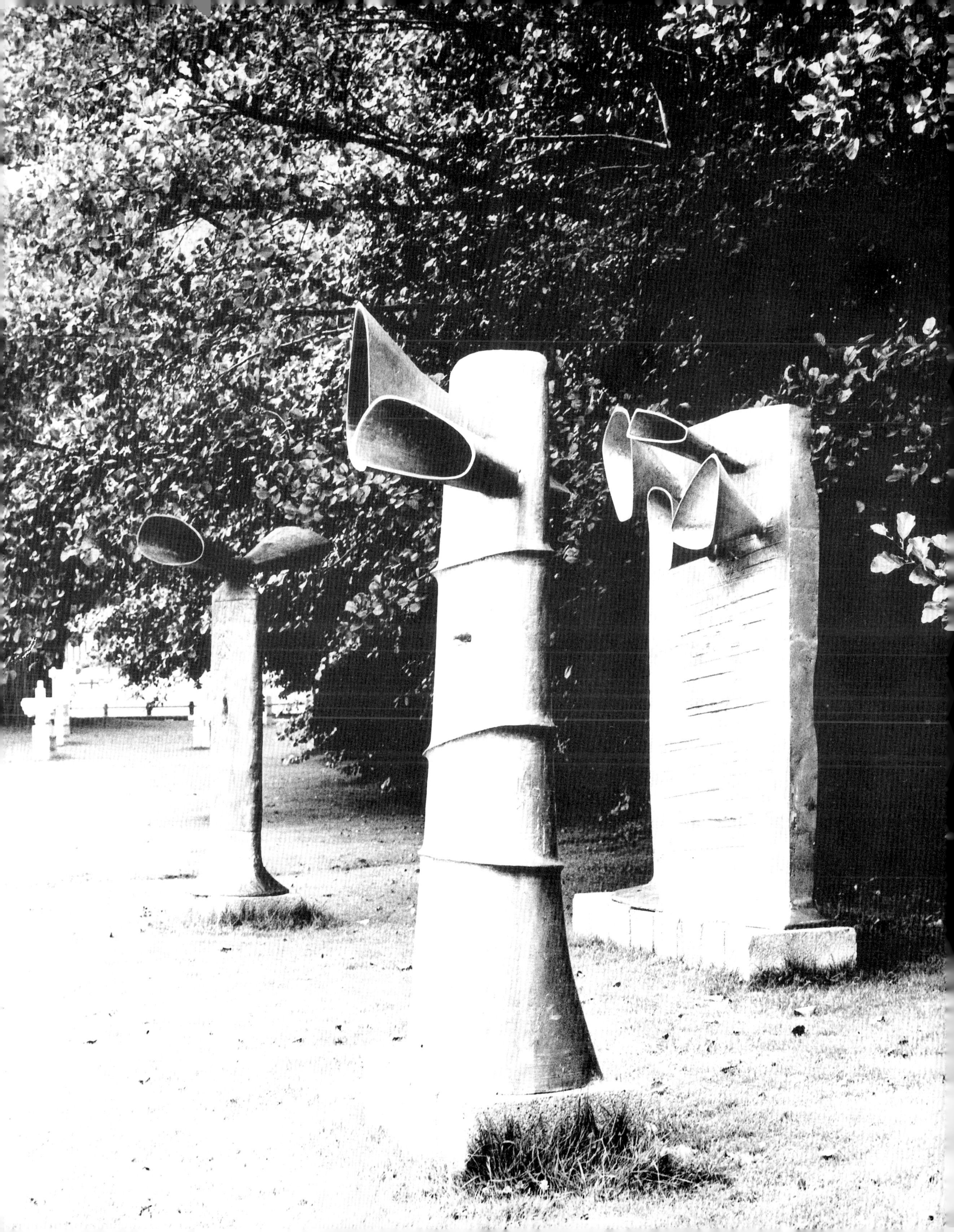

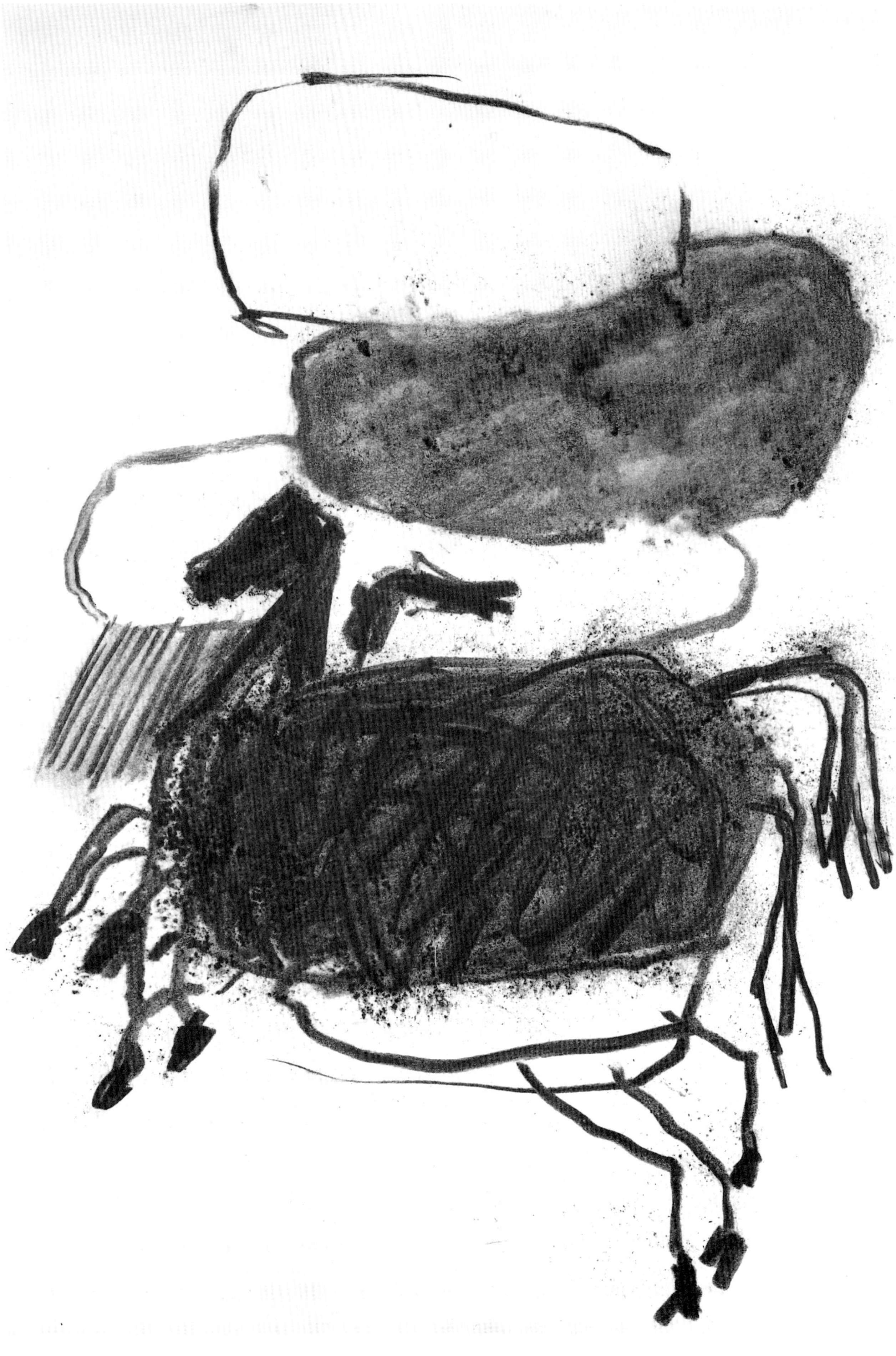

In 1963 I was approached by an Italian publisher, Edizione del Cinquale of Petrasanta, who had the idea of publishing my drawings in relation to poetry. I was very interested. I did not read much contemporary poetry but I have always read Geoffrey Chaucer with the greatest enjoyment and I suggested that my charcoal drawings in relation to the Chaucer text would be a good combination. The publisher thought this would be ideal. He was killed shortly after in a car crash and the firm was closed.

My favourite Chaucer of all, 'Troilus and Cressida', was far too long for me to attempt to do drawings in relation to. So I chose instead 'The Reves Tale', mainly because it is short and very funny in a medieval, slapstick music-hall sort of way. The style is different from 'Troilus' – it is a very saucy piece. But another thing which was very important for me was that the action takes place in the bedroom of a mill and the characters are all there, but have nothing on, so that I did not have to attempt period costume, which I loathe doing. Instead I was on my home ground, which is nude figures. First of all I visited churches or cathedrals of the same date as Chaucer to look at stained-glass windows, and I made some drawings based on the heavy black lines of the lead which holds the glass. I did not want to illustrate the story, but instead I wanted to make drawings in relation to Chaucer, not depicting the details of all the incidents in the story.

The characters are the miller and his wife, the two clerks, John and Aleyn, a baby in the cradle and the daughter of the house, and the star of the story, 'swete Malin', of 'buttokes brode and brestes rounde and hye'; she has fair hair and all the things that the medieval person might relish, and is stockily built and very sturdy. I let myself draw in my natural way using charcoal and wash. Some people regard my drawings as humorous anyhow, so this seemed to me to be suitable for 'The Reves Tale'.

My drawings are mostly of two kinds – (a) an activity as natural as breathing, committing onto paper fleeting thoughts or ideas as doodles or sketches, so numerous they are often discarded but, even so, forming the most useful references for future sculpture; (b) at the same time, more considered but less frequent drawings which are complete in themselves with no further purpose in mind.[4]

I worked on 'The Reves Tale' intermittently from 1964, and when I was working in Berlin, where I stayed for a year and a half, I was approached in 1968 by a marvellous art publisher, Propyläen Verlag. I wanted to have a large edition and for the price to be kept low, but the publishers wanted the very opposite – so the project fell through.

(*opposite*) Illustration for 'The Reves Tale' by Geoffrey Chaucer, plate II (begun in 1964):
'The clerk's horse
Goth to the fen
with wild mares
As fast as he may go'

In 1963 I went to Venezuela. The invitation came from Miguel Aroyo, Director of the Museo de Bellas Artes, Caracas, who had asked if I would make a visit to help the sculptors there who were less familiar with international art than the painters were. I dithered initially but at last agreed, partly because I wanted to meet the forest Indians, for I had a lifelong interest in anthropology. Aroyo came to London to discuss details: the British Council would cover the cost of the return air fare. Hans Neumann, a very rich Venezuelan, would cover the cost of my living expenses there. All this was under the aegis of the museum. Not wanting to teach or give a series of lectures I agreed to the idea that I would work with a group of the best sculptors under one roof so we would all benefit from close association. A workshop had been found

4. See *Drawings Towards Sculpture*, exh. cat. Isis Gallery and Arts Institute, Leigh-on-Sea, Essex, 1993

(*opposite*) Makiritari women and children, Venezuela, and forest Indians. Two stills from the 'home movie' made by Hans Neumann, who joined up with KA's party during the expedition to the rain forest of southern Venezuela, 1963-4

with excellent top light and with washing and toilet facilities attached. We would thus be self-contained.

The seven or eight sculptors settled down in the workshop. I liked them and we got on well. They each worked on their own and I began another version of the *Pandarus* series which I had started in London – life-size with funnels. After a month I felt it was time to organise the jungle trip, the details of which were slowly taking shape.

I could not stay for a year as they wanted, but we agreed on four to six months, which was all the time I could spare.

On the second night Hans gave a party for me to which the British Ambassador came, together with a few people I would need to meet, including an attractive young woman, Barbara Braendli. Barbara was a top Venezuelan photographer, but better, she had a passionate interest in the forest Indians and had befriended a legendary figure: Daniel de Marandarian, a Little Brother of Jesus. Father Daniel gave medicine to the Indians daily and lived alone with them. Barbara was the link to Father Daniel, and her architect husband had a radio transmitter so they were in radio contact with him. On the first attempt to get there we found there had been an outbreak of malaria, and on the second, all the warriors had gone off on a hunting trip, leaving only old men, boys, women and children. As this sort of trip needed a great deal of organisation we decided to go anyway. Meanwhile, Hans Neumann wanted to join us.

At 9 o'clock one morning, Barbara, Hans and I, plus Harry Gibson, the very experienced pilot, flew off in a Cessna light aircraft together with sufficient food for a short visit and Scotch, heading for the ancient capital Ciudad Bolivar, where we had our last civilised meal. Then we set off five degrees east of south, past the huge iron mountain, a giant ranch and then the vast, flat and very hot Llanos, through which the Orinoco winds its way. This, I felt, was the heart of Venezuela, with cattle and contrapuntal 'folkloric' music. We reached the mountains – the 'mesas', flat-topped with precipitous sides and the longest narrow unbroken waterfall in the world, discovered by Harry Gibson on a previous flight. Then the equatorial rain forests appeared and extended to the horizon and into Brazil. We landed in a small clearing with grass huts and were welcomed by a group of Indians, the Makiritari, a superior Carib nation, similar to those found by Columbus on his discoveries.

Hans and I shared a grass hut, and Barbara joined Father Daniel. So the days began. Each morning the women and children would queue at Daniel's hut for medicine. We made several expeditions; one was to the Shiri-Shana, a very primitive sub-tribe with no pottery, no musical instruments, where again the warriors had gone on a walk-about, leaving the chief, who eyed us very carefully. We stayed for lunch, which was hand-caught freshwater crabs, uncooked – all of which appears in the film *Kanarakuni* made by Hans. It all seemed, and was, very far away from Caracas – about 20,000 years – where there were elections, with bombs every hour or so and bursts of machine-gun fire. This was the first democratic election in Venezuela and they were very pleased that only twenty men had been killed.

Some of the hut walls had been daubed with mud, on which crude drawings had been made – some with men on horses, which was surprising, for no horse could get through the jungle and this could perhaps only be explained by a tribal memory handed on even from the conquistadors centuries before. A feature that surprised me was the moon, for in Europe

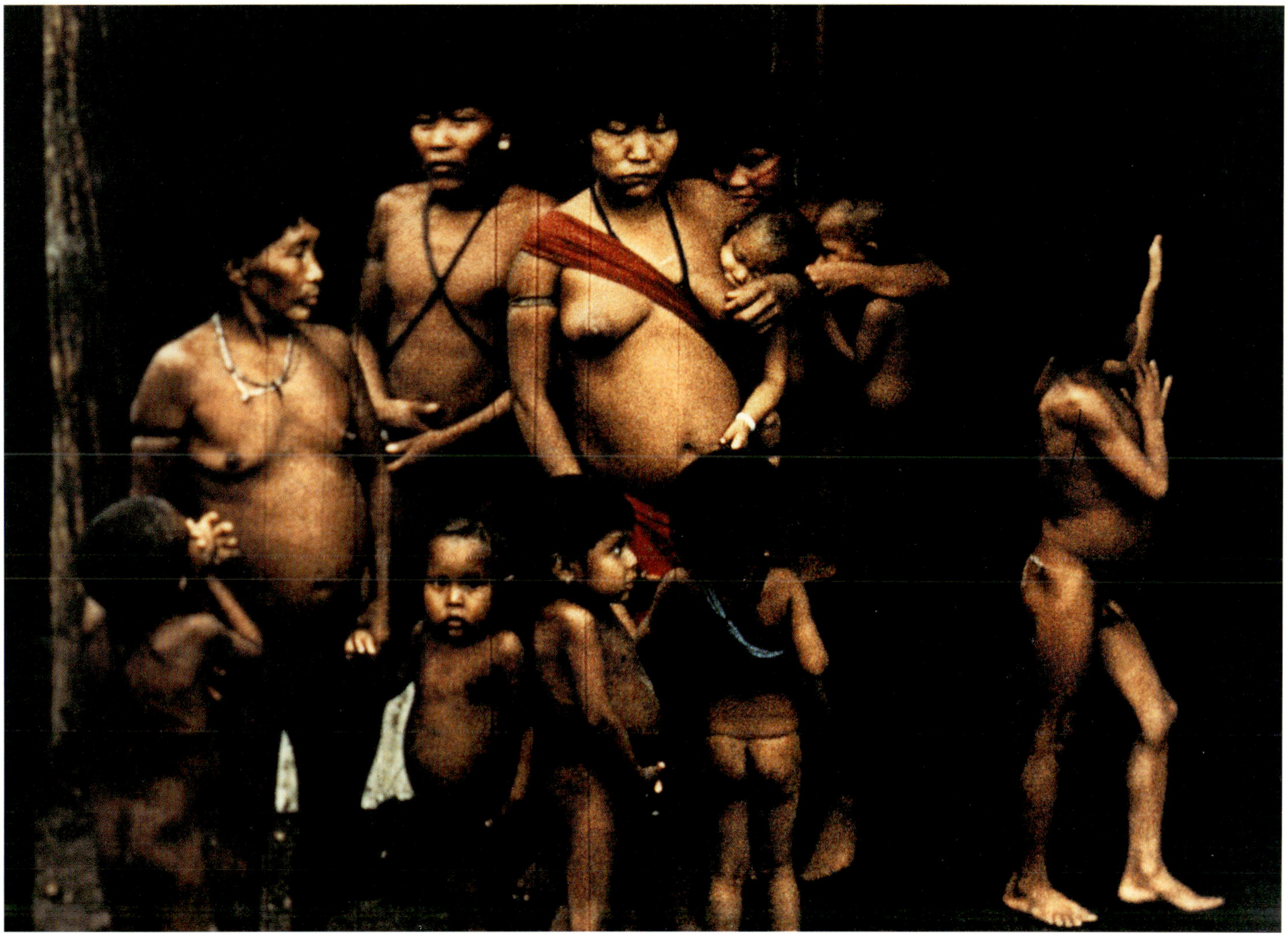

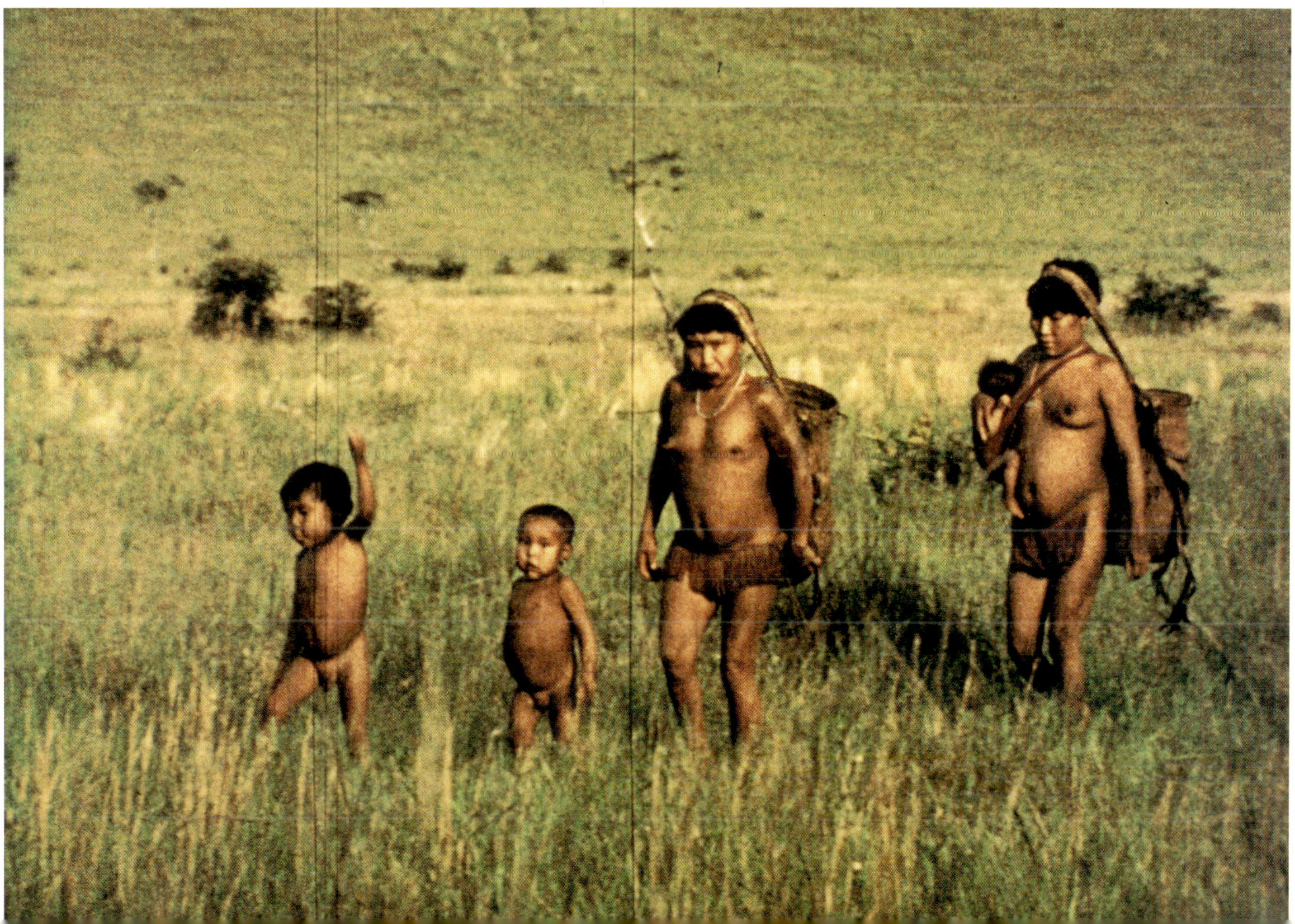

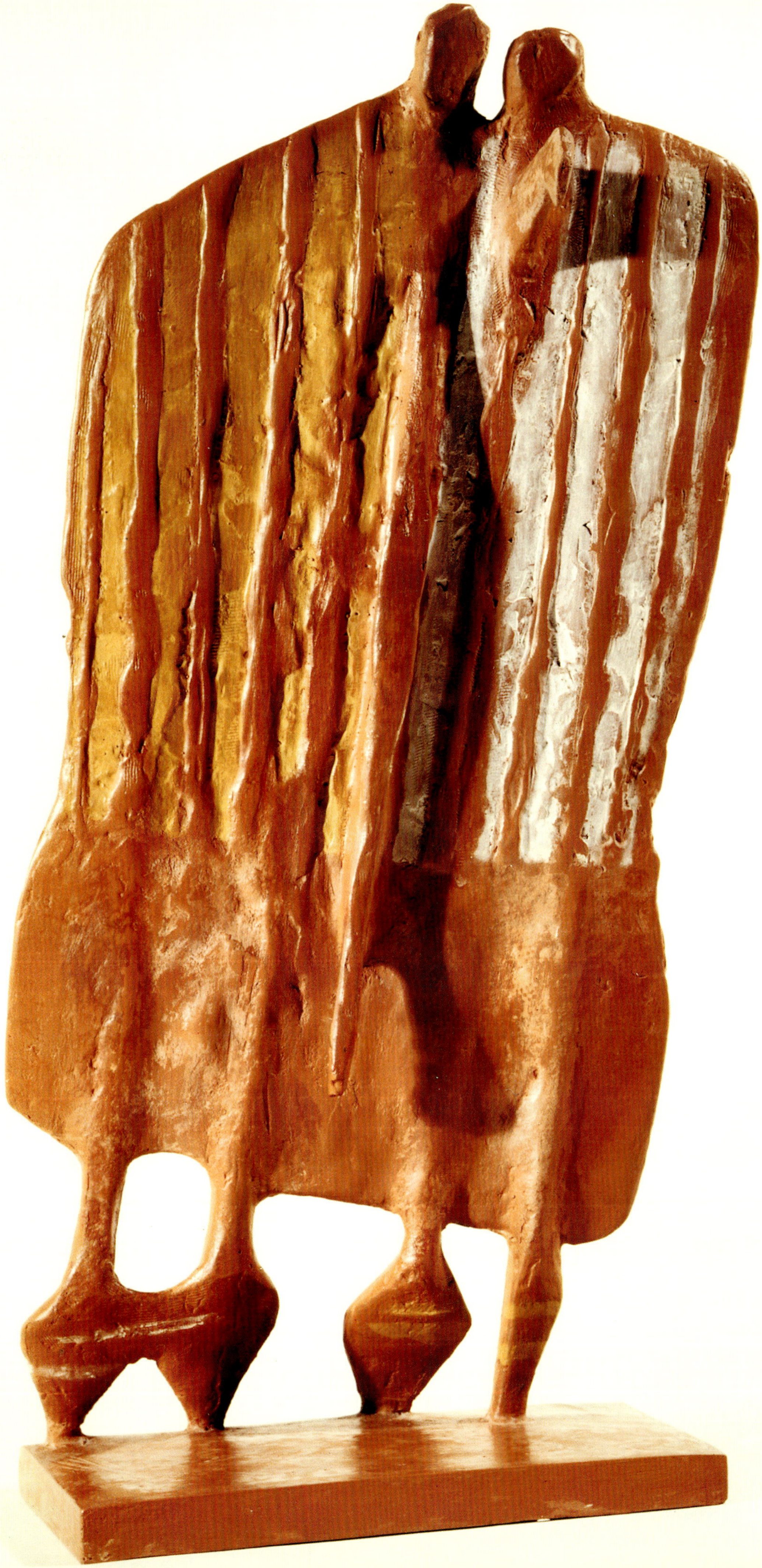

(opposite) Footballers, plaster 1953, cast 1986 (KA34)
H 51 cm (20 in), resin cast

Mouton Sun 1959-63 (KA86a)
L 269 cm (106 in), bronze with gold leaf

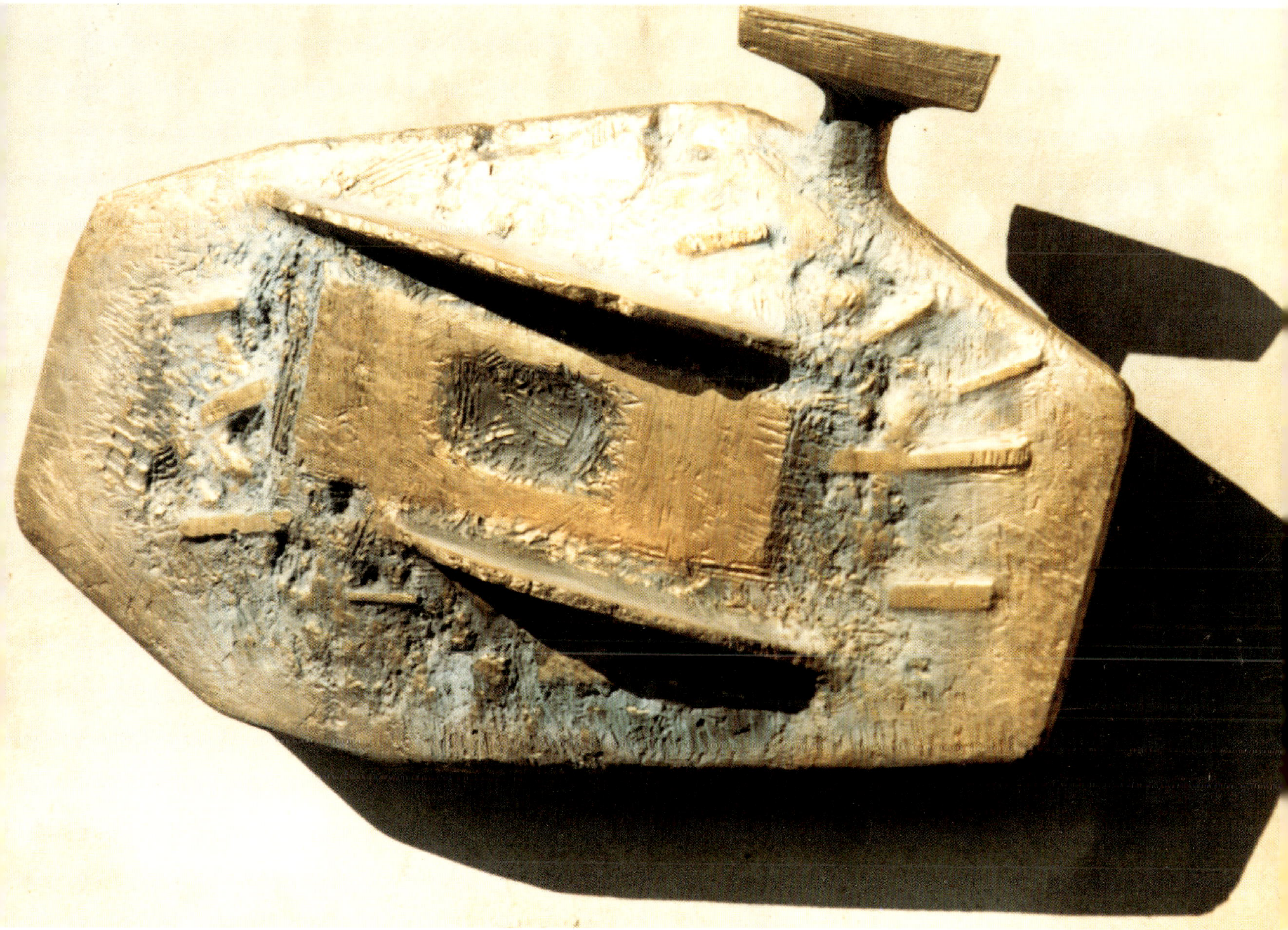

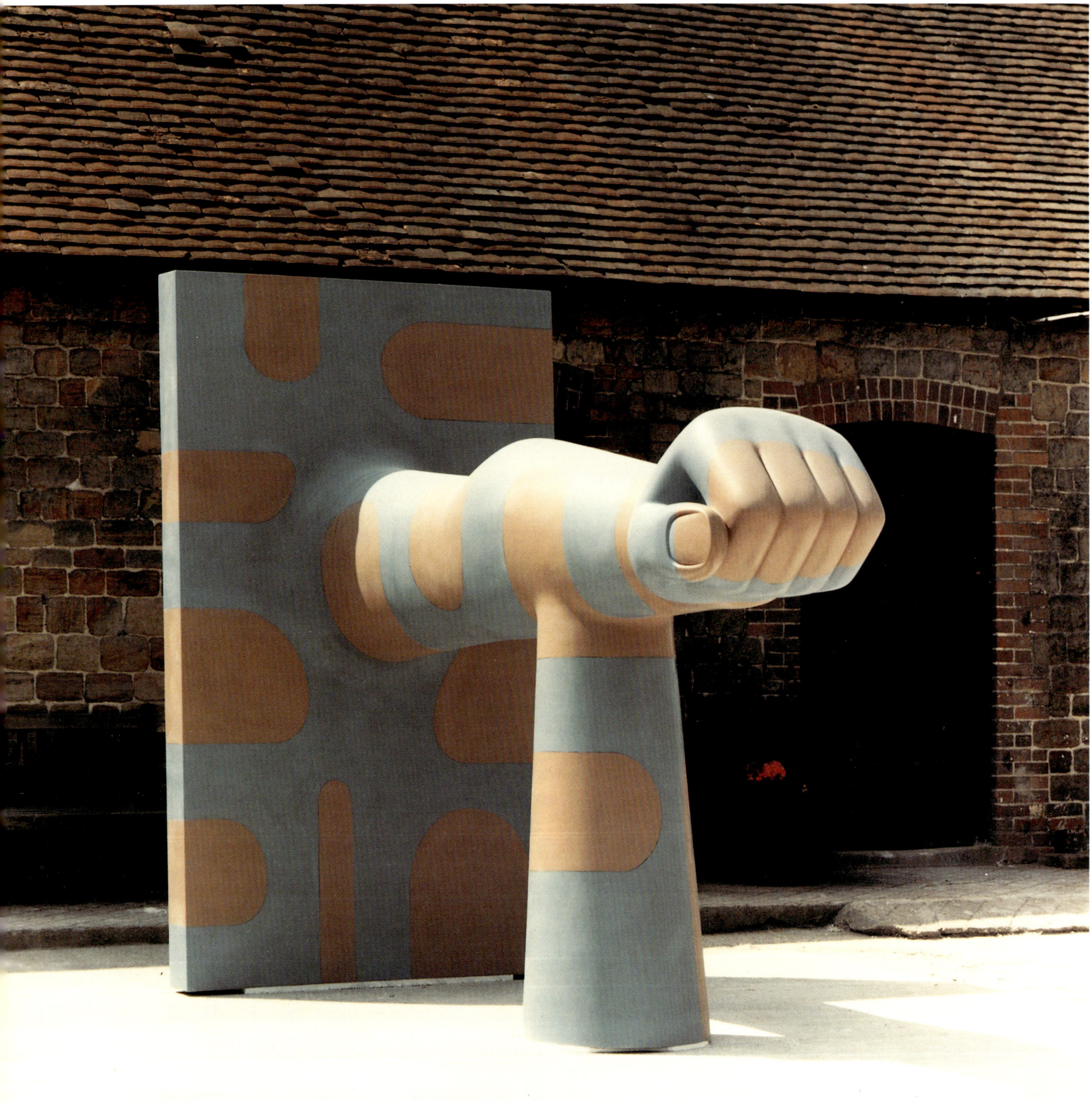

Two views of *Arm* 1967-8 (KA163)
H 386 cm (152 in), resin and fibreglass (paint-sprayed)

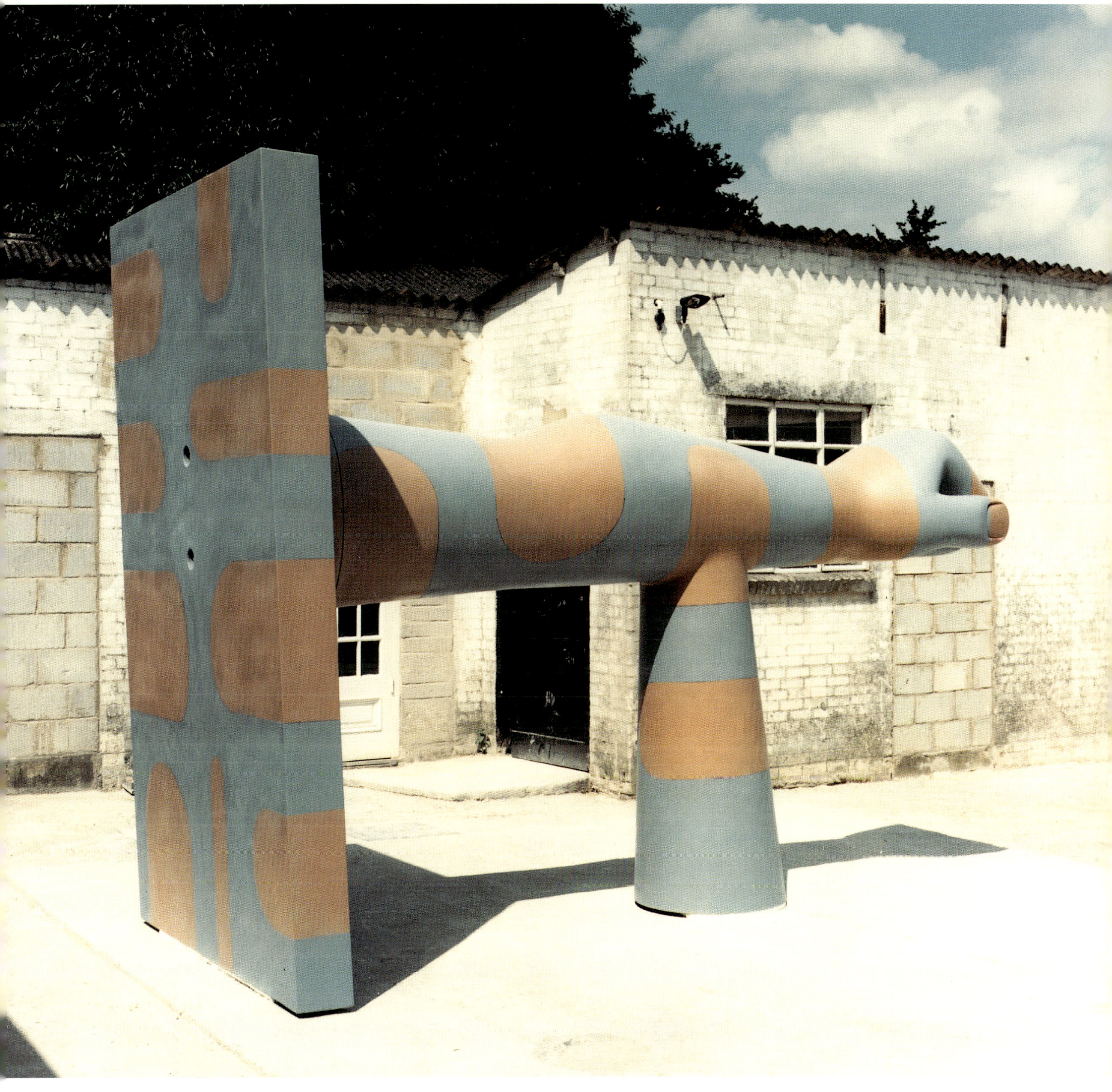

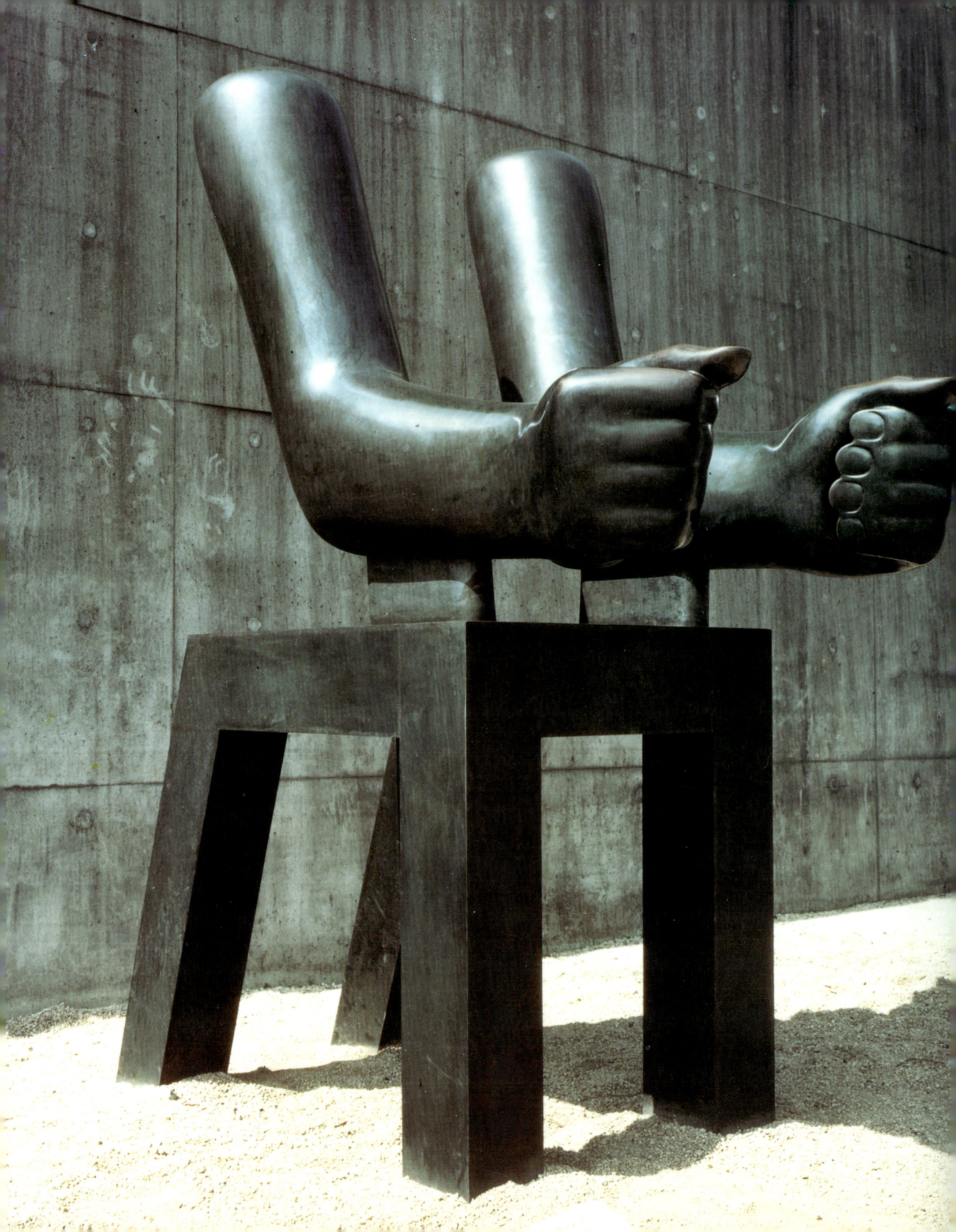

(*opposite*) *Both Arms* 1969 (KA172)
H 232 cm (91$\frac{1}{2}$ in), bronze

Rose-red City (version 1) 1982 (KA249)
L 42 cm (16$\frac{1}{2}$ in), bronze

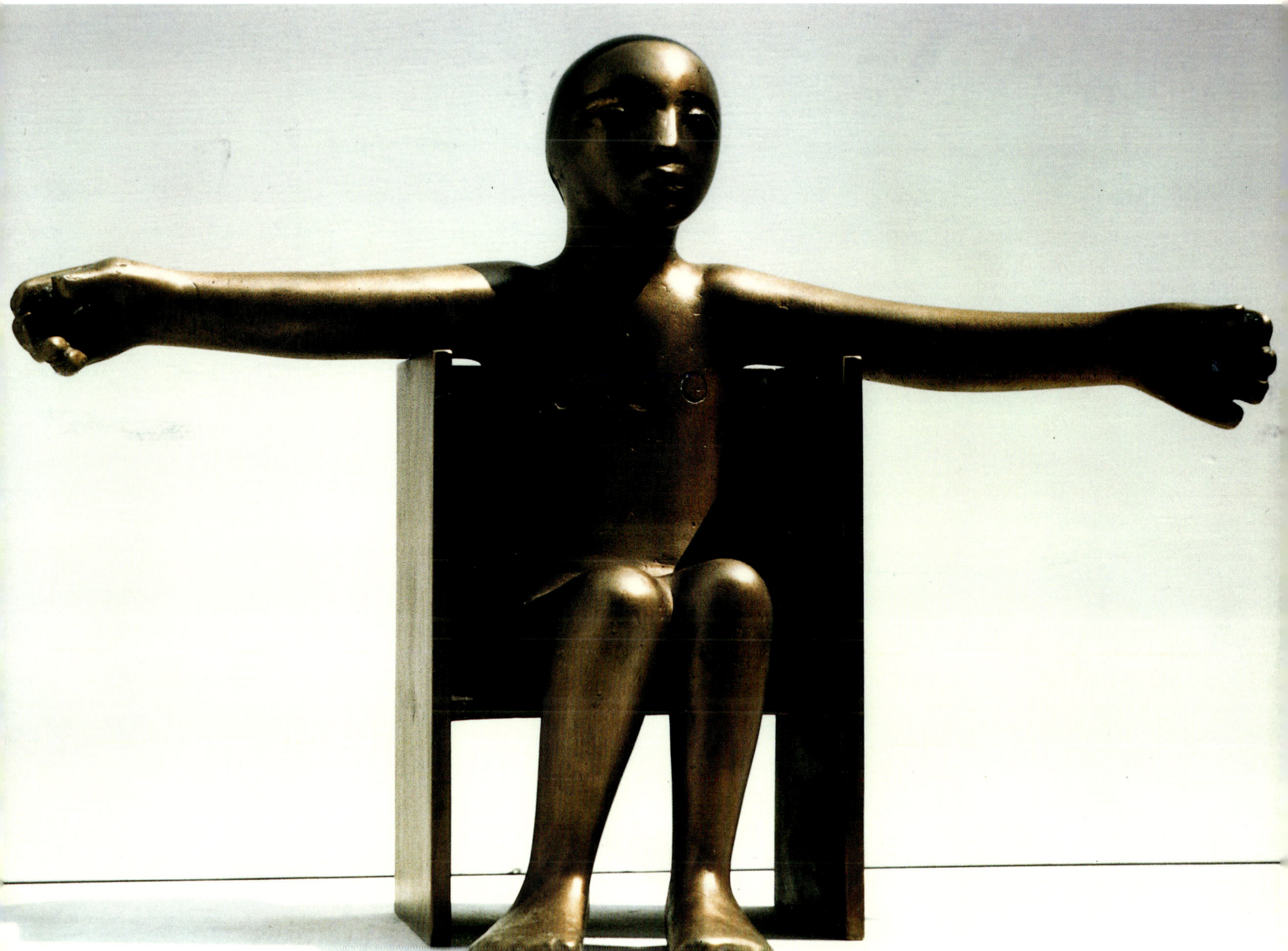

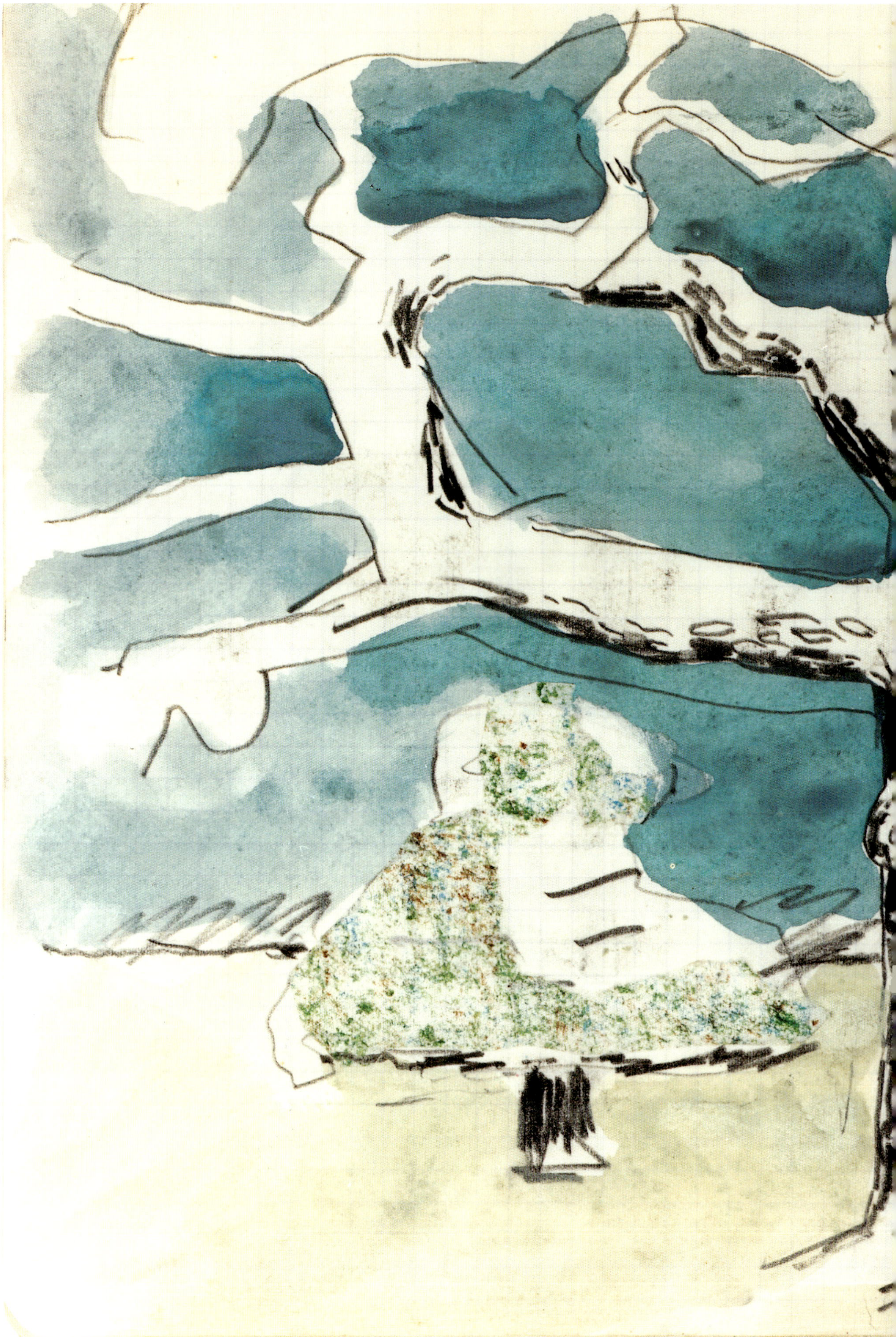

Richmond Oak,
from a sketchbook about 1975

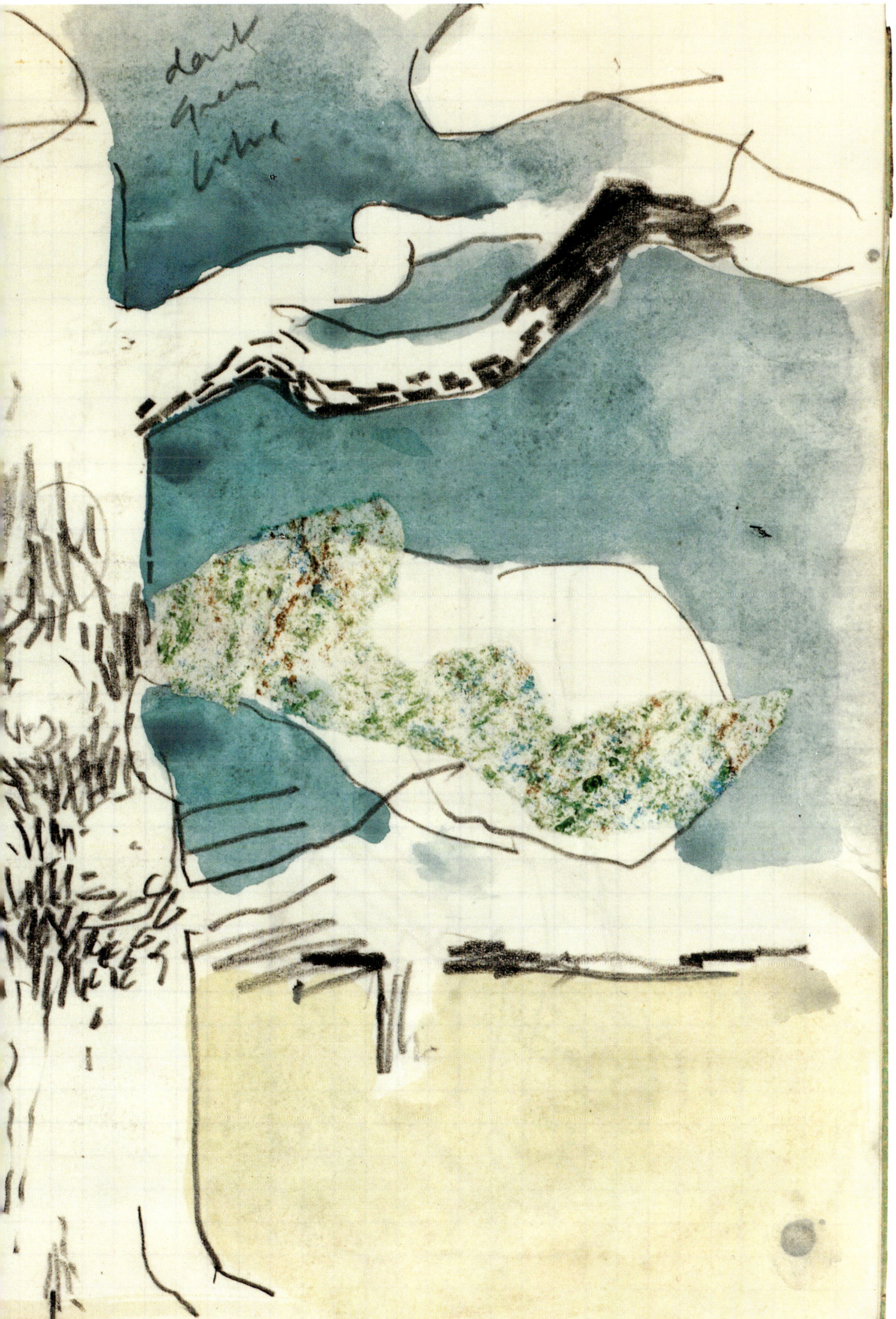
dark
green

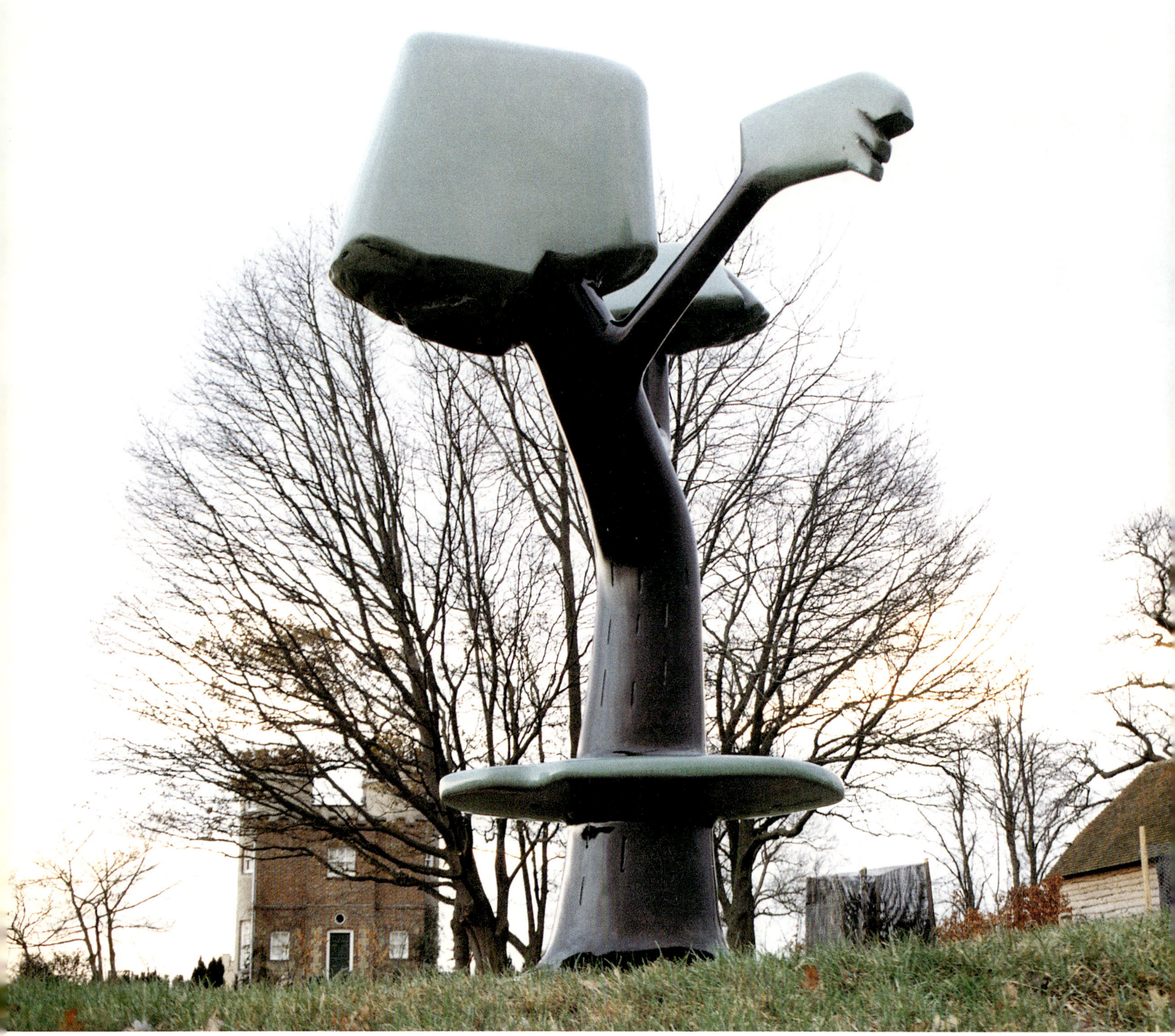

Richmond Oak 1985 (KA261)
H 300 cm (118 in), black and green bronze, sited temporarily at the Deer Tower, Shillinglee Park

(*opposite*) Another view of *Richmond Oak*

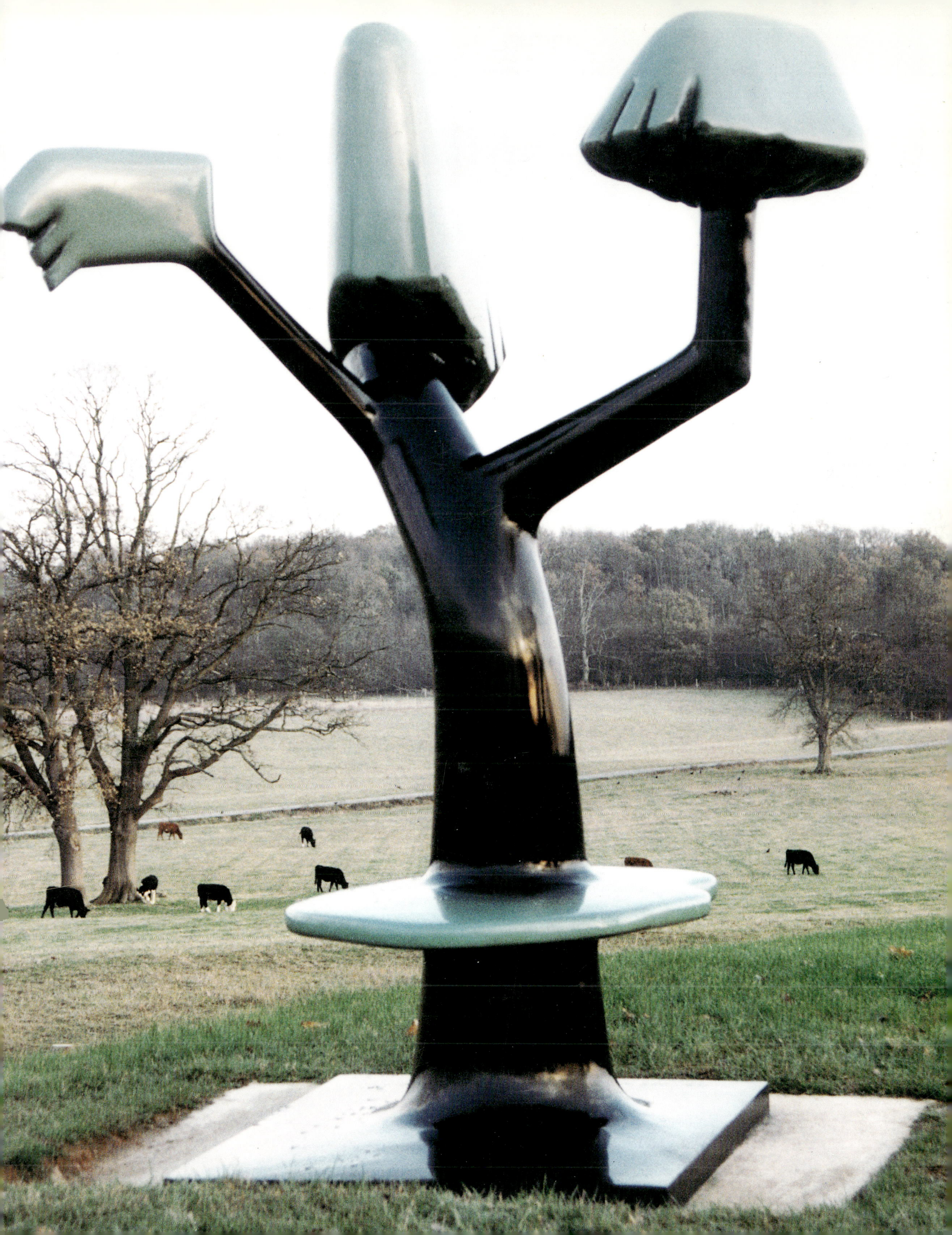

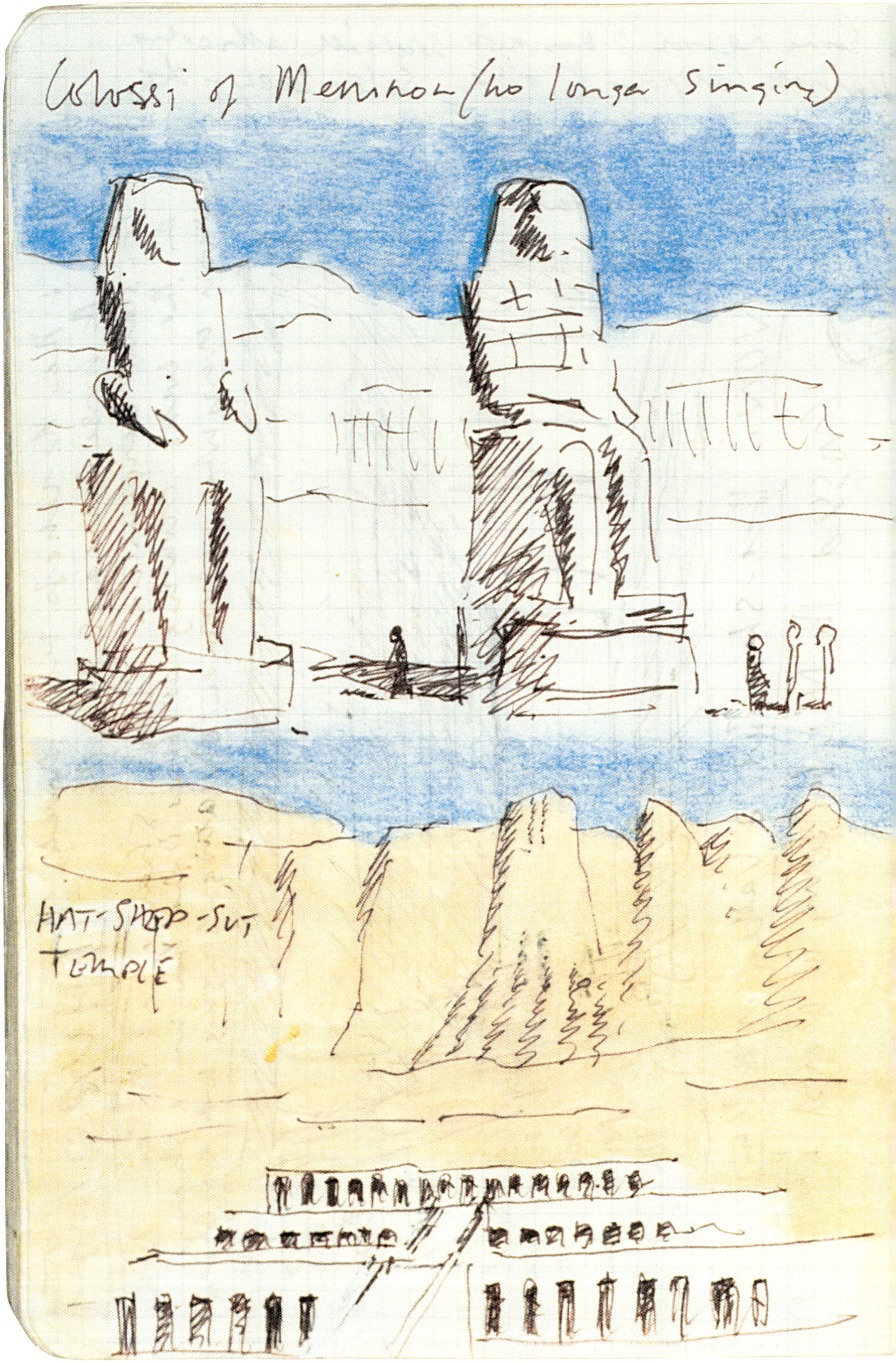

In 1985, KA toured Egypt with his friends.
This is a double-spread from his tour sketchbook

It was a morning of such light
The god spoke to his chisels
Sang with them
In choirs of ringing hammers,
Stone birds flew from the marshlands,
Gazelles cropped among the flowers,
Breasts were hard with milk

How soon upstream
The chisels turn their points
To fearful hurried work
Kings fed huge with blood
Sweet lotus bloated
Into magnificent colonnades
Osiris in the dark
His coffin sealed with lead

Dogs among the stones
Eat the food we have brought
Dogs themselves with the form of a god
Anubis son of Seth destroyer of Osiris
And see how big they are
These dogs how well fed
These dogs of Saqqara

Written by Terence Griffin during visit to Egypt 1985

For K.A

TG.

The Egypt party '85

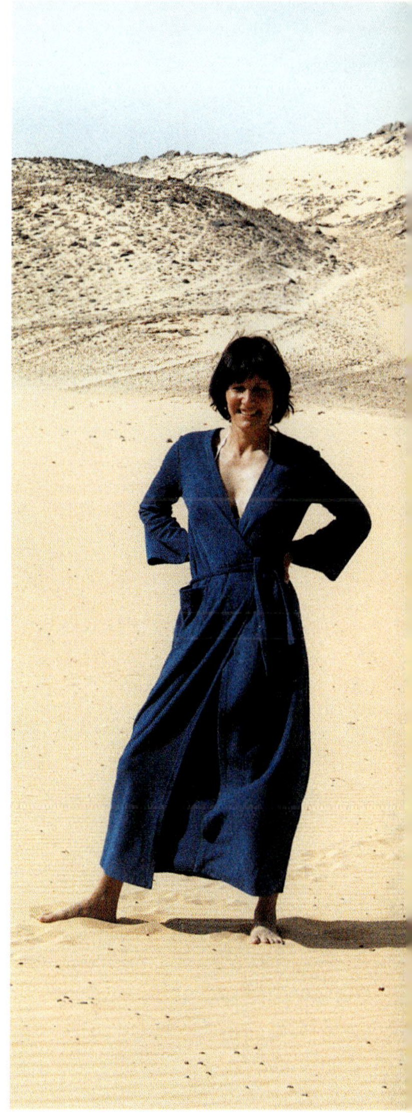

Josceline Dimbleby after a swim in the Nile

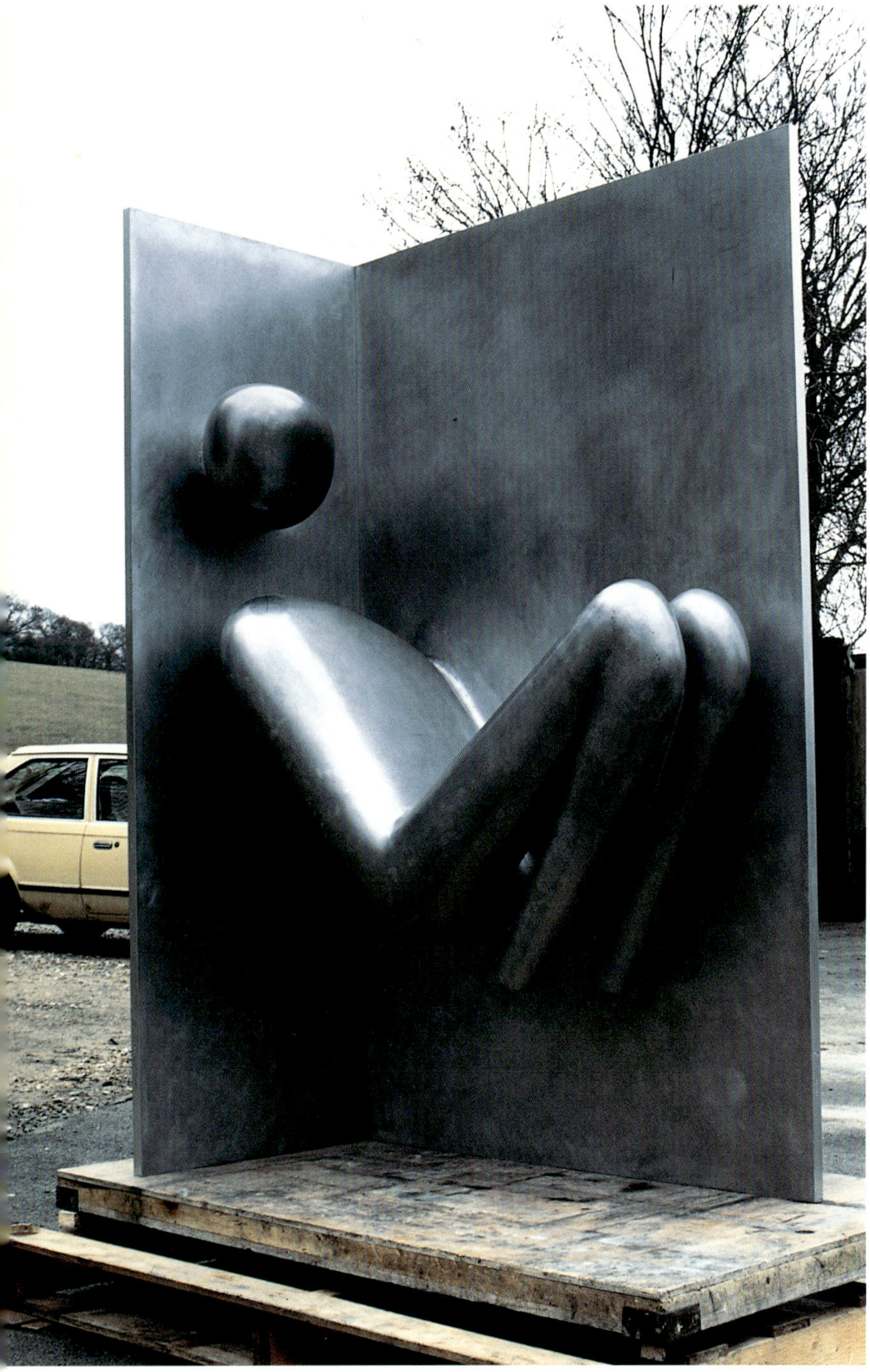

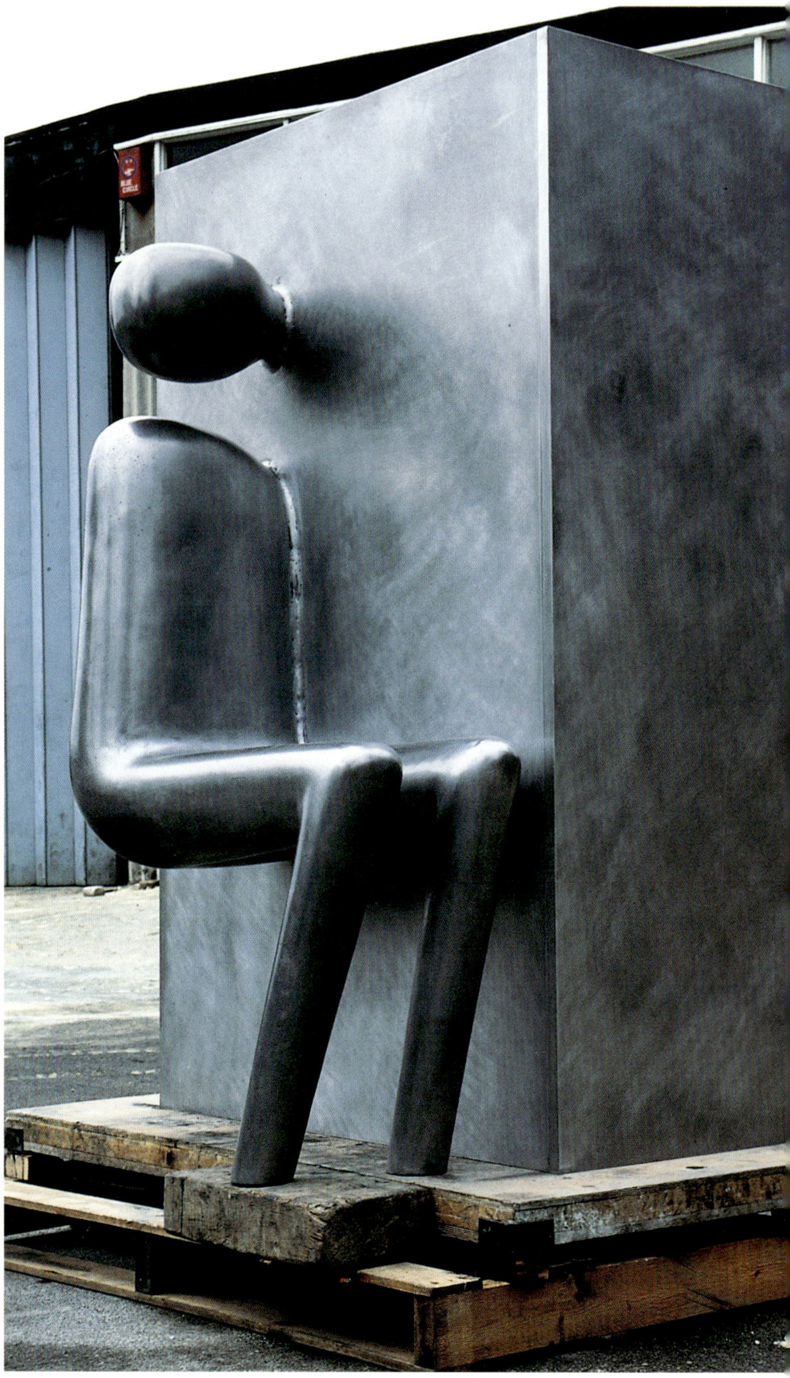

Three views of *L-shaped Screen* 1991 (KA268)
H 180 cm (71 in), plate and cast aluminium

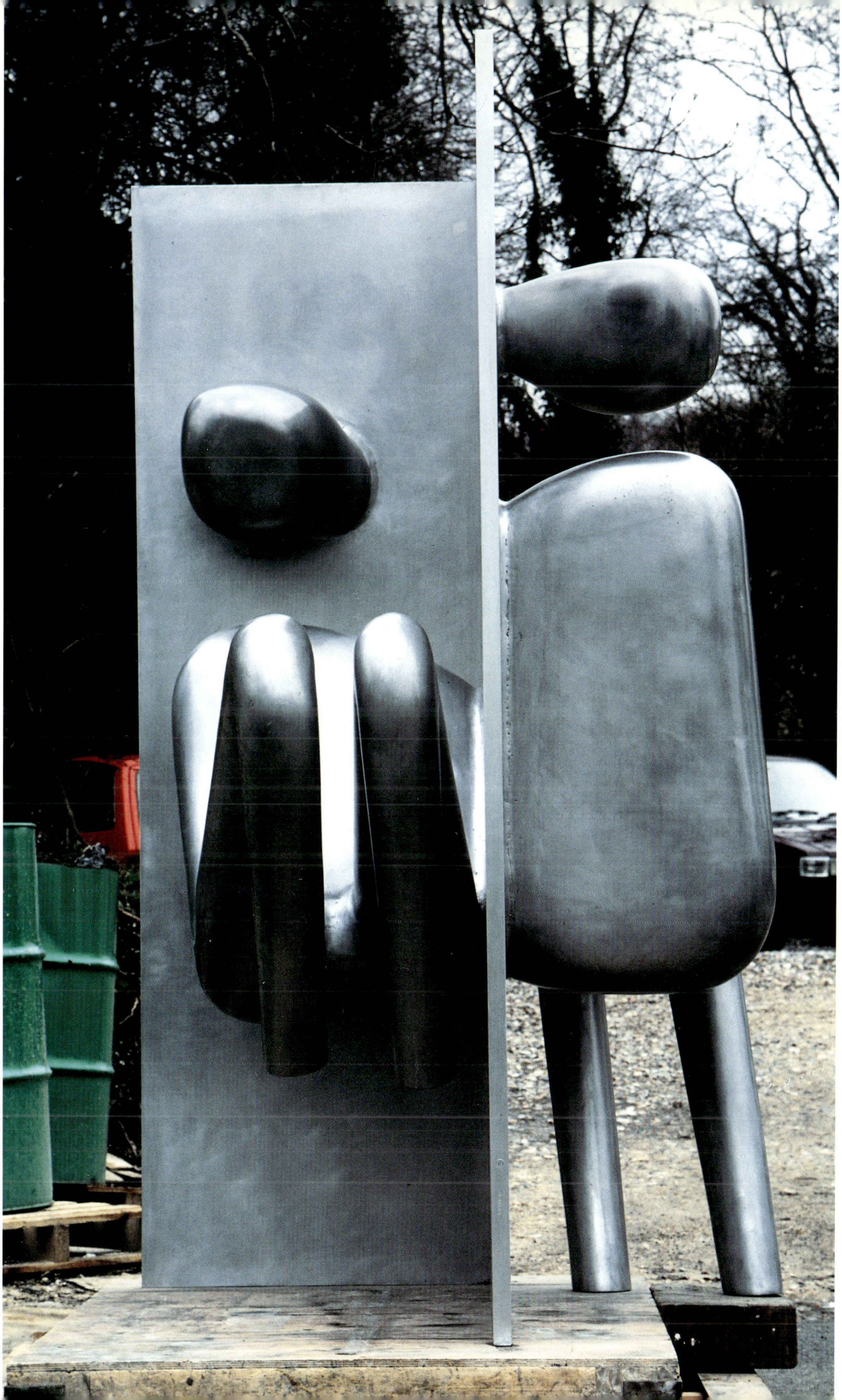

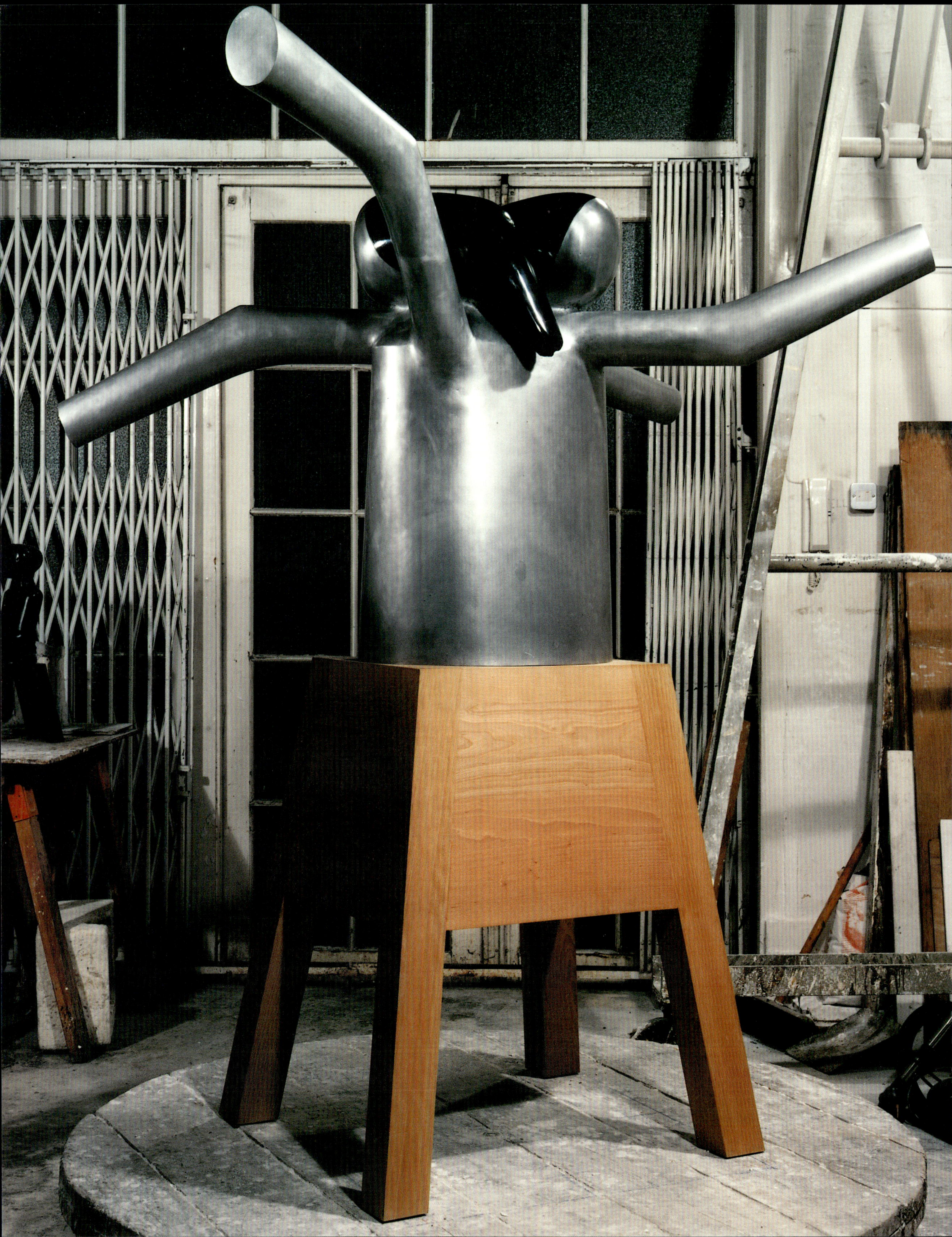

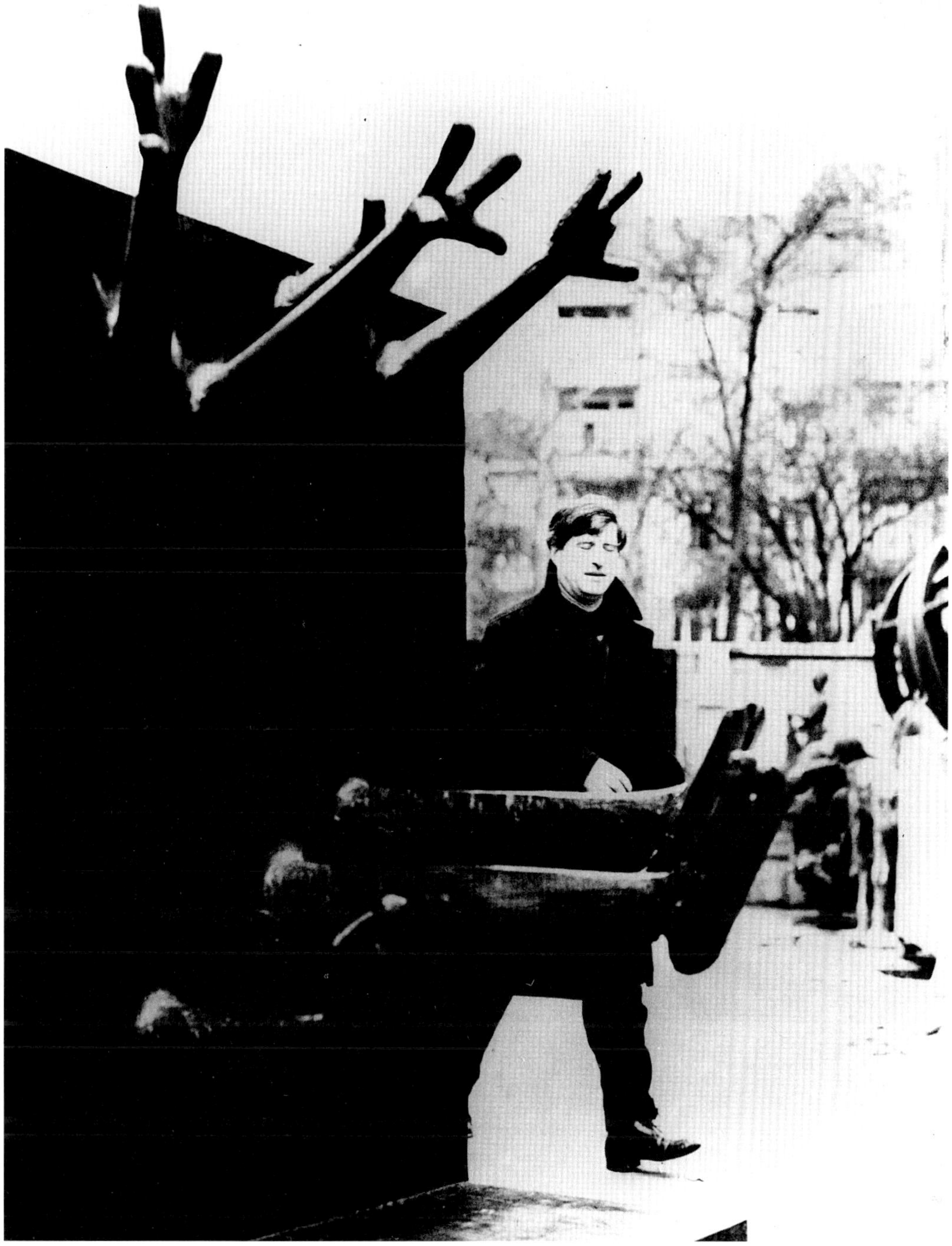

The Forest 1965 (KA154)
H 163 cm (64 in), bronze
with KA in the background

(*opposite*) *The Dagda* 1996 (KA270)
H 198 cm (78 in), aluminium and beech wood

it turns on a vertical axis with the shadow spreading left to right, while there it turned on a horizontal axis with the shadow up and down, due to the situation almost on the Equator. The trip was cut short when we received a radio report informing us that there had been an explosion at one of Hans's factories and some men had been killed. Hans was distraught and we had to leave. I could not afford to have a second plane to collect me, but Barbara consoled me – I could make another trip later.

This expedition left a lasting and vivid impression. One result was a fairly large sculpture, *The Forest* (1965), with extended arms and legs from a plain vertical slab. For me, work rarely results from visits, but in this case there was a direct influence. In the equatorial rain forest it is not congested at ground level; the congestion is in the canopy above, with these enormous trees and great buttresses holding them up. But if there is a clearing, then there are dense thickets so thick that you cannot put your hand in. This inspired the bronze – I made two maquettes first and then the large piece.

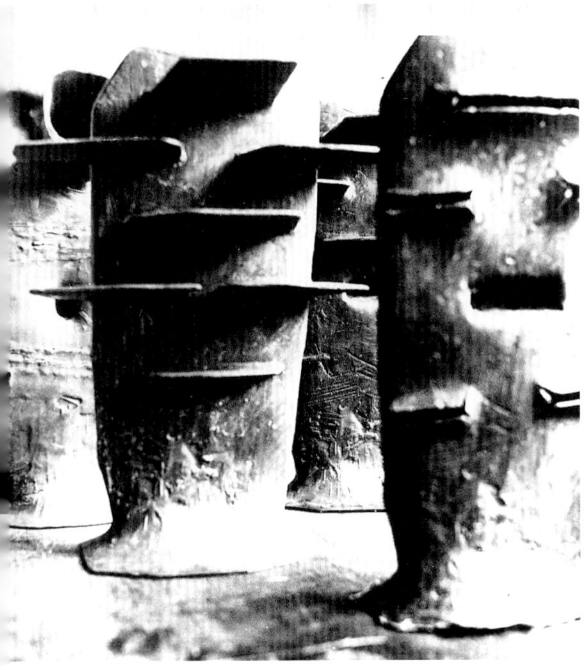

Still from the film *Five British Sculptors Work and Talk* (1964) directed by Warren Forma, showing models by KA

(*opposite*) Detail of *The Legend of Skadar* (version 2) 1965 (KA138)
H 56 cm (22 in), brass

In Caracas, the sculptors ended their work and I had my *Pandarus* model cast, to be bought by the Museo de Bellas Artes. Hans asked if I could have a second cast made for him, which he would not pay me for but would give the money to the sculptors in the form of a mini Armitage 'Fundacion'. So ended one of the most fascinating episodes of my life. I later made three visits to Caracas. Harry Abend, one of the sculptors who worked with me, became a lifelong friend, and we have met many times both in Venezuela and London.

I made an etching and gave a print to the many friends I left behind. The British Council representative, Sydney Whitaker, brought a bottle of champagne and glasses to the airport runway and drank my health on departure.

In the mid-1960s I found the tide turning against me. I had been very lucky in the 1950s due to the British Council exhibitions abroad, and as a result I was better known and received outside Britain than I was here. At this time, the English habit was to follow American ideas on art, and people thought that I was wrong on two counts. Firstly, I was wrong for being figurative. People thought figurative art was dead, which was of course nonsense. I didn't like the idea of having a figure with two arms, five fingers on each hand and five toes, for example, so I would use a simple element of the curved surfaces of the arm and body, which I combined with severe geometric shapes; this has in fact gone on in my work until this day.

The other thing people attacked me for was for using bronze casting: I think they felt it was an ancient technique (four-and-a-half thousand years old!) and this worried people. It is very strange that people accept that the technique of painting is much the same as it ever was. Oil paint is still used, but whereas oil painting has no corporeal reality – just marks on a surface – sculpture has a three-dimensional reality; it has substance and takes up room.

When I first went to Corsham I went to a technical school in Bath and hammered out two things there in steel, but I didn't do it for long. Noticing the famous artist Gonzalez and all the other sculptors who welded sculpture, I saw that their raw material was rod and plate, which when assembled gave a jerky, slightly cruel quality. If the sculpture is abstract, the content relies on the medium, rod and plate steel, and the result is spiky and fearful. Naturally the medium one uses in sculpture does affect the appearance of the work. César, the French sculptor, obtained a plastic quality occasionally by using hundreds of small segments welded together which he would then smooth over in places, but this was an extremely laborious way of doing it. I found bronze was an excellent medium for making the sensual, plastic surfaces which I was concerned with, and to hell with what other people thought, for I have never had any interest in fashion.

In 1965 I started another extended project which I called *The Legend of Skadar*, after Skadar on the River Ljubljana. I have always worked listening to classical music on Radio 3, and once I heard a terrible singing – so terrible that I had to stop working and listen to it. It was a recording made by Alan Lomax, who went all over the world recording people singing. This particular piece was a recording of a blind beggar who went around the mountains of Yugoslavia singing of ancient myths, for which, after six hours non-stop, he would be given enough bread and wine to see him through that day. There are several versions of the Skadar myth spread throughout southern Europe. The story is of three brothers who were building a

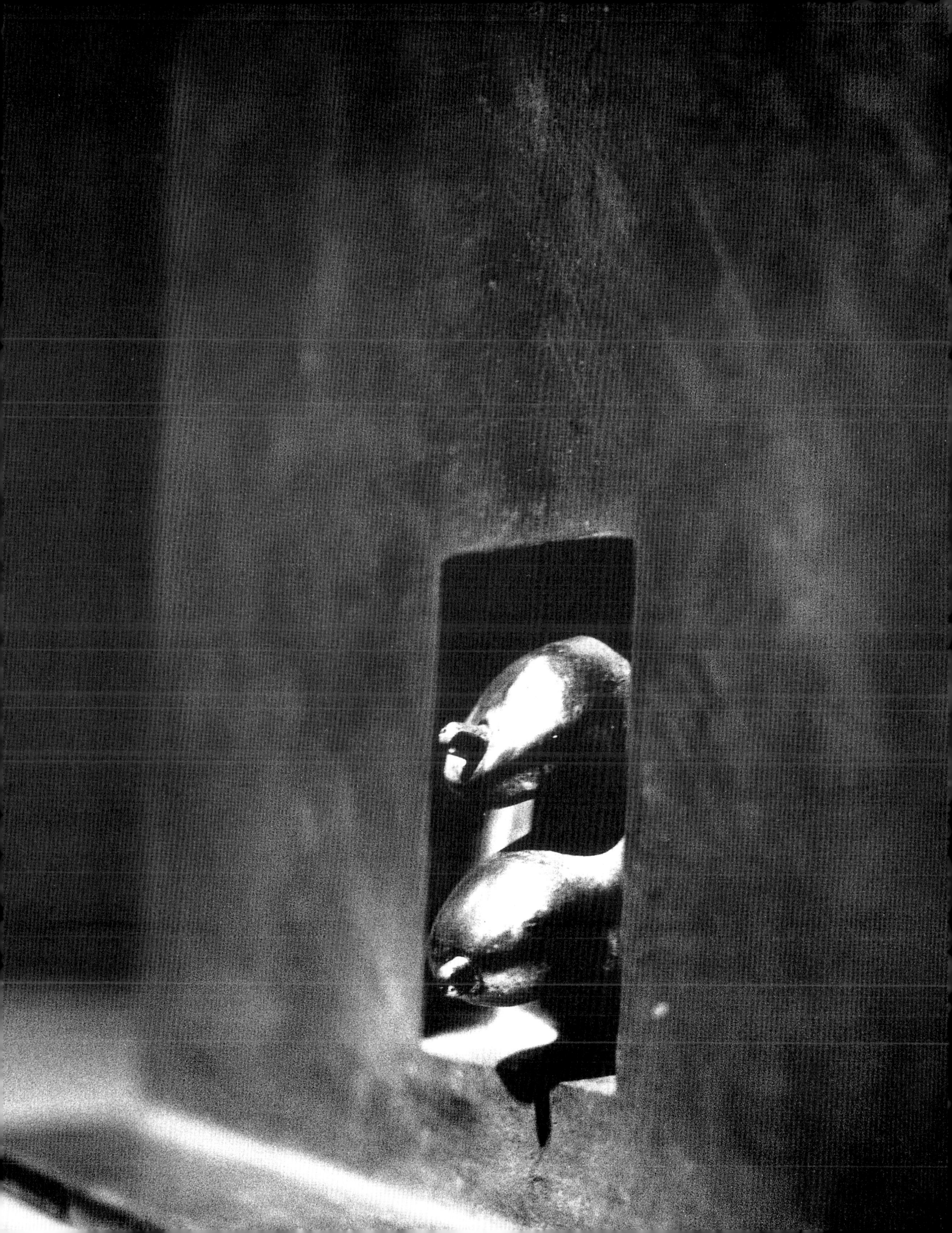

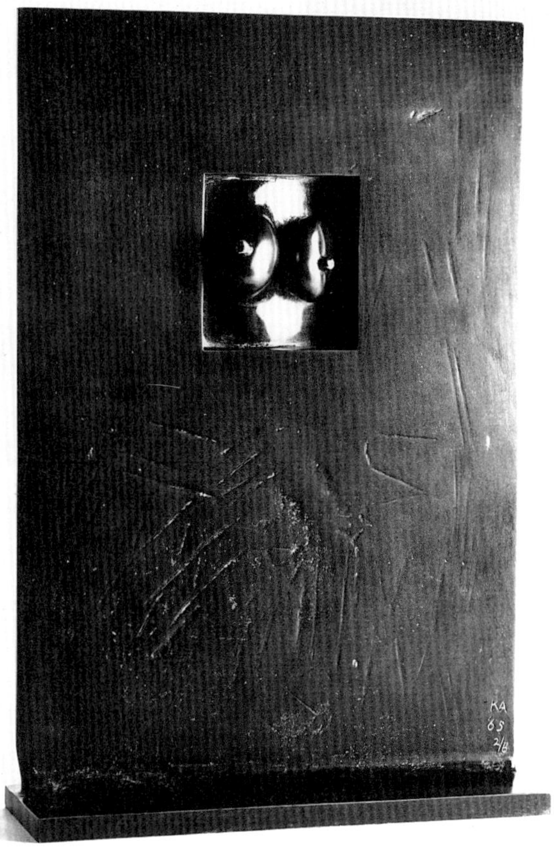

(*above*) *The Legend of Skadar* (version 3) 1965 (KA139)
H 43.5 cm (17 in), bronze

(*opposite*) *The Legend of Skadar* (version 4) 1965 (KA140)
H 60.5 cm ($23\frac{3}{4}$ in), bronze

fort, and every night a female mountain spirit threw down what they had built during the day. After three years the spirit eventually said: 'The only way that I will let the wall remain is if you brick up alive one of your wives in the wall', which they did. They had an awful problem choosing which wife it should be, but the wife of Gojko, one of the brothers, was selected and she had to go through with it. She had recently given birth. At first she thinks it's a joke as the stones rise to her knees, and she laughs. But when the stones rise to her waist, she shrieks in fury, and begs to be spared. In desperation she says her mother will provide a slave girl to sacrifice in her stead. The legend has a strange repetitive character which I have never come across before and it was described thus in an article sent to me by an Englishman living in Japan: 'But when the slender bride has seen that no prayer she prays will do her good, then she begs Rade the master builder, "Brother in God, Rade, master builder, leave me only a window at my breasts, and push my white breast through it when Jovo [her son] comes. When my little one comes, when he comes let him suck my breasts." Rade accepted it in brotherhood. He left a window at her breasts. She pushed her white breasts out at the window. And so they built her into the town, and carried out the child in the cradle, and she gave her milk for seven days, and after seven days her voice had gone. And still the child fed at the breast, and she gave him her milk through a year ... And so it was, and so it has remained. Look, even now the white milk [is] running down, like a great miracle and medicine for any woman who can give no milk.' And so it turned into a sacrifice that was a miracle, and was of help to women with fertility problems.

I made about ten models, all approximately two to three feet high; it took that much time for me to get it out of my system.

A couple of years after *Skadar*, in 1967, I was invited by the DAAD, the German Academic Exchange, to go to Berlin for the City of Berlin Künstlerprogramm (Artists' Programme). The DAAD attracted the best people they could find: for example, I met Dallapiccola, the very well known Italian composer, under the same scheme. There were poets and painters there: William Scott went before me, and the American sculptor George Rickey was there at the same time as I was. He became a great friend whom I often see.

I already knew Berlin from my visits to the Noack bronze foundry before the Wall had been built, but by the time of my lengthy visit the Wall was in place.

The idea of going to Berlin attracted me. The other thing was the fact that I felt that things were going against me in Britain, it was getting tougher; and I idly thought that I might put myself in exile and live abroad for a bit to overcome this problem.

In the late 1960s people were reacting against both figurative art and the use of bronze. There has been figurative art since almost the beginning of humanity – the Lascaux caves, for example, are 15,000 years old – so that did not worry me so much, but the reaction to bronze casting made a little more sense. Although bronze was for me a very important material, I do agree that stainless steel is the more splendid metal because it is very hard, and resistant to the weather. But it is cold and you can't patinate it so easily, if at all. And this cold shiny metal would not suit my work. Bronze was ideal for me; it was softer to work, it was a warmer metal, and it would take patinations of different colours, which is why I have used it to this day.

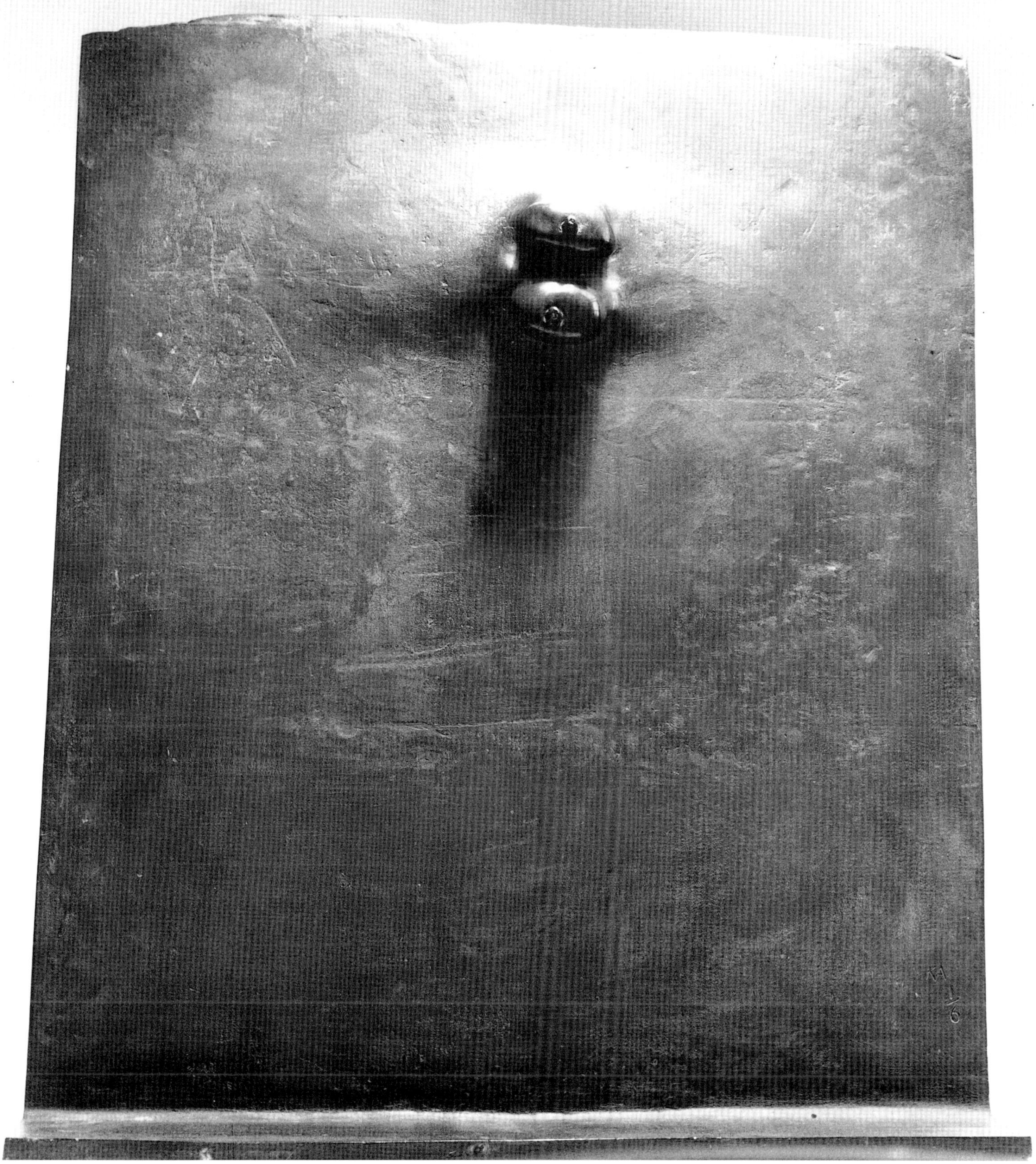

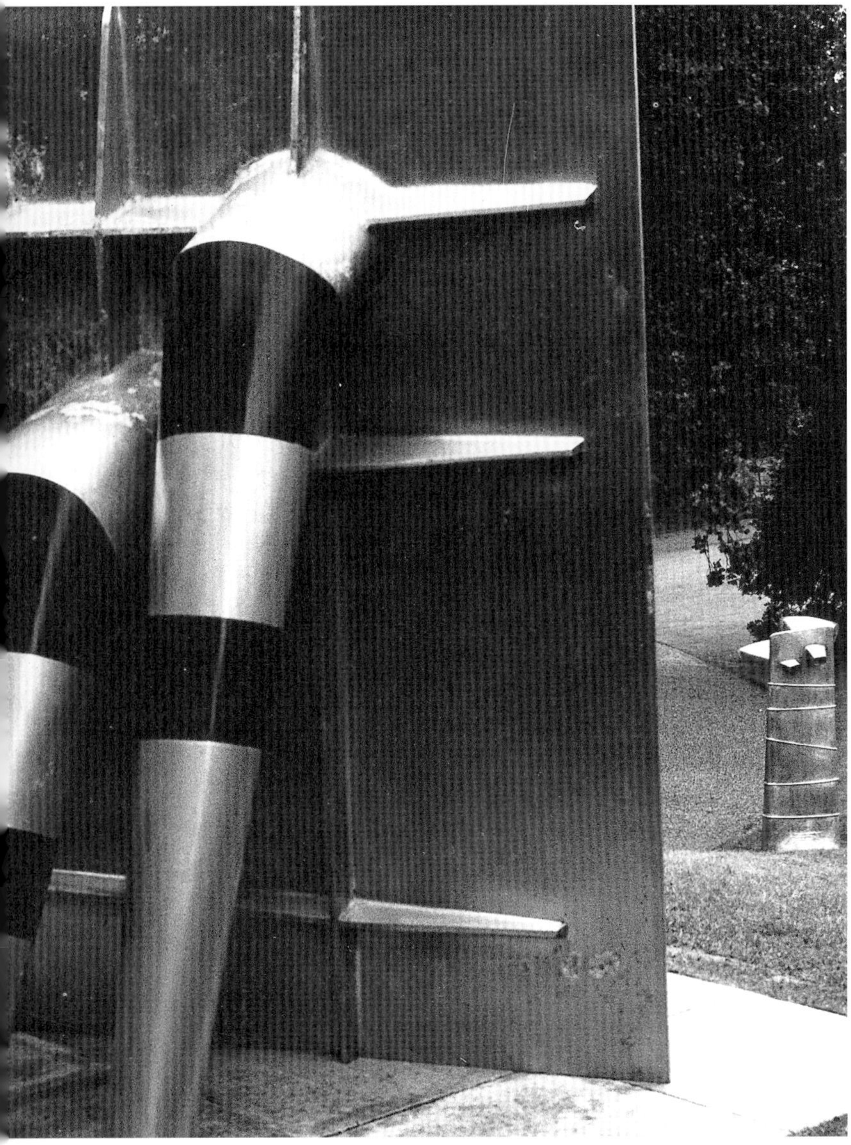

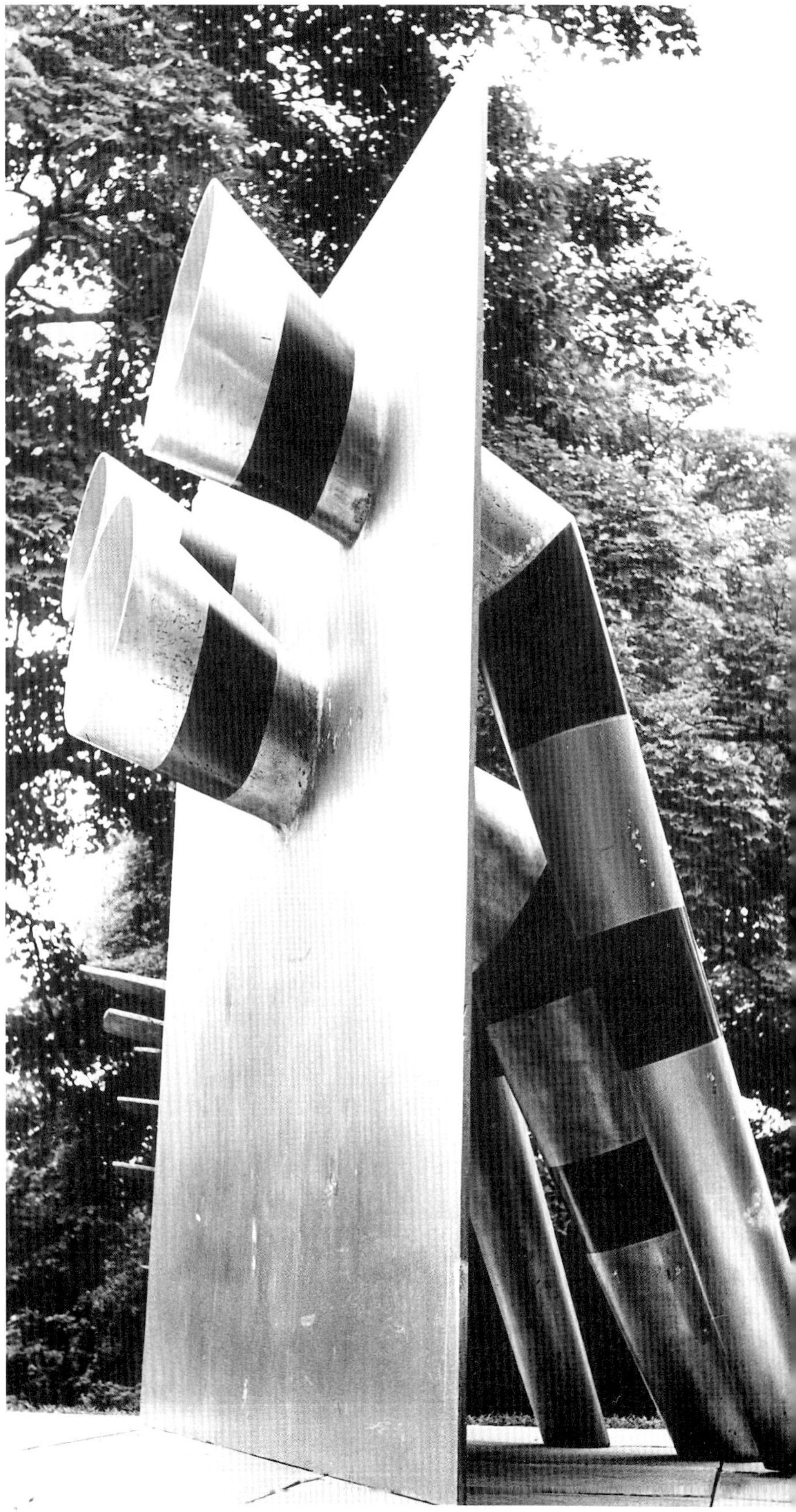

Tiger Tiger 1966 (KA158)
H 218 cm (85¾ in), cast and plate aluminium, painted stripes, exhibited Battersea Park, London, 1966

(*right*) Another view of *Tiger Tiger*

(*opposite*) Battersea Park, London, 1966:
On the hill: *Tiger Tiger* 1966
In the foreground: *Pandarus* (version 11) 1964 (KA133)
H 224 cm (88 in), brass

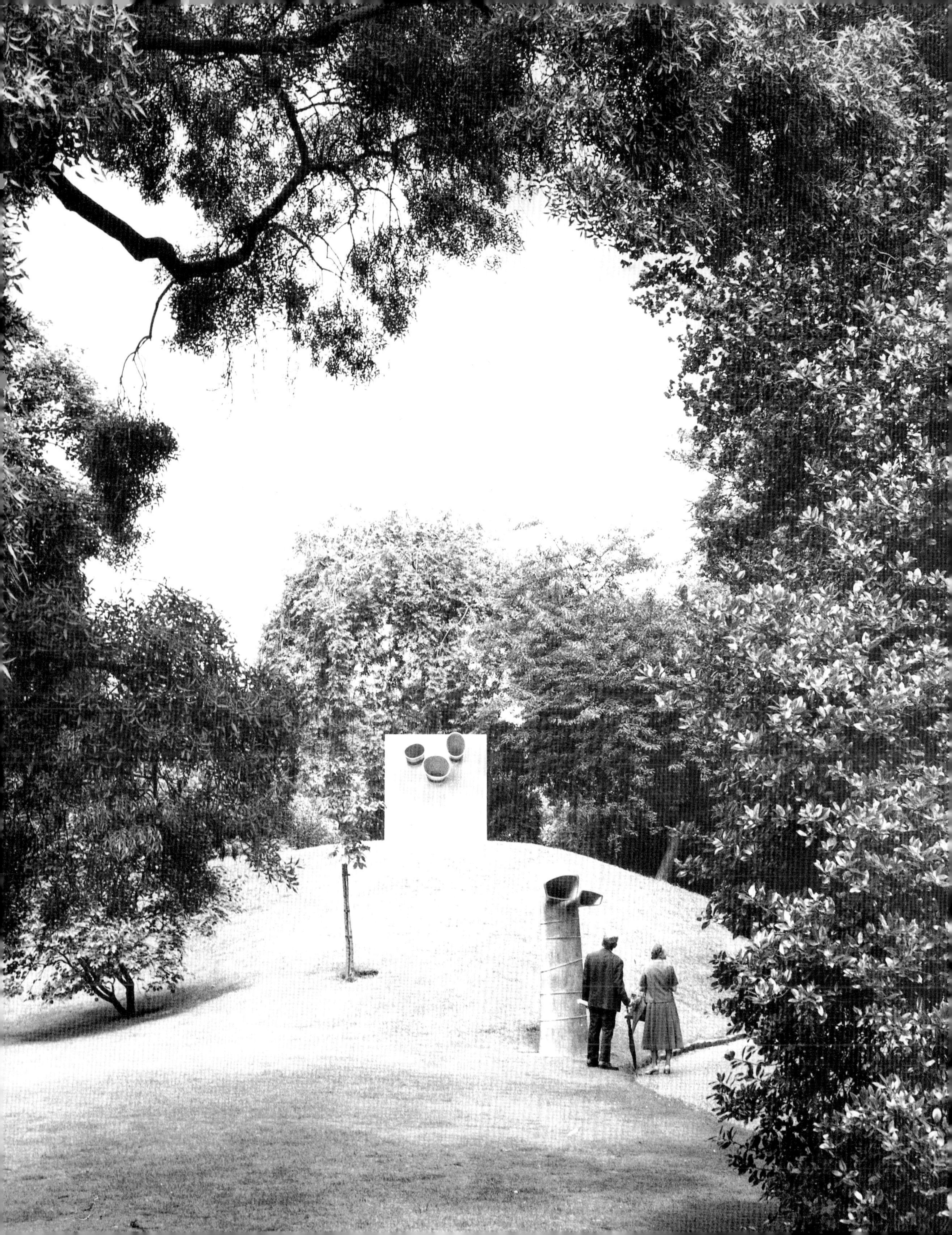

At that time, people began almost to detest the 1950s, and one became labelled with it, as certain writers and poets, like Stephen Spender, are associated with the Spanish Civil War. It is something you get stuck with.

There was something else I had come to realise from travels abroad – that art was not generally accepted in England. Although we have marvellous things here – the National Gallery, the British Council and the Arts Council, the good artists – the general attitude to art is not as natural as it is, say, in France or Latin America, especially with sculpture. During my time with the Gregory Fellowship at Leeds, a neighbour, on seeing what I was making and hearing that they were figures, said 'We send people to hospital like that. We pay money to have them put right.' When I told him they were already sold to a museum in the USA, he said 'Ah, you sell them do you?', which for him was meaningful in the sense that if I could sell them then he could overlook the 'badness' of the work.

In this context, Virginia Woolf, in her biography of Roger Fry many years ago, wrote: 'The English, it appeared to him, always attack an original idea, then debase it, and when they have rendered it harmless, proceed to swallow it whole. Fry deplored the extraordinary indifference of the English to the visual arts – among the undergraduates of his day, even the more thoughtful, the most speculative, this indifference seems to have been universal.'

Everything was laid on in Berlin; I had a marvellous studio, a flat ten minutes' walk away, and money. No teaching, no duties except to get on with my work.

When I left for Berlin in 1967 I took maquettes with me, knowing what I was going to make. I started joining different parts together. *Both Arms* (1969) was on a kind of table welded out of sheet metal, the two arms cast in the normal way. I also had a big plaster model of *Screen with Folded Arms* (cast 1967) and I had the idea of putting it onto the wall of a building. There would be two massive, heavy, rounded arms coming out of the wall, as though the building behind was the body of the person, with its folded arms sticking out in front. I cast the piece in aluminium and welded it onto a screen, and as aluminium does not weather well, Noack sprayed it with car paint.

Then I started a big piece, *Arm* (1967-8) – a huge twelve-feet-long arm growing out of a large ten-feet-high plate, resting on a circular column near the front. On one of my many visits to the British Museum, in the Egyptian Room, my eye had suddenly caught sight of this fragment of a colossal statue, part of the forearm, resting on two blocks. And this fitted in entirely with my idea behind the work I was doing, figurative work combined with geometric shapes. I had wanted to have it cast in Corten steel, which had only been invented some years previously. Its great attraction then was that it formed a skin when left outside, sealing the surface, so then it would not rust any more. I could not get US Steel to give me permission to cast it, as it was a secret formula, so I abandoned the idea and Noack cast it reluctantly in resin as a temporary measure – resin reinforced with glass fibre. In fact, during that long visit to Berlin, where my main foundry was, I did very little bronze casting and used mostly resin at the time; I got over that and came back to bronze later. The big *Arm* was later exhibited at *Expo 88* in Australia and is now in the Yorkshire Sculpture Park.

Later, in 1974 or 1975 I was approached by the Department of the Environment PSA to make a large piece of sculpture for the new Royal Marines Commando Training Centre at

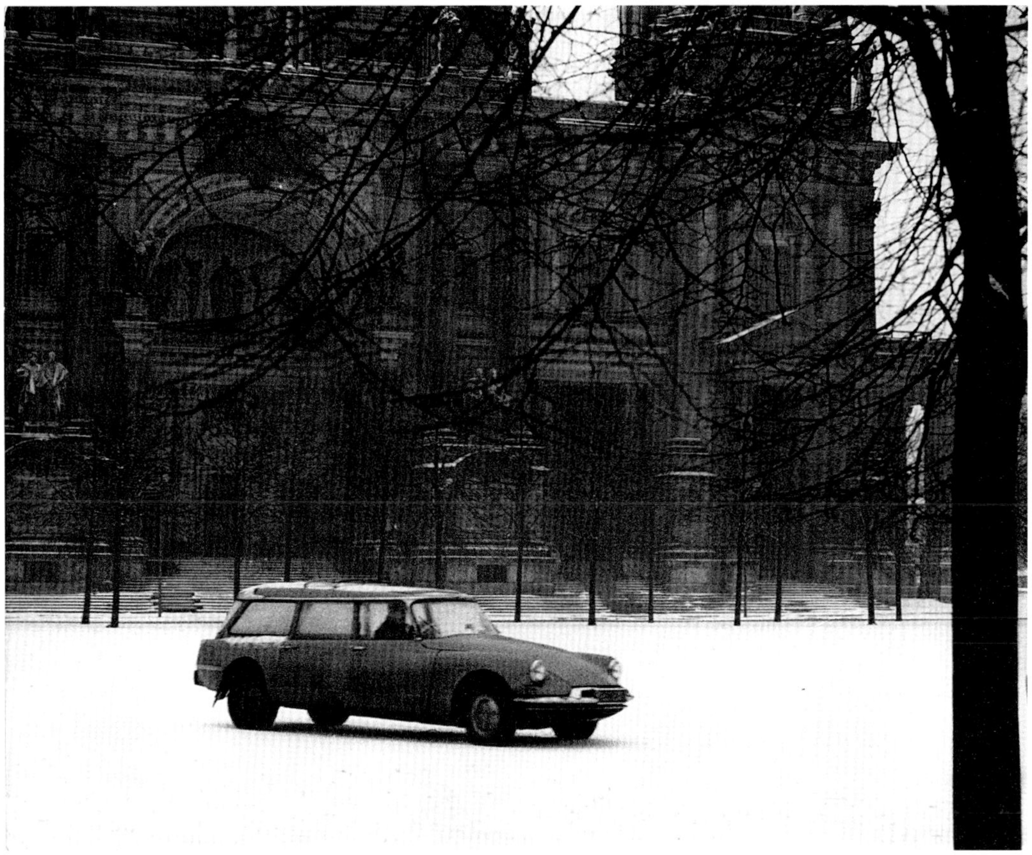

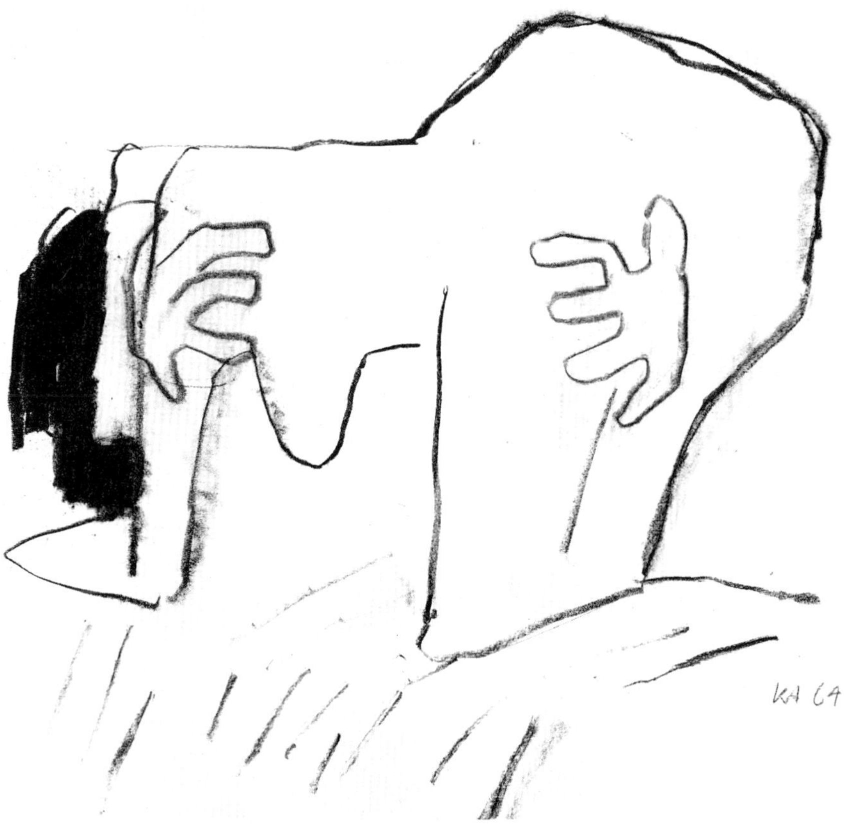

(*top*) KA in Berlin, 1968/9
In the background is the Reichstag building.

(*bottom*) Drawing (untitled) 1964
charcoal

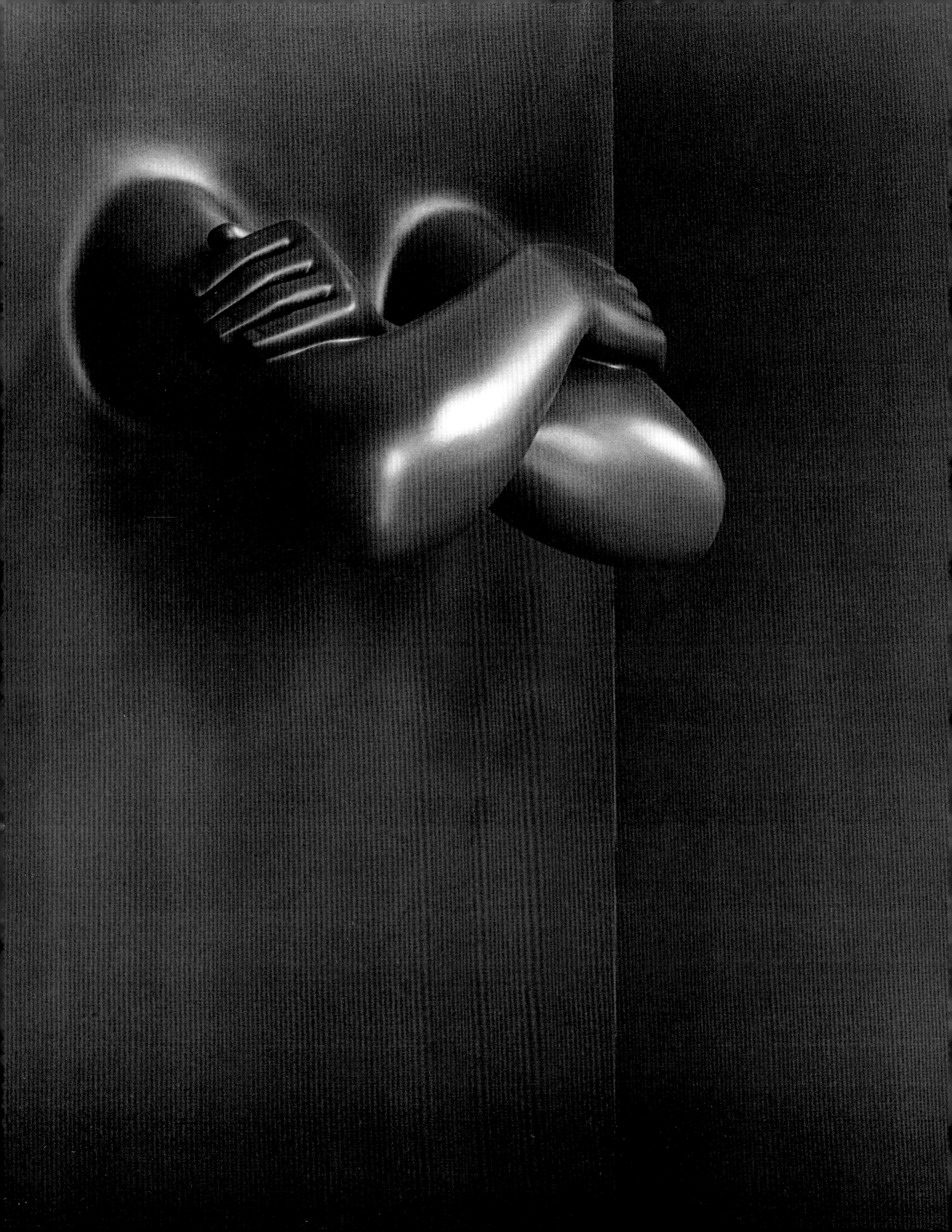

Lympstone, Devon, and it was to be a gift from the PSA to the Marines. I was a bit nervous about this. Although I had been six-and-a-half years in the Army in the Second World War, I didn't want to make a piece with buttons and boots and rifles and all the rest of it. There was a very good senior architect; I showed him photographs of *Both Arms* (1969), which had been first shown in Japan and purchased by the Hakone Open Air Sculpture Museum, and he said: 'You have done it! Here is a piece that's ideal. It is called *Both Arms*, which illustrates the dual role of the Marines, Army and Navy, embodying strength and power.' This proposal was accepted and a slightly modified second cast was made which went to Lympstone, to the Commandant's court, within the complex of barracks which was not open to the public. *Both Arms* remained there for several years, until it was decided that a more representational sculpture would be better understood by the rank and file. The piece was later moved to a better, open site at the Combined Operations Centre, Poole, Dorset, where students in the Army and Navy came from all over the world to study.

There was another work which I made in Berlin which I called *Big Doll* (1969); the table was made by a Berlin cabinet-maker and the figure cast in resin. This was one of the first times I used a graphic image on sculpture – the eyes.

My work was starting to change: together with using the plastic rounded shapes and geometry, I also started including drawing when I made sculpture, but I never really succeeded with this. Later on I used a silkscreen print on the back plate and hand-printed hair on the figure *Single Figure with Drawing* (1972). In *Return to Eden* (1988-9), a resin piece, the face of the end figure was screen-printed. That was my last resin piece.

It was very exciting being in Berlin in the late 1960s. The new National Gallery, designed by Mies van der Rohe, was finished just before I left. I was given German lessons by Renata Sami at the German Language Institute. 'Sami' was an excellent person, a tremendous radical enthusiast. She taught me all about politics and lent me books. This was the beginning of the enormous student unrest in Berlin and in Paris and later in the USA. It was very difficult to be in Berlin at that time without taking sides, and naturally I was on the side of the students because they were for reform. I met Rudi Dutschke briefly, and a few of the students who were the leaders at the time. Every Sunday there were great demonstrations, which I used to join, and sometimes police dispersed them with water cannon.

Through Rudolf Prinz zur Lippe I met a girl called Dorothea ('Dodo') Bantzer (whose maiden-name was von Haeften) and one day she asked me if I would like to go to Plötzensee. I had seen snowdrops in front of her father's photograph in her room, and had thought that very touching. We went to Plötzensee: a big lake, with a huge prison next to it. Outside the prison was a shrine; inside was a huge room where there was a cross-beam with hooks. The door was open, and she said, 'My father must have seen that tree', and then she told me all about it. She had kept it secret until then. Her father was a diplomat, and he was in the small group of people in the von Stauffenberg bomb plot to assassinate Hitler, which all the world knows was unsuccessful. Her father and his fellow collaborators were hanged by thin piano wire, and filmed for Hitler to see later on the same day. Dodo was later given a state pension and an honorary seat in the Reichstag.

In Berlin I came across a marvellous cross-section of German life, from the radical Sami to the von Trotts and other people involved in the von Stauffenberg bomb plot.

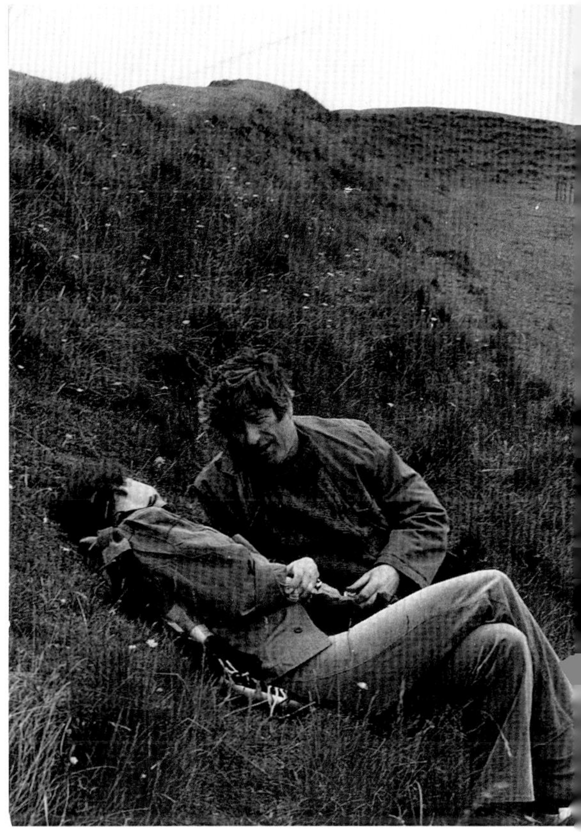

KA with Dorothea von Haeften on Maiden Castle, Dorset, in the mid-1970s. The photograph was taken by Dorothea's first husband, Christof Bantzer.

(*opposite*) Detail of *Screen with Folded Arms* 1967 (KA160)
H 195.5 cm (77 in), nickel bronze
Intended to form part of a continuous wall, but
in the meantime incorporated in a screen for display

(*opposite*) *Arm* 1967-8 (KA163)
L 386 cm (152 in)
resin and fibreglass (paint-sprayed)

Because of the student revolts I was asked to teach in the *Hochschule;* the students were out talking politics in the bars, and going on demonstrations. It was felt that if I, as a known name in the city, went into the school to do some teaching it might have the effect of encouraging the students to return to work. Although I did not particularly want to teach, I taught one day a week for one semester, which was really very interesting because I liked the students, and it did have an effect on them. Somehow I tried to make it clear to them that this was the one time in their lives when they could work unhindered, and that they should keep on working, whatever their politics were.

While I was there I met a woman called Wibke von Bonin, who was the Director of Films for Cologne television, and she asked if she could make a film on my work. I said: 'No, let's do it on my visit to Berlin'.[5] I took the film crew to see the students and to the Noack foundry, and to see the Wall and to the Wannsee – my favourite walk where the swans swam by one's side. I also took the team to East Berlin, where Sami had introduced me to Wolf Biermann, a famous singer, who even though a great Communist, attacked the East German government in a political-style cabaret they had in Berlin and in Paris. The government didn't like what he sang, and he was under house arrest. I was allowed to go and see him at his home, but I could not take the film crew. Dodo came with me and took photographs that could be used in the film as stills, and we wandered around the city. Returning from the East I had to go through Checkpoint Charlie. The German film crew went through their separate gate in the Wall, but when I got to mine I was stopped and taken to the back room where two officers went through my pockets, found my diary, and went through it page by page. One of them said: 'I see you have been several times to East Berlin. What are you doing?'. So I quickly thought and told him that I was a sculptor, visiting the sculptors of East Berlin, and I mentioned the name of a sculptor I had met who was a very devout Communist. I was held there for two hours. There was no diplomatic protection in East Berlin and I was lucky to be released; it was a warning and I never went back to the East.

I must say that Berlin was terrific, but I did get a mysterious malaise after about two or three months in the city. Then all I needed was to go by car to Hanover, for example, not far away in West Germany, and it would all fall off my shoulders. It was something to do with the claustrophobic nature of Berlin, and that is the only ill-effect that I found. But now the Wall has gone, and it is marvellous to feel that they are all now one people in a country called Germany, Deutschland, and not East and West Germany.

From Berlin I made journeys all over the place: I went to Moscow, and to Lübeck, where there is a marvellous brick Romanesque cathedral where Buxtehude, who taught Bach, had played the organ. And I went to a North Sea island called Sylt, which was beautiful with 'Daz'-white sand. I also went to Hamburg, where we sat at the Baroque organ where Bach had played, and to Heidelberg.

Suddenly I received a telegram and then a letter, asking if I would accept the CBE. And it was rather a shock because I was, as it were, in exile, and yet after all someone was thinking about me.

When I returned to England I had an invitation to teach at Boston University, Massachusetts and I went for one semester only in 1970.

5. 'Armitage in Berlin', Westdeutsche Rundfunk. First TV broadcast in late 1969, West Germany (30 minutes colour)

(*overleaf p.102*) left to right: *Big Doll* 1969 (KA175)
H 183 cm (72 in), resin and wood
Table G 1971 (KA184)
H 170 cm (67 in), wood
Table H (with round arms) 1971 (KA185)
H 152 cm (60 in), wood, plaster and bromide paper
A drawing from 'The Reves Tale' appears in the background.

(*overleaf p.103*) Another view of *Big Doll*

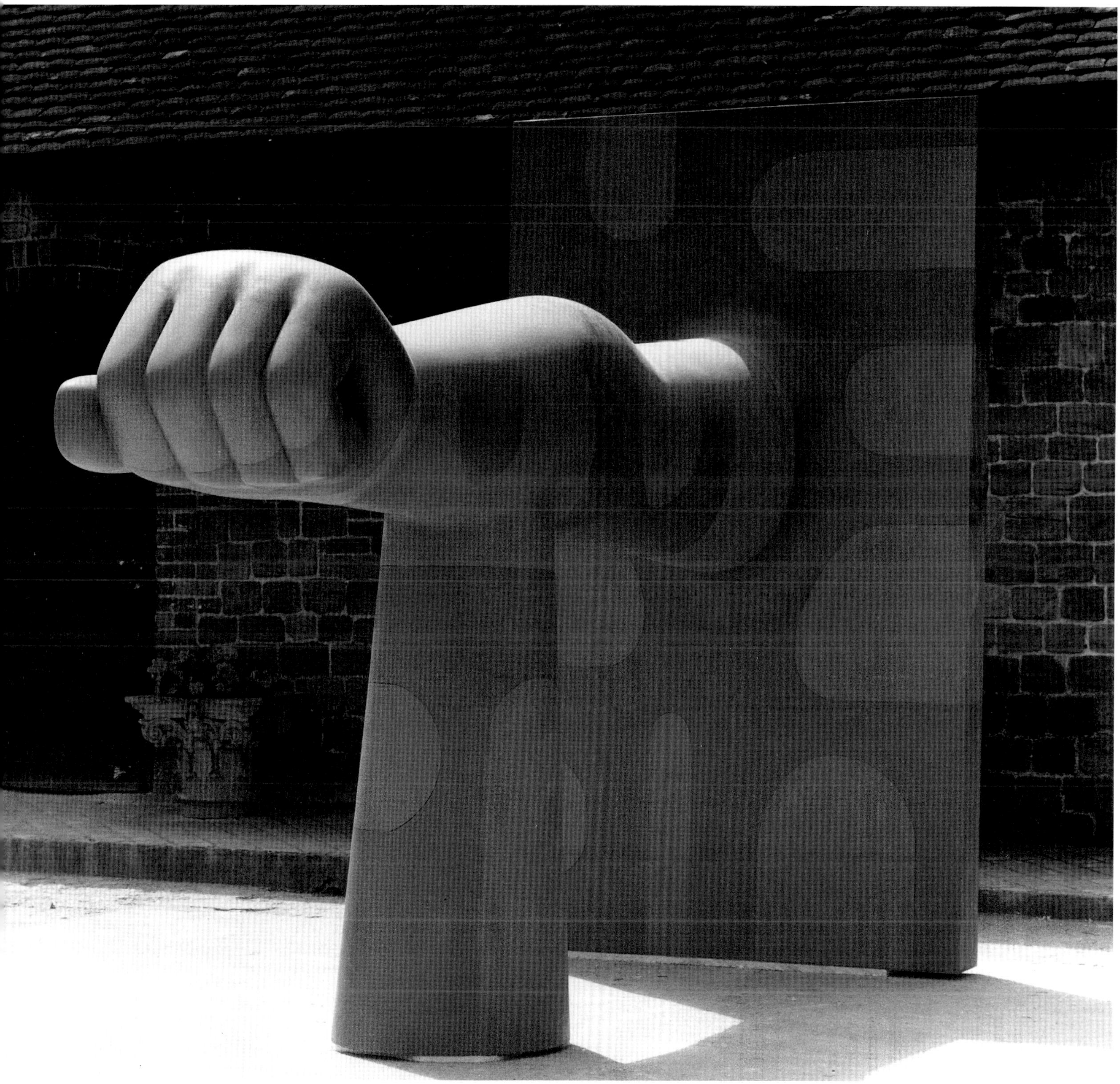

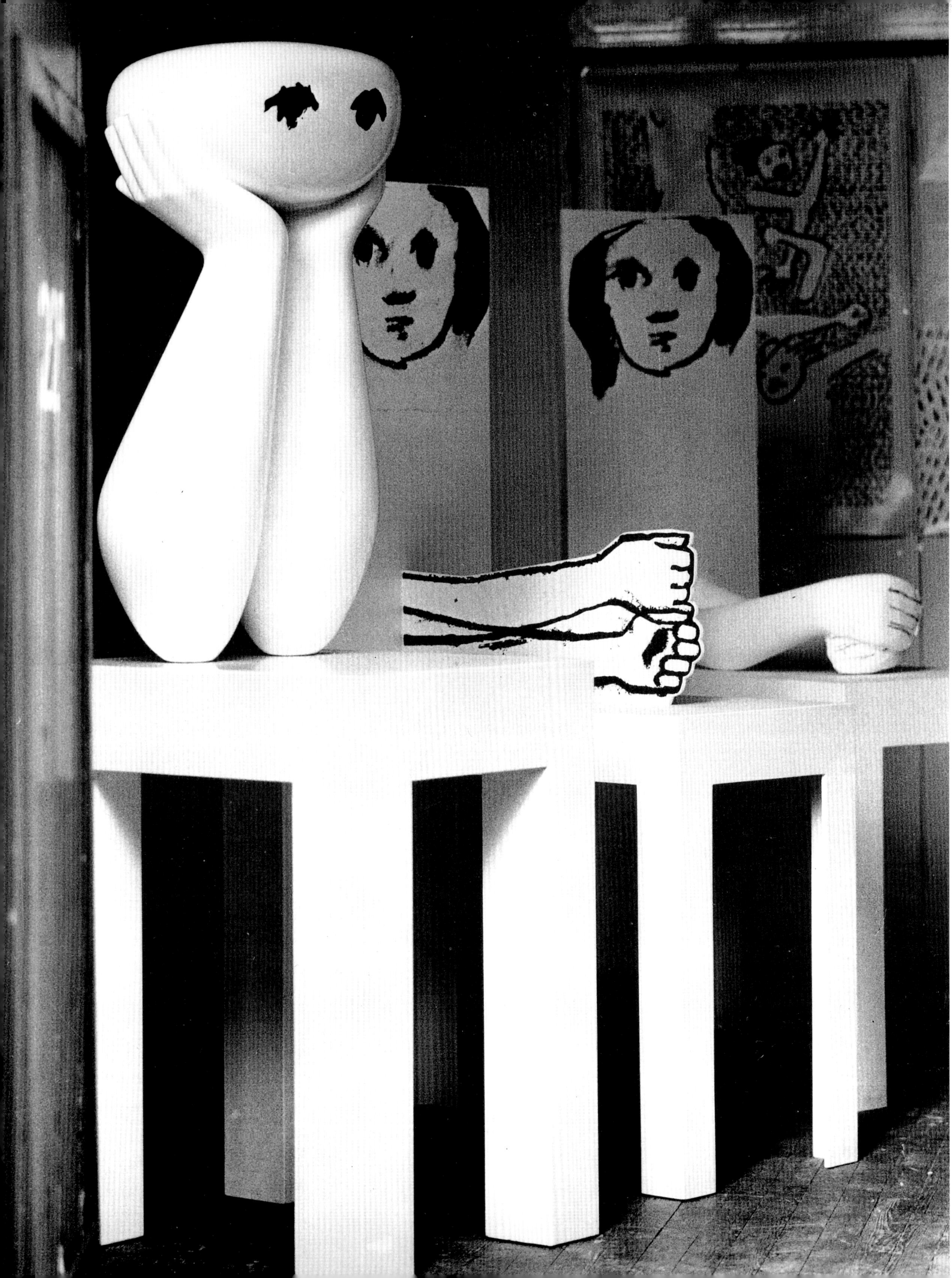

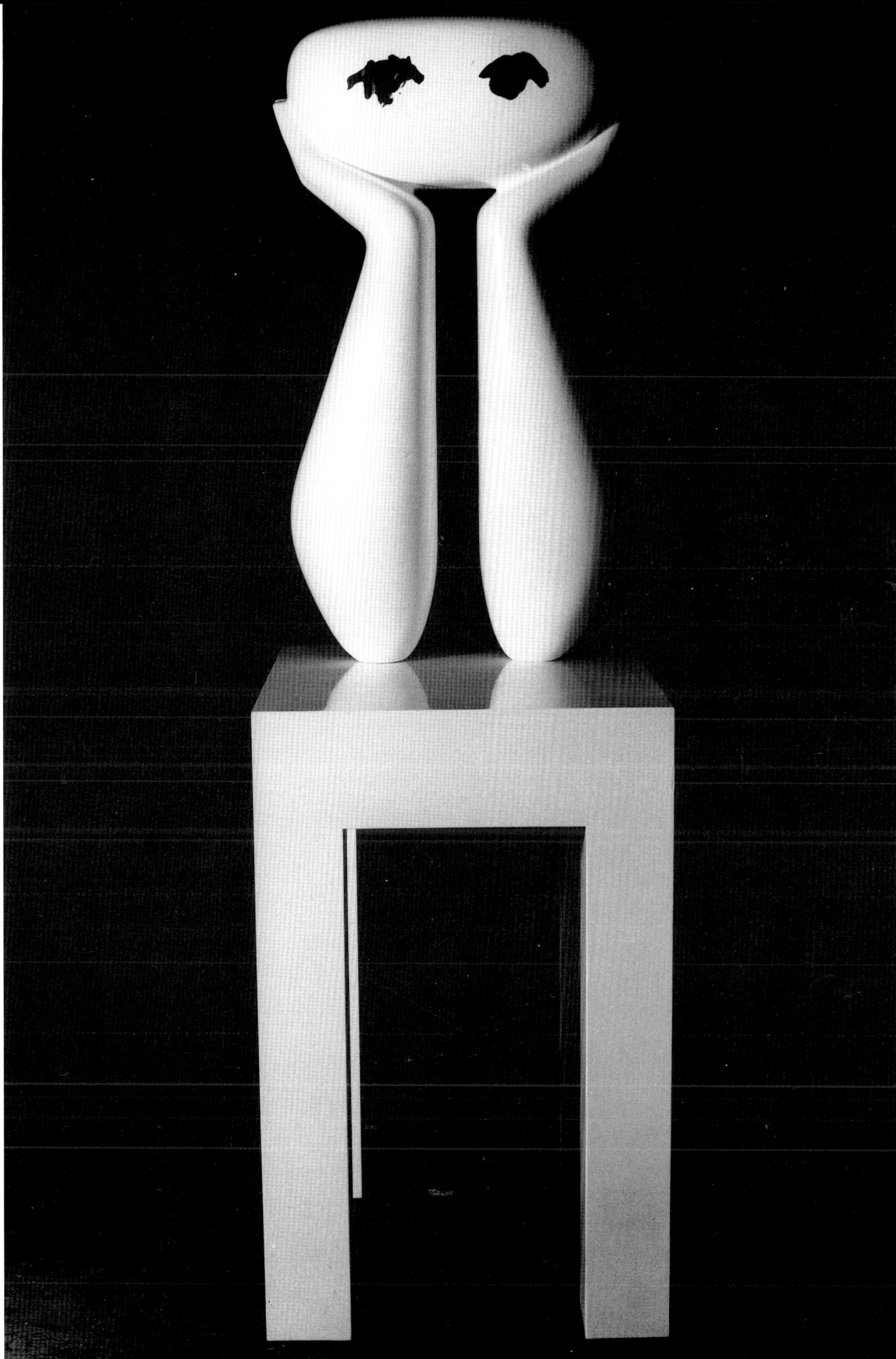

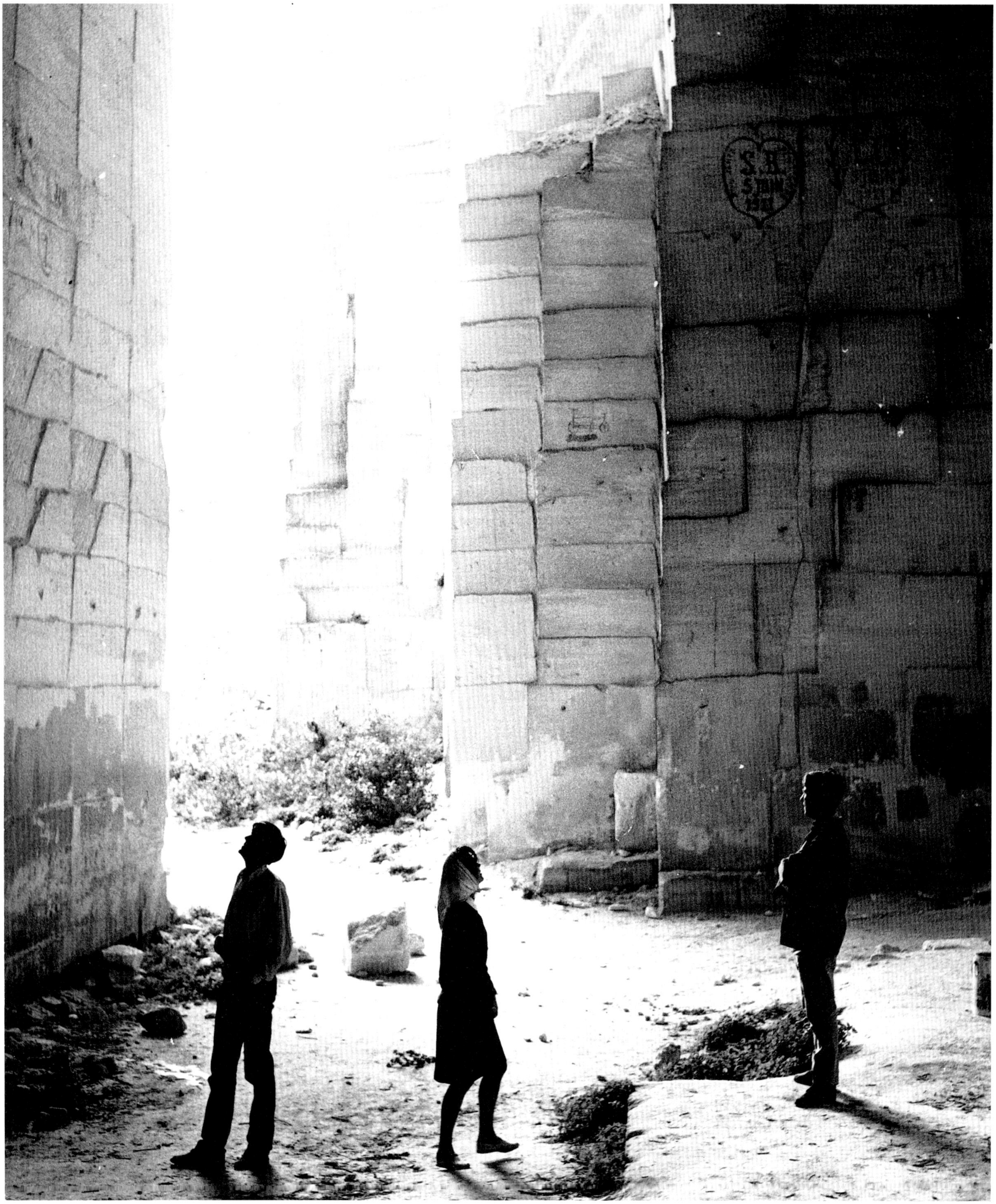

Quarries at Les Baux, Vaucluse, France, during a visit by Rory and Romana McEwen and KA (on the right) in the mid-1960s. KA believed that the rectangular shapes characteristic of the work of the artist Nicolas de Stael, who lived nearby, were influenced by the extraction squares in the quarries.

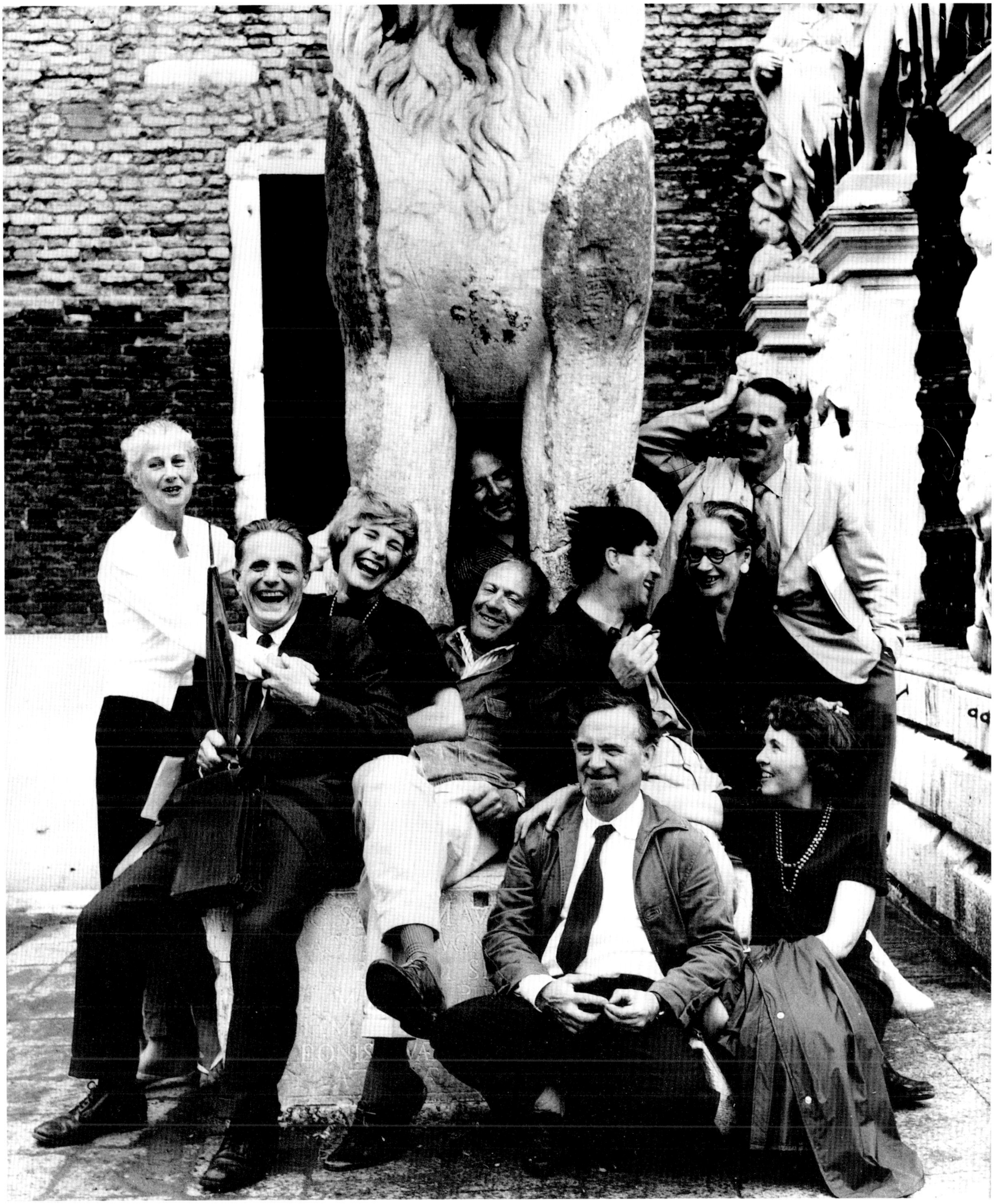

At the Venice Biennale, 1958:
back row: Beth and F. E. McWilliam, with Sir Philip Hendy between the sculpture's legs; centre row, left to right: S. W. Hayter, Frances and Lynn Chadwick, KA, Lilian Somerville; front row: William and Mary Scott

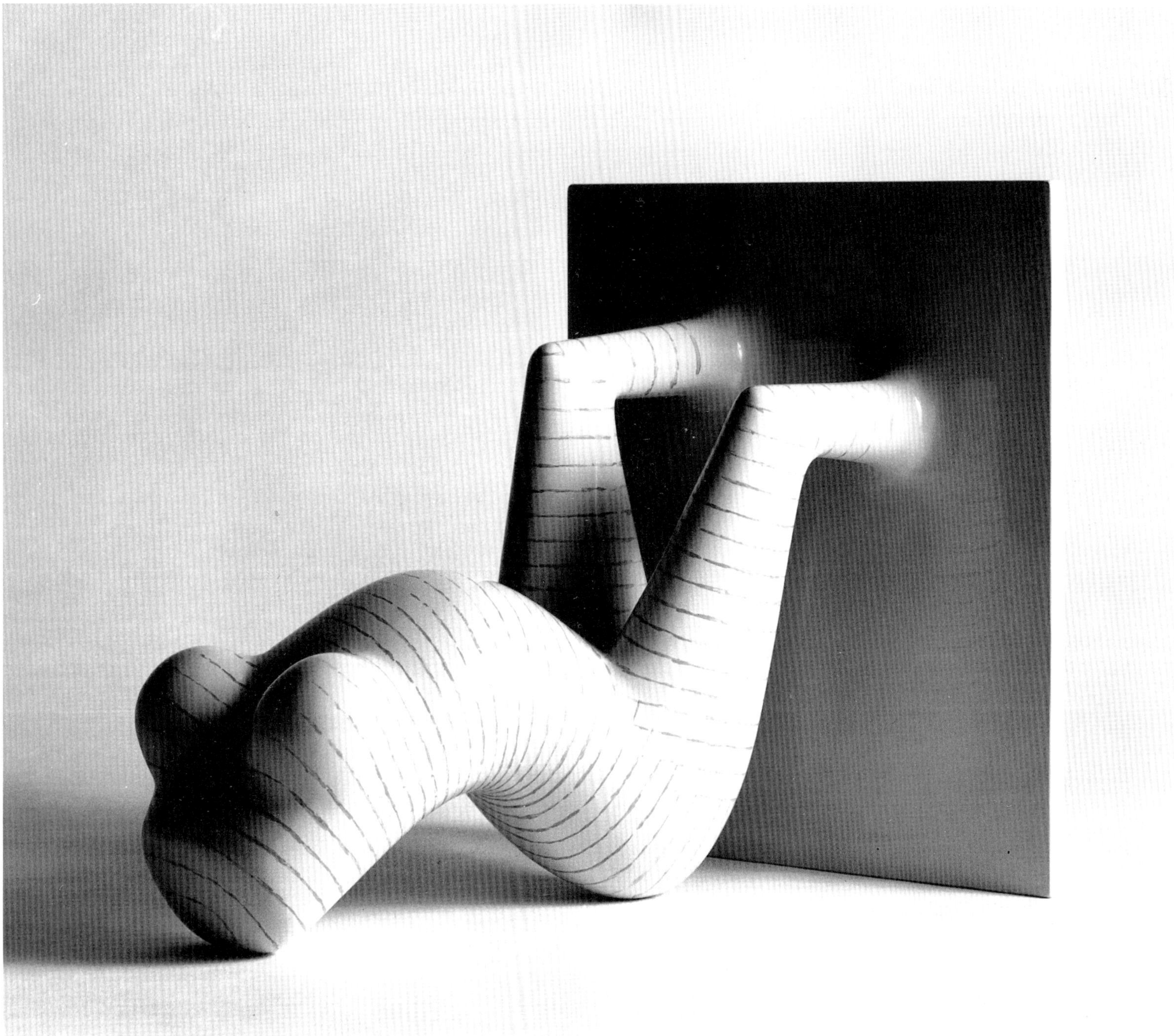

(*above*) *Figure on its Back* 1965-77 (KA155)
L 24 cm (9½ in), painted aluminium

(*opposite top*) Drawing (untitled) 1962
charcoal

(*opposite bottom*) Drawing (untitled) 1960
charcoal and wash

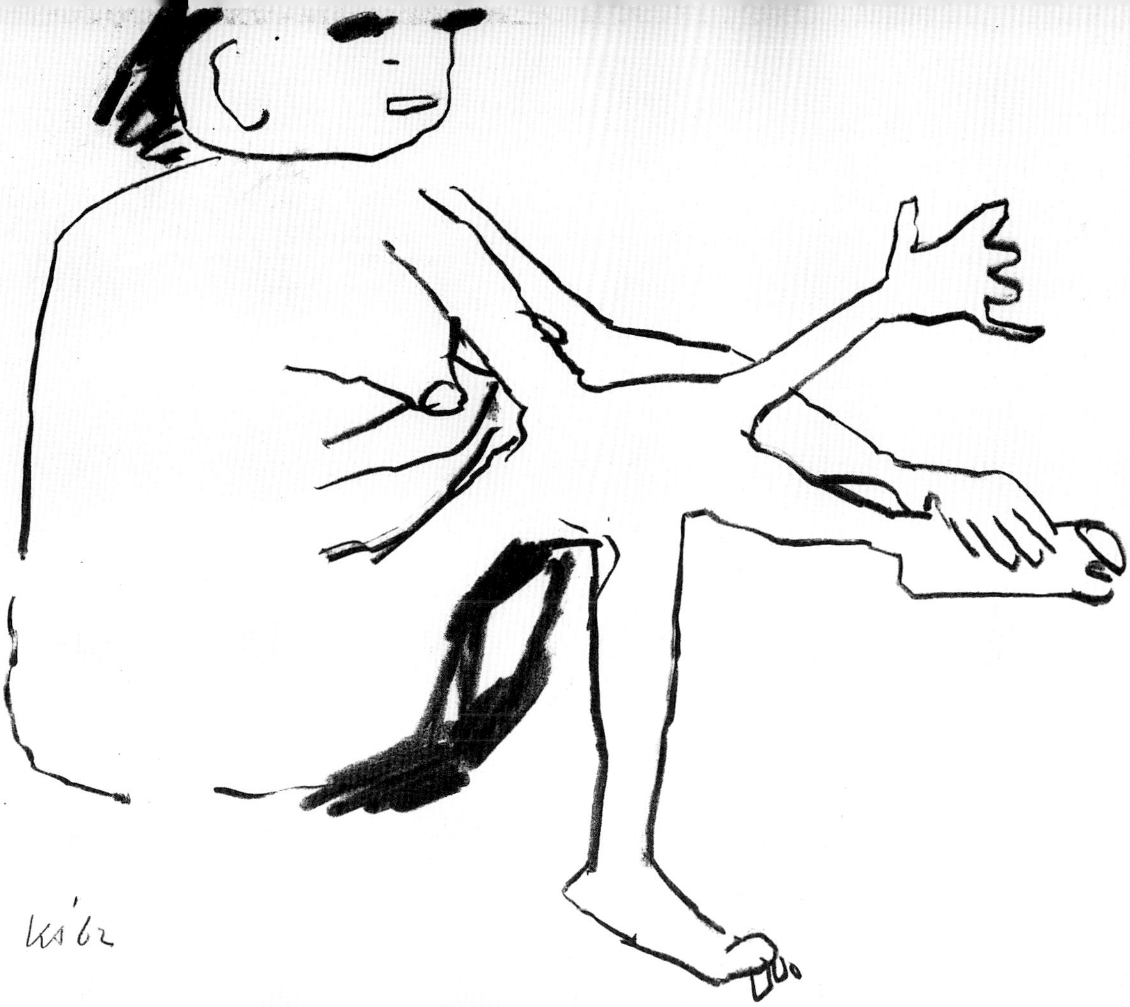
KA'62

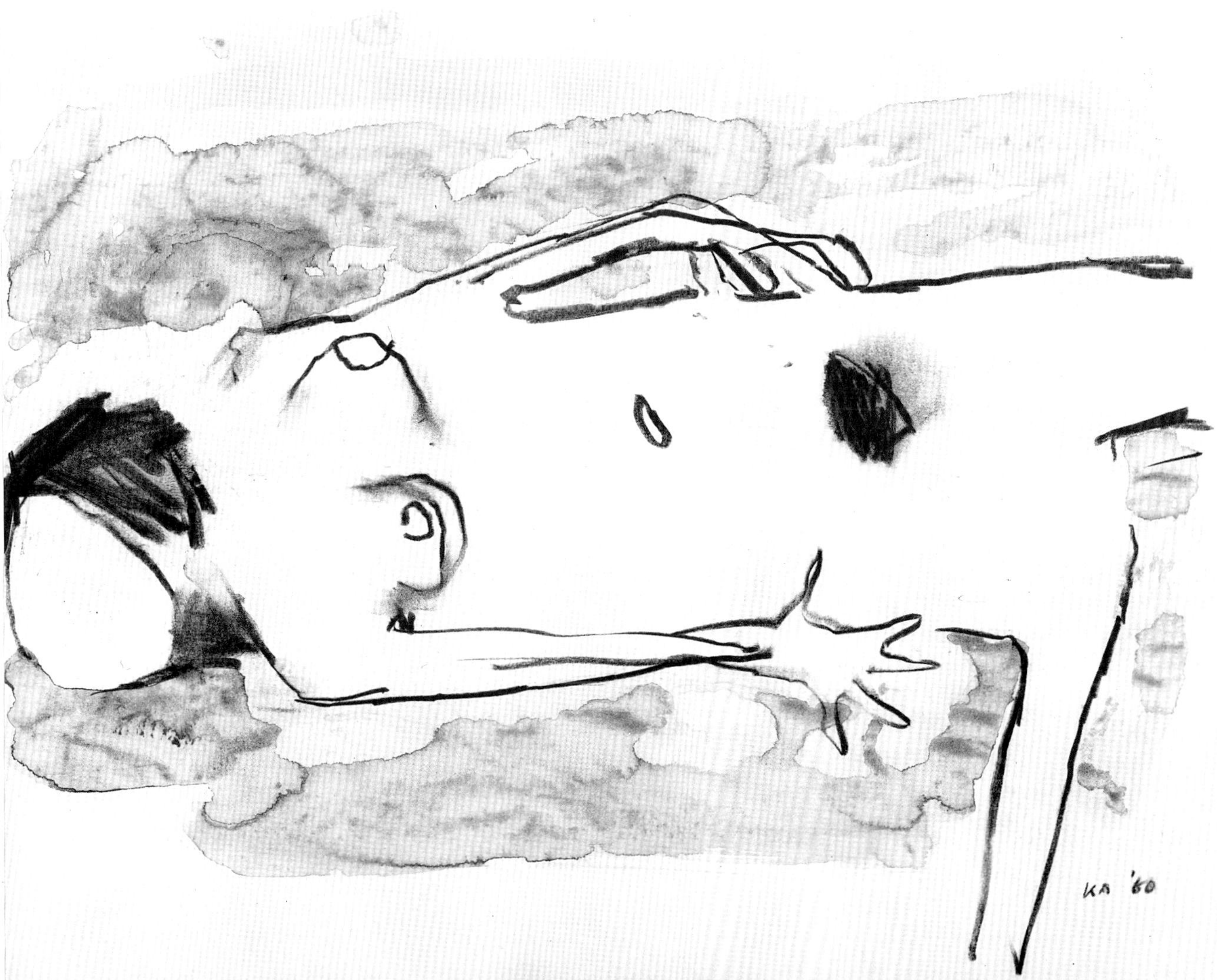
KA '60

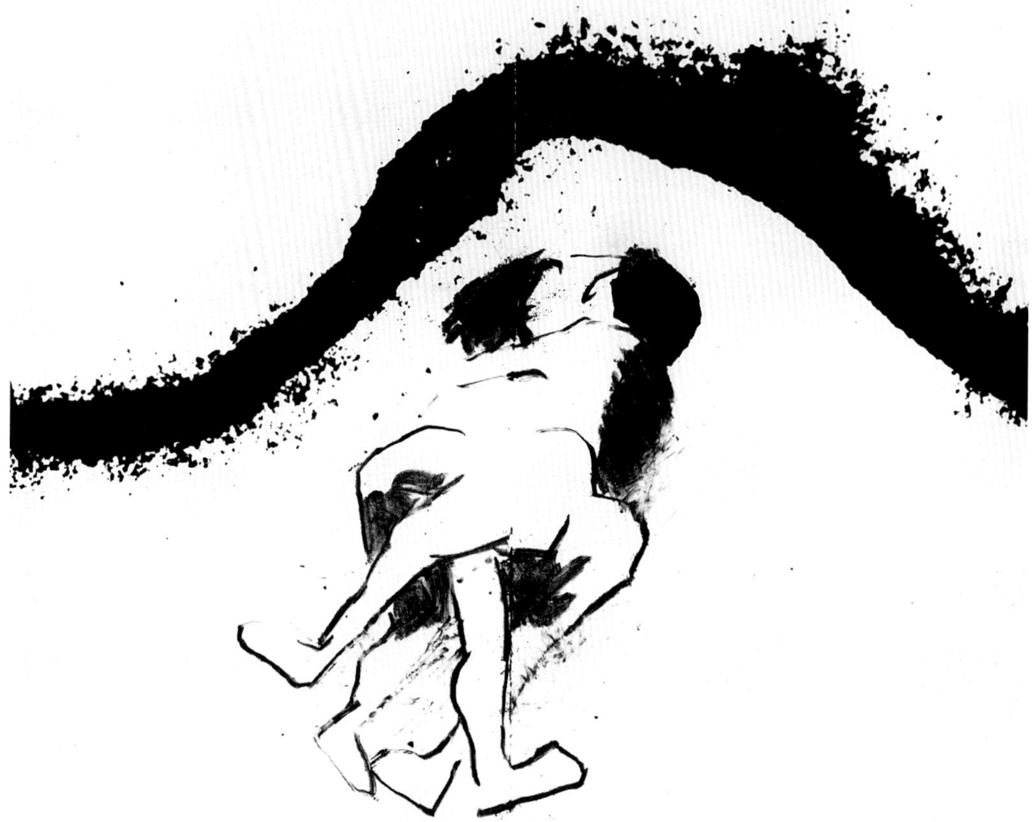

Sand Dune 1972
drawing and collage

In 1972 I resigned from the Marlborough Gallery. I had been with them for twelve years and I found that to have a major sculpture show every three or four years was a bit much really. It was a treadmill, leaving one little time to feel one's way. At that time I was experimenting with bits of bent cardboard, as Picasso had done with drawing, and I made screens with printed images. I felt they would be unacceptable to Marlborough, so when eventually I resigned, I knew they would not say no. So I left, and was happy, although I didn't know where the next penny would come from. I was absolutely penniless, having depended on them for twelve years, but in my heart relieved. And then slowly, bit by bit, things picked up. There was an exodus from the Marlborough. Henry Moore left, Lucian Freud also left and James Kirkman became Freud's dealer, remaining so until recent years. Lynn Chadwick remained. It was the end of my longest association with a gallery and I have not had a full-time exclusive gallery in London since then.

Bernard Meadows gave me a day a week teaching at the Royal College for about five years, which helped financially. I took a lodger and sold my car. Then things improved.

This was a time when, as a result of my experiments with bits of paper, I became obsessed with folding screens. These were *real* folding screens, to be used as such. I made two mock-ups out of a timber frame, faced with plywood with photographic images printed on them, but nothing came of these.

Shortly afterwards, the Arts Council commissioned me to make a piece for the new library at Nottingham University. Instead of making a conventional three-dimensional piece I decided that I would make a big screen, and they were surprised. I spent every penny of the £2000 commission on the cost of the production of a five-panel, seven-feet-high and nine-feet-long folding screen. The screen had continuous nickel-plated hinges, and an enlarged drawing of striding figures was printed by silk-screen onto the surface, the same image repeated in reverse on both sides. In the architectural design of the library, the windows appeared as long, vertical dark stripes on the façade, and I introduced this motif into the design.

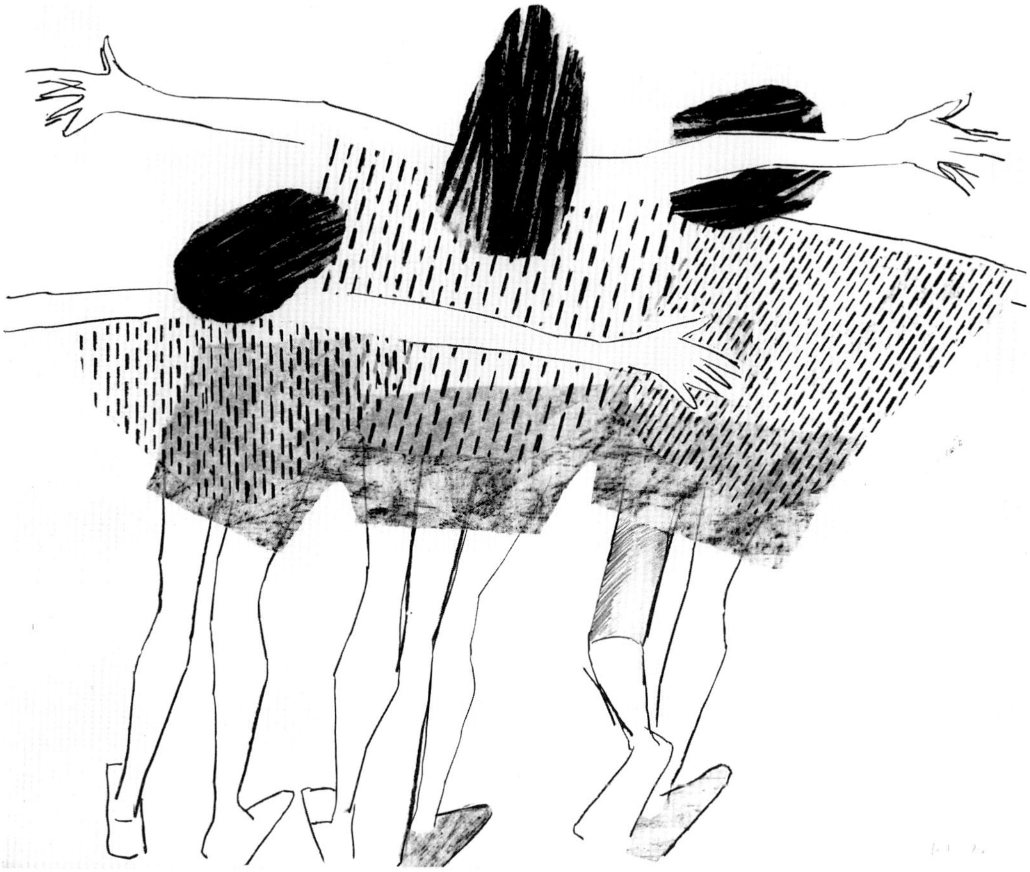

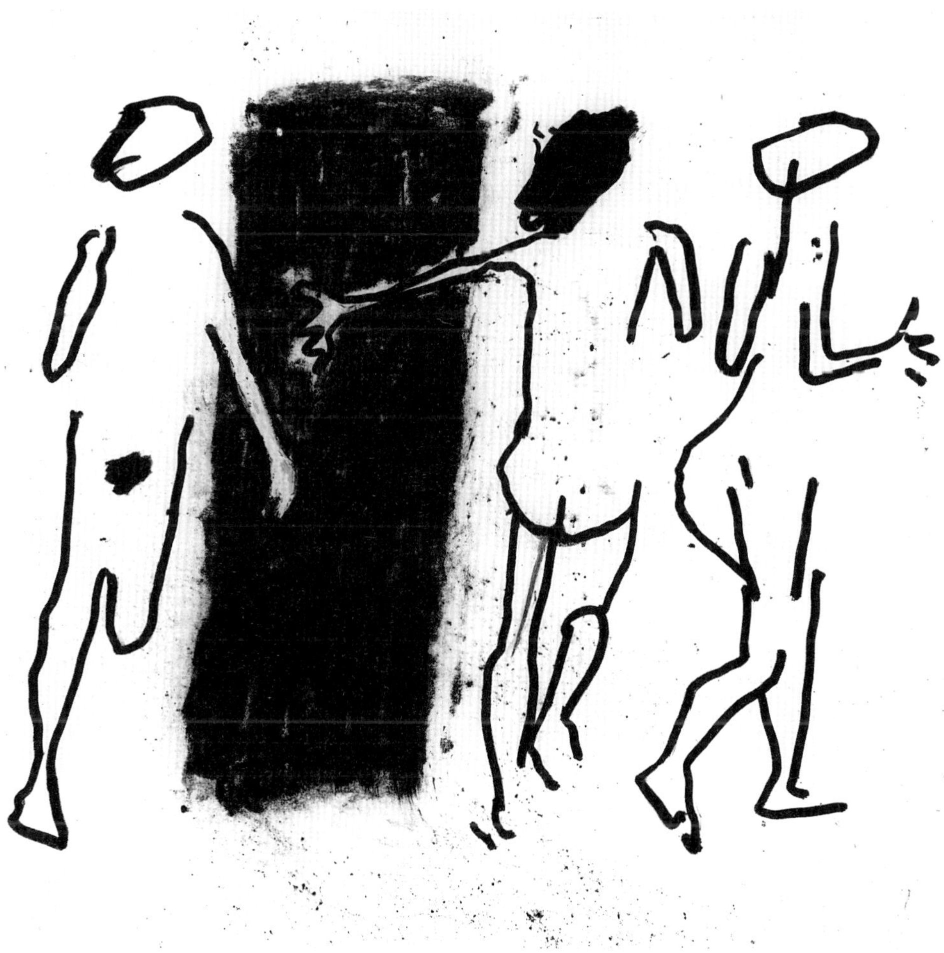

(*top*) *Children playing c.*1972
charcoal and collage

(*bottom*) *People running* 1970s
ink and wash

(*overleaf p.110*) *Table H* (with round arms) 1971 (KA185)
H 152 cm (60 in), wood, plaster and bromide paper

(*overleaf p.111*) *Folding Screen* 1971 (KA183)
H 182.9 cm (72 in), plywood, foam core and bromide paper

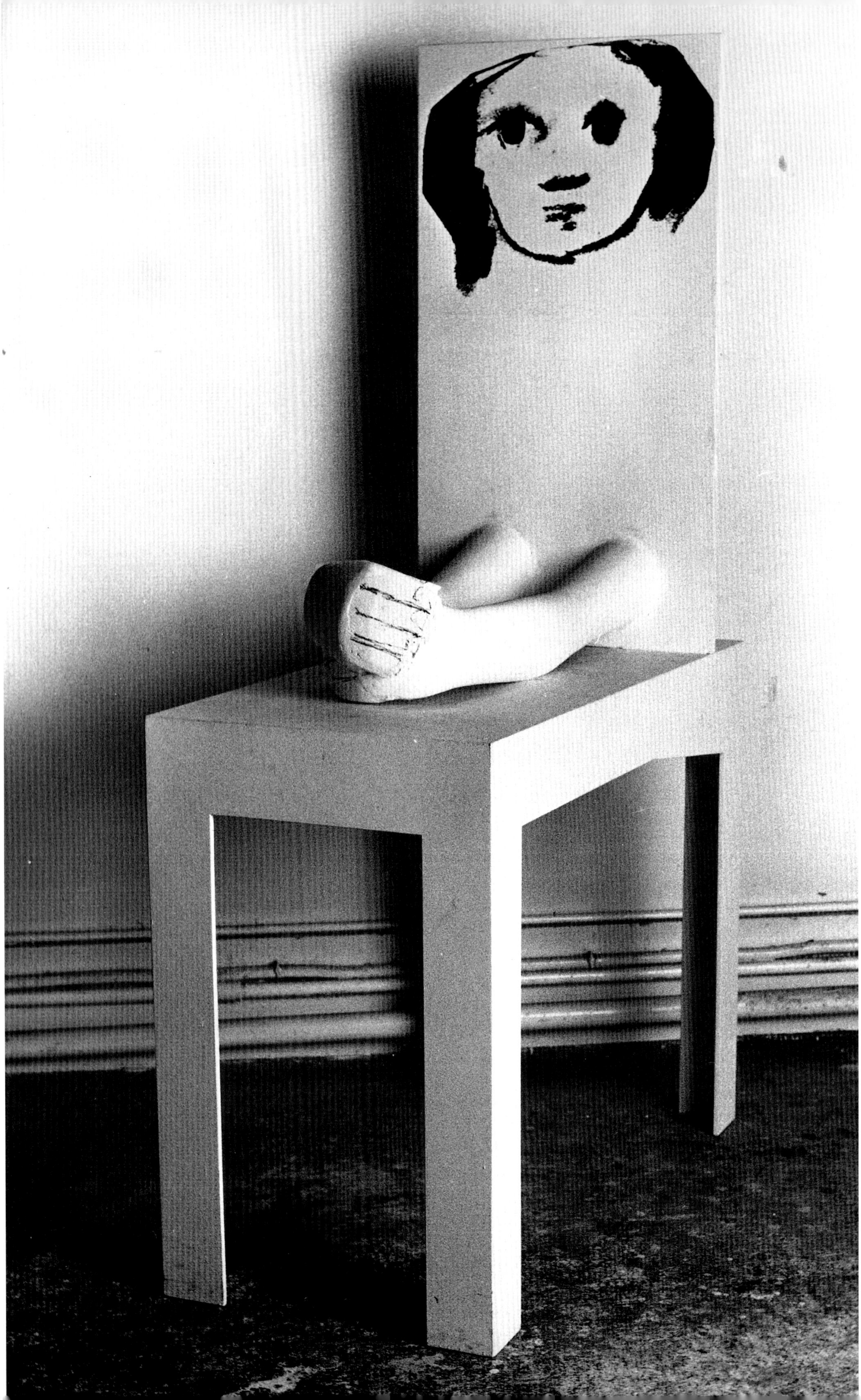

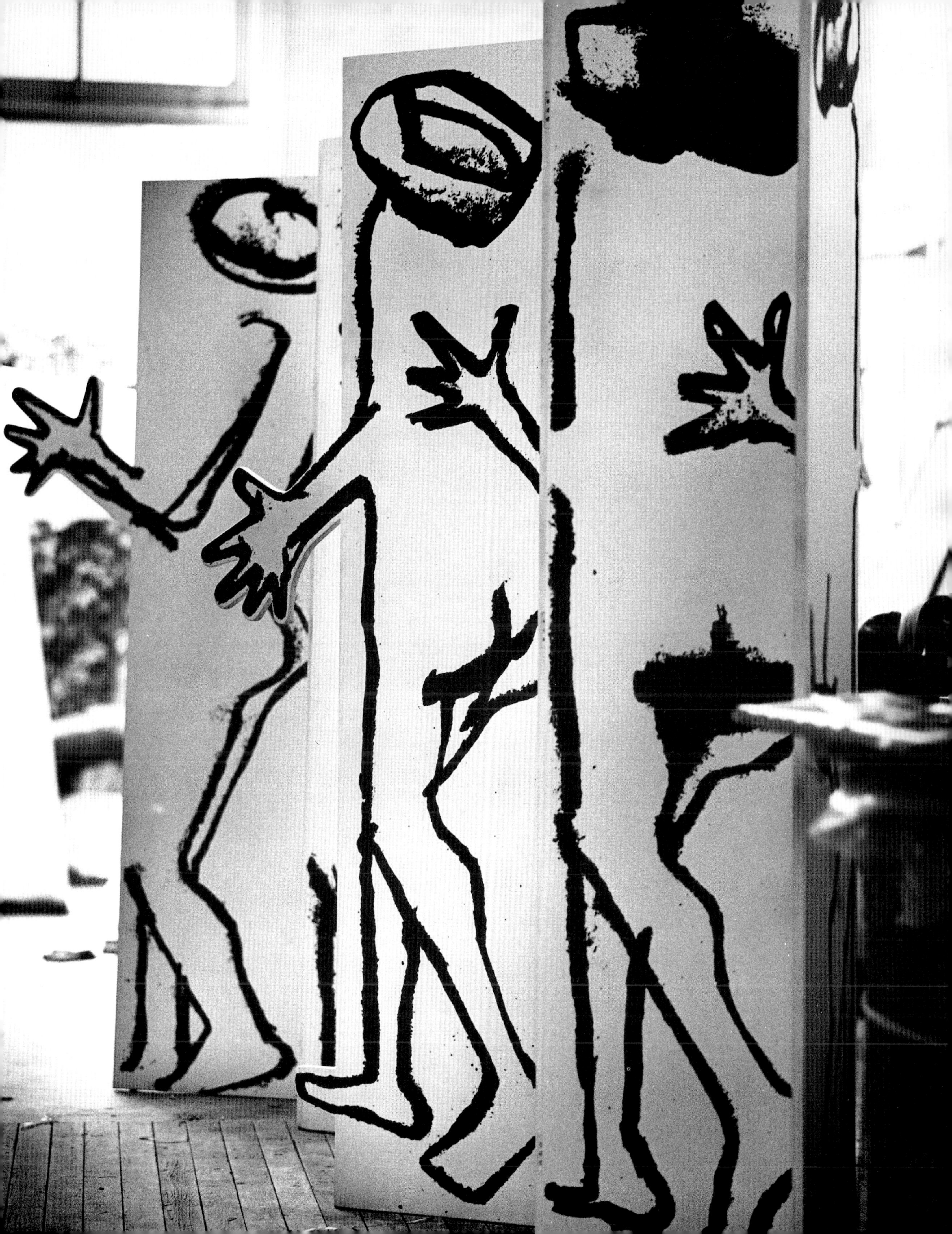

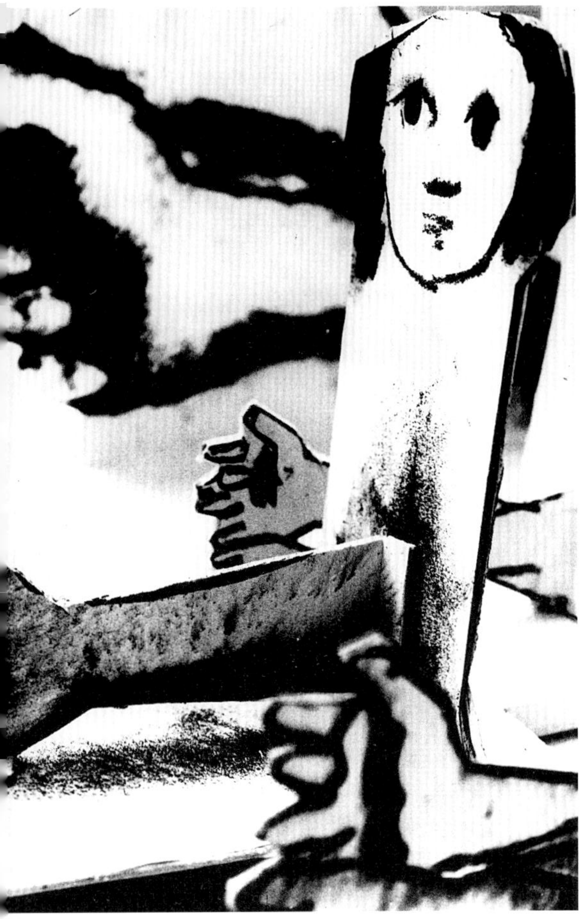

(*above*) *Face* (with screenprint) 1971 (KA187)
H 70 cm ($27\frac{1}{2}$ in), wood and bromide paper

(*opposite*) *Nottingham Screen* 1973 (KA203a)
L 275 cm ($108\frac{1}{4}$ in), plywood, foam core and bromide paper

The *Nottingham Screen* (1973) was a one-off piece, and I enjoyed the fact that I had realised something with the drawings I had previously drawn on bits of paper. The screen shape is an extraordinary form: very economical, and self-supporting because of its zig-zag plan, and yet there is no body or bulk.

This work was not recognised at the time. Now it's different. I had a letter about two years ago from the Director of the Musée des Arts Décoratifs, Paris, asking if I had modern sculpture based on, or related to, domestic objects such as tables, chairs, and screens, which I had. I sent him a whole lot of photographs, and he said 'Marvellous!'. But he died or left and nothing came of it.

In 1972, just before I made the screen for Nottingham, I had made a small piece of sculpture called *Bernadette going to Wales*. The idea came about because a friend left London to go and live in a tiny cottage under Snowdon. The work consists of a hooded, striding woman, cast in aluminium, welded to and leading a square of plate aluminium, onto which I stencilled male figures running in the opposite direction. It was only $14\frac{1}{2}$ inches in length. It combined, once again, a figure with a geometric shape, as well as drawing. In 1974 I made *How many Miles to Babylon?*. The title was taken from Walter de la Mare's poem. It was cast in bronze, patinated black, again with sturdy 'table' legs, and is yet another work with plastic rounded figures and geometric shapes.

There then followed a series of figures which are different from the others: they don't combine geometry, and I call them *July Figures*. They were made from 1975 to 1982 and were all standing figures with one feature in common: the forearms were sticking out in front. The reason for this was that we had heatwaves for several summers; it was so hot that I noticed I was walking round in the studio sticking out my arms rather than folding them. My sculptures followed that. They were bronze figures with black hair.

There had been another series (1971-2) which I had called *Design for a Wilderness*. The origin of this came from visiting John McEwen's sister, Lady Hesketh, who lived at Easton Neston in Northamptonshire. In the grounds was a wonderful, high, almost black yew hedge, and behind that a place called 'The Wilderness'. I visualised a large slab-like bronze with a gesticulating figure, not unlike the Bernadette piece, but more dramatic, behind which was a rectangular buttress which would jut out from the yew hedge. Only the maquette was made. It is my kind of bestiary.

I had a long association with the McEwen family. I first met Rory McEwen and his wife Romana at Bronwen Pugh's marriage to Bill Astor at Cliveden and they became lifelong friends. It was through them that I met my close friend Josceline Dimbleby (née Gaskell). Rory's younger brother John occupied my house from 1968 to 1969 while I was living in Berlin.

In 1982, I made a visit to Ireland, where I had not been since my student days. I was nervous and thought I would not like to go back because surely it would all be changed, but I found it was much the same. My main purpose was to visit the Burren, an area of limestone exposed by the Ice Age, which is unlike anything one has ever seen. I had read about it in the book by Praeger I came across before the war (see p.16).

I stayed first at a place called Lisdoonvarna, which was almost in the Burren, and then at a hotel called The Falls Hotel at Ennistimon, which was owned by the MacNamara family

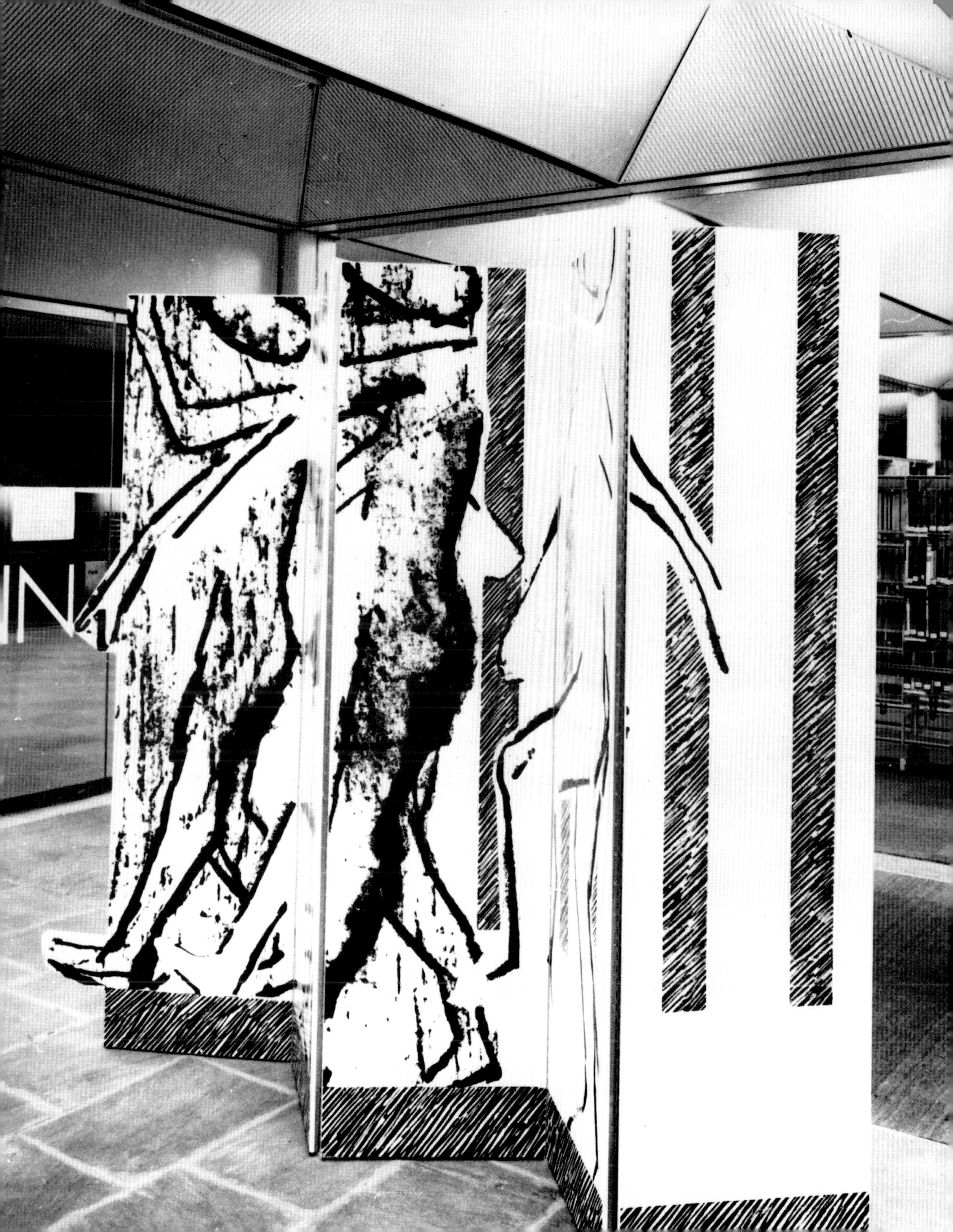

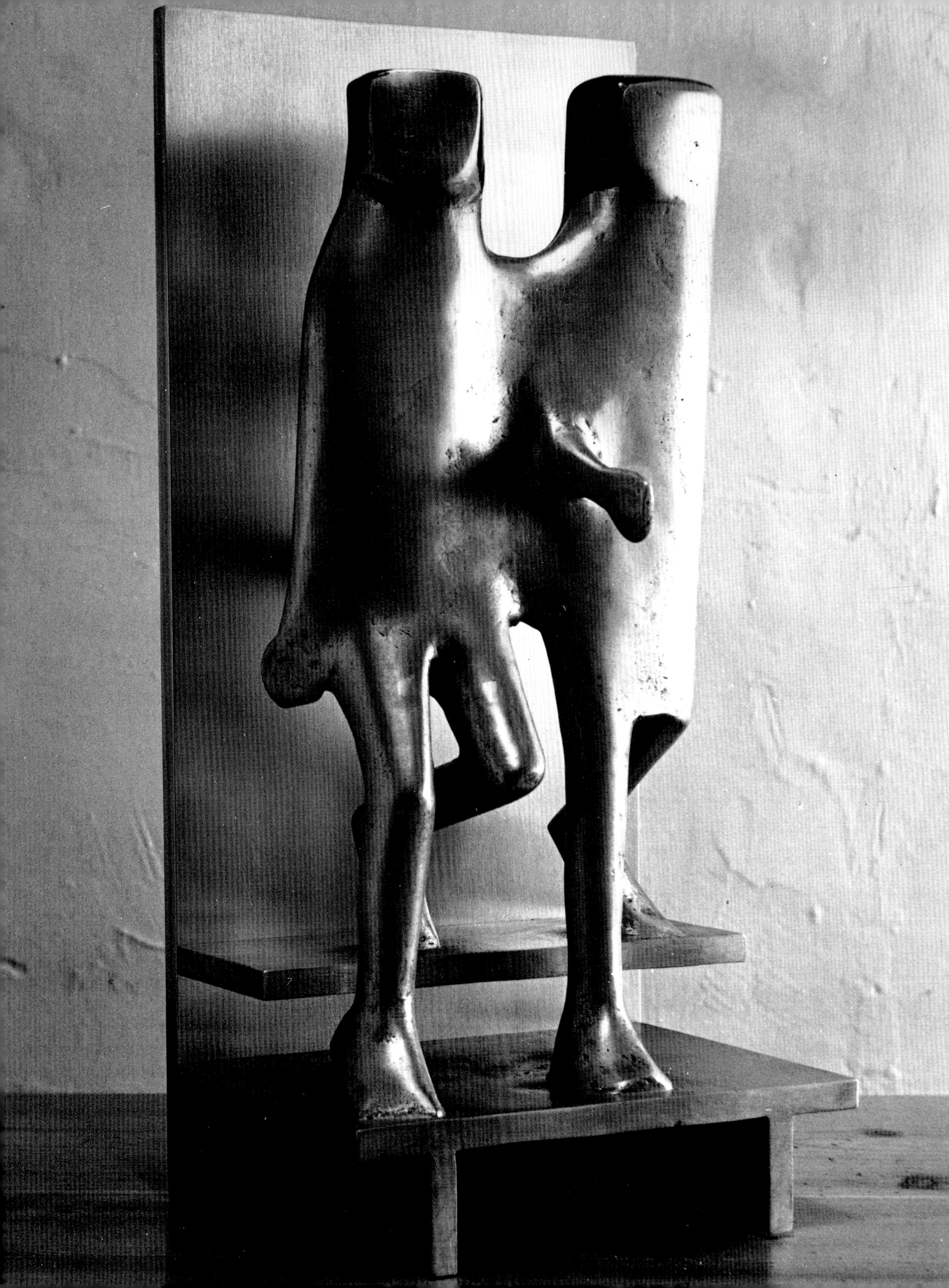

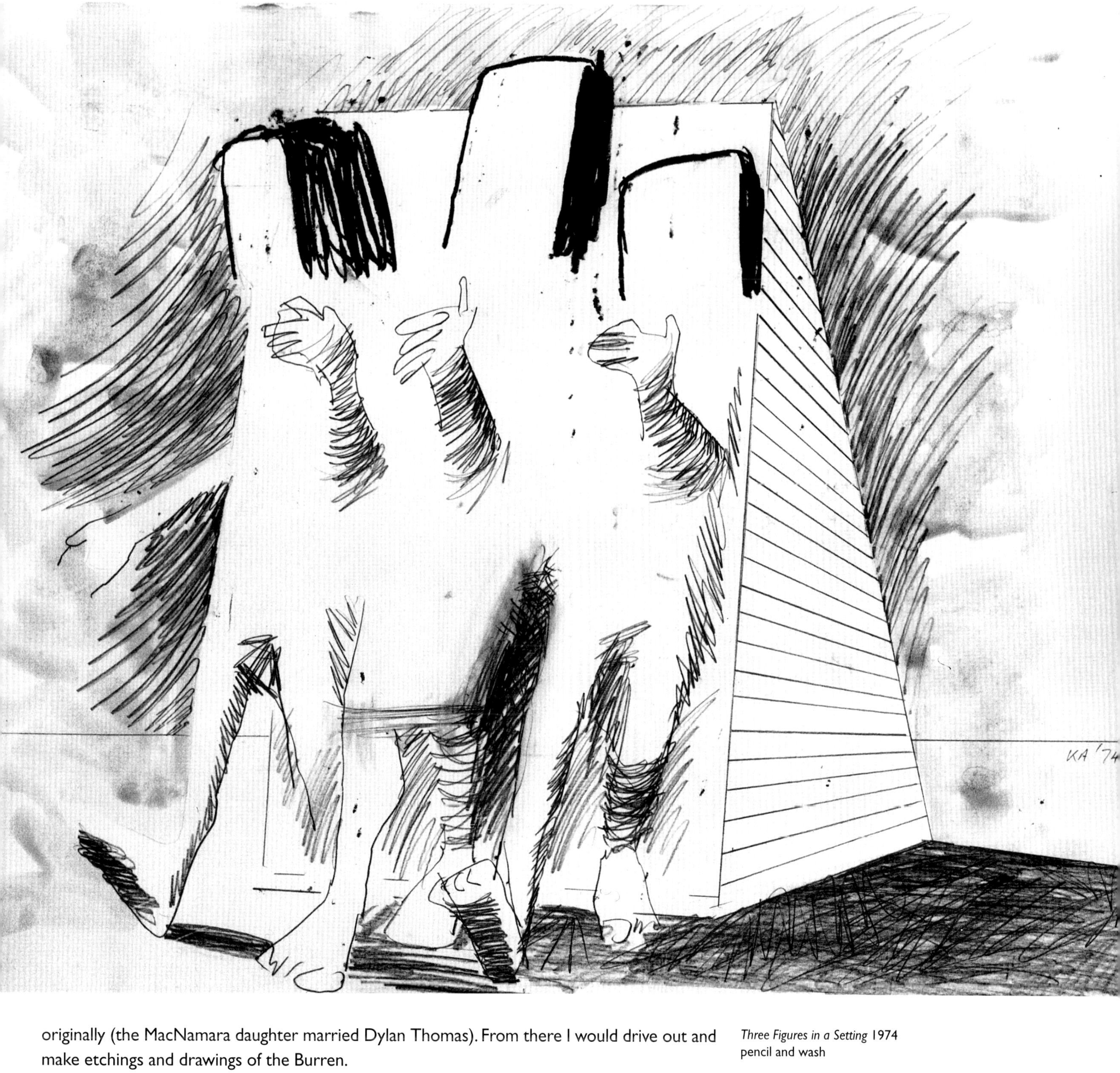

originally (the MacNamara daughter married Dylan Thomas). From there I would drive out and make etchings and drawings of the Burren.

On my most recent visit to Ireland, with Alastair and Zandria Service, Alastair, being very occupied with archaeology, wanted to go to New Grange, the amazing walk-in barrow tomb north of Dublin. Driving west I was very sad to find that Lackan had been razed to the ground. This was the end of the very successful farming period when some of the farmers had become very rich.

Three Figures in a Setting 1974
pencil and wash

(*opposite*) *Nottingham Group* 1973 (KA203)
H 34 cm ($13\frac{1}{2}$ in), painted aluminium

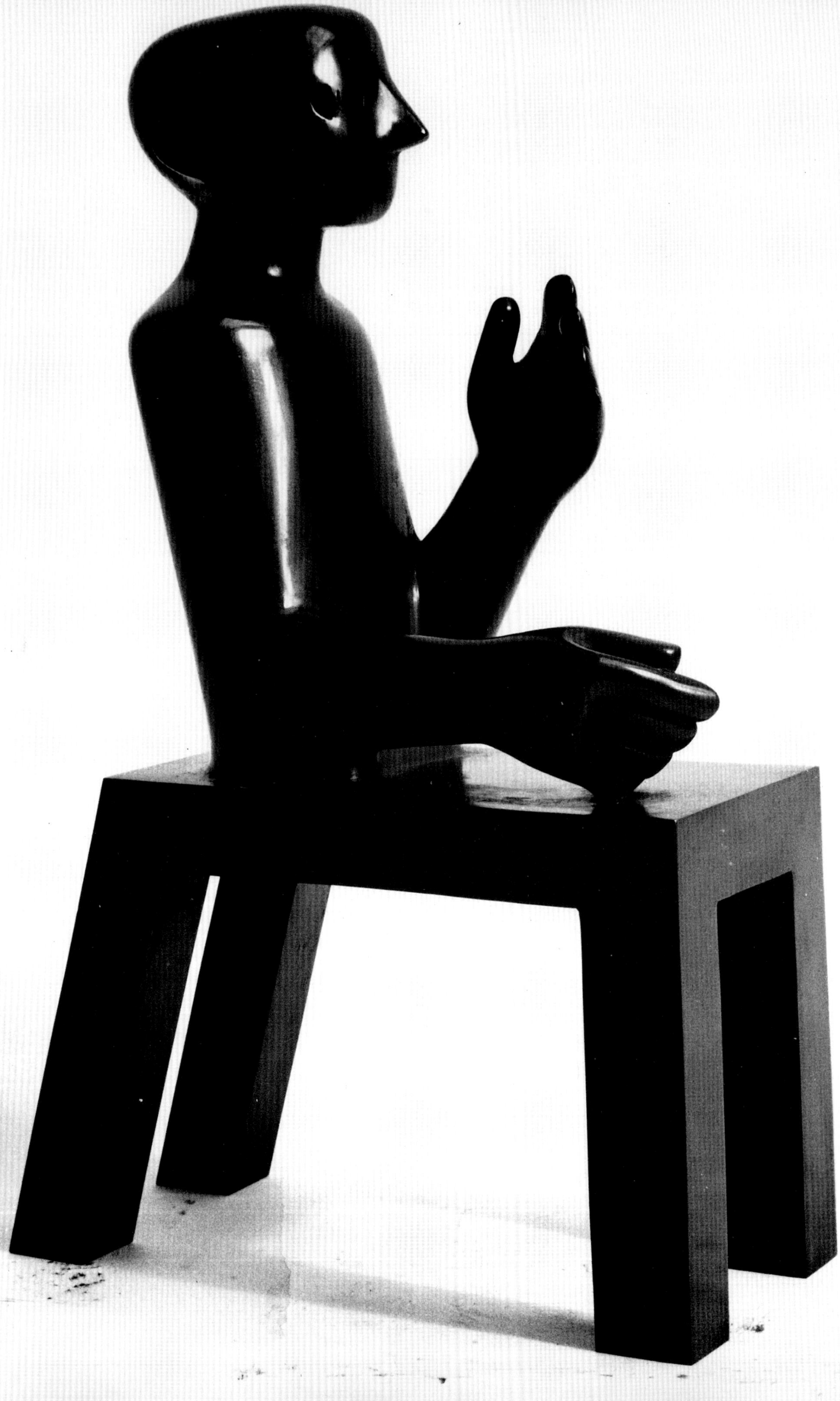

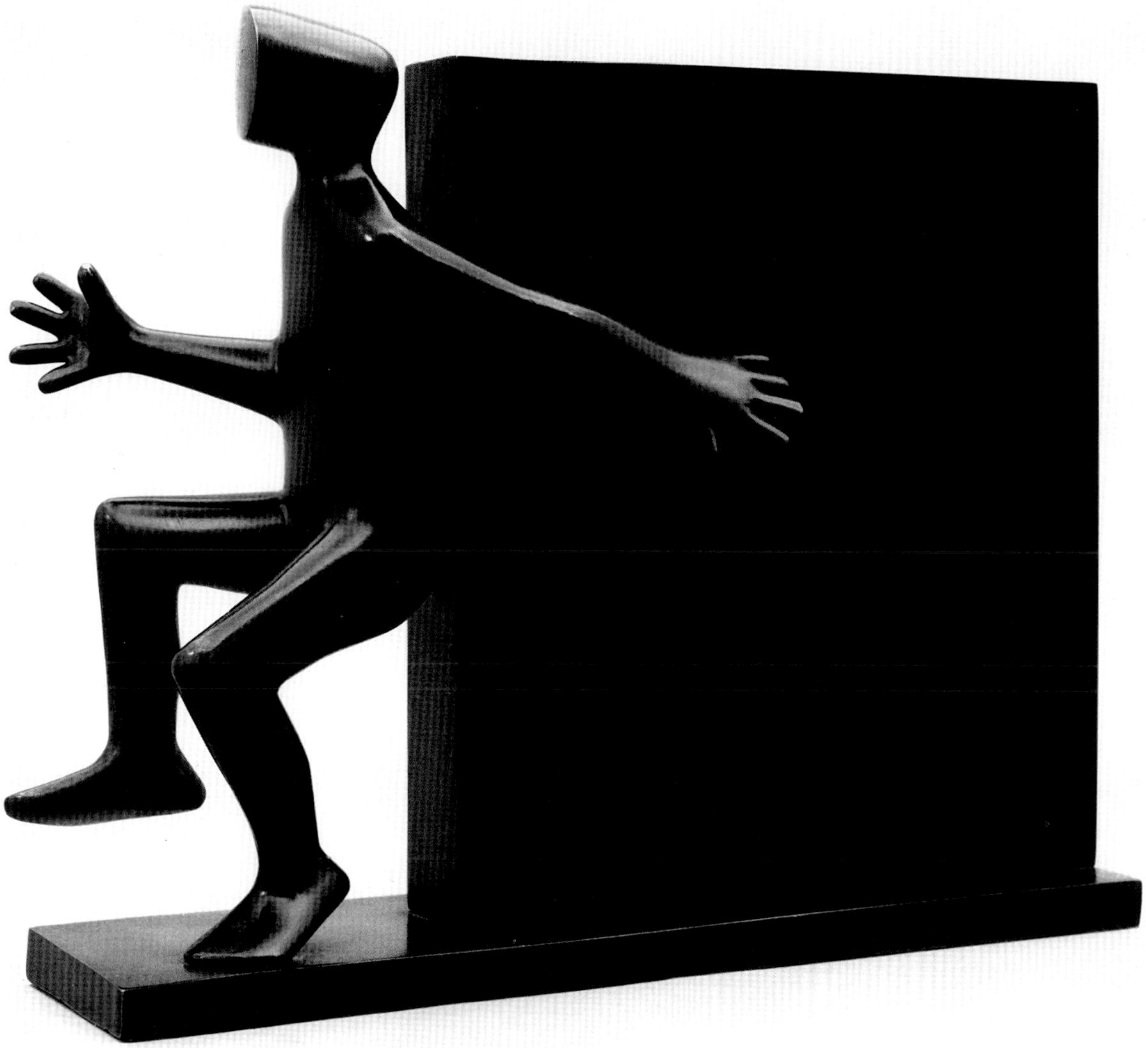

(opposite) *How many Miles to Babylon?* 1974 (KA208)
H 57 cm (22½ in), bronze

(top) *Design for a Wilderness No. 1* 1971 (KA190)
L 44 cm (17½ in), bronze

(bottom) *Bernadette going to Wales* 1972 (KA194)
L 36 cm (14¼ in), aluminium with painted image both sides

(overleaf p. 118) *July Figure* 1975 (KA209)
H 77 cm (30½ in), bronze

(overleaf p. 119) *July Figure 2* 1979 (KA224)
H 86 cm (34 in), bronze

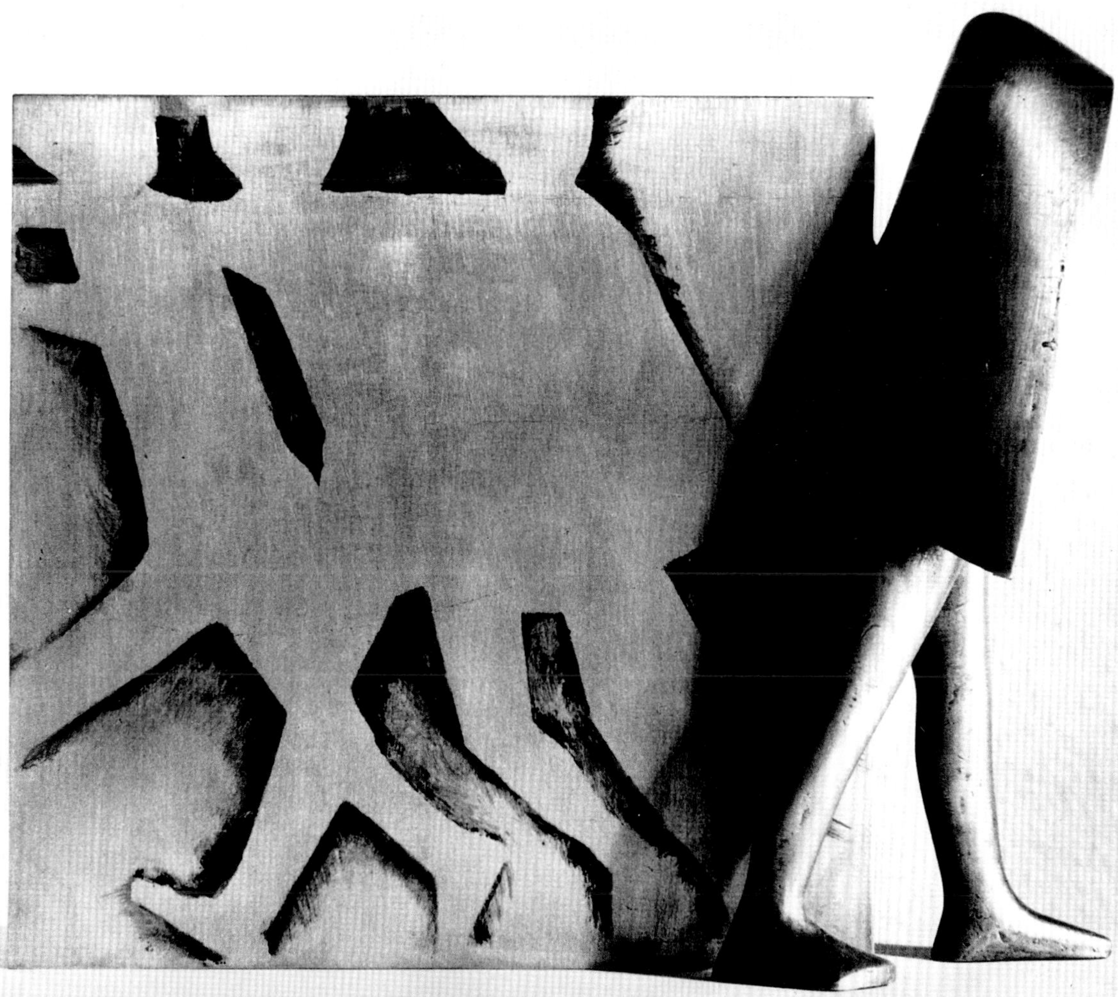

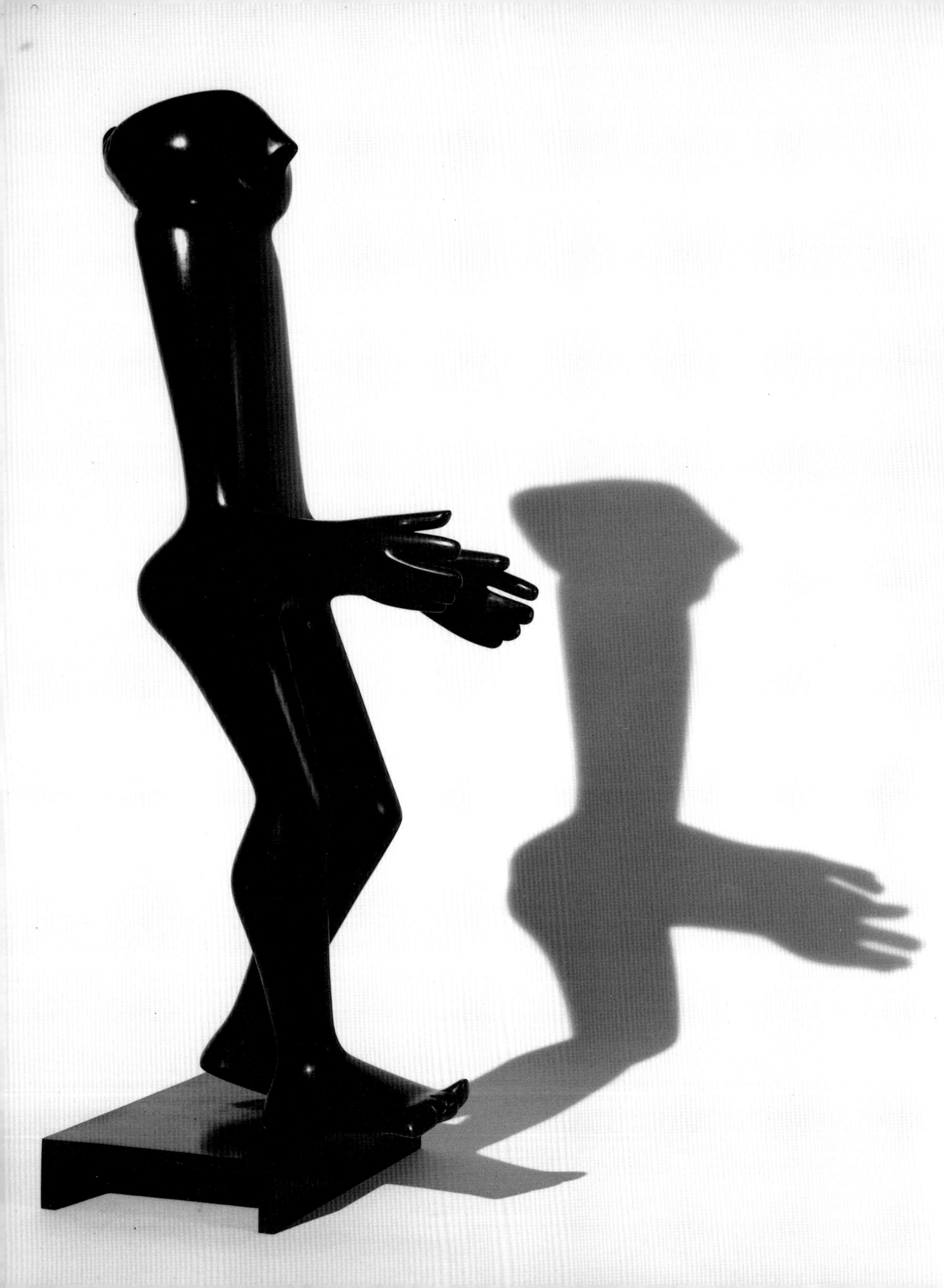

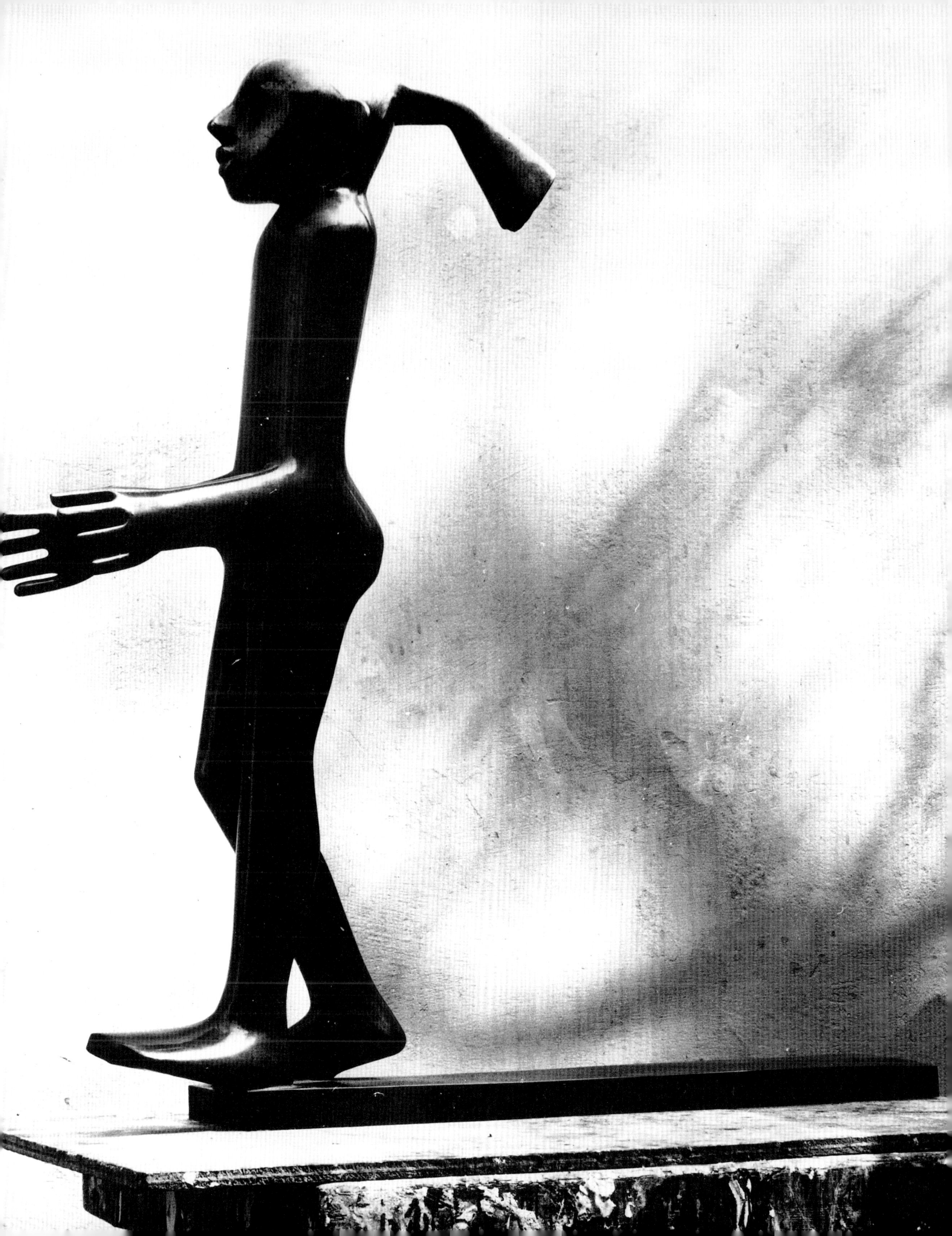

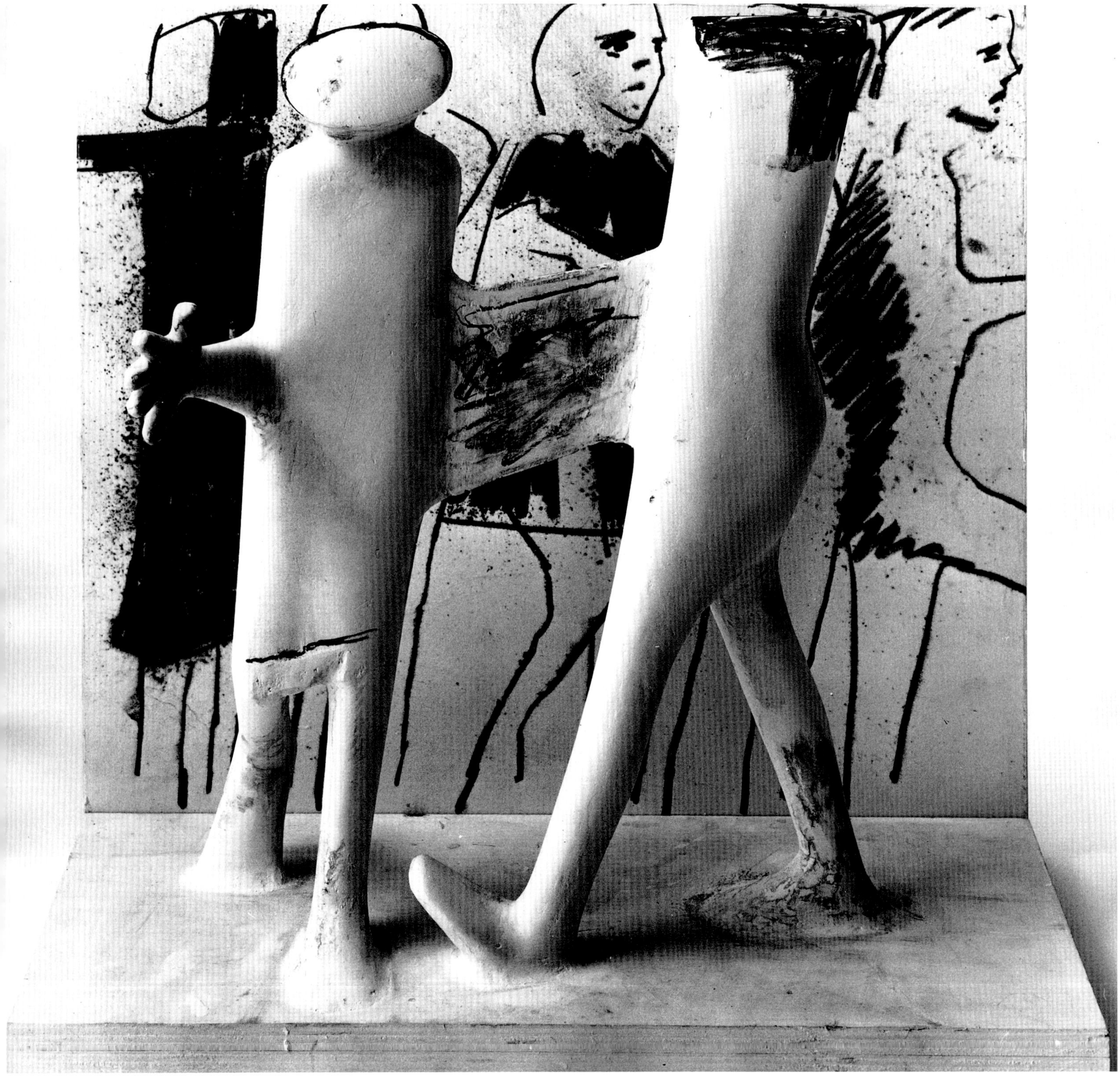

In 1975, a phase began which was very important for me. Ever since I have lived in London, I have been to Richmond Park, an ancient royal hunting park of some six square miles, with rough undulating grassland and numerous oak trees, some of very great age. It is near my home and I made many visits, with friends but often by myself. I had noticed of course that there were trees all over the park, but they did not really mean anything to me until one day in 1975, in the spring, I suddenly *saw* them. It was a bright spring day with blue sky and little white clouds, and everywhere I looked it was a revelation, the trees were alive. There was a slight breeze and the leaves were moving slightly.

From then on I was absolutely hooked, and I went usually about three times a week, mostly very early, as early as I could before the main gates were open. I was invited to write about the park in the Fuji Television Gallery Catalogue: 'I found you could walk through a wicket-gate and the park was empty at which early time the red and fallow deer regarded with unperturbed interest a solitary visitor. At that time they hardly noticed you, they did not run away and even foxes crossed my path.'

An oak tree can live for 800 years, so some of the oldest oaks there could have been acorns at the time of King John. I got books out on the oak trees, their extraordinary growth rate, their right-angular growth. The little branches shoot out at right-angles, so the shape is always zig-zagging and not curvaceous.

... Out of so many trees, some became special favourites, but all are eloquent, their trunks and branches sometimes lopped (pollarded) adding even greater character. The strange peculiarities are well-known – branches of massive girth, growing out horizontally, and even in places weighted down – or branches of considerable length showing no appreciable tapering or the jerky, right-angled twists and turns, as though convulsed by electric shock, and deeply fissured bark textures accentuating like intermittent traffic markings on a motorway, marking every bend. I like best the late summer and autumn, when presumably due to drying and shrinking the leaves separate into heavy, definable clusters. Otherwise certain winter days, with a white low lying mist and each black tree standing free in space, isolated, awesome, still, with limbs in frozen gestures.[6]

I took sketch-books and eventually made etchings on the spot. It made me very happy to be there: once inside the gates one could throw off all the petty worries of the outside world. This love affair with Richmond Park lasted for a decade, from 1975 to 1985.

In 1977, in the Queen's Silver Jubilee year, there was the last of the great Battersea Park open-air sculpture exhibitions. We were the first country to have such exhibitions. Battersea Park was suitable because it had a self-contained area with a fence, and a green grassy area in the middle. Bernard Meadows and myself were appointed to organise the exhibition of 1977, and the committee invited American sculptors to take part. I toyed with the idea of showing a large bronze tree of my own, to go with God's trees in the park, but of course it would be extremely expensive to cast; I was also nervous of making one without having done a lot of preparatory work, so I sent one of my figurative pieces instead.

Meanwhile I got on with making bronze tree maquettes; I must have made about twenty or more of them, about eighteen inches high, experimenting, using acid, for example, for a green patina for the leaves.

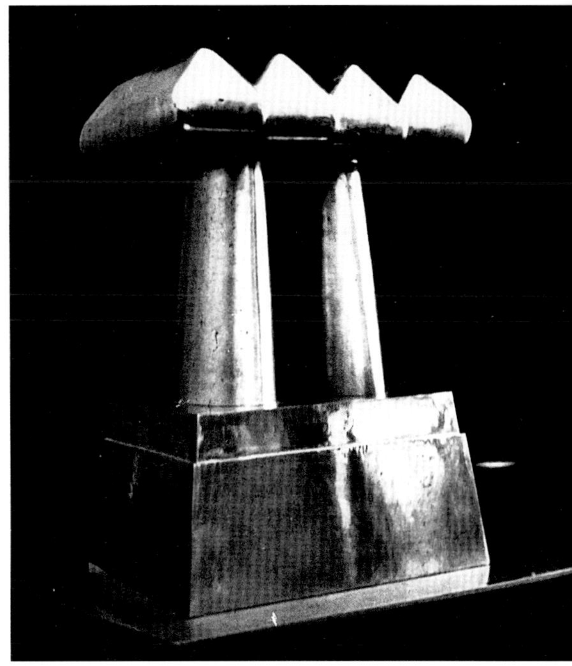

Monument or Memorial Design 1970s (KA223)
H 50 cm ($19\frac{3}{4}$ in), aluminium

(*opposite*) *Two Figures with Drawing* 1972 (KA200)
H 38 cm (15 in), plaster original

6. Extracts based on Kenneth Armitage, 'Notes on the Oak Trees', in *Armitage*, exh cat. Fuji Television Gallery, Tokyo, Gallery Humanité, Nagoya and Gallery Kasahara, Osaka, 1978

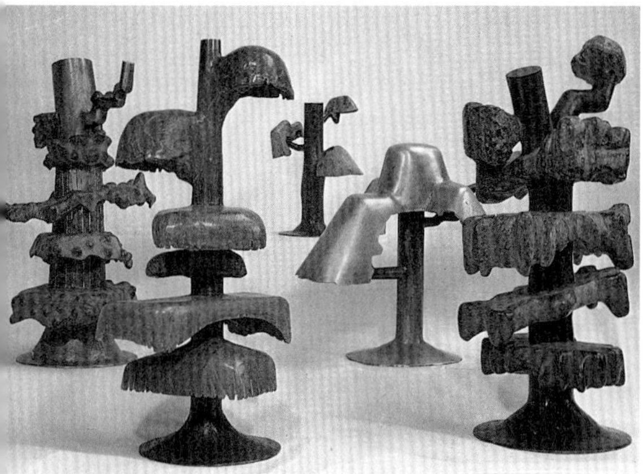

Richmond oaks:
from left to right:
Tall Oak (nobbles) 1980-1 (KA241)
H 61 cm (24 in), bronze
Tall Oak 1979-80 (KA237)
H 72 cm ($28\frac{1}{2}$ in), bronze
Oak (three clusters) 1979 (KA234)
H 36 cm (14 in), bronze with green
Single Oak (canopy) 1979 (KA235)
H 46 cm (18 in), bronze with green
Tall Oak 1980 (KA239)
H 62 cm ($24\frac{1}{2}$ in), bronze

(*opposite*) Oak trees in Richmond Park

My trees were shown all over the place – both drawings and sculpture in Japan in 1978. Several trees were sent to Caracas, others to Gimpel Fils in London, to Paris and elsewhere.

Much later, in 1985, I was commissioned to make a piece of sculpture for the new British Embassy in Brasilia. To my great delight Dr Wendy Baron and her committee from the Government Art Collection selected the first tree maquette, which gave me an opportunity to make a tree on a bigger scale. Noack in Berlin was enormously helpful, giving me the use of a workshop in his foundry; I could not have done it without him. I made *Richmond Oak* in 1985 by modelling directly with plaster over a steel skeleton. Polystyrene was used to fill out the shapes, over which I then modelled with plaster to the necessary thickness. I stayed with Noack in Berlin and worked absolutely flat out from 8.30 am to 5.30 pm each day, and managed to complete my work in six weeks. The cast was then sent to Brasilia, where I went for the installation. And when I was setting up the tree a man approached me who said he was an engineer, and asked me if I had made provision for the extraordinary temperature changes there. I said no, I didn't know about that. 'Well', he said, 'you are going to be in trouble', and this indeed was the case.

Following the decade of the 'Richmond Oaks' I made a version called *Blasted Oak* (1986), based on an ancient hollow tree, black inside with shoots of green growth here and there, amazingly showing that an apparently dead tree can still have life.

We made a second cast of the *Richmond Oak*, and as I had been asked by the Fuji Television Gallery in Japan to send a cast to the Women's Forum which had a park in Yokohama (a civic commission), I felt it would do nicely. Another cast was shown at the National Garden Festival, Gateshead in 1990, and joined my exhibition at the Yorkshire Sculpture Park in 1996.

In 1978 I had a touring exhibition in Japan. The two galleries I was most involved with in Japan were the powerful Fuji Television Gallery (Channel 8 Tokyo) owned by Mr Shikenai (who also founded the first and largest open-air sculpture park at Hakone and acquired the whole of the collection), and the excellent Gallery Kasahara in Osaka.

I wanted to see for myself the immensely hard-working Japanese and so I visited a giant steel works, Nippon Kohan Kaihin. The visit was arranged by the British Council, who let me borrow their car and driver. The main factory produced eighteen million tons of steel a year, although the peak had then passed. As most of the Japanese coast was fully occupied, they built a man-made island off-shore with a communicating tunnel under the sea for trucks and buses. Calling ships unloaded raw material on one side, while on the other, ships loaded up with finished rolled plate and sailed away. This island is called Ogishima.

Although it was a steel works, we had a very sophisticated lunch with the highly intelligent and sensitive Director in a smart building with a pond containing carp. With me was Kasuo Amano of the Gallery Kasahara and the British Council provided an interpreter. Although it was a high-tech factory and ultra-modern, tradition was not forgotten. As we left it was raining and, our car being a British Council one with a blue diplomatic number-plate, all the secretaries were brought out with their umbrellas and, standing in a row, made simultaneously a deep bow!

I also went to a Sumo training centre (I saw a real fight later in Osaka). I saw the 'Noh' theatre twice, once in Tokyo and the other time in Kyoto, the ancient capital.

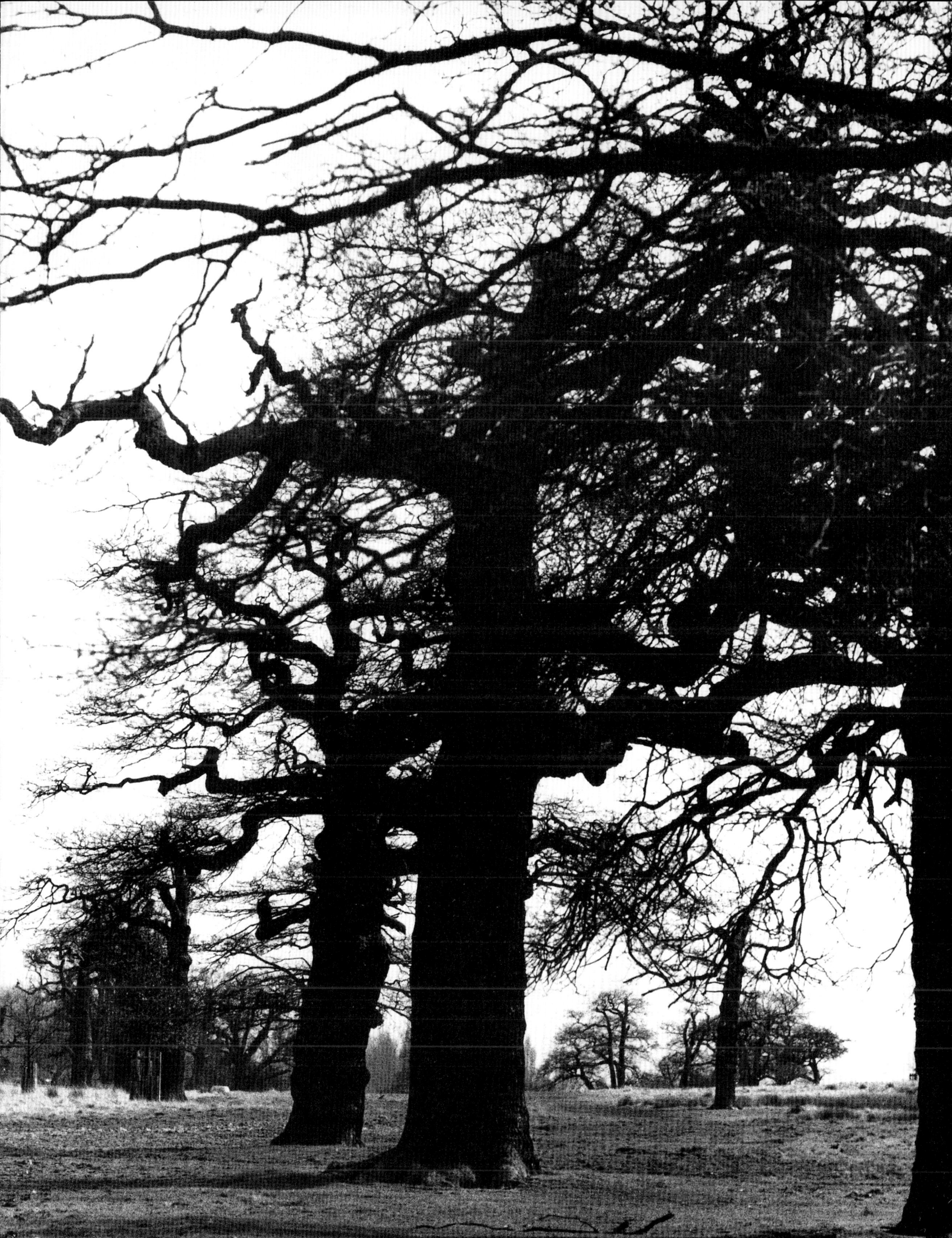

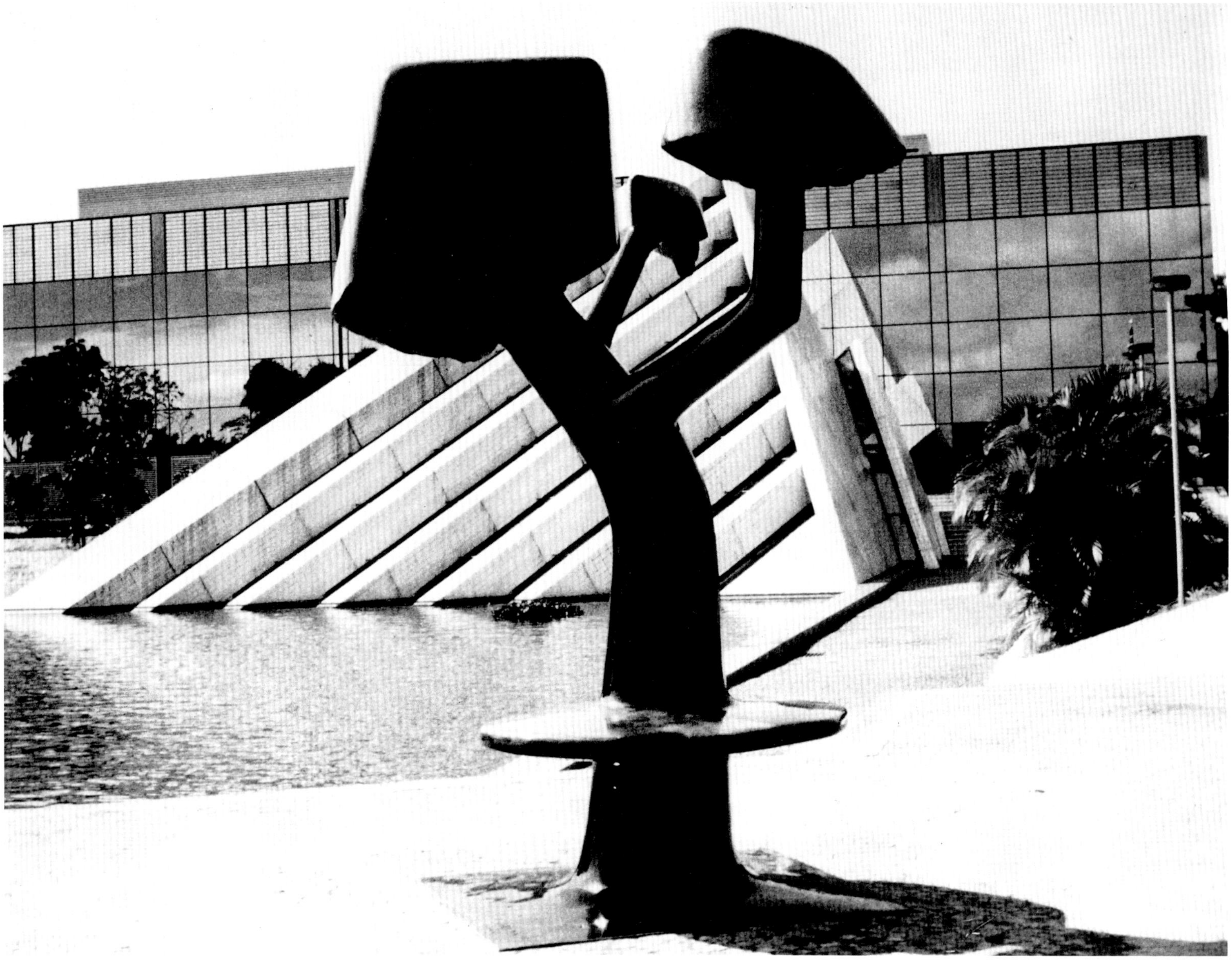

A view of the *Richmond Oak* at the
British Embassy, Brasilia

(*right*) *Large White Figure with Arm across Sky*
1978-81, collage

(*opposite*) *Blasted Oak* 1986 (KA264)
H 79 cm (31 in), bronze
patinated grey and green, with black interior

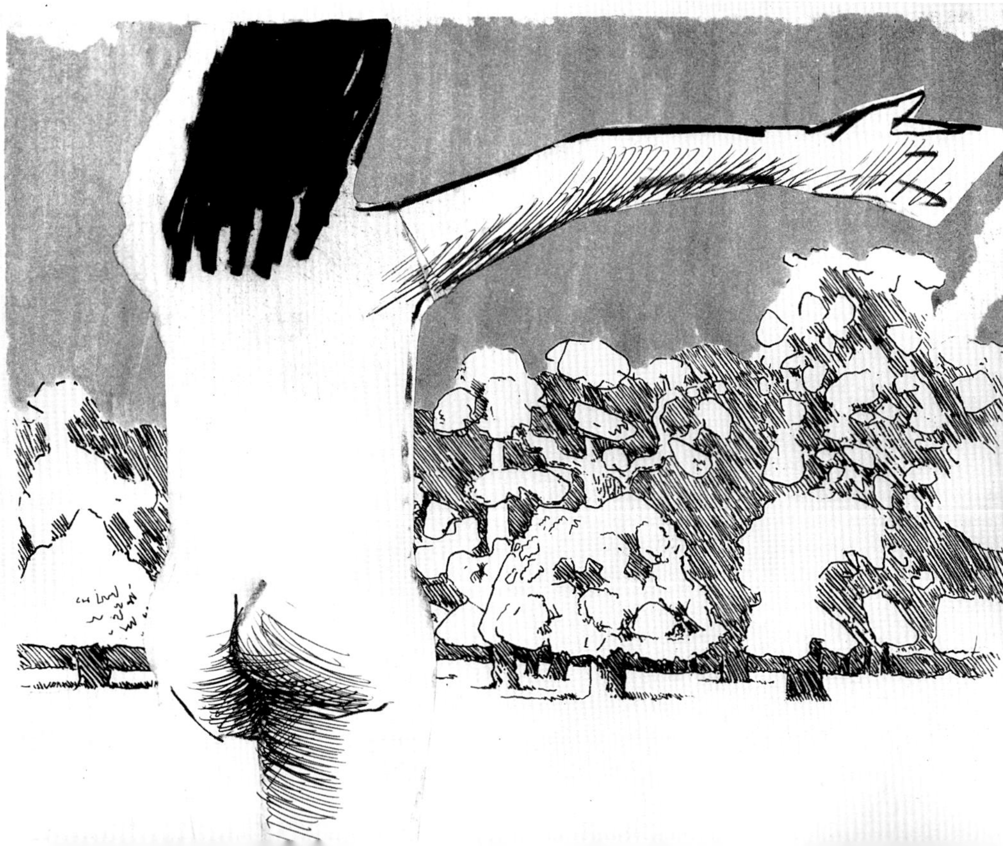

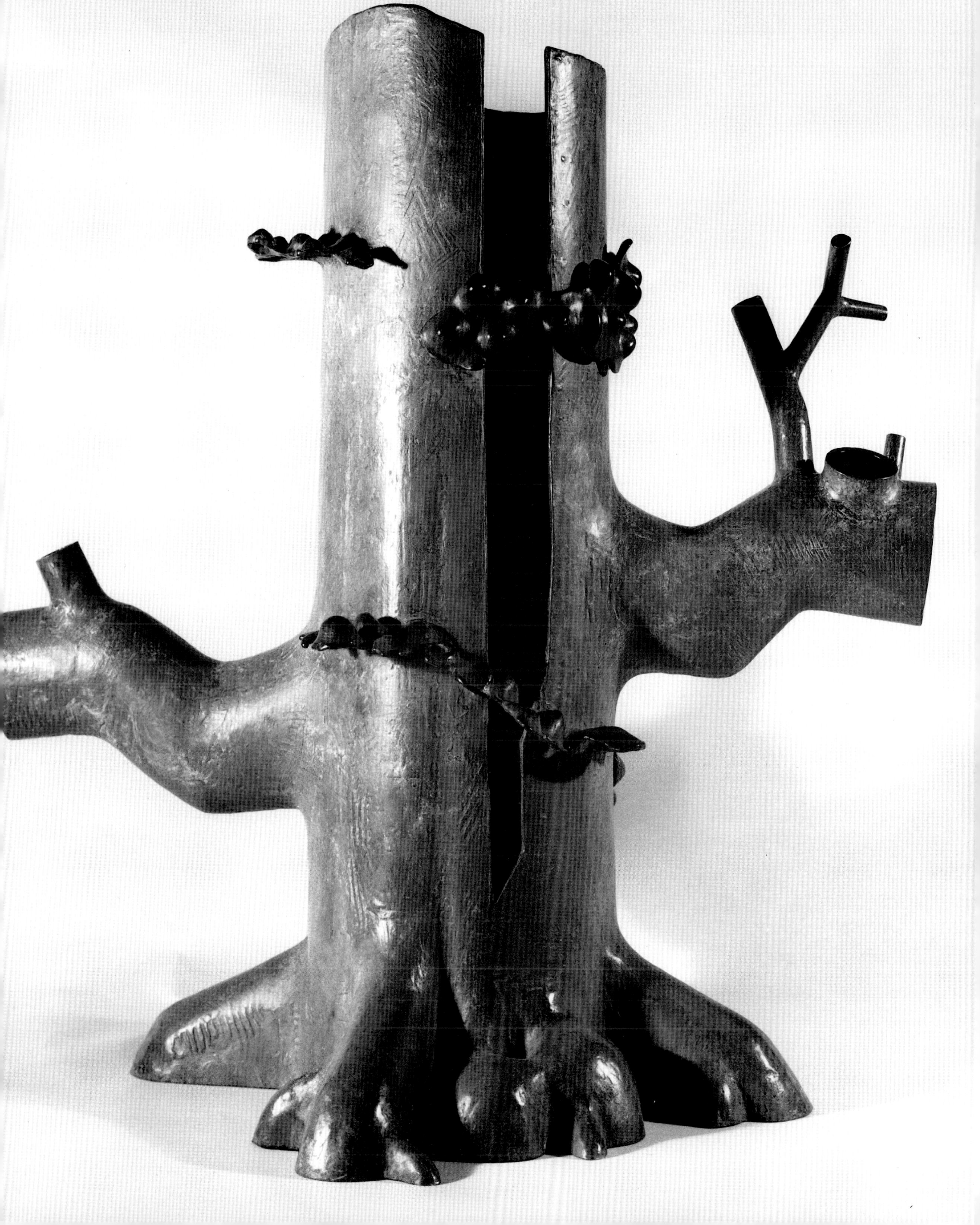

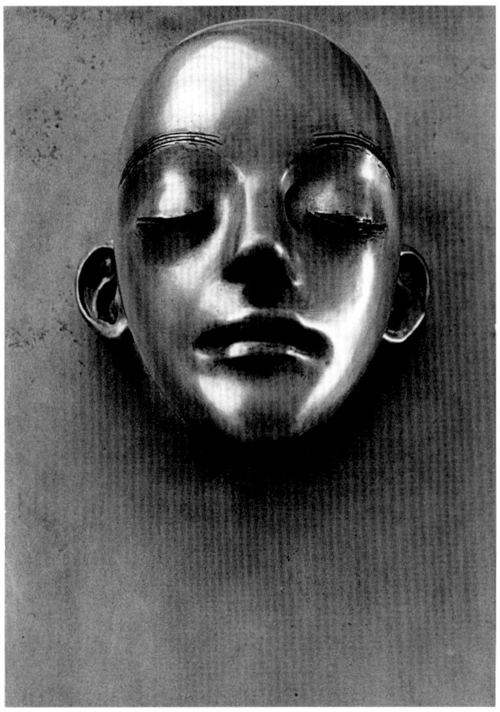

Detail of *Chair* 1983-91

(*opposite*) *Chair* 1983-91 (KA259)
H 152 cm (60 in), bronze

Through the Gallery Kasahara I borrowed Kasuo Amano again, hired a car and we drove through this land of contrasts from high mountains with snow to lush valleys with paddy fields everywhere. We took the car on the ferry to the island of Sado in the Japanese Sea facing China. It still retained the life it had always had. The coast was very volcanic with sharp, vertical columns extending down into the sea like marching giants. The people dressed in traditional costume. I loved the traditional folk songs of Sado. Following this visit I was asked to write an article describing my impressions for the *Yomiori* newspaper of Osaka.

In my bedroom I have had since the end of the Second World War a wooden farmhouse armchair which I like very much, and I made many drawings of it in the 1950s. In 1983 I made some sculptures: one big one, which is not at all like the chair, but before it the three small ones which were like it. The three small ones were made directly in wax; the big one was made in a rather complicated way. It was like a throne with a tall, curved back plate, a seat, forearms, lower legs and head, but no body, all welded together, 152 centimetres high in bronze. By this assembly method and separate modelling of head, arms and legs, it was possible to achieve greater detail than if it had been made in one piece. The cast was sold to the Brisbane Town Hall, Australia in 1989.

I had always had in my heart a longing to go to the Middle East. Those of us who have been brought up in England, and especially Ireland, where there is a lot of rain, have a hankering after the dry desert. The British Council had lent their collection of sculpture to Jordan's new National Gallery, who asked if one of the artists could attend the opening in case there were any questions from visitors. I was the artist selected, to my great delight. This took place in 1981.

The opening was attended by Queen Noor, who incidentally was American and had studied at art school and consequently was familiar with contemporary American art. She was, as everybody knows, very beautiful and charming, and took a great interest in the exhibition. I felt a slight unease because the collection was all bronze, mainly from the 1950s, so that it had an antique look, whereas she had been more recently in New York. I was introduced to the man in charge of the Ministry of Tourism, who offered me a car with driver and guide.

We went to Jarash, with its great Roman remains: temples and a huge amphitheatre. We also went to the mountains of Moab where, standing on a rise, you could look over the Jordan valley, and just see Jericho in the distance. The guide said this was where Moses had stood after the forty years in the wilderness, when he saw the Promised Land. There was something wonderful about that view, the same view that Moses had seen. The most vivid impressions came from my trip to Petra, described in Dean Burgon's celebrated poem as 'Rose-red city, half as old as Time', and discovered about 150 years ago. Previously it was guarded by the Bedouin and no one went there. At the edge of the mountains, just at the entrance to a gorge, we had to leave the car and get on horses to ride down the extremely narrow chasm; the walls each side were about 200 feet high. We got down to an opening, and facing us in the sun was the famous rose-red classical façade.

I found the place terribly exciting. I suppose the architecture was what you would call

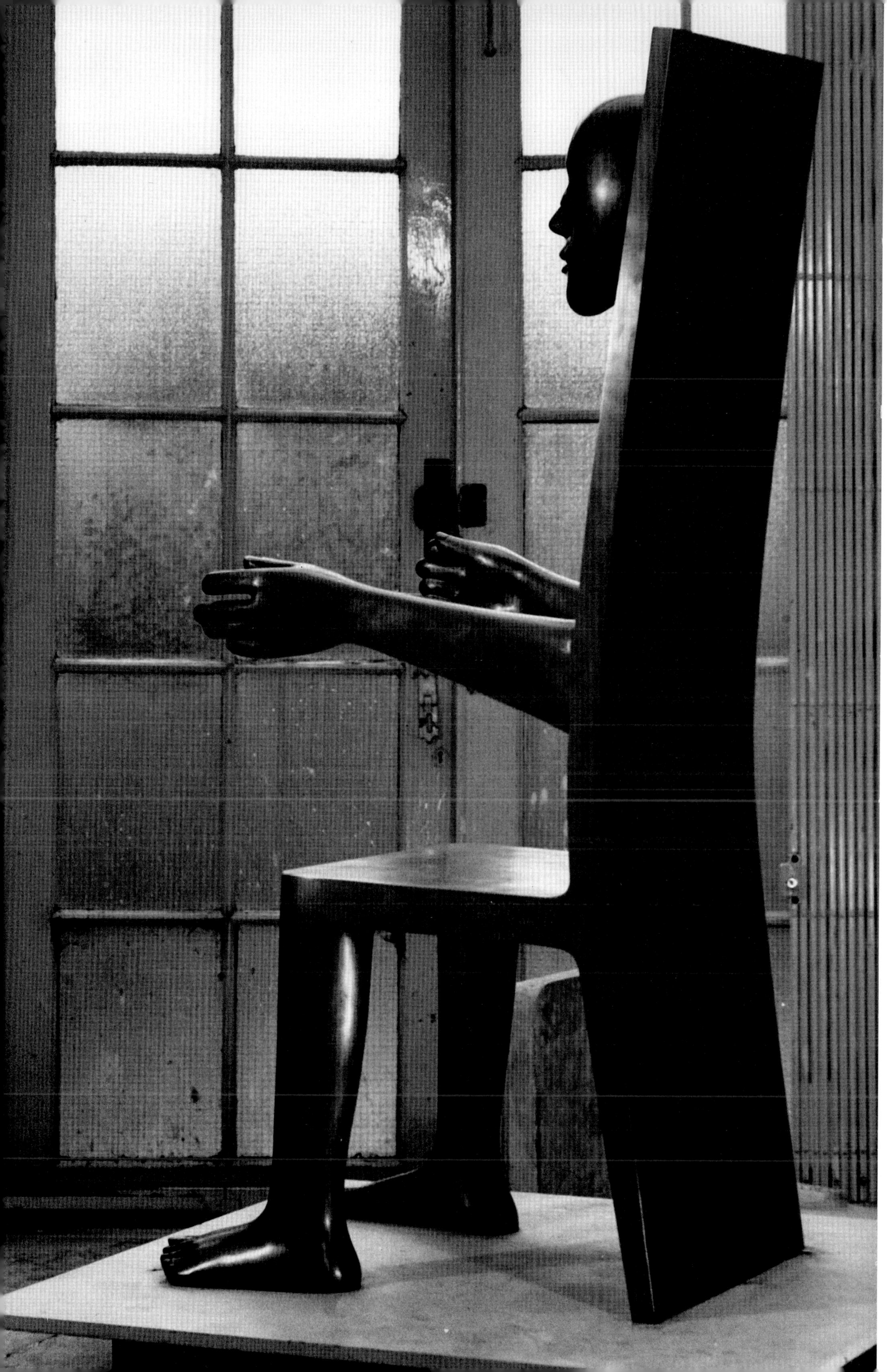

(*opposite*) *Fleeing Figure* 1977 (KA216)
L 283 cm (111 in), cast and plate aluminium

colonial classical: not quite as pure as the Parthenon, or Rome, but very clearly classical, and no doubt they had architects from Rome, or even from Greece, as designers. And this was so exciting that I did a rare thing: I made three small figures when I came back, nothing more than a girl sitting on a bench or a chair with her arms out sideways, and her eyes painted in the Egyptian manner. I called this *Rose-red City* and made two or three versions.

In 1985 I went at last to Egypt with a small group which included my old friend Jossy Dimbleby and Katarina Gascoigne. The latter had been born in Baghdad and spoke fluent Arabic. We went south by train to Aswan, rather than via the traditional boat on the Nile, which is always full of tourists, and glided along through the night almost silently, with the Nile by our side and the dark sky with the moon. In Aswan we hired a felucca, which sailed up and down the Nile. From there we got a plane south to Abu Simbel; it was there that I first saw what are probably the most spectacular sculptures I have ever seen – two colossal carvings of Rameses, about forty feet high – and I made sketch-book notes of them. We saw the main tourist attractions and also the wonderful Cairo Museum in which were two absolutely beautiful statues of female guardians from outside Tutankhamun's tomb, covered with gold-leaf.

My last visit to the Middle East was a trip I made to Baghdad. I had received an invitation to attend the Baghdad International Festival of Art in 1986. I thought I would go, especially because I knew that as Iraq was still at war with Iran, no tourists were allowed at all, and so one would have the sites to oneself.

There were five of us: Tom Phillips, David Elliott (then Director of the Museum of Modern Art, Oxford), an archaeologist (part of the British Council team), and a driver. We drove to Babylon, which was wonderful, being deserted. We wandered around the ruins, saw everything under the blue sky, and I shall never forget that trip. We also went to Samarra, a very high minaret with a spiral bank rising round it, which in itself is staggering. On the way there we stopped at a castle next to the east bank of the Tigris where we were told the history of how the caliph had fallen in love with a Bedouin girl who couldn't live in a city. So he had built a castle for her there in the desert, which was called by the people in Baghdad 'The Castle of the Lovers'. The caliph lived with this girl until she died.

The first trip I made with Alastair and Zandria Service was to Carnac in about 1986, where we saw the mystifying great lines of stones. A few miles outside Carnac we visited Er Grah, a fallen megalith reputed to have been over sixty feet high, which is enormous for a single carving. It had an oval section, not polished but smooth, and it was in four pieces on the ground. There was a reference to a sighting of it in a ship's log in 1650, when it was used as a navigational guide. There was also a drawing from the eighteenth century showing it on the ground. So in between those two dates it had toppled, due either to lightning or, more likely, Alastair said, to earth tremors, because there was a rumour of earth tremors there. It was a remarkable achievement to have erected this monolith in the Stone Age.

In 1990 we made a trip to Orkney, off the north of Scotland, which has many megalithic sites. The climate was milder in those days and the weather better, so there could be astronomical sightings which were related to religious ceremonies. We went to see the stone

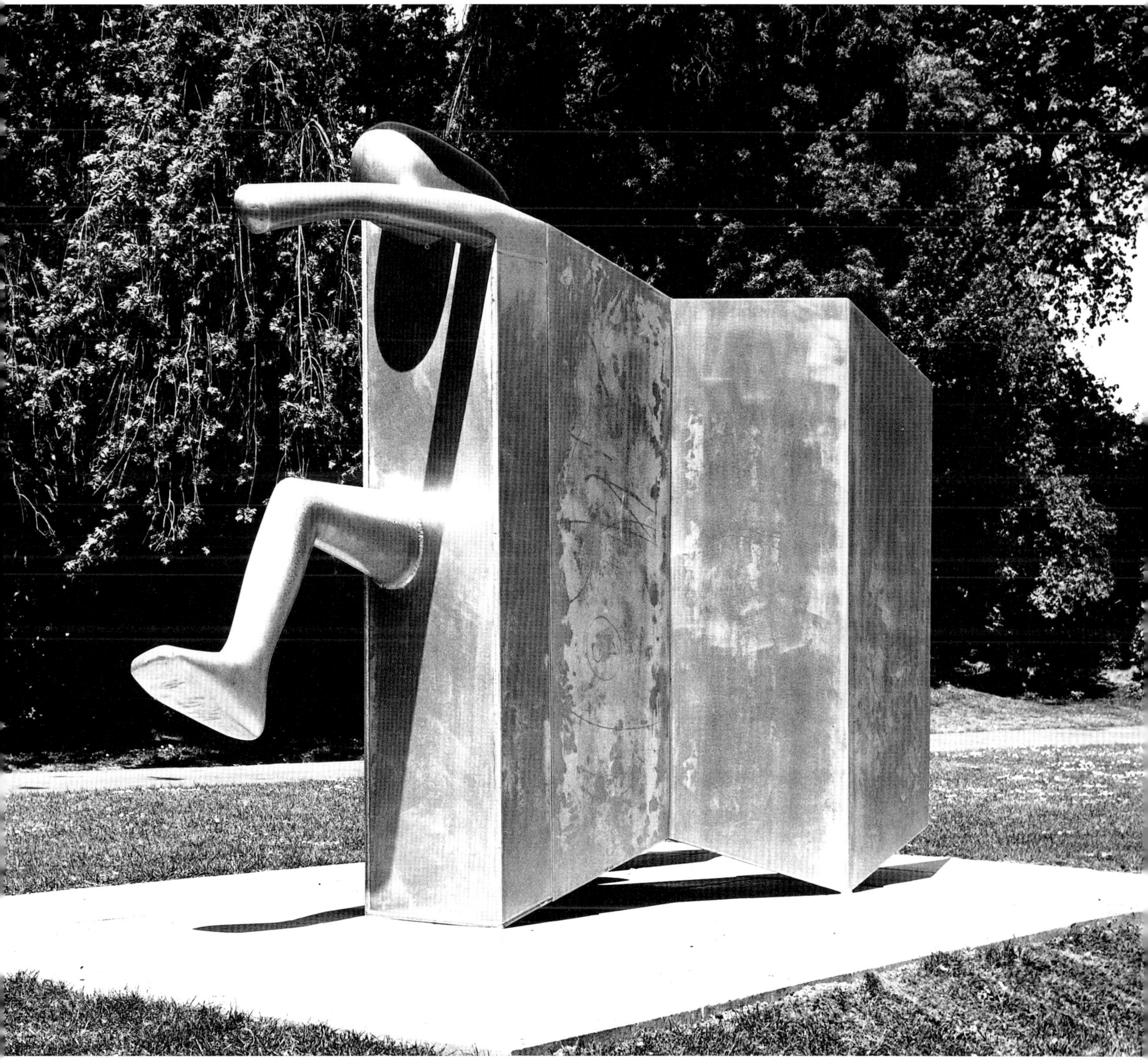

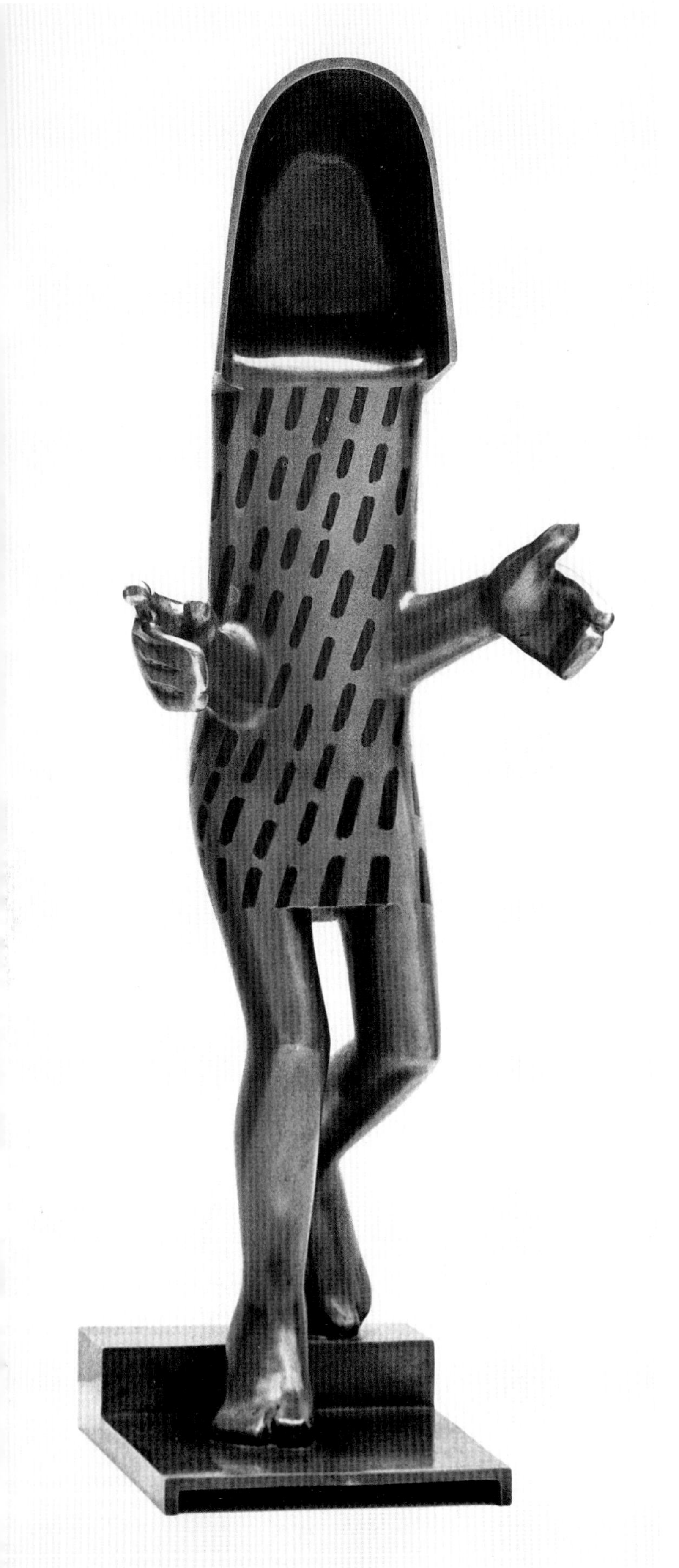

Girl without a Face (version 2) 1982 (KA251)
H 74 cm (29 in), bronze and enamel with painted stripes

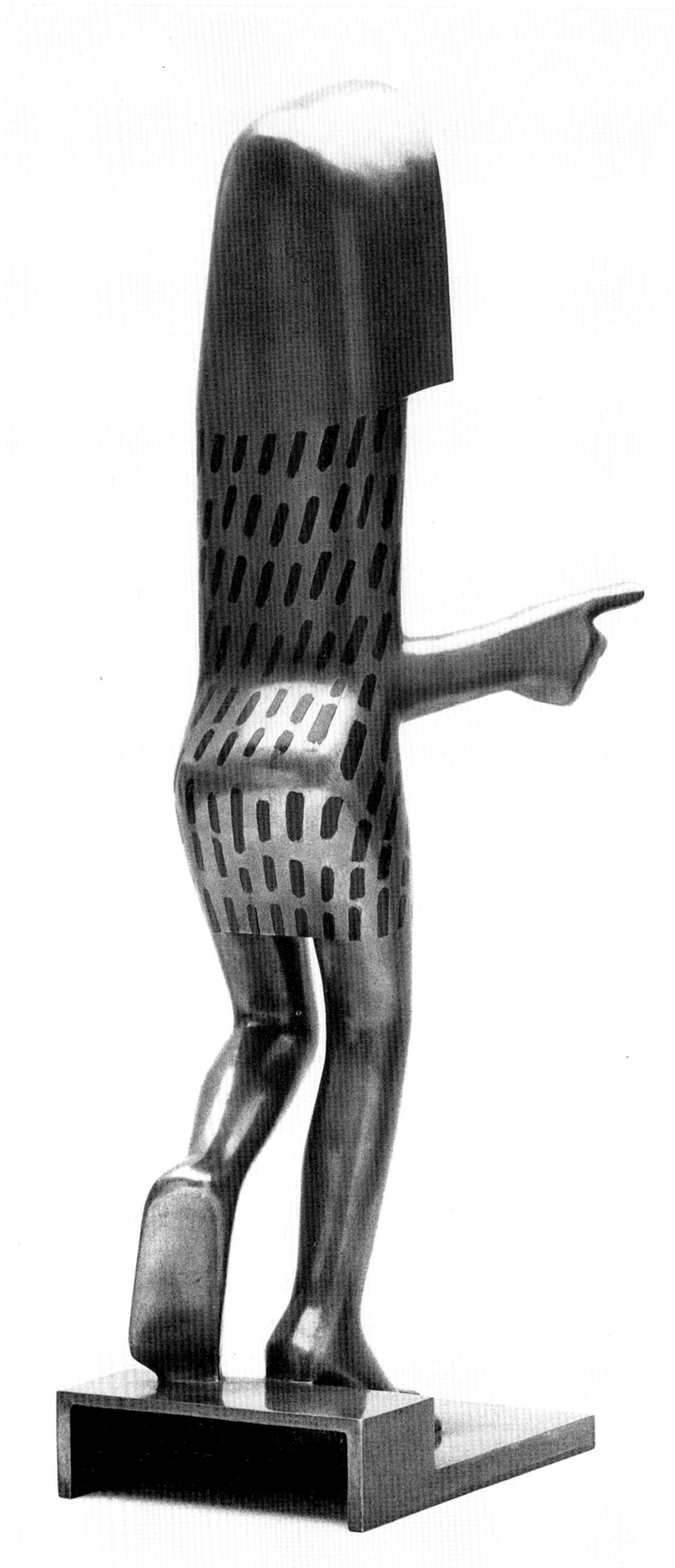

Rear view of *Girl without a Face* (version 2)

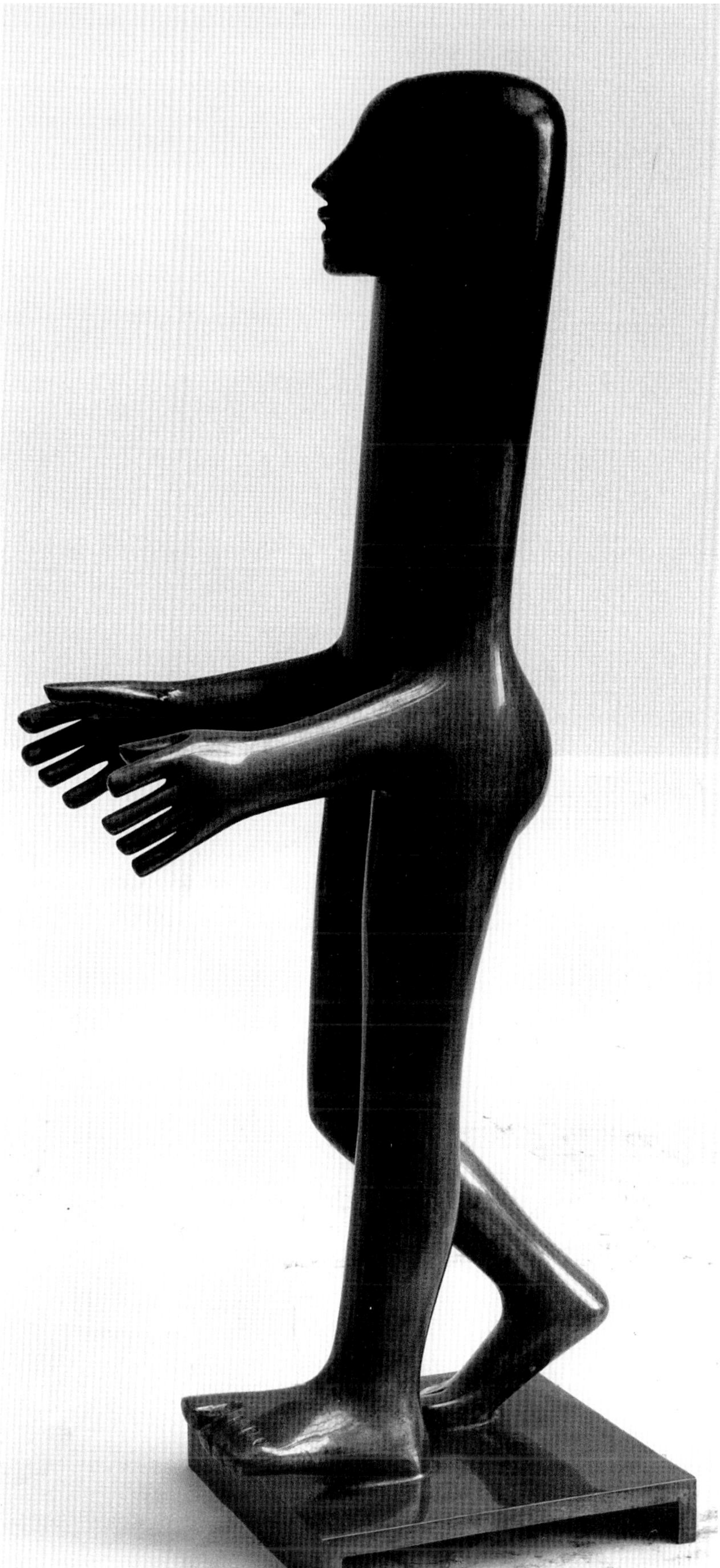

July Figure 3 1980 (KA240)
H91 cm (36 in), bronze

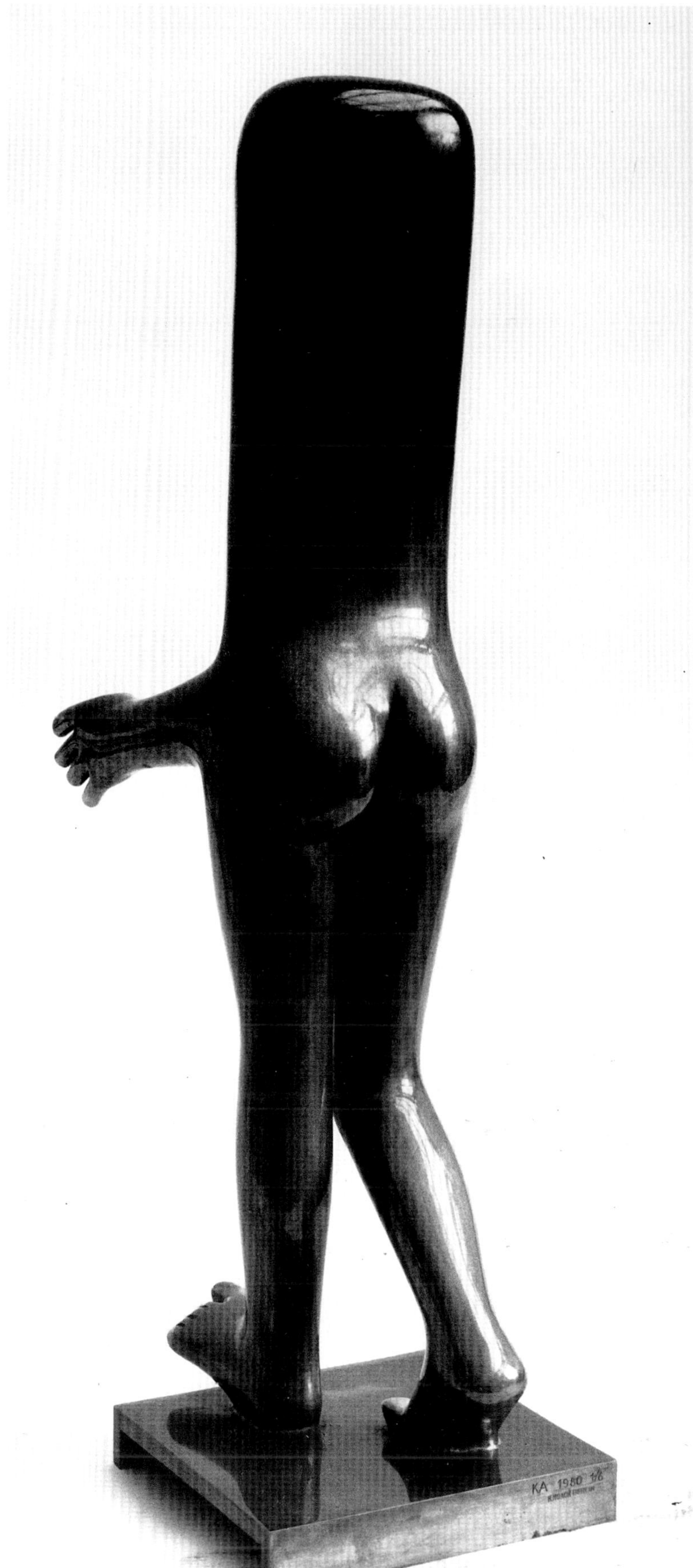

Rear view of *July Figure 3*

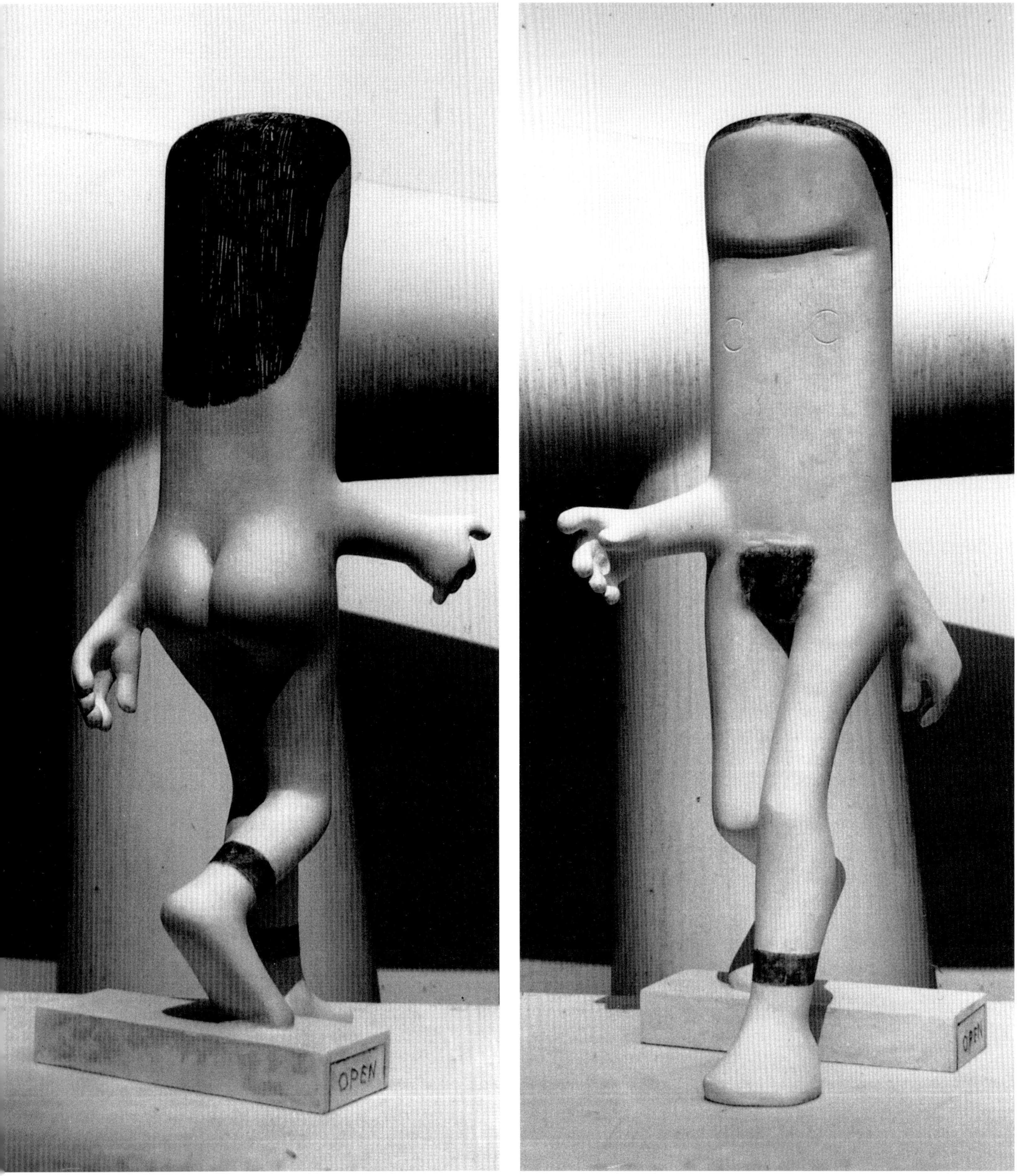

Two views of *July Figure 4* 1982 (KA248)
H 88 cm (34½ in), plaster model

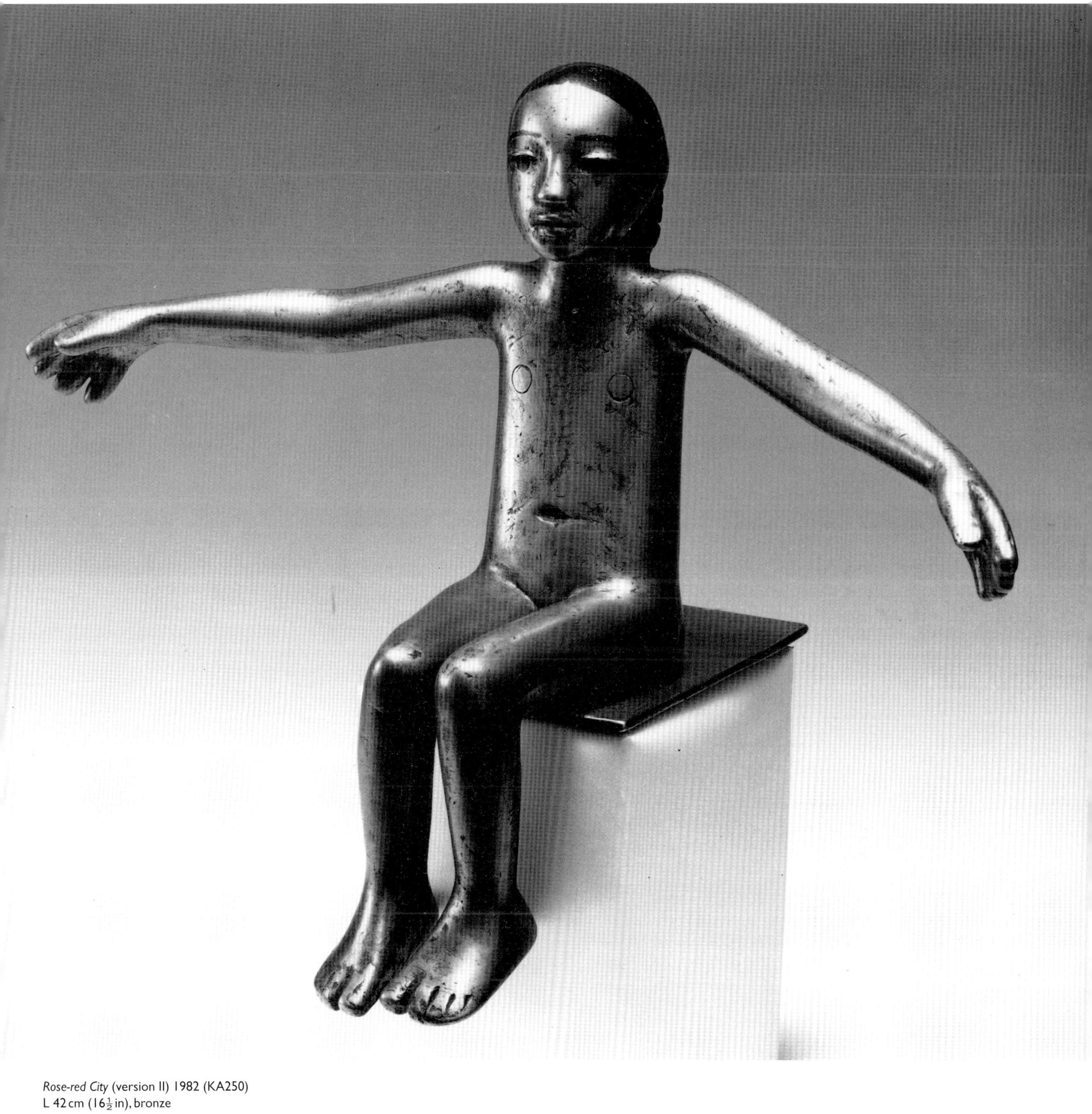

Rose-red City (version II) 1982 (KA250)
L 42 cm ($16\frac{1}{2}$ in), bronze

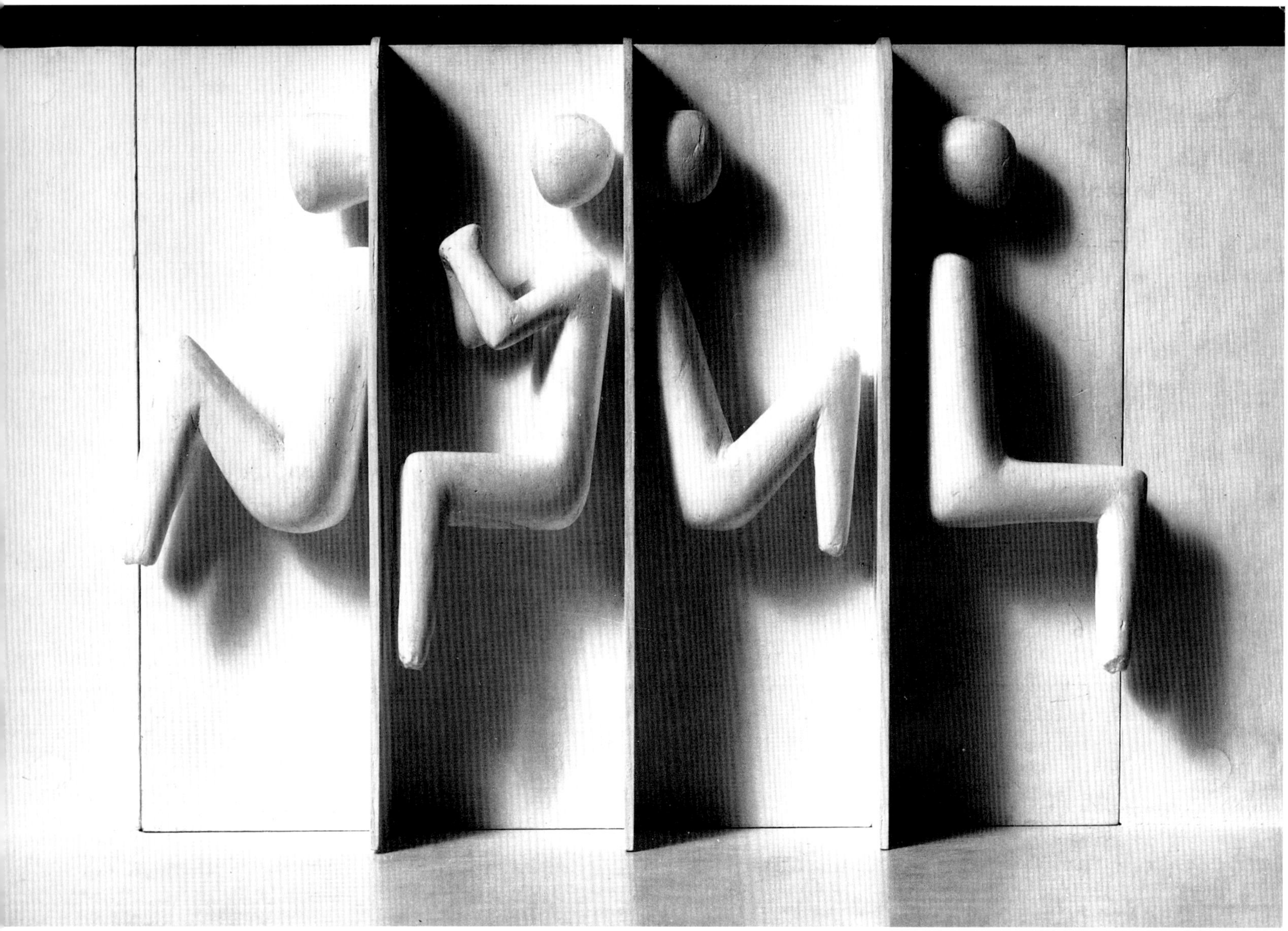

(*above*) *Isolated Seated Figures* (model) 1990 (KA267)
L 55 cm (21$\frac{1}{2}$ in), wood and plaster

(*opposite*) *Return to Eden* (model) 1983 (KA258)
L 48 cm (19 in), plaster

circles and a large walk-in burial ground, Maes Howe. Also Skara Brae, a 5000-year-old little hamlet of about ten small houses, which had been smothered by sand in a gale and not uncovered until 1850, so that it is very well preserved with walls, niches and tables in stone.

The next large piece I made was for the 1988 Seoul Olympics, the 24th Olympiad, and I called it *Garden Game*. I do not know why I gave it that name but one could imagine it set in a hedge at the end of a garden. It is in seven pieces bolted together and was made in resin; it is very much a relief.

Another large piece I made was of a group of figures, again a relief, which I called *Return to*

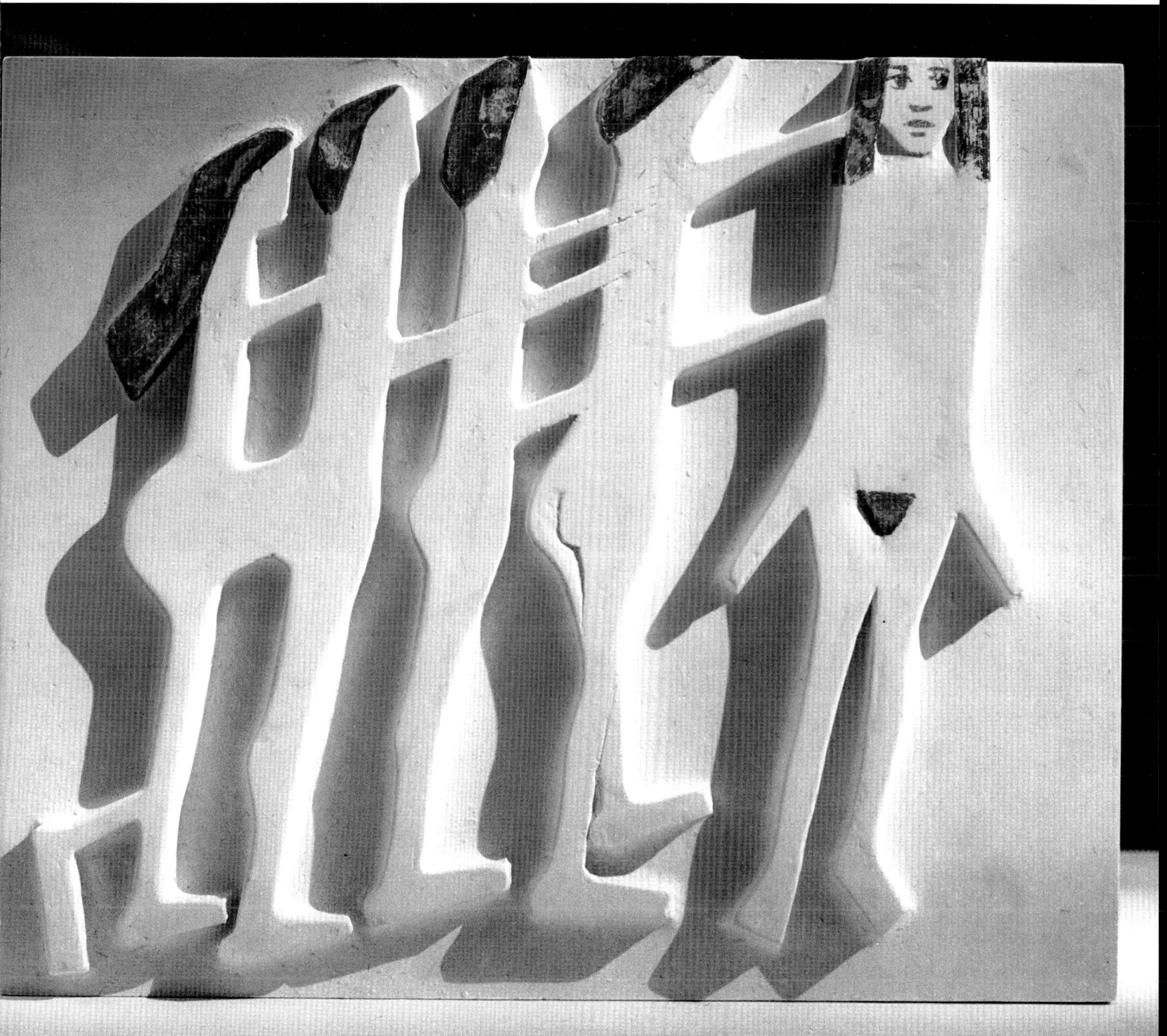

Alastair Service and KA on the Burren, Co. Clare, Ireland, 1987

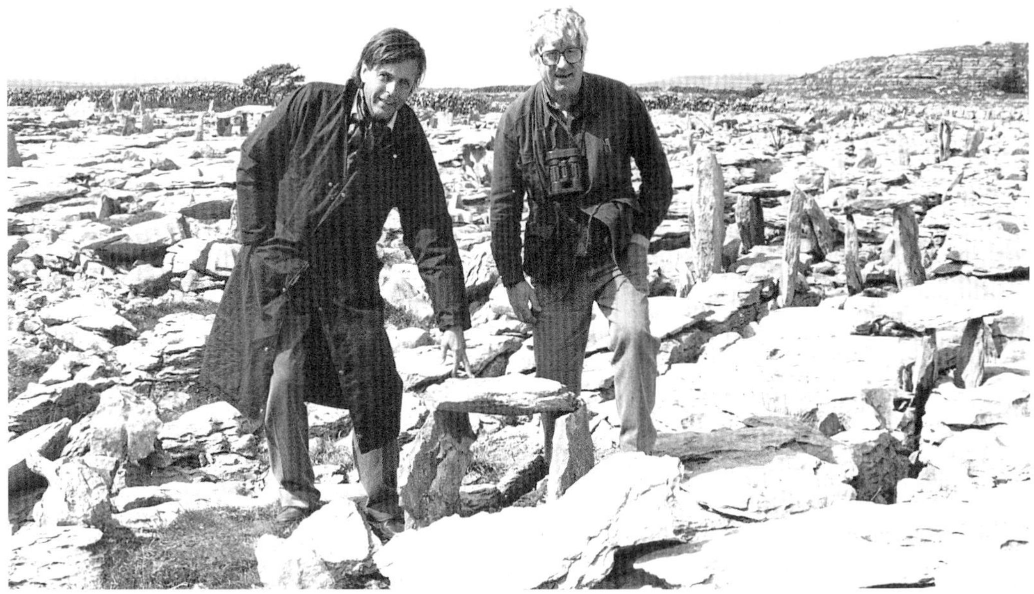

Eden (1988-9). As the name implies it is about figures sneaking back: a group of four figures on the left, facing one on the right, with a screen-printed face.

L-shaped Screen (1991) fits in with the work I was making at that time: rounded organic shapes combined with geometric shapes. And this was once again a screen. This version was made in aluminium, because to have used a bronze plate one inch thick would have been too heavy.

I now come to my most recent work, *The Dagda* (1992-6). For most of us who are steeped in Greek clarity, the Celtic myths, like the spirals of Celtic art, are a tangle of stories concerning gods, heroes, magic, women, poetry, land and nature, hunger for power. Of the several invading peoples it was the last that concerns us here – the Tuatha De Danaan. The Dagda were very prominent. Although the name appears to be plural it is treated as a single deity: the Good God combining Night and Day, North, South, East and West, Lord of Knowledge, the Creative All-Father, Lord of Life and Death. Numerous stories survive from the oral tradition (I have a book of Celtic myths) which were recorded by early scholars in about 1000 AD. But I am mainly attracted to the name Dagda, which inspires awe. This can be felt by walking into the inner chamber of the vast megalithic passage grave called Newgrange, in County Meath, which dates from approximately 3200 BC, thus making it older than Avebury, Stonehenge and the Egyptian pyramids. And older than the Tuatha.

Not knowing what to call my piece, I felt it might have to be 'Untitled' – which is just feeble, especially as it seems to signify something. When recently visiting my wife in Highgate I saw a Christmas card I had made for her in 1981 and thought it could be developed. The card had been made after several visits to the Burren – a vast area of exposed grey fissured rock strata

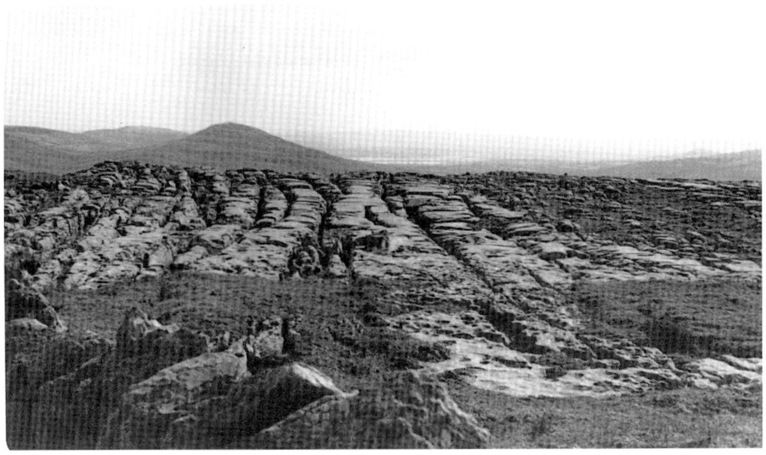

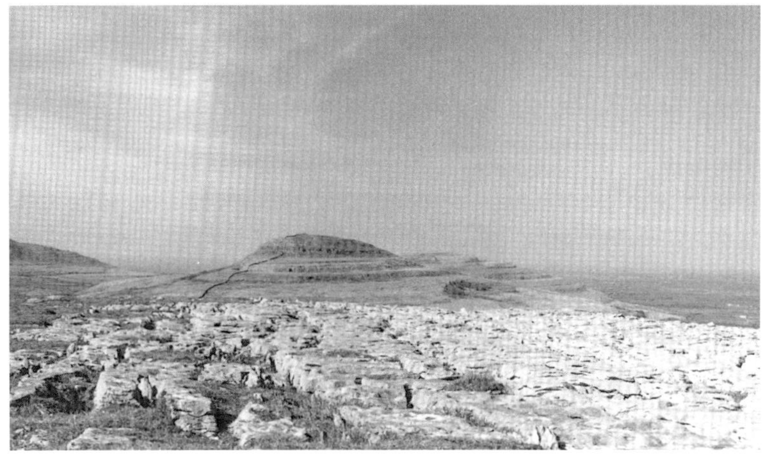

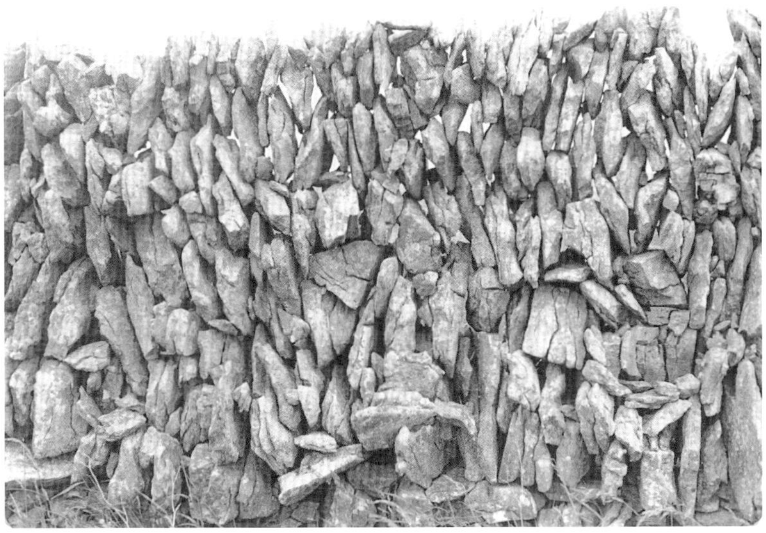

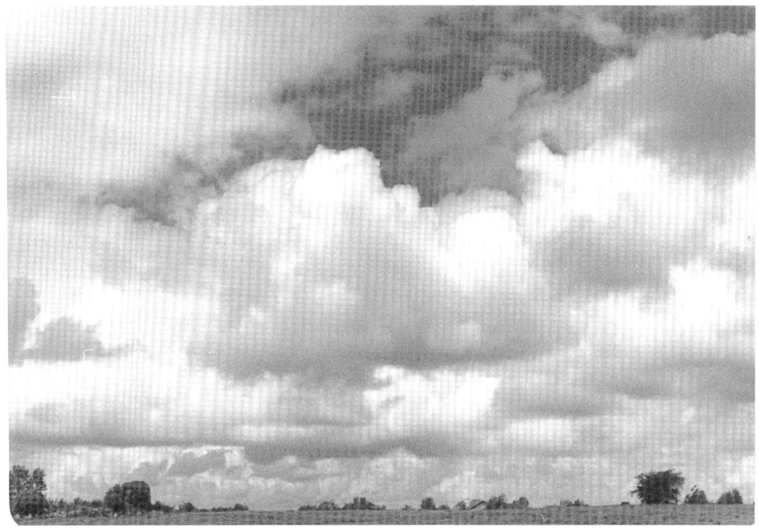

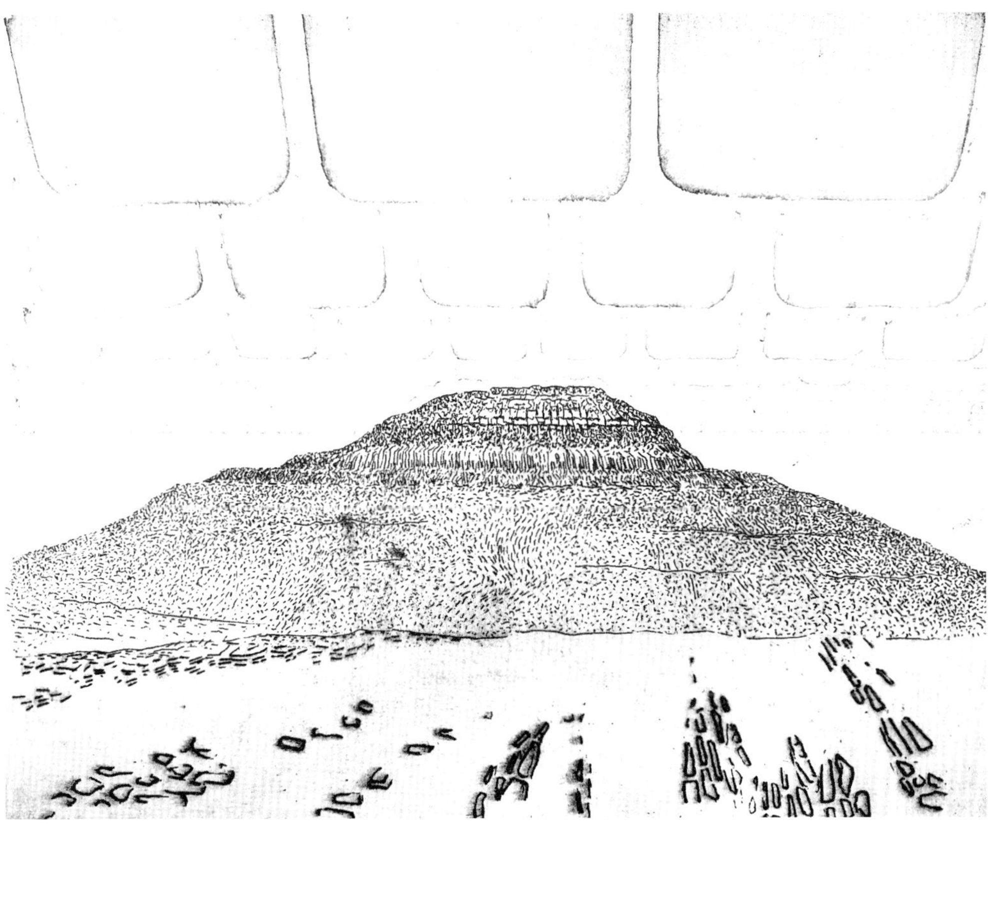

(*above*) Four views of the Burren 1979-80

(*left*) *The Turloughmore Mountain, Co. Clare, with clouds*, etching

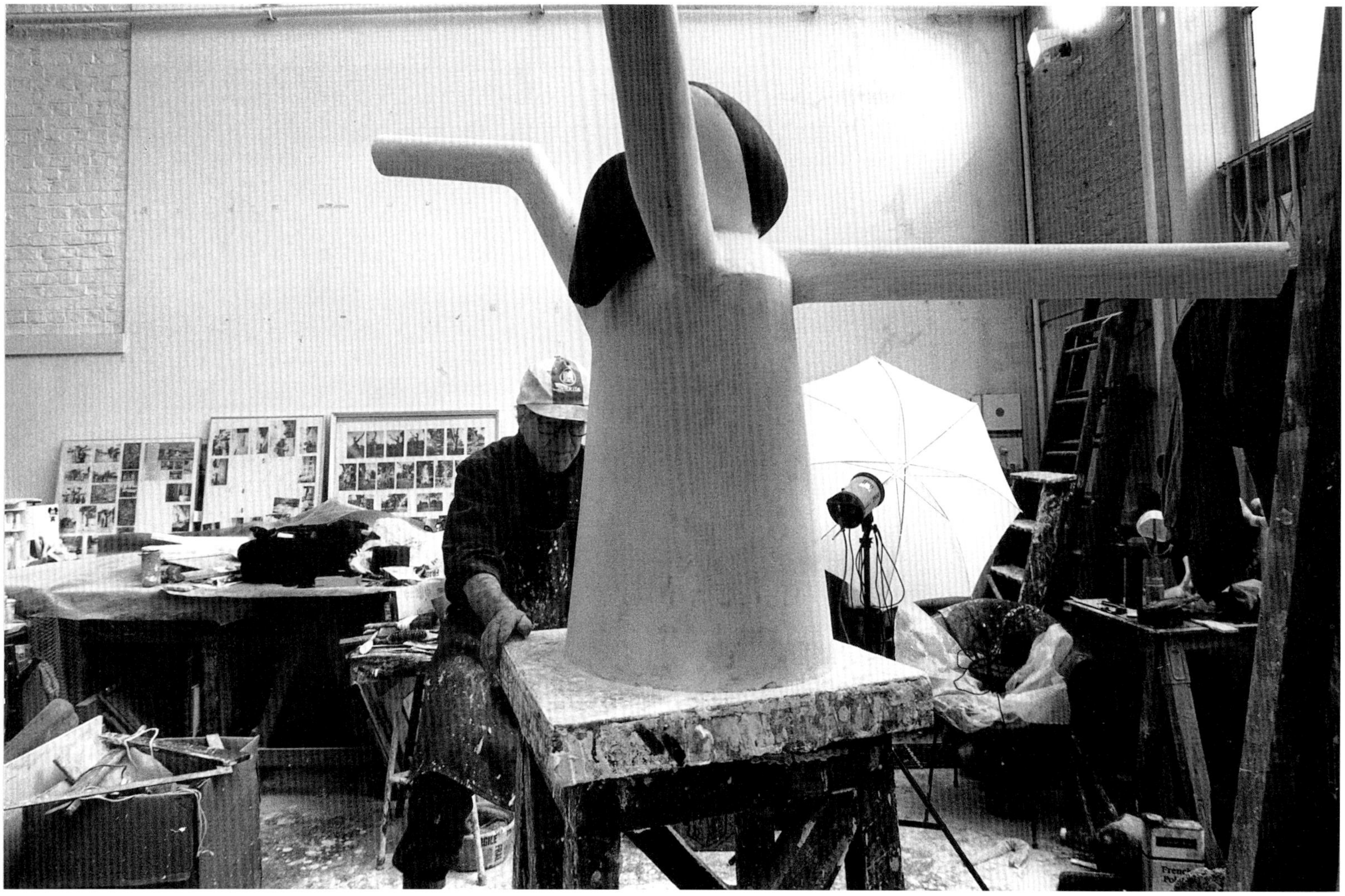

Work in progress on *The Dagda* 1995

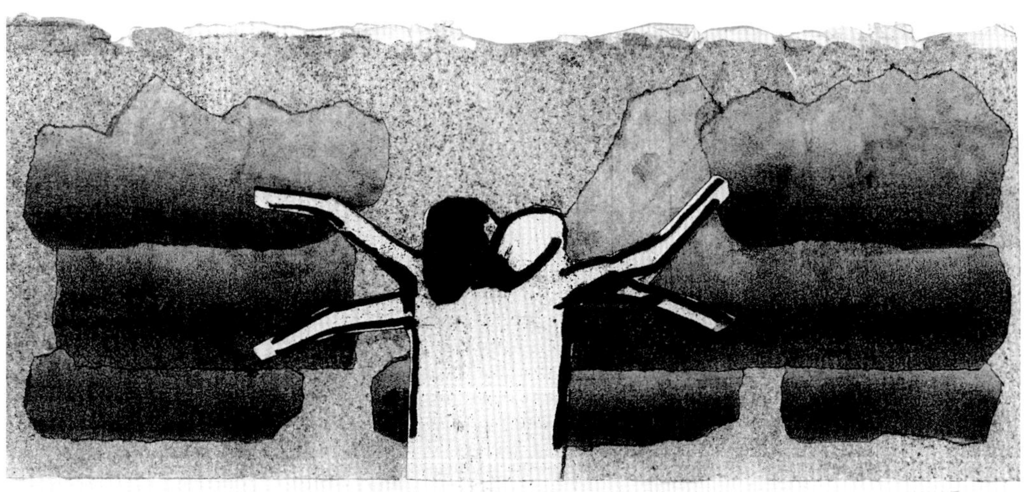

(*right*) Christmas Card 1981
This was produced following a visit to the Burren, Co. Clare, Ireland, in the same year. The idea was used as a basis for *The Dagda* of 1992-6.

in County Clare, facing Galway Bay. Because of its excellent drainage, nourishing limestone and mild climate, special plants flourished in the fissures, and the area was made famous by visiting botanists. But I love the bare and haunting moon landscape and made many etchings and drawings, and took several friends there. The second feature was the sky, clouds ranked in diminishing layers extending to the horizon. I had drawn the clouds on that card and added figures (four arms like sign-posts springing from a supporting mass). This card was the origin of the idea for *The Dagda*.

Several times in my life I have found that an odd, casual occurrence or idea, quite unimportant at the time, can, if accepted, take on much greater significance later. This was the case with *The Dagda*. Similarly, I mentioned the officer in the mess at Deepcut camp, who casually passed me the *Times* advertisement for the art-school teaching job at Bath, which I applied for, and I eventually went to teach at Bath, and that really became almost a way of life; it was a very important accident to have happened. Accidents, trivial things, seem to have happened a lot in my life, and can also happen in my work. A little thing that appears not to be important can lead to much greater things if one takes it up. So that if anyone asks me to give an item of advice, I would say that it is to heed the faint whisper, the hunch that can cut right across intended or conscious activities.

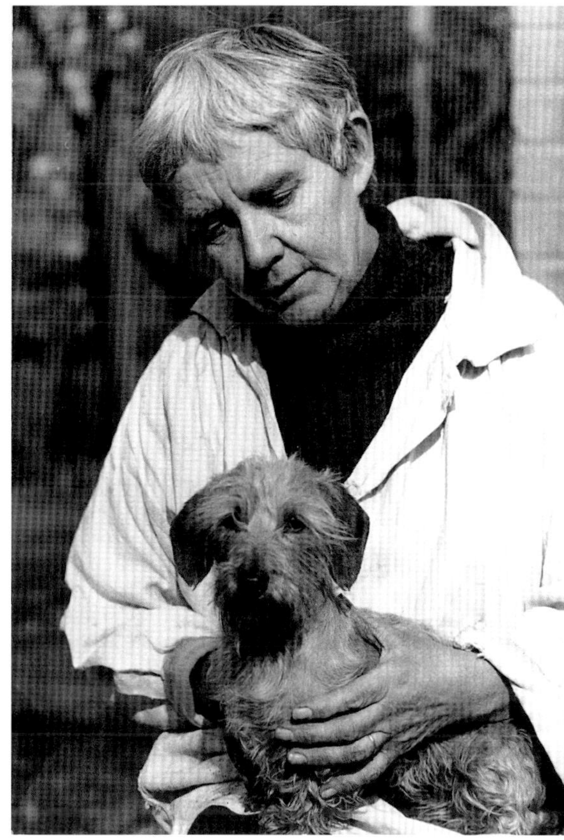

Joan Moore, wife of the artist,
born 1909, died 14 October 1996

On my numerous visits to the British Museum, which I regard as a museum of life, I see of course regularly what is obvious, the sculpture halls with Egyptian, Cycladic and archaic Greek sculpture. But I also visit a tiny room on a mezzanine floor containing a handful of Stone Age artefacts, items of pre-history. There is the whole skeleton a few thousand years old that might, by a billion to one chance, be one's own direct forebear. Or the small, rather wonderful chalk drums, only a few inches high, cylindrical, beautifully carved in relief, found in a girl's barrow made 4000 years ago, and for which there is no known purpose; they appear to be unique. But what I find most interesting is a fragment of reindeer antler, only eight inches long, on which is engraved the head and antlers of a reindeer, so clear, direct and fresh that it might have been made today by a student at the Royal College of Art. It is estimated to date back unbelievably to 12,000 BC, thus relating in date to the Lascaux caves (which I was privileged to see before they were closed to the public) containing the fabulous cave paintings. It gave me a thrill, shaking hands, so to speak, with another artist unbelievably of nearly 14,000 years ago, in spite of differences of race, language and way of life. It is an example of the role of art, a form of direct communication quite independent of other human activities.

The art industry is enormous: the National Gallery, the Tate Gallery, the Royal Academy, the Hayward Gallery, Whitechapel Art Gallery, the numerous civic galleries right through the country stuffed with paintings and very little sculpture. The auction houses: Sotheby's, Christie's, Bonhams, Phillips; the hundreds of commercial galleries dealing with current art production. The art writers and critics, the magazines, the paint, frame and paper manufacturers; the bronze foundries; the hundred or so art schools giving employment. Underneath this activity involving an annual turnover of millions are many tiny dots. These, the artists, are mainly anonymous, but a few reach star status, mostly for excellence of work but not always so. Individual artists are of course vastly important, but can be lost in the mass of activity we call art. This is all like a benevolent goddess, fading or emerging with circumstance, but always there, indestructible, and continuing for all time. This strange activity occurs only in the human species and nowhere else in life.

I would like, finally, to refer to a book I read recently which I found fascinating. It is by an American called Richard Coe and was published in 1984 by Yale University Press. Coe tries to analyse the child's mind, which I certainly was not doing as I was working. He called the book *When the Grass was Taller*. But what interested me was that he felt there were two categories of human thinking or understanding. There was the part of the mind involved with what he calls a 'real' dimension, with useful consequences, practical, material, and of benefit to the performer: let us say business or building. The other part was a 'play' dimension, which was wholly gratuitous, generating no direct consequence, throwing off a feeling. And these two things can combine; we all do both. In fact, he refers to two thinkers or philosophers: Johan Huizinga, who thought that the two dimensions were equally important in our minds, and Roger Caillois, who thought that the play element was the more important of the two. And Coe says that the play dimension is the foundation for all culture, all art, all religion, and what we call the aesthetic. He says that the fun or playing resists all analysis, all logical interpretation, and cannot be reduced to any other category.

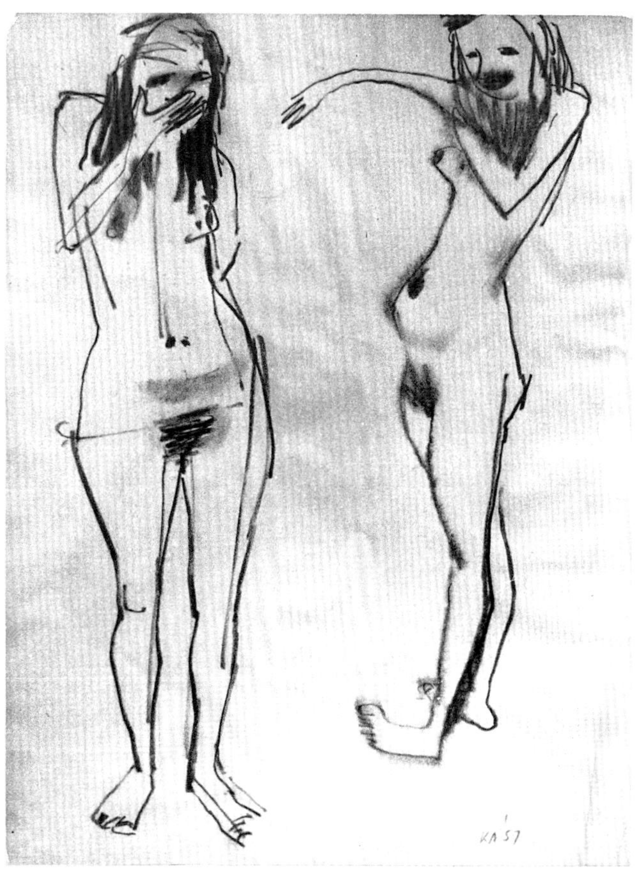

Life drawing (Ulla) 1957
charcoal

A selection of untitled drawings by the artist is reproduced between pages 141 and 160.

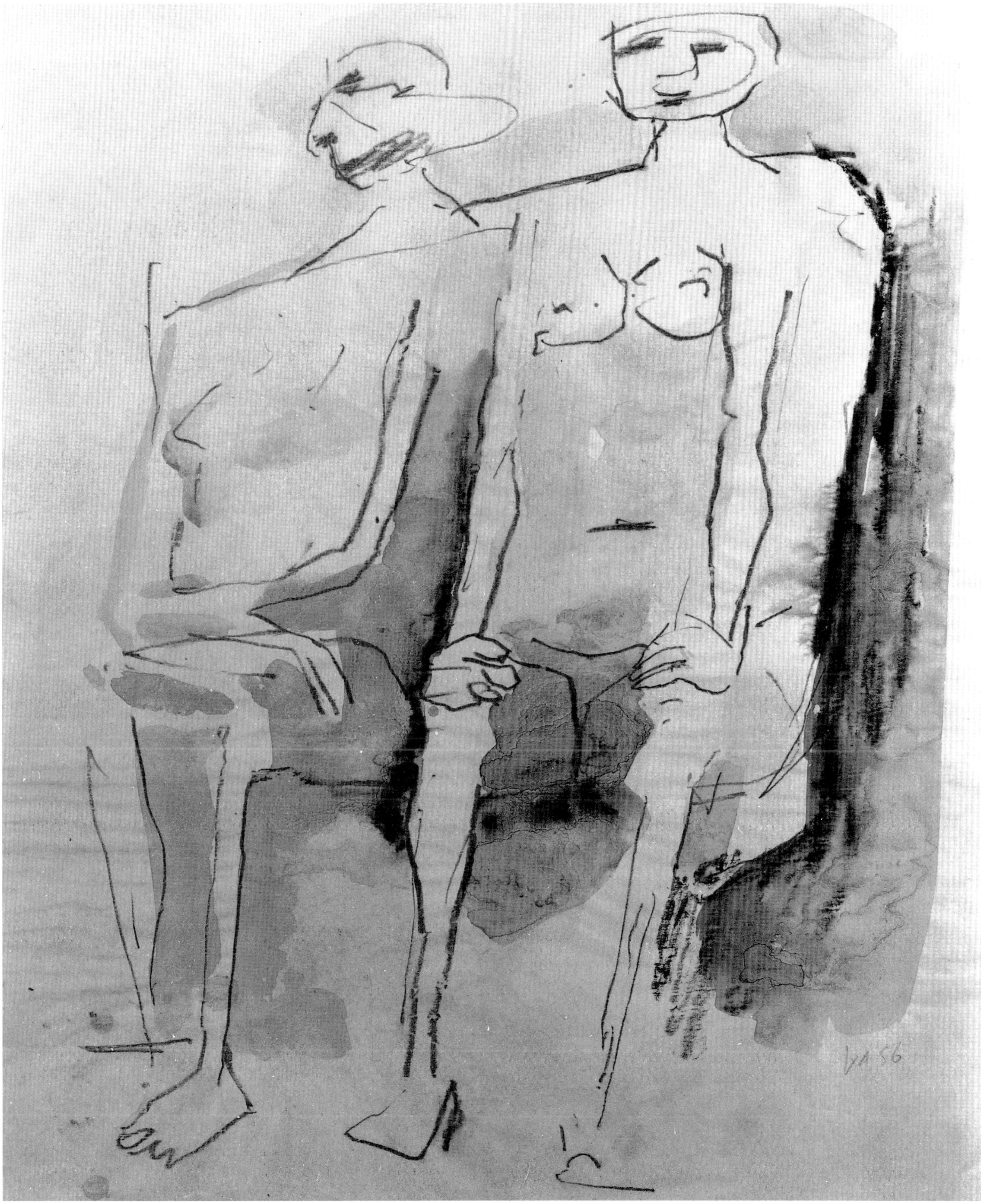

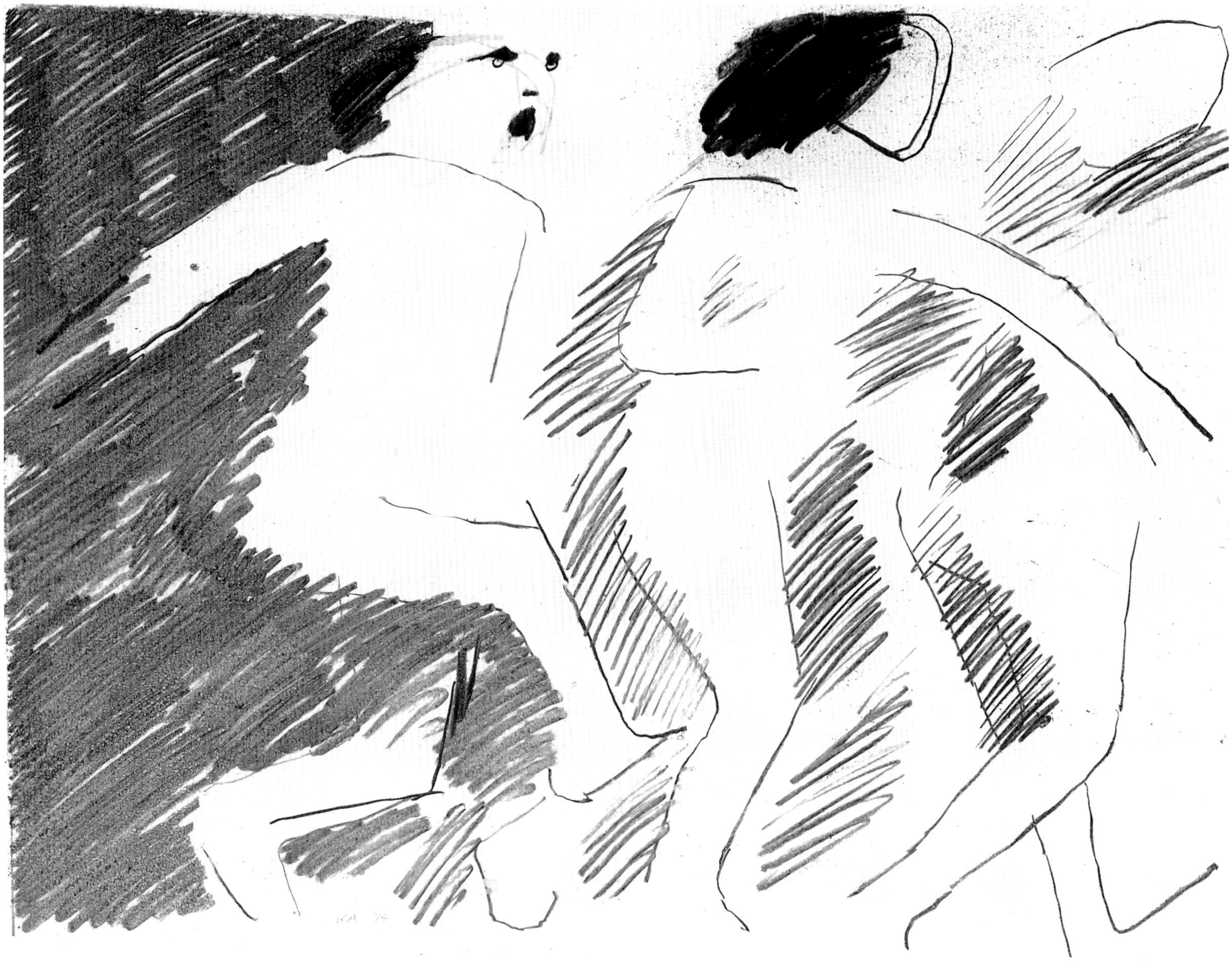

Catalogue of Sculpture

This list has been compiled from the artist's records and other sources. It is not complete, since the artist's output spans a period of fifty years and a number of pieces have disappeared or been destroyed. It is hoped that it provides as useful a list as is possible in the circumstances.

Page numbers in brackets indicate where in this volume a work is illustrated.

In all cases the largest dimension of a work is given: either height (H) or length (L).

KA1 **Angela Walker** (portrait head), plaster 1938, cast 1985
H 36 cm (14 in), bronze
(page 19)

KA2 **Standing Woman** 1947
H 62 cm (24 in), bronze

KA3 **Moon Figure** 1948
H 86 cm (34 in), plaster
(page 23)

KA4 **Moon Figure** 1948
H 86 cm (34 in), bronze
(page 24)

KA5 **Linked Figures** 1949, cast 1960
H 28 cm (11 in), bronze
(page 25)

KA6 **Two Linked Figures**, plaster 1949, cast 1985
H 104 cm (41 in), bronze

KA7 **People in the Wind** 1950
H 65.5 cm (25½ in), plaster
(page 29)

KA8 **People in the Wind** 1950
H 65.5 cm (25½ in), bronze
(page 28)

KA9 **People in the Wind** 1950
Two variations, one with arms at rear, one without arms at rear

KA10 **People in the Wind** (small version) 1950
H 23 cm (9 in), bronze

KA11 **People in the Wind** (small version 2) 1950
H 20 cm (8 in), bronze

KA12 **Standing Group** 1950
H 20 cm (8 in), bronze

KA13 **Linked Figures** 1951
H 99 cm (39 in), bronze
(page 27)

KA14 **Two Standing Figures** (small version) 1951
H 23 cm (9 in), bronze

KA15 **Family going for a Walk** 1951
H 74 cm (29 in), bronze
(page 31)

KA16 **Two Standing Figures** 1951
H 18 cm (7 in), bronze

KA17 **Two Standing Figures** 1951
Large version: plaster of large version since destroyed

KA18 **Walking Group** 1951
H 23 cm (9 in), bronze

KA19 **Standing Group** 1951
H 74 cm (29 in), bronze

KA20 **Family going for a Walk** (small version) 1952
H 23 cm (9 in), bronze

KA21 **Family going for a Walk** (small version 2) 1952
H 20 cm (8 in), bronze

KA22 **Flat Standing Figure** 1952
H 23cm (9 in), bronze

KA23 **Seated Group listening to Music** 1952
L 117 cm (46 in), bronze
(page 32)

KA24 **Man holding Shirt** 1952
H 20 cm (8 in), plaster

KA25 **People sitting** (large version) 1952
H 80 cm (31½ in), bronze

KA26 **Friends walking** 1952
H 56 cm (22 in), bronze
(page 33)

KA27 **Man with Arms Up** (small version) 1952
H c.24 cm (9½ in), unique bronze

KA28 **Standing Group 2** (large version) 1952
H 104.5 cm (41¼ in), bronze
(page 35)

KA29 **Standing Group 2** (small version) 1952
H 74 cm (29 in), bronze

KA30 **Man in a Coat** 1952
H 25 cm (10 in), bronze

KA31 **Children playing** 1953
L 42 cm (16½ in), bronze
(page 36)

KA32 **Standing Figure** (small version) 1953
H 13 cm (5 in), bronze

KA33 **Standing Figure (Life Study)** 1953
H 110 cm (43½ in), bronze
(page 37)

KA34 **Footballers**, plaster 1953, cast 1986
H 51 cm (20 in), resin
(page 74)

KA35 **Mother and Child** 1953
H 22 cm (8½ in), bronze

KA36 **Standing Figure** 1953
H 17 cm (6½ in), bronze

KA37 **Seated Figure** 1953
H 22 cm (8½ in), bronze

KA38 **Seated Figure** (version 2) 1953
Dimensions unknown, bronze

KA39 **Standing Group** 1953
H 152 cm (60 in), plaster

KA40 **Two Standing Figures** 1953
Dimensions unknown, unique plaster

KA41 **Figure with Coat** 1953, cast 1957
H 27 cm (10½ in), bronze

KA42 **Children by the Sea** 1953
H 44.5 cm (17½ in), bronze

KA43 **Standing Group** 1953
H 104.5 cm (41¼ in), bronze

KA44 **Standing Group** 1954
H 50 cm (19½ in), bronze

KA45 **Seated Figure** 1954
H 44 cm (17½ in), bronze

KA46 **Seated Group** 1952-4
H 80 cm (31½ in), bronze

KA47 **Reclining Figure** 1953-4
H 69 cm (27 in), bronze relief
(page 39)

KA48 **Square Figure** 1954
H 107 cm (42 in), bronze relief

KA49 **Seated Woman with Square Head** 1954
H 37 cm (14½ in), bronze

KA50 **Standing Figure** 1954
H 76 cm (30 in), bronze

KA51 **Standing Figure** 1954
H 49.5 cm (19½ in), bronze

KA52 **Several Standing Figures** 1954
Dimensions and media unknown

KA53 **Roly-poly** 1955
H 36 cm (14 in), bronze

KA54 **Seated Woman with Square Head** 1955
H 61 cm (24 in), bronze
(page 46)

KA55 **Standing Group** 1955
Dimensions unknown, bronze

KA56 **The Sentinels** 1955-6
H 114 cm (45 in), bronze
(page 53)

KA57 **Standing Woman** 1955
H 48 cm (19 in), bronze

KA58 **Standing Figure** 1955
H 71 cm (28 in), bronze

KA59 **The Seasons** 1956
H 86 cm (34 in), bronze (partly painted)
(page 45)

KA60 **Reclining Figure** 1956
L 43 cm (17 in), bronze

KA61 **Two Seated Figures (Sunbathers)** 1956
L 33 cm (13 in), bronze

KA62 **Model for Krefeld Monument** 1956
H 34 cm ($13\frac{1}{2}$ in), bronze
(pages 55, 56, 57)

KA63 **Standing Woman with Arms Sideways** 1956-7
H 42 cm ($16\frac{1}{2}$ in), bronze

KA64 **Standing Figure** 1956-7
H 122 cm (48 in), bronze
(page 48)

KA65 **Figure lying on its Side** (version 3) 1957
L 79 cm (31 in), bronze

KA66 **Figure lying on its Side** (version 4) 1957
L 118 cm ($46\frac{1}{2}$ in), bronze

KA67 **Figure lying on its Side** (version 5) 1957
L 84 cm (33 in), bronze
(page 47)

KA68 **Two Seated Figures** (large version) 1957
L 140 cm (55 in), bronze
(page 43)

KA69 **Two Seated Figures**
(small model with straight arm) 1957
L 38 cm (15 in), bronze

KA70 **Two Seated Figures**
(small model with arms crossed) 1957
L 43 cm (17 in), bronze

KA71 **Seated Woman** 1955-7
H 61 cm (24 in), bronze

KA72 **Two Seated Figures (Square)** 1957
L 30 cm (12 in), bronze

KA73 **Seated Figure with Arms Raised**
(small version) 1957
H 33 cm (13 in), bronze

KA74 **Seated Figure with Arms Raised**
(large version) 1957
H 122 cm (48 in), bronze
(page 52)

KA75 **Two Striding Figures** (version 1) 1957
L 127 cm (50 in), bronze

KA76 **Two Striding Figures** (version 2) 1957
L 146 cm ($57\frac{1}{2}$ in), bronze

KA77 **Model for Large Seated Group** 1957
L 38 cm (15 in), bronze

KA78 **Model for Diarchy** (small version) 1957
H 30cm (12 in), bronze

KA79 **Diarchy** 1957
H 174 cm ($68\frac{1}{2}$ in), bronze
(page 41)

KA80 **Sprawling Woman** (small version) 1957
H 67 cm ($26\frac{1}{2}$ in), bronze

KA81 **Sprawling Woman** (large version) 1957
L 258 cm ($101\frac{1}{2}$ in), bronze
(page 43)

KA82 **Square Seated Figures** 1957
L 30 cm (12 in), bronze

KA83 **Triarchy** (model) 1957
L 38 cm (15 in), bronze

KA84 **Girl without a Face** (small model) 1958-9
H 38 cm (15 in), bronze

KA85 **Girl without a Face** (large version) 1958-9
H 166 cm ($65\frac{1}{2}$ in), bronze
(page 49)

KA86 **Triarchy** 1958-60
L 247 cm ($97\frac{1}{4}$ in), bronze
(page 42)

KA86a **Mouton Sun** 1959-63
L 269 cm (106 in), bronze with gold leaf
(page 75)

KA87 **Standing Man** 1960
H 178 cm (70 in), bronze
(page 62)

KA88 **Figure on its Back** 1960
L 56 cm (22 in), bronze

KA89 **Small Torso** 1960
L 28 cm (11 in), bronze

KA90 **Two Standing Figures** 1960
H 57 cm ($22\frac{1}{2}$ in), bronze

KA91 **Children playing** (second model) 1960
Dimensions and medium unknown

KA92 **Balanced Figure** 1961
H 130 cm (51 in), bronze
(page 59)

KA93 **Wall Group** 1961
L 58 cm (23 in), bronze

KA94 **Guardians** 1961
H 97 cm (38 in), bronze

KA95 **The Visitors** 1961
H 58.5 cm (23 in), bronze

KA96 **Standing Figure** 1961
H 173 cm (68 in), bronze
(page 61)

KA97 **Little Monitor** 1961
L 38 cm (15 in), bronze

KA98 **Monitor** 1961
L 198 cm (78 in), bronze
(page 51)

KA99 **Playful Figure** 1961
H 24 cm ($9\frac{1}{2}$ in), bronze

KA100 **Kneeling Figure** 1961
H 53 cm (21 in), bronze

KA101 **Little Box Figure** 1961
H 30 cm (12 in), bronze

KA102 **Winged Figure** (version 1) 1961
L 51 cm (20 in), bronze

KA103 **Figure with its Arms Up** (version 2) 1961
H 61 cm (24 in), bronze

KA104 **Anvil** 1961
L 85 cm ($33\frac{1}{2}$ in), bronze

KA105 **Slab Figure** 1961
H 72 cm ($28\frac{1}{2}$ in), bronze
(page 58)

KA106 **Sibyl** (version 1) 1961
H 116 cm ($45\frac{1}{2}$ in), bronze

KA107 **Sibyl** (version 2) 1961
H 102 cm (40 in), bronze

KA108 **Sibyl** (version 3) 1961
H 103 cm ($40\frac{1}{2}$ in), bronze
(page 64)

KA109 **Prophet** 1961
H 163 cm (64 in), bronze

KA110 **Figure on its Back** (version 2) 1961
L 69 cm (27 in), bronze

KA111 **Figure on its Back** (large version) 1961
L 163 cm (64 in), bronze
(page 65)

KA112 **Sculpture No.105** 1961
H 74 cm (29 in), bronze

KA112a **Little Winged Figure,** plaster 1961, cast 1966
H 18 cm (7 in), aluminium

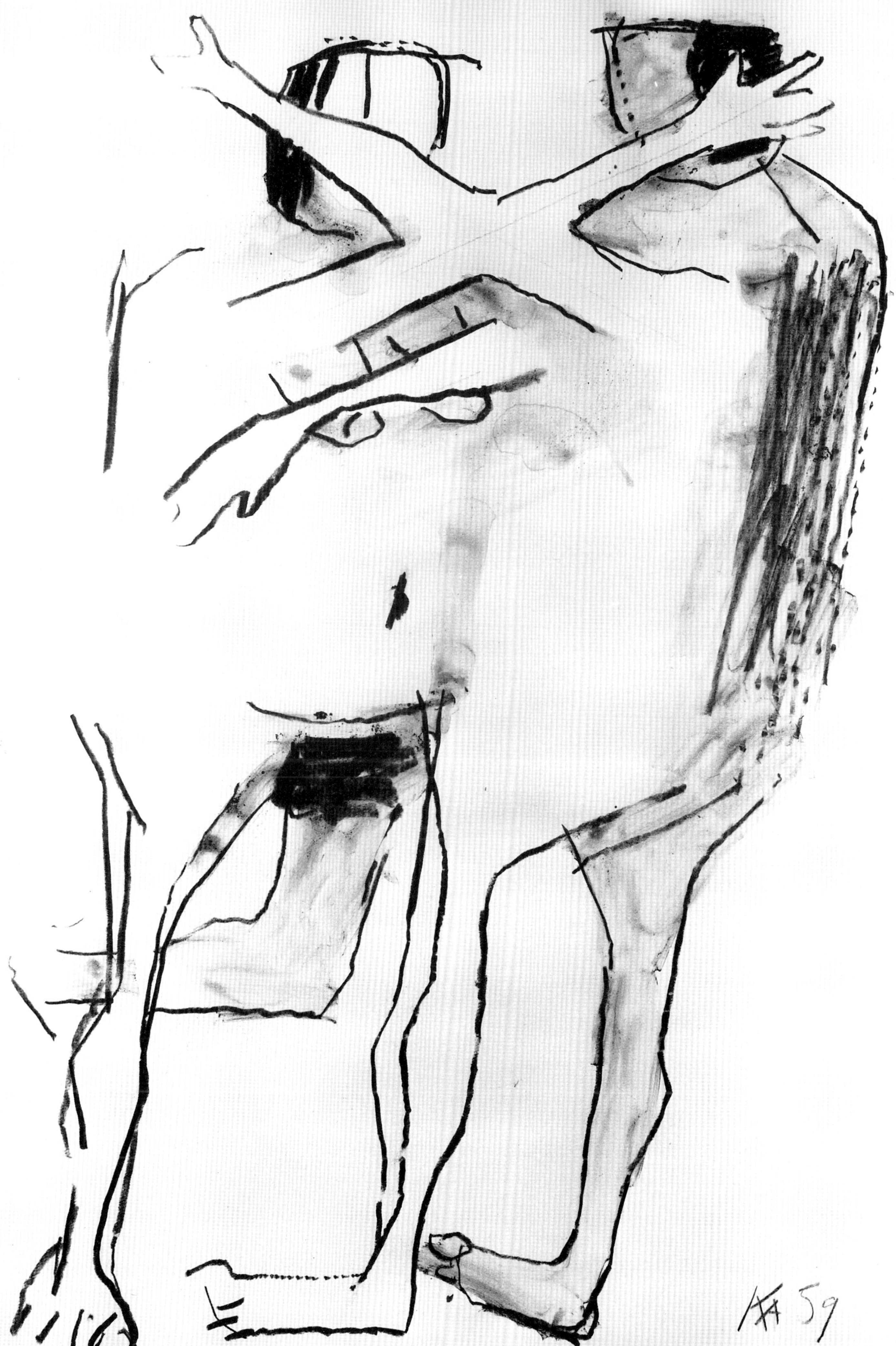

KA112b **Two Seated Figures,** plaster 1961, cast 1989
L 32 cm ($12\frac{1}{2}$ in), bronze

KA113 **Whistle** 1961-2
H 48 cm (19 in), bronze

KA114 **Prophet** (small version 1) 1962
H 36 cm (14 in), bronze

KA115 **Prophet** (small version 2) 1962
H 32 cm ($12\frac{1}{2}$ in), yellow bronze
(page 64)

KA116 **Figure on its Back** (flat version) 1962
L 81 cm (32 in), bronze

KA117 **Model for Large Work** (version A) 1962
L 41 cm (16 in), bronze

KA118 **Pandarus** (version 1) 1962
H 173 cm (68 in), aluminium

KA119 **Pandarus** (version 2) 1962
H 192 cm ($75\frac{1}{2}$ in), plaster model and bronze
(page 66)

KA120 **Pandarus** (version 3) 1963
H 61 cm (24 in), brass

KA121 **Pandarus** (version 4) 1963
H 56 cm (22 in), brass

KA122 **Pandarus** (version 5) 1963
H 67 cm ($26\frac{1}{2}$ in), brass

KA123 **Pandarus** (version 6) 1963
H 71 cm (28 in), brass

KA124 **Pandarus** (version 7) 1963
H 52 cm ($20\frac{1}{2}$ in), bronze

KA125 **Pandarus** (version 8) 1963
H 178 cm (70 in), brass
(pages 67, 69)

KA126 **Model for Large Work** (version B) 1963
L 88 cm ($34\frac{1}{2}$ in), bronze

KA127 **Model for Large Work** (version C) 1963
L 51 cm (20 in), bronze

KA127a **Mouton Variation** (small version 1) 1963
H 34.5 cm ($13\frac{1}{2}$ in), brass

KA128 **Small model with 6 flanges** 1963
H 34.5 cm ($13\frac{1}{2}$ in), brass, unique

KA129 **Small model with 5 flanges** 1963
H 33 cm (13 in), brass, unique

KA130 **Pagoda** (alternative title **Tower**) 1963
H 91.5 cm (36 in), brass

KA131 **Pandarus** (version 9) 1964
H 185 cm (73 in), brass
(pages 68, 69)

KA132 **Pandarus** (version 10),
plaster 1964, cast 1979
H 90 cm ($35\frac{1}{2}$ in), black bronze

KA133 **Pandarus** (version 11) 1964
H 224 cm (88 in), brass
(pages 66, 95)

KA133a **Mouton Variation** 1964
H 252 cm (99 in), brass
(page 65)

KA134 **Small model with funnel** (A) 1964
H 34.5 cm ($13\frac{1}{2}$ in), brass

KA135 **Screen with Folded Arms** (model) 1964
H 32 cm ($12\frac{1}{2}$ in), plaster

KA136 **Pandarus** (version 12) 1965
H 168 cm (66 in), bronze

KA137 **The Legend of Skadar** (version 1) 1965
second cast 1976
H 40.5 cm (16 in), bronze

KA138 **The Legend of Skadar** (version 2) 1965
H 56 cm (22 in), brass
(page 91)

KA139 **The Legend of Skadar** (version 3) 1965
H 43.5 cm (17 in), bronze
(page 92)

KA140 **The Legend of Skadar** (version 4) 1965
H 60.5 cm ($23\frac{3}{4}$ in), bronze
(page 93)

KA141 **The Legend of Skadar** (version 5) 1965
H 43 cm (17 in), bronze

KA142 **The Legend of Skadar** (version 6) 1965
H 41.5 cm ($16\frac{1}{4}$ in), bronze

KA143 **The Legend of Skadar** (version 7) 1965
H 21.5 cm ($8\frac{1}{2}$ in), brass

KA144 **The Legend of Skadar** (version 8) 1965
H 123 cm ($48\frac{1}{2}$ in), brass

KA145 **The Legend of Skadar** (version 9) 1965
H 126.5 cm ($49\frac{3}{4}$ in), brass

KA146 **Wall** (small model A), plaster 1965, cast 1978
H 20 cm (8 in), bronze and pewter

KA146a **Wall** (small model B) 1965
H 24 cm ($9\frac{1}{2}$ in), bronze

KA147 **Wall** (small model C) 1965
L 20.5 cm (8 in), plaster

KA147a **Wall** (small model D) 1965, second cast 1976
H 47 cm ($18\frac{1}{2}$ in), bronze

KA148 **Wall** 1965
H 190.5 cm (75 in), bronze
(pages 67, 69)

KA149 **The Bed** 1965
L 174 cm ($68\frac{1}{2}$ in), fibreglass

KA150 **The Bed** (small model A), first cast 1965,
second cast 1976
L 22 cm ($8\frac{1}{2}$ in), bronze

KA151 **The Bed** (small model B), first cast 1965,
second cast 1976
L 24 cm ($9\frac{1}{2}$ in), bronze

KA152 **The Forest** (small model A) 1965
H 35.5 cm (14 in), bronze

KA153 **The Forest** (small model B) 1965
H 35.5 cm (14 in), bronze

KA154 **The Forest** 1965
H 163 cm (64 in), bronze
(page 89)

KA155 **Figure on its Back** 1965, cast 1977
L 24 cm ($9\frac{1}{2}$ in), painted aluminium
(page 106)

KA156 **Eyes** (relief) 1966
H 104 cm (41 in), aluminium

KA157 **Pearly Gates** 1966
H *c.*91.5 cm (36 in), aluminium

KA158 **Tiger Tiger** 1966
H 218 cm ($85\frac{3}{4}$ in), cast and plate aluminium,
painted stripes
(pages 94, 95)

KA159 **Kneeling Woman** 1967
H 141 cm ($55\frac{1}{2}$ in), bronze
Destroyed

KA160 **Screen with Folded Arms** 1967
H 195.5 cm (77 in), nickel bronze
(page 98)

KA161 **Arm** (model), plaster 1967, cast 1986
L 32 cm ($12\frac{1}{2}$ in), nickel bronze

KA162 **Arm** (small model) 1967-8
L 29 cm ($11\frac{1}{2}$ in), bronze

KA163 **Arm** 1967-8
H 386 cm (152 in), resin and fibreglass
(paint-sprayed)
(pages 76, 77, 101 and front of jacket)

KA164 **Screen** 1967-8
L 195 cm (77 in), painted aluminium
(page 98)

KA165 **The Bed** (version 3) 1968
H 50 cm ($19\frac{1}{2}$ in), aluminium

KA166 **Table A** 1968
H 152 cm (60 in), resin

KA167 **Table B** 1968
H 153 cm (60 in), resin

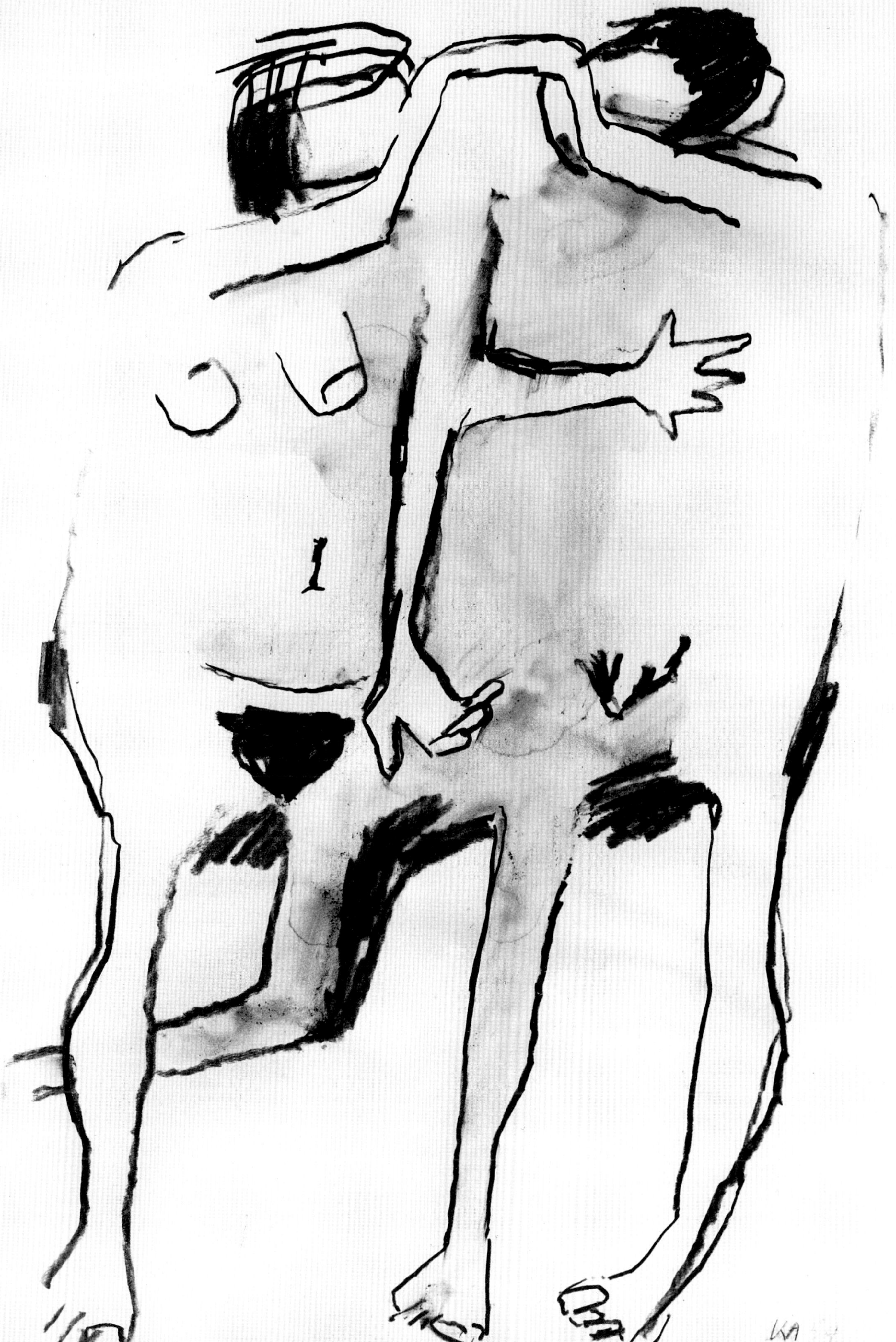

KA168 **Table C** 1968
H 153 cm (60 in), resin

KA169 **Table D** 1968
H 186 cm (73 in), resin

KA170 **Table E** 1969
H 183 cm (72 in), aluminium

KA171 **Table F** 1969
H 170 cm (67 in), aluminium

KA172 **Both Arms** 1969
H 232 cm ($91\frac{1}{2}$ in), bronze
(page 78)

KA173 **Model for Both Arms** 1969-72
H 24 cm ($9\frac{1}{2}$ in), bronze

KA174 **Angle Figure with Photos** 1969
H 137 cm (54 in), wood and bromide paper

KA175 **Big Doll** 1969
H 183 cm (72 in), resin and wood
(pages 102, 103)

KA176 **Model for Table E** 1969
H 27.3 cm ($10\frac{3}{4}$ in), brass and stove enamel

KA177 **Small Table with Arms and Eyes** 1970
H 28.5 cm ($11\frac{1}{4}$ in), wood and plaster

KA178 **Small Table with Flat Head** 1970
H 19.7 cm ($7\frac{3}{4}$ in), wood and plaster

KA179 **Design for a Multiple Small Screen** 1970
H 32.4 cm ($12\frac{3}{4}$ in), card and bromide paper

KA180 **Sculptural Screen** (version 1) 1970-1
H 211 cm (83 in), wood and bromide paper

KA181 **Sculptural Screen** (version 2) 1970-3
H 211 cm (83 in), wood and bromide paper

KA182 **Small folding Screen** 1971
H 38.7 cm ($15\frac{1}{4}$ in), card and bromide paper

KA183 **Folding Screen** 1971
H 182.9 cm (72 in), plywood, foam core and bromide paper
Eight panels, each 47 cm ($18\frac{1}{2}$ in) wide
(page 111 and back of jacket)

KA184 **Table G** 1971
H 170 cm (67 in), wood
(page 102)

KA185 **Table H** (with round arms) 1971
H 152 cm (60 in), wood, plaster and bromide paper
(pages 102, 110)

KA186 **Table H** (with flat arms) 1971
H 152 cm (60 in), aluminium

KA187 **Face** (with screenprint) 1971
H 70 cm ($27\frac{1}{2}$ in), wood and bromide paper
(Several versions)
(page 112)

KA188 **L-shaped Model with Legs Inside** 1971
H 61 cm (24 in), plywood and bromide paper

KA189 **L-shaped Model with Legs Outside** 1971
H 62.2 cm ($24\frac{1}{2}$ in), plywood and bromide paper

KA190 **Design for a Wilderness No.1** 1971
L 44 cm ($17\frac{1}{2}$ in), bronze
(page 117)

KA191 **Design for a Wilderness No.2** 1971
H 33 cm (13 in), bronze

KA192 **Design for a Wilderness No.3** 1971 cast 1972
L 38 cm (15 in), wood and plaster

KA193 **Design for a Wilderness No.4** 1972
L 43 cm (17 in), bronze

KA194 **Bernadette going to Wales** 1972
L 36cm ($14\frac{1}{4}$ in), aluminium with printed image both sides
(page 117)

KA195 **Children** 1972
L 17 cm ($6\frac{1}{2}$ in), cast in gold for deposit in bank

KA196 **Little L-shaped Screen** 1972
H 22 cm ($8\frac{1}{2}$ in), bronze

KA197 **Crouching Figure** 1972
L 19 cm ($7\frac{1}{2}$ in), aluminium

KA198 **Flat Figure** (extended legs front, arms back) 1972
H 135 cm (53 in), wood, plaster and bromide paper

KA199 **Single Figure with Drawing** 1972
H 51 cm (20 in), enamelled aluminium and screenprinted plaster

KA200 **Two Figures with Drawing** 1972
H 38 cm (15 in), enamelled aluminium and screenprinted plaster
(page 120)

KA201 **Figure with Clouds** 1972
H 39 cm ($15\frac{1}{2}$ in), enamelled aluminium and screenprinted plaster

KA202 **Figure against a Wall** 1973
H 28 cm (11 in), plaster

KA202a **Wallflower** 1973-80
H 23 cm (9 in), silver multiple

KA203 **Nottingham Group** 1973
H 34 cm ($13\frac{1}{2}$ in), aluminium
(page 114)

KA203a **Nottingham Screen** 1973
L 275 cm ($108\frac{1}{4}$ in), plywood, foam core and bromide paper
Five panels
(page 113)

KA204 **Children**, plaster 1973, cast 1977
H/L 18 cm (7 in), bronze

KA205 **Six Arms** 1973
H 41 cm (16 in), bronze

KA206 **Scurrying Figures,** plaster 1974, cast 1980
L 47 cm ($18\frac{1}{2}$ in), bronze

KA207 **Girl in a Striped Skirt** 1974
H 42 cm ($16\frac{1}{2}$ in), aluminium sprayed with white paint, with drawing

KA208 **How many Miles to Babylon?** 1974
H 57 cm ($22\frac{1}{2}$ in), bronze
(page 116)

KA209 **July Figure** 1975
H 77 cm ($30\frac{1}{2}$ in), bronze
(page 118)

KA210 **Oak Tree** 1977
H 27 cm ($10\frac{1}{2}$ in), bronze

KA211 **Single Oak Tree** (version A) 1977
H 44 cm ($17\frac{1}{2}$ in), bronze

KA212 **Single Oak Tree** (version B) 1977
H 50 cm ($19\frac{1}{2}$ in), bronze

KA213 **Single Oak Tree** (version C) 1977
H 46 cm (18 in), bronze

KA214 **Single Oak Tree** (version E) 1977
H 43 cm (17 in), bronze

KA215 **Fleeing Figure** 1977
H 66 cm (26 in), bronze

KA216 **Fleeing Figure** 1977
L 283 cm (111 in), cast and plate aluminium
(page 129)

KA217 **Milton Keynes Project** 1977
H 39 cm ($15\frac{1}{2}$ in), bronze and stainless steel

KA218 **Three Trees** 1977
L 56 cm (22 in), yellow bronze

KA219 **Single Oak** (with three crowns) 1977
H 27 cm ($10\frac{1}{2}$ in), bronze

KA220 **Single Oak** (with three crowns) 1977-9
H 27 cm ($10\frac{1}{2}$ in), bronze with green patina

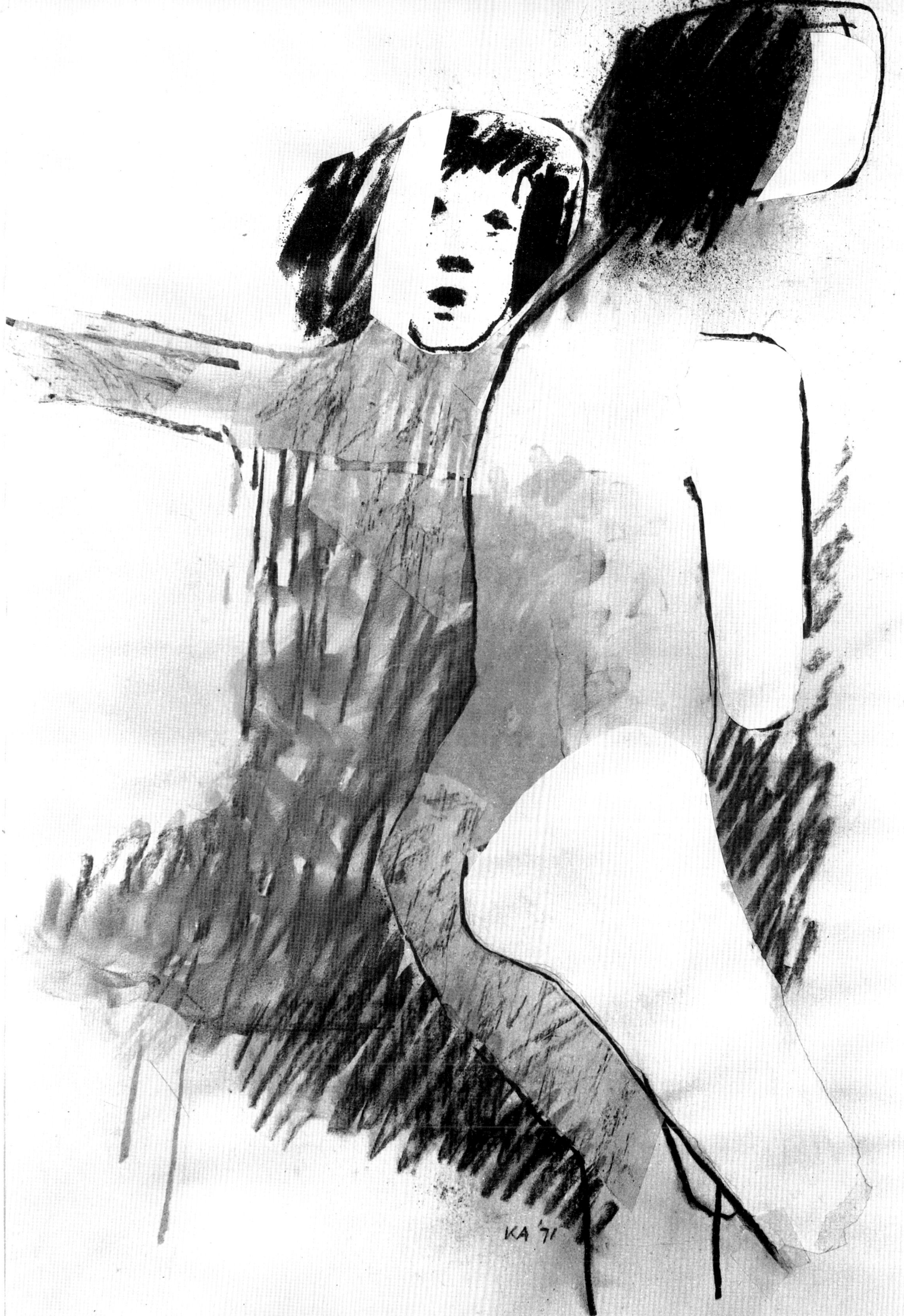
KA '71

KA221 **Oak Tree** 1978
H 27 cm ($10\frac{1}{2}$ in), bronze

KA222 **Milton Keynes model** 1978-9
H 51 cm (20 in), bronze and stainless steel

KA223 **Monument or Memorial** 1970s
H 50 cm ($19\frac{3}{4}$ in), aluminium
(page 121)

KA224 **July Figure 2** 1979
H 86 cm (34 in), bronze
(page 119)

KA225 **Hollow Oak 2** 1979
H 64 cm (25 in), bronze

KA226 **Oak** 1979
H 38 cm (15 in), bronze

KA227 **Hollow Oak 3** (1979)
H 37 cm ($14\frac{1}{2}$ in), bronze

KA228 **Oak** 1979
H 46 cm (18 in), bronze

KA229 **Oak** (thick trunk) 1979
H 46 cm (18 in), bronze

KA230 **Hollow Oak 4** 1979
H 56 cm (22 in), bronze

KA231 **Oak** (single trunk) 1979
H 44 cm (17 in), bronze

KA232 **Oak** (with three crowns) 1979
H 30 cm (12 in), bronze

KA233 **Single Oak** (four clusters) 1979
H 25 cm (10 in), green bronze

KA234 **Oak** (three clusters) 1979
H 36 cm (14 in), bronze with green
(page 122)

KA235 **Single Oak** (canopy) 1979
H 46 cm (18 in), bronze with green
(page 122)

KA236 **Single Oak** (canopy filigree) 1979
H 97 cm (38 in), bronze with green

KA237 **Tall Oak** 1979-80
H 72 cm ($28\frac{1}{2}$ in), bronze
(page 122)

KA238 **Tall Oak** (trunk) 1980
H 61 cm (24 in), bronze

KA239 **Tall Oak** 1980
H 62 cm ($24\frac{1}{2}$ in), bronze
(page 122)

KA240 **July Figure 3** 1980
H 91 cm (36 in), bronze
(page 131)

KA241 **Tall Oak** (nobbles) 1980-1
H 61 cm (24 in), bronze
(page 122)

KA242 **Children's Oak** 1981
H 52 cm ($20\frac{1}{2}$ in), bronze

KA243 **Oak** 1981
H 47 cm ($18\frac{1}{2}$ in), bronze

KA244 **Standing Figure** 1981
H 22 cm ($8\frac{1}{2}$ in), bronze

KA245 **Chair I** 1981
H 46 cm (18 in), bronze

KA246 **Chair II** 1981
H 46 cm (18 in), bronze

KA247 **Chair III** 1981
H 57 cm ($22\frac{1}{2}$ in), bronze

KA248 **July Figure 4** 1982
H 88 cm ($34\frac{1}{2}$ in), bronze
(page 132)

KA249 **Rose-red City** (version I) 1982
L 42 cm ($16\frac{1}{2}$ in), bronze
(page 79)

KA250 **Rose-red City** (version II) 1982
L 42 cm ($16\frac{1}{2}$ in), bronze
(page 133)

KA251 **Girl without a Face** (version 2) 1982
H 74 cm (29 in), bronze and enamel with painted stripes
(page 130)

KA252 **Arm (Arch)** 1982
H 58 cm (23 in), German silver

KA253 **Little Arm (Arch)** 1982
H 22 cm ($8\frac{1}{2}$ in), German silver

KA254 **Jesus and Two Angels** 1982
H 15-18 cm (6-7 in), bronze

KA255 **Little Fort** 1982
L 13 cm (5 in), bronze

KA256 **Green Park, Piccadilly** (version 1) 1983
H 42 cm ($16\frac{1}{2}$ in), bronze

KA257 **Green Park, Piccadilly** (version 2) 1983
H 39 cm ($15\frac{1}{2}$ in), bronze

KA258 **Return to Eden** (model) 1983
L 48 cm (19 in), plaster
(page 135)

KA259 **Chair** 1983-91
H 152 cm (60 in), bronze
(pages 126, 127)

KA260 **Alice through the Looking Glass** 1984
H 19 cm ($7\frac{1}{2}$ in), nickel bronze

KA261 **Richmond Oak** (for Brasilia) 1985
H 300 cm (118 in), black and green bronze
(pages 82, 83, 124)

KA262 **Garden Game** (model), plaster 1985, cast 1988
H 43 cm (17 in), nickel bronze

KA263 **Richmond Oak** 1986
H 82 cm (32 in), bronze

KA264 **Blasted Oak** 1986
H 79 cm (31 in), bronze, patinated grey and green, with black interior
(page 125)

KA265 **Garden Game** 1988
L 274 cm (108 in), resin (in seven pieces)

KA266 **Return to Eden** 1988-9
L 230 cm ($90\frac{1}{2}$ in), resin and screenprint on aluminium

KA267 **Isolated Seated Figures** (model) 1990
L 55 cm ($21\frac{1}{2}$ in), wood and plaster
(page 134)

KA268 **L-shaped Screen** 1991
H 180 cm (71 in), plate and cast aluminium
(pages 86, 87)

KA269 **The Dagda** (model) 1992
H 27 cm ($10\frac{1}{2}$ in), plaster

KA270 **The Dagda** 1992-6
H 198 cm (78 in), aluminium and beech wood
(pages 88, 138)

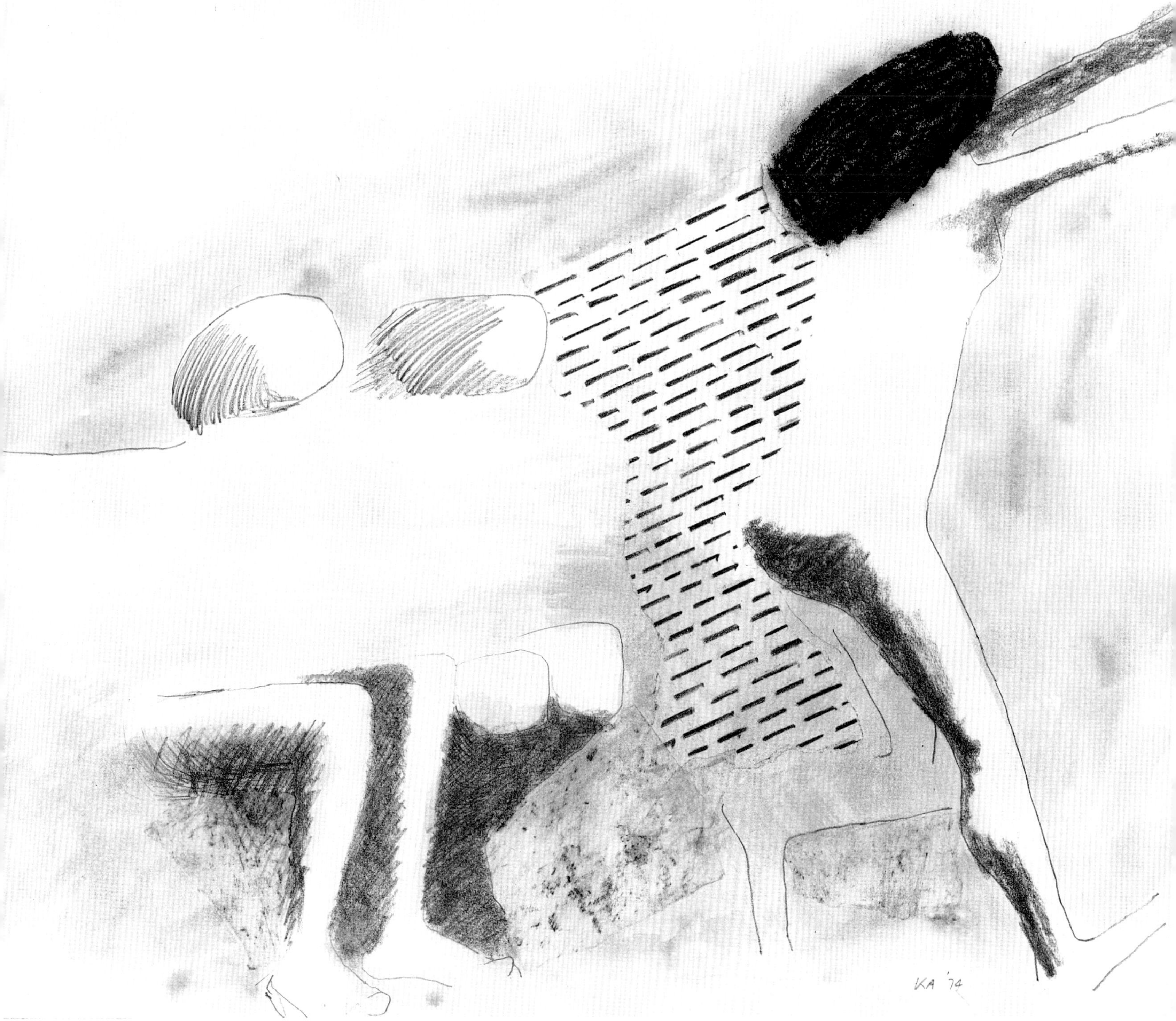
KA '74

Biography

1916	Born Leeds July 18
1933-37	Leeds College of Art
1937-39	Slade School of Fine Art, London
1939-46	Served in the Army
1946-56	Head of Sculpture, Bath Academy of Art, Corsham
1953-55	Gregory Fellow in Sculpture, Leeds University
1956	First Prize, International War Memorial Competition, Krefeld, West Germany
1958	David E. Bright Foundation Award, Venice Biennale
1964	Visiting Professor, University of Caracas, Venezuela
1967-69	Berlin Artists' Programme Fellowship, West Germany
1969	Awarded CBE
1970	Visiting Professor, Boston University, Massachusetts
1974-79	Visiting Tutor, Royal College of Art, London

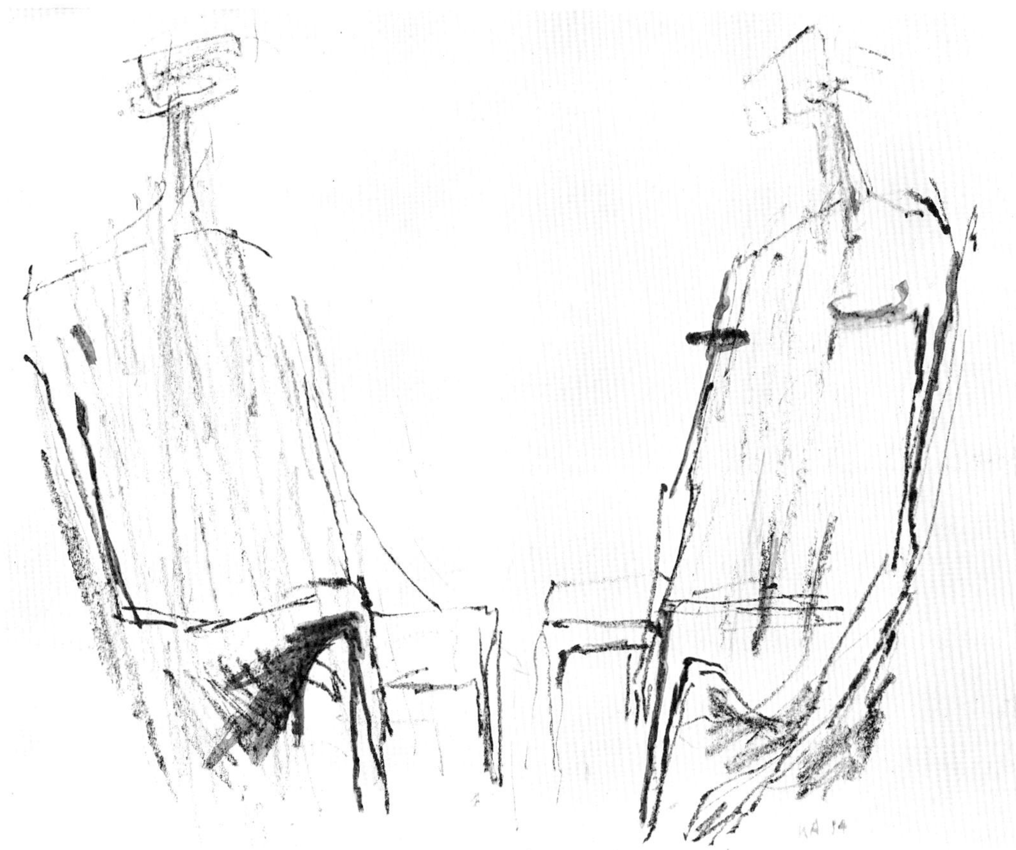

One-man Exhibitions

1952-57 Various exhibitions at Gimpel Fils, London
1954-56 Various exhibitions at Bertha Schaefer Gallery, New York
1958 Paul Rosenberg & Co, New York
Venice Biennale (with William Scott and S. W. Hayter), subsequently toured in 1958-9 by British Council to Musée National d'Art Moderne, Paris, Wallraf-Richartz Museum, Cologne, Palais des Beaux-Arts, Brussels, Kunsthaus, Zürich and Boymans Museum, Rotterdam
1959 *Retrospective*, Whitechapel Art Gallery, London
1960 Kestner-Gesellschaft, Hanover (with Chadwick, touring Europe and Japan)
1962 Paul Rosenberg & Co, New York
Marlborough Fine Art, London
Galerija Suvremene Umjetnosti, Zagreb
1963 Galerie Charles Lienhard, Zürich
Galerie Wilhelm Grosshennig, Düsseldorf
Galleria Blu, Milan
1965 Arnolfini Gallery, Bristol
Marlborough Fine Art, London
1972 Arts Council exhibition (touring 10 British cities)
1974 *Kenneth Armitage: Drawings*, Hester van Royen Gallery, London
Gallery Kasahara, Osaka and Tokyo
1975 New Art Centre, London
1978 Fuji Television Gallery, Tokyo
Galerie Humanité, Nagoya
Gallery Kasahara, Osaka
1980 Gimpel Fils, London
1981 Stoke-on-Trent City Museum and Art Gallery
1982 Sala Mendoza, Caracas
Taranman, London
1985 *Retrospective*, Artcurial, Paris
1996-97 *Kenneth Armitage: 80th Birthday Survey*, Yorkshire Sculpture Park
1996 *Works on Paper*, Friends Room, Royal Academy of Arts, London
1997 *Works on Paper*, Victoria City Art Gallery, Bath

Selected Group Exhibitions

1952 Venice Biennale (with Adams, Butler, Chadwick, Clarke, Meadows, Paolozzi, Turnbull)
1953 2nd Open Air Sculpture Exhibition, Middelheim Sculpture Park, Antwerp
1954 *Documenta I*, Kassel, Germany
1955 *The New Decade*, Museum of Modern Art, New York
1957 São Paulo Bienal, Brazil
1958 5th International Drawing and Engraving Exhibition, Lugano
1959 *New Images of Man*, Museum of Modern Art, New York
Documenta II, Kassel, Germany
1960 *International Sculpture Exhibition*, di Tella Institute, Buenos Aires
1962 *British Sculpture Today*, San Francisco Museum of Art (and USA tour)
1964 *Contemporary British Painting and Sculpture*, Albright-Knox Art Gallery, Buffalo, New York
Documenta III, Kassel, Germany
54-64: Painting and Sculpture of a Decade, organised by the Calouste Gulbenkian Foundation at the Tate Gallery, London
1965 *British Sculpture in the Sixties*, Tate Gallery, London
1966 *Sculpture in the Open Air*, Battersea Park, London
1967 International Sculpture Exhibition, Guggenheim Museum, New York
1972 *British Sculptors '72*, Royal Academy of Arts, London
1981 *British Sculpture in the Twentieth Century*, Whitechapel Art Gallery, London
1988 *World Expo 88*, Brisbane, Australia
1988 *Seoul Olympiad of Art*, Korea
1993 Chelsea Harbour Sculpture Exhibition, London
1995/96 Summer Exhibition, Royal Academy of Arts, London
1995/96 New Art Centre Sculpture Garden, Salisbury

Public Collections

Austria: Museum des 20. Jahrhunderts, Vienna
Australia: City Hall, Brisbane; National Gallery of Victoria, Melbourne
Belgium: Middelheim Sculpture Park, Antwerp; Musée Royale des Beaux-Arts, Brussels
France: Château Mouton Rothschild, Bordeaux; Musée National d'Art Moderne, Paris
Finland: National Gallery, Helsinki
Germany: Berlin Opera House; Kunsthalle, Hamburg; Sammlung Spengel, Hanover; Kunstmuseum Duisburg; Nationalgalerie, Berlin; Städtische Galerie, Hanover; Von-der-Heydt Museum, Wuppertal
Israel: Billy Rose Sculpture Garden, Israel Museum, Jerusalem
Italy: Galleria Nazionale d'Arte Moderna, Rome; Municipal Museum of Modern Arts, Carrara; Museo Civico, Turin; Peggy Guggenheim Museum, Venice
Japan: Civic Commission, Yokohama; Hakone Open Air Sculpture Museum; Museum of Modern Art, Hyogo; National Museum of Art, Osaka
Korea: Seoul Olympic National Park
Mexico: Museo Rufino Tamayo, Mexico City
Netherlands: Rijksmuseum Kröller-Müller, Otterlo
Sweden: Arkiv for Decorativ Kunst, Lund University; Konstmuseet, Gothenburg
Switzerland: Villa Ciani, Lugano
United Kingdom: Arts Council of England, London; Bristol City Museum & Art Gallery; British Council, London; Ferens Art Gallery, Hull; Fitzwilliam Museum, Cambridge; Government Art Collection, London; Laing Art Gallery, Newcastle-upon-Tyne; Leeds City Art Gallery; Royal Academy of Arts, London; Royal Marines, Dorset; Tate Gallery, London; Ulster Museum, Belfast; University of Nottingham; Victoria & Albert Museum, London; Whitworth Art Gallery, Manchester
USA: Albright-Knox Art Gallery, Buffalo, New York; Brooklyn Museum, New York; Des Moines Institute of Fine Arts, Iowa; Hirshhorn Museum and Sculpture Garden, Washington DC; The Museum of Modern Art, New York; Museum of Modern Art, Philadelphia; University of Michigan, Ann Arbor; University of Nebraska, Lincoln; Wichita State University, Kansas
Venezuela: City Metro, Caracas; Museo de Bellas Artes, Caracas

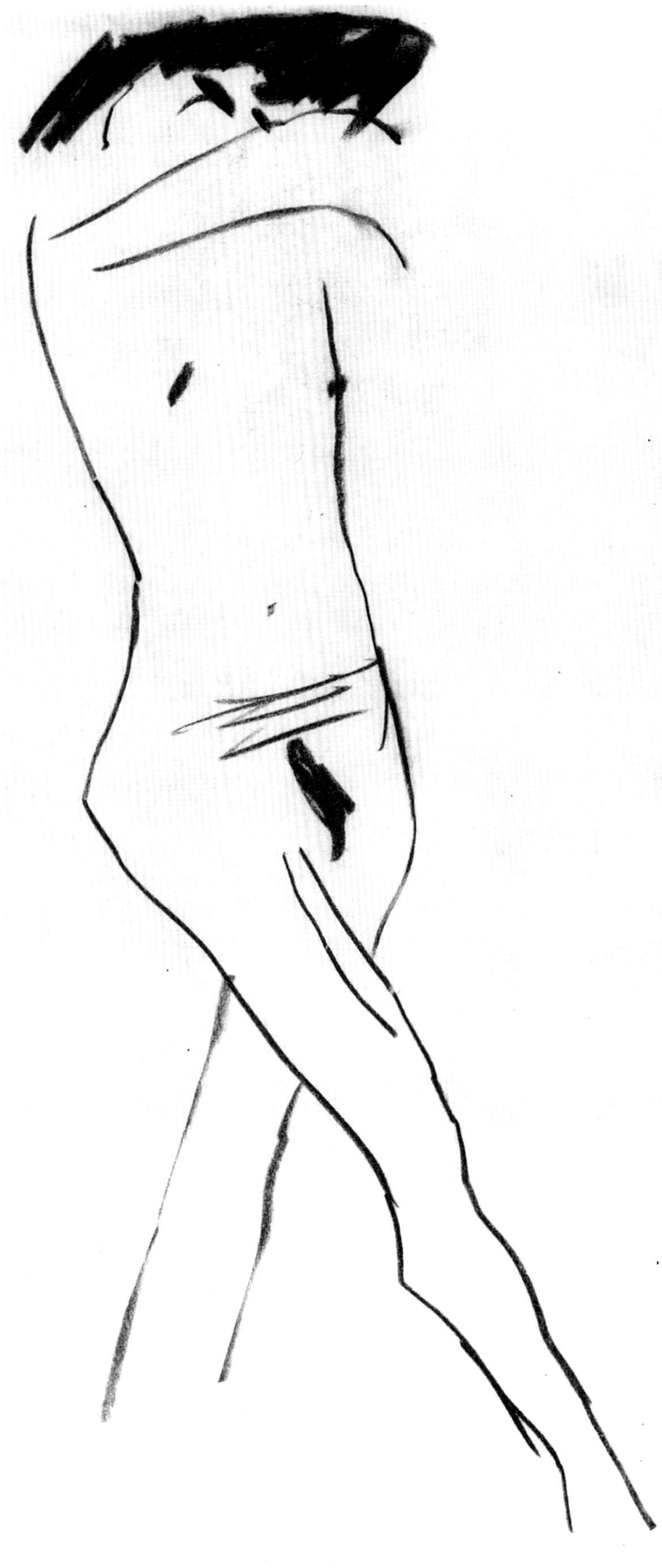

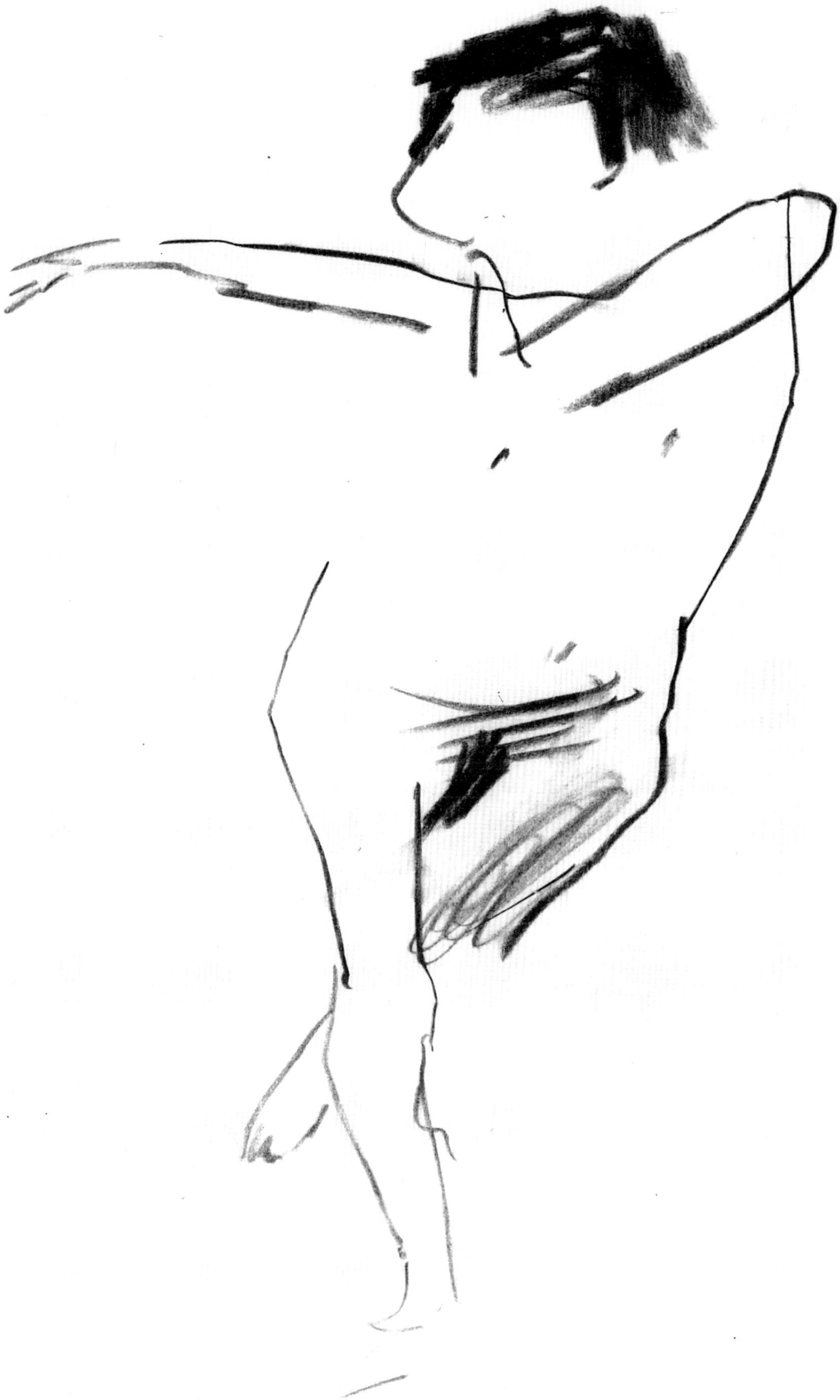

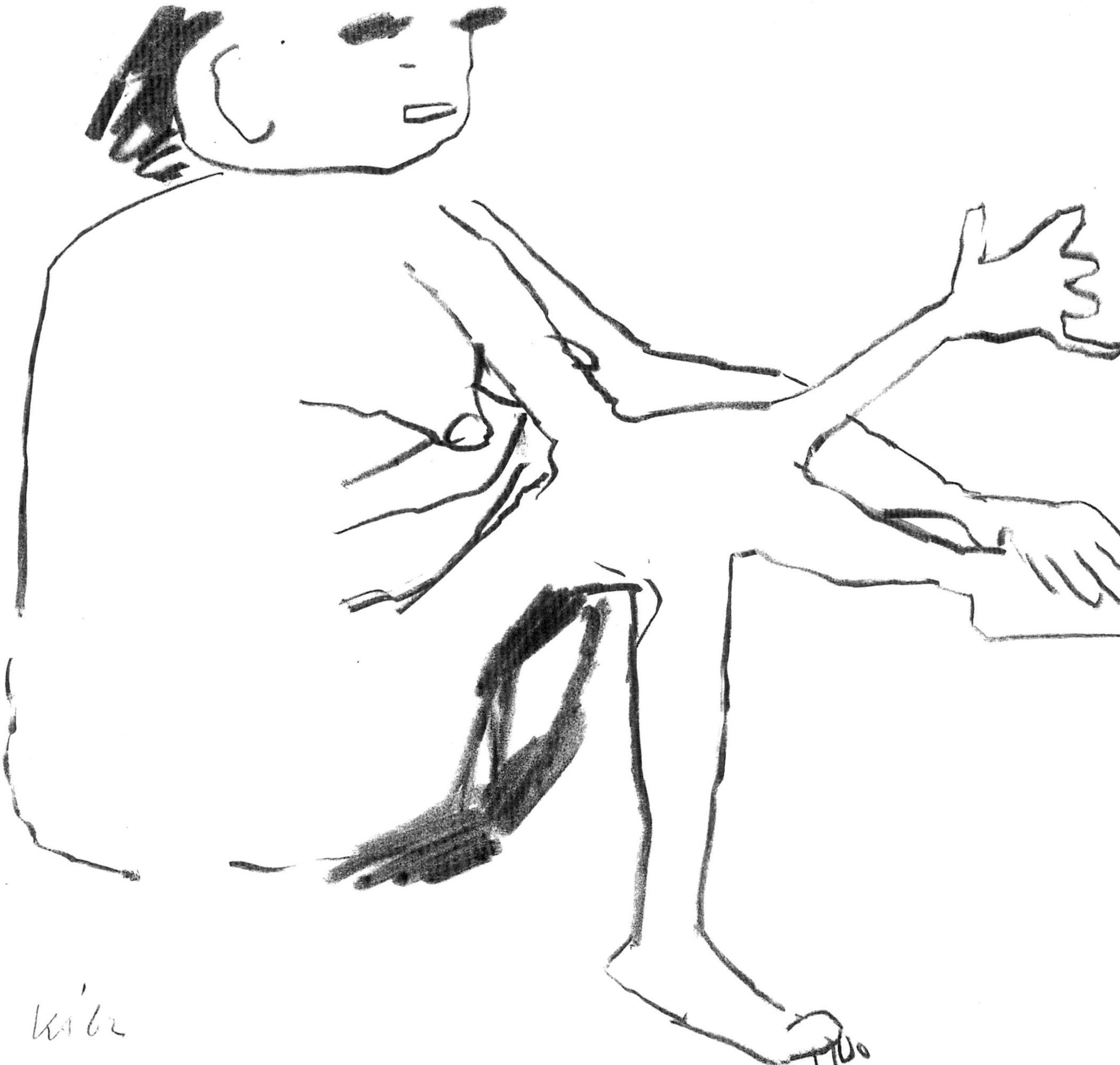

Selected Bibliography

Books and Articles

1955 Kenneth Armitage, statement in the catalogue of the exhibition *The New Decade*, Museum of Modern Art, New York.

1957 Pierre Rouve, 'Armitage or the Anti-Draughtsman', *Arts News & Review*, London, October.

1957 David Sylvester, 'Kenneth Armitage', *New Statesman*, London, 26 October.

1957 Patrick Heron, 'Kenneth Armitage', *Arts*, New York, December.

1958 Herbert Read, foreword in the catalogue of the British Council touring exhibition *Armitage, Hayter, Scott.*

1958 Alan Bowness, *Four English Artists*. Catalogue of the exhibition at Galleria Blu, Milan.

1959 Kenneth Armitage, statement in the catalogue of the exhibition *New Images of Man*, Museum of Modern Art, New York.

1959 Alan Bowness, *Kenneth Armitage*. Catalogue of the exhibition at the Whitechapel Art Gallery, London.

1959 Alan Bowness, 'Armitage's retrospective at Whitechapel', *Arts*, New York, November.

1960 Roland Penrose, *Kenneth Armitage*. Artists of Our Time, Vol.VII, Bodensee-Verlag, Amriswil, Switzerland.

1962 Norbert Lynton, *Kenneth Armitage*. Art in Progress series, Methuen, London.

1963 Alan Bowness, 'Kenneth Armitage: His recent sculpture', *Motif* No.11.

1964 Warren Forma (ed.), *Five British Sculptors (Work and Talk)*. Grossman Publishers, New York.

1972-3 Alan Bowness, introduction to *Kenneth Armitage*. Catalogue of the Arts Council touring exhibition.

1972-3 Kenneth Armitage, statement in *Kenneth Armitage*. Catalogue of the Arts Council touring exhibition.

1978 Roland Penrose, foreword to *Kenneth Armitage*. Catalogue of the Gallery Kasahara touring exhibition.

1978 Kenneth Armitage, 'Notes on the Oak Trees', in *Kenneth Armitage*. Catalogue of the Gallery Kasahara touring exhibition.

1979 John Glaves-Smith, 'Kenneth Armitage', *Artscribe* No.16.

1980 John McEwen, introduction to *Kenneth Armitage: Richmond Oaks and other Works*. Catalogue of the Gimpel Fils exhibition.

1980 Roger Berthoud, 'Kenneth Armitage: Sculptural vigour even in neglect', *The Times*, 29 October.

1981 John Glaves-Smith, 'Sculpture in the 1940s and 1950s – the Form and the Language', in *British Sculpture in the Twentieth Century*, Whitechapel Art Gallery.

1982 Constance Glenn, 'A Conversation with Kenneth Armitage', *The Architectural Digest*, March.

1982 Stephen Duncan, 'Figurative Sculpture of the Fifties', *Artscribe* No.35, June.

1982 John McEwen and Roland Penrose, introductions to the catalogue of the Taranman exhibition.

1985 John McEwen, introduction to the catalogue of the Artcurial exhibition.

1996 John McEwen, foreword to *Kenneth Armitage: 80th Birthday Tribute*. Catalogue of the Yorkshire Sculpture Park exhibition.

Film

1960 John Read, *Kenneth Armitage*. One of six BBC Television films in a series *The Artist Speaks*.

1963 Hans Neumann, *Armitage Expedition to Kanarakuni*. Equatorial Rain Forests of Southern Venezuela.

1964 Warren Forma, *Five British Sculptors Work and Talk*, USA.

1969 *Armitage in Berlin*, a Facta film for television. Westdeutsche Rundfunk.

Acknowledgements

A list of public collections containing works by the artist is given on page 153. Some of the illustrations reproduce works to be found in public collections, including the following:

Page 31 *Family going for a Walk*
The Museum of Modern Art, New York
(acquired through the Lillie P. Bliss Bequest)
Sammlung Spengel, Hanover

Page 35 *Standing Group 2* (large version)
Victoria & Albert Museum, London

Page 37 *Standing Figure* (Life Study)
Hirshhorn Museum and Sculpture Garden, Smithsonian Institution, Washington
(gift of Joseph H. Hirshhorn, 1966)

Page 39 *Reclining Figure*
Gift to the Royal Academy of Arts, London, 1995

Page 41 *Diarchy*
Tate Gallery, London
The Museum of Modern Art, New York

Page 47 *Figure lying on its Side* (version 5)
Arts Council Collection, Hayward Gallery, London

Page 58 *Slab Figure*
British Council, London

Page 64 *Sybil* (version 3)
Tate Gallery, London

Page 66 *Pandarus* (version 2)
On loan to Margam Sculpture Park

Page 78 *Both Arms*
Hakone Open Air Sculpture Museum

Page 113 *Nottingham Screen*
Nottingham University Library

Page 124 *Richmond Oak*
Government Art Collection (British Embassy in Brasilia)

Photographic Credits

Sue Adler *frontispiece*, p.138
Christof Bantzer p.99
Theo Bergstrom p.94
Corry Bevington pp.107, 110
Graham Bishop/Corry Bevington pp.38, 120
Ronald Chapman p.51
Nobby Clark p.119
Harriet Crowder pp.58, 59,64,66, 79, 93, 114, 129, 131(2), 132(2)
Josceline Dimbleby p.104
Sandra Flett pp.46, 55, 56, 57
Giacomelli, Venice p.45
John Gill p.76
Gimpel Fils p.122
Douglas Glass, © J. C. C. Glass p.105
Denis E. Harvey p.82
Lidbrooke pp.33, 47, 52, 53
Roger Mayne pp.22, 40
Rory McEwen p.97
© Lee Miller Archives p.44
Hans Neumann p.73
Frieda Ollamans p.17
Zandria Pauncefort p.136
RAF Film Production Unit, Air Ministry p.54
Stephen Spender p.75
Rodney Todd-White p.88
Dorothea von Haeften p.98
Erhard Wehrmann pp.48, 69, 91, 95
Rodney Wright-Watson pp.108, 109, 115

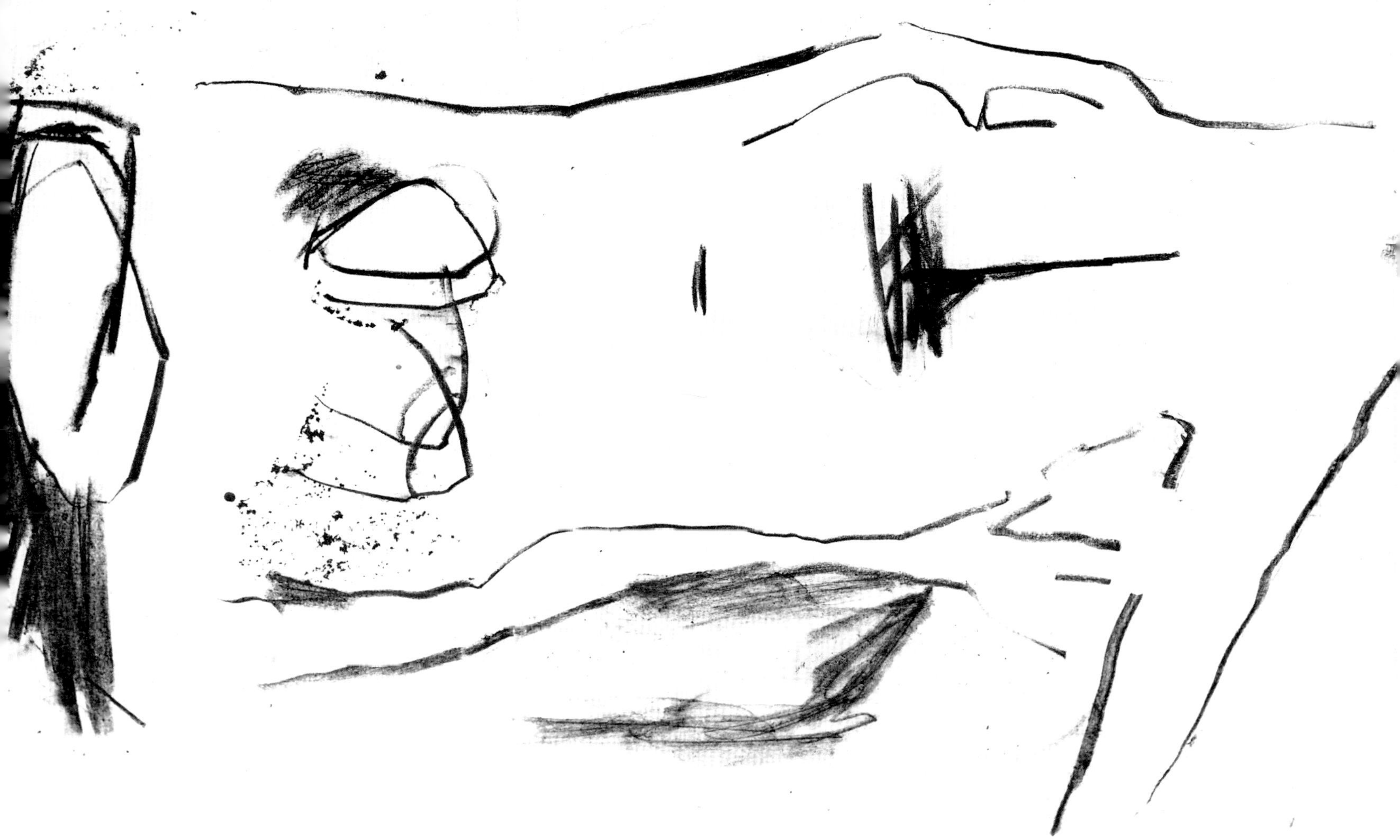

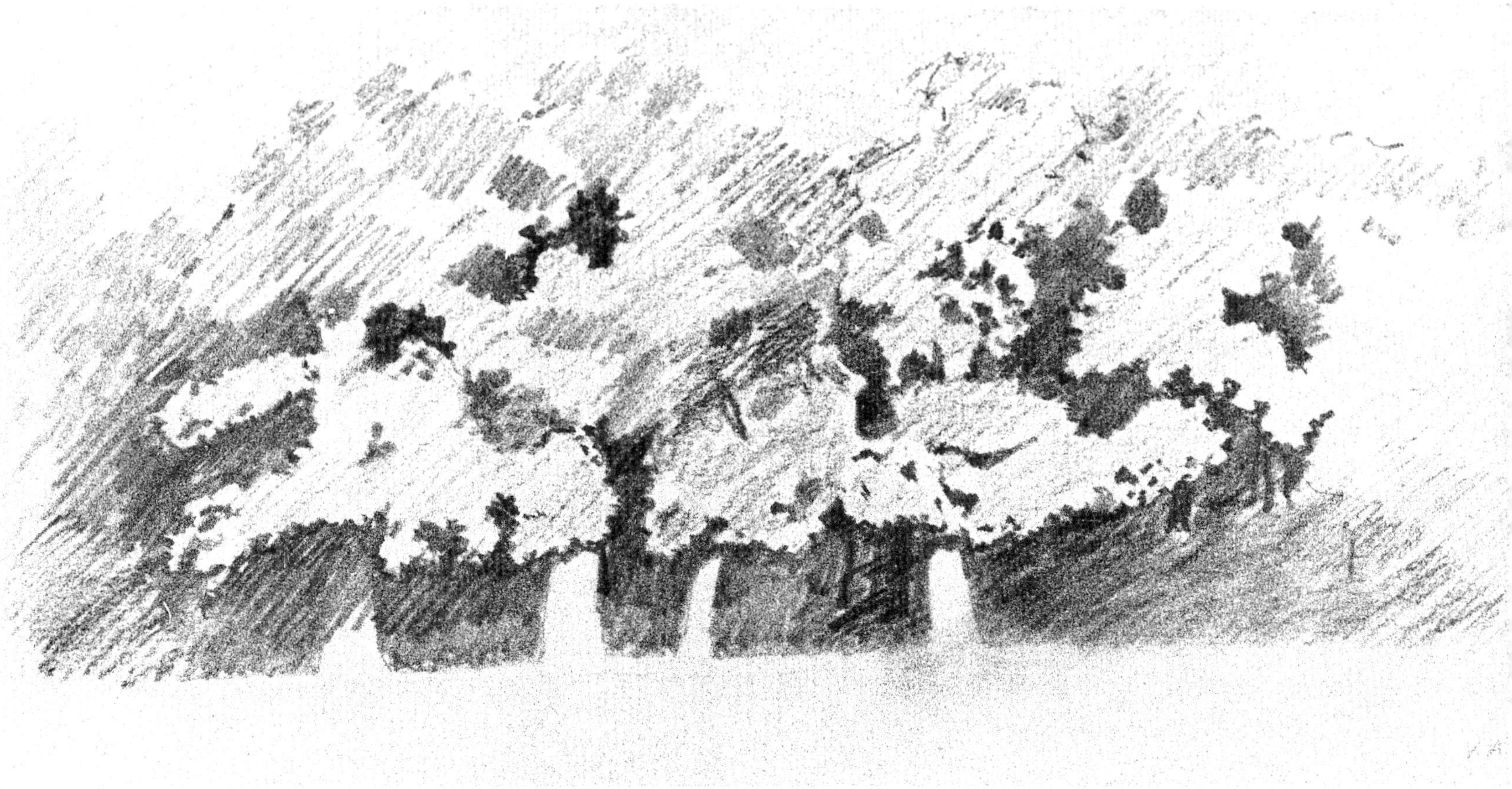

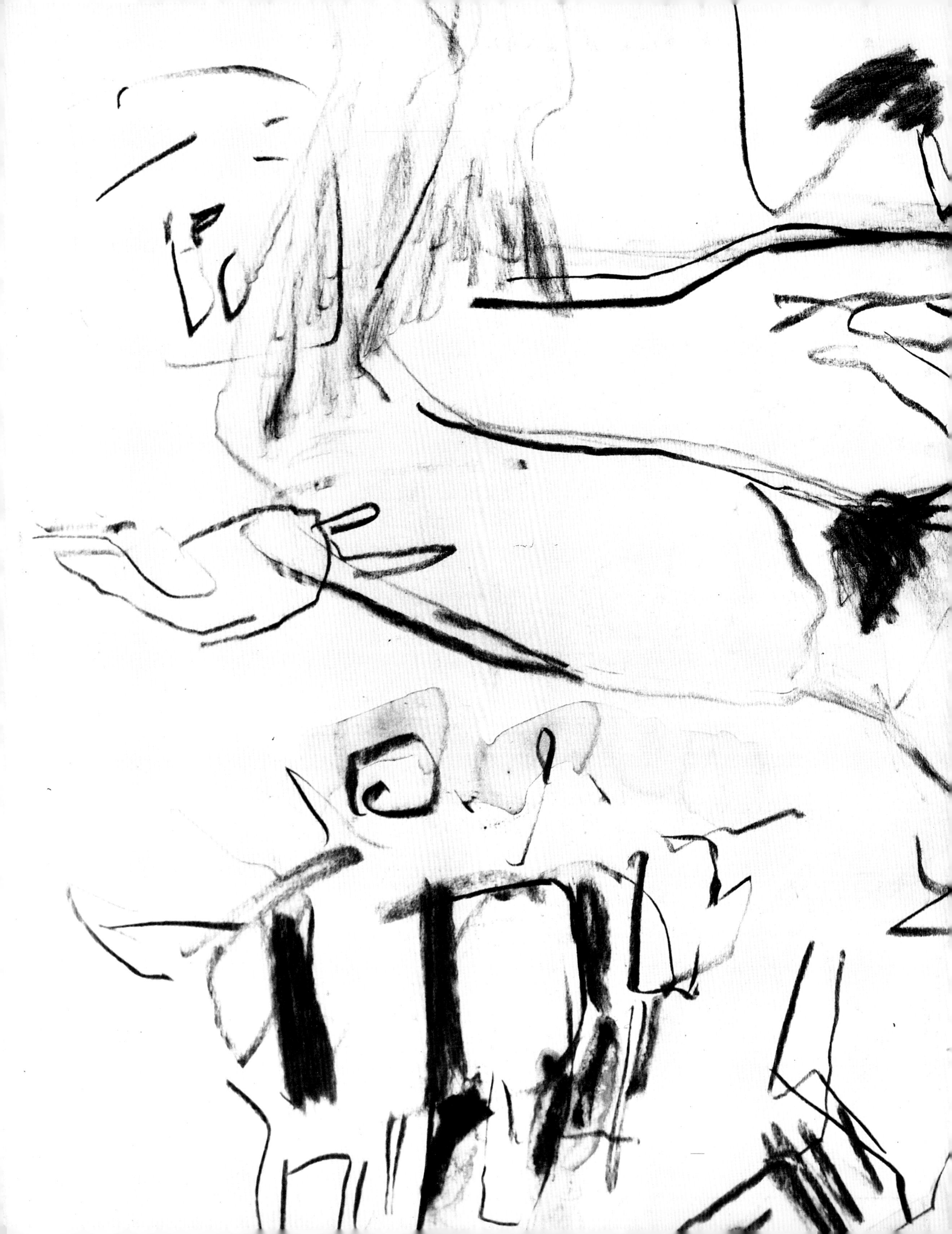